AQA Religious Studies B
Catholic Christianity
with Islam and Judaism

Peter Wallace
Marianne Fleming
Peter Smith
David Worden

Series editor
Cynthia Bartlett

OXFORD
UNIVERSITY PRESS

Great Clarendon Street, Oxford, OX2 6DP, United Kingdom

Oxford University Press is a department of the University of Oxford. It furthers the University's objective of excellence in research, scholarship, and education by publishing worldwide. Oxford is a registered trade mark of Oxford University Press in the UK and in certain other countries

© Oxford University Press 2016

The moral rights of the authors have been asserted

First published in 2016

All rights reserved. No part of this publication may be reproduced, stored in a retrieval system, or transmitted, in any form or by any means, without the prior permission in writing of Oxford University Press, or as expressly permitted by law, by licence or under terms agreed with the appropriate reprographics rights organization. Enquiries concerning reproduction outside the scope of the above should be sent to the Rights Department, Oxford University Press, at the address above.

You must not circulate this work in any other form and you must impose this same condition on any acquirer

British Library Cataloguing in Publication Data
Data available

978-0-19-837038-3

10 9 8 7 6 5 4 3 2

Paper used in the production of this book is a natural, recyclable product made from wood grown in sustainable forests. The manufacturing process conforms to the environmental regulations of the country of origin.

Printed in Great Britain by Bell and Bain Ltd., Glasgow.

Links to third party websites are provided by Oxford in good faith and for information only. Oxford disclaims any responsibility for the materials contained in any third party website referenced in this work.

> Nihil obstat: The Rev Jonathan Veasey, Censor Deputatus
> Imprimatur: + Bernard Longley, Archbishop of Birmingham 10th May 2016
>
> The Nihil obstat and Imprimatur are a declaration from within the Catholic Church that the parts of this publication concerned with doctrine and morals are free from error. The Nihil obstat and imprimatur apply to Part One and Part Three. It is not implied that those who have granted the Nihil obstat and Imprimatur agree with the contents, opinions or statements expressed.

Approval message from AQA

This textbook has been approved by AQA for use with our qualification. This means that we have checked that it broadly covers the specification and we are satisfied with the overall quality. Full details of our approval process can be found on our website.

We approve textbooks because we know how important it is for teachers and students to have the right resources to support their teaching and learning. However, the publisher is ultimately responsible for the editorial control and quality of this book.

Please note that when teaching the AQA GCSE Religious Studies course, you must refer to AQA's specification as your definitive source of information. While this book has been written to match the specification, it cannot provide complete coverage of every aspect of the course.

A wide range of other useful resources can be found on the relevant subject pages of our website: www.aqa.org.uk.

Please note that the Practice Questions in this book allow students a genuine attempt at practising exam skills, but they are not intended to replicate examination papers.

Contents

Introduction 8

PART ONE: CATHOLIC CHRISTIANITY

Chapter 1: Creation

1.1	Michelangelo's *Creation of Adam*	10
1.2	Other Christian art that depicts creation	12
1.3	Creation and the nature of God in Genesis 1	14
1.4	Creation and the nature of humans in Genesis 2	16
1.5	The significance of the creation stories for Catholics	18
1.6	The origins and structure of the Bible	20
1.7	Inspiration and the Bible as the word of God	22
1.8	Interpreting the Genesis creation stories	24
1.9	Natural law and Catholic attitudes towards science	26
1.10	Caring for the environment	28
1.11	The meaning of stewardship	30
1.12	CAFOD and sustainability	32
	Assessment guidance	34

Chapter 2: Incarnation

2.1	Jesus as God incarnate	36
2.2	God's message to Joseph	38
2.3	Jesus, the Word of God	40
2.4	Jesus as both fully human and fully God	42
2.5	Christian symbols	44
2.6	How the incarnation affects Catholic attitudes towards religious art	46
2.7	Interpreting statues of Jesus	48
2.8	The moral teachings of Jesus	50
2.9	Tradition and St Irenaeus' writings about Jesus	52
2.10	Different understandings of the incarnation	54
2.11	Grace and the sacramental nature of reality	56
2.12	The seven sacraments	58
2.13	*Imago dei* and abortion	60
	Assessment guidance	62

Chapter 3: The Triune God

3.1	Psalms and the use of music in worship	64
3.2	Music in the liturgy	66
3.3	Acclamations used in the Mass	68
3.4	The Triune God explained in the Bible	70
3.5	The Trinity in the Nicene Creed and Genesis 1	72
3.6	The influence of the Trinity on Christians today	74
3.7	The Trinity in the Bible	76
3.8	The Trinity and God's love	78
3.9	The authority of the Magisterium and its views on the Trinity	80
3.10	Baptism	82
3.11	Traditional and spontaneous prayer	84
3.12	Prayer and posture	86
	Assessment guidance	88

Chapter 4: Redemption

4.1	How church architecture reflects Catholic beliefs	90
4.2	The main parts of a Catholic church	92
4.3	Contrasting features and artefacts used by Catholics	94
4.4	The role of Jesus in restoration through sacrifice	96
4.5	The significance of Jesus' death, burial, resurrection and ascension	98
4.6	Salvation (past, present and future)	100
4.7	Redemption in the Bible (1)	102
4.8	Redemption in the Bible (2)/St Irenaeus' & St Anselm's thoughts on salvation	104
4.9	The importance of conscience for Christians	106
4.10	Redemption and the Mass	108
4.11	Different Christian understandings of the Eucharist	110
4.12	Prayers in the Mass and adoration	112
	Assessment guidance	114

Chapter 5: Church and the Kingdom of God

5.1	Pilgrimage and the Stations of the Cross	116
5.2	Pilgrimage to Rome, Lourdes and Walsingham	118
5.3	Mission and evangelism in drama	120
5.4	The Kingdom of God and the Lord's Prayer	122
5.5	Signs of the Kingdom: justice, peace and reconciliation	124
5.6	The hierarchy of the Catholic Church and the Second Vatican Council	126
5.7	The importance of Mary and the Magnificat	128
5.8	The four marks of the Church and apostolic succession	130
5.9	The counciliar and pontifical nature of the Church	132
5.10	The Church as the Body of Christ: the importance of charity for Catholics	134

5.11	Kingdom values in different vocations	136
5.12	Kingdom values in the life of a Catholic	138
	Assessment guidance	140

Chapter 6: Eschatology

6.1	The Paschal candle	142
6.2	Michelangelo's *The Last Judgement*	144
6.3	Memorials for the dead	146
6.4	Eschatology and life after death	148
6.5	The four last things	150
6.6	Purgatory and judgement	152
6.7	The Parable of the Rich Man and Lazarus	154
6.8	Cosmic reconciliation	156
6.9	The Church's teachings on the end of time	158
6.10	The last rites	160
6.11	The funeral rite	162
6.12	The care of the dying and euthanasia	164
	Assessment guidance	166

PART TWO: WORLD RELIGIONS

Chapter 7: Islam: beliefs and teachings

7.1	The Oneness of God and the supremacy of God's will	168
7.2	Key beliefs of Sunni Islam and Shi'a Islam	170
7.3	The nature of God	172
7.4	Angels	174
7.5	Predestination	176
7.6	Life after death	178
7.7	Prophethood and Adam	180
7.8	Ibrahim	182
7.9	Muhammad and the Imamate	184
7.10	The holy books in Islam	186
	Assessment guidance	188

Chapter 8: Islam: practices

8.1	The Five Pillars, the Ten Obligatory Acts and the Shahadah	190
8.2	Salah: the daily prayers (1)	192
8.3	Salah: the daily prayers (2)	194
8.4	Sawm: fasting during Ramadan	196
8.5	Zakah: almsgiving	198
8.6	Hajj: pilgrimage (1)	200
8.7	Hajj: pilgrimage (2)	202

5

8.8	Jihad	204
8.9	The festivals of Id-ul-Fitr and Id-ul-Adha	206
8.10	The festival of Ashura	208
	Assessment guidance	210

Chapter 9: Judaism: beliefs and teachings

9.1	The nature of God: God as one	212
9.2	The nature of God: God as creator	214
9.3	The nature of God: God as lawgiver and judge; the divine presence	216
9.4	Life after death, judgement and resurrection	218
9.5	The nature and role of the Messiah	220
9.6	The Promised Land and the covenant with Abraham	222
9.7	The covenant at Sinai and the Ten Commandments	224
9.8	Key moral principles in Judaism	226
9.9	Sanctity of life	228
9.10	Free will and mitzvot	230
	Assessment guidance	232

Chapter 10: Judaism: practices

10.1	The importance of the synagogue	234
10.2	Interior features of a synagogue	236
10.3	Worship in Orthodox and Reform synagogues	238
10.4	Daily services and prayer	240
10.5	Shabbat in the synagogue	242
10.6	Shabbat in the home	244
10.7	Worship in the home; the written and oral law	246
10.8	Ceremonies associated with birth	248
10.9	Bar and Bat Mitzvah	250
10.10	Marriage	252
10.11	Mourning for the dead	254
10.12	Dietary laws	256
10.13	Rosh Hashanah and Yom Kippur	258
10.14	Pesach	260
	Assessment guidance	262

PART THREE: THEMES

Chapter 11: Religion, relationships and families

11.1	Human beings as sexual, male and female	264
11.2	Pope John Paul II's 'Theology of the Body'	266
11.3	Human sexuality and its expression	268
11.4	A valid marriage in the Catholic Church	270

11.5	The nature of marriage, marriage promises, and cohabitation	272
11.6	Annulment, divorce and remarriage	274
11.7	Family planning and contraception	276
11.8	The nature and purpose of the family	278
11.9	Roles and responsibilities within the family	280
11.10	Gender equality in the Bible	282
11.11	Catholic teaching on the equality of women and men	284
11.12	Gender prejudice and discrimination	286
	Assessment guidance	288

Chapter 12: Religion, peace and conflict

12.1	Biblical perspectives on violence and bullying	290
12.2	Forgiveness and reconciliation	292
12.3	Justice	294
12.4	The just war theory	296
12.5	Nuclear war and weapons of mass destruction	298
12.6	The consequences of modern warfare	300
12.7	Religion as a reason for violence and war	302
12.8	Pacifism	304
12.9	The role of religion in conflicts of the twenty-first century	306
12.10	Terrorism	308
12.11	Torture, radicalisation and martyrdom	310
12.12	Conflict resolution and peacemaking	312
	Assessment guidance	314

Chapter 13: Religion, human rights and social justice

13.1	Human dignity and religious freedom	316
13.2	Human rights	318
13.3	Rights and responsibilities	320
13.4	Responsibilities of wealth	322
13.5	Wealth creation and exploitation	324
13.6	Greed, materialism and the sacrifice of wealth	326
13.7	Catholic teachings about poverty	328
13.8	Contrasting views on fighting poverty	330
13.9	The work of CAFOD and Christian Aid	332
13.10	Racial prejudice and discrimination	334
13.11	Equality	336
13.12	Justice, racial equality and racial prejudice	338
	Assessment guidance	340
	Glossary	342
	Acknowledgments	347
	Index	349

AQA GCSE Religious Studies: Catholic Christianity

Introduction

This book has been written to support GCSE students studying the AQA Religious Studies Specification B: Catholic Christianity.

The book covers everything that you need to know to complete Specification B Papers 1 and 2A:

- Chapters 1 to 6 cover beliefs, teachings, practices, forms of expression and sources of authority related to Catholic Christianity for the following six topics: Creation, Incarnation, the Triune God, Redemption, Church and the Kingdom of God, and Eschatology.
- Chapters 7 to 8 explore beliefs, teachings and practices for Islam.
- Chapters 9 to 10 examine beliefs, teachings and practices for Judaism.
- Chapters 11 to 13 cover religious, philosophical and ethical issues, including Religion, relationships and families, Religion, peace and conflict, and Religion, human rights and social justice.

For this course you must study two world religions: Catholic Christianity and either Islam or Judaism. You may either study two of the three religious, philosophical and ethical themes, or the two textual studies themes. The textual studies themes are supported by a separate book in this series, *St Mark's Gospel*.

Assessment guidance

Each chapter has an assessment guidance section that helps you to familiarise yourself with the AQA paper. There are multiple choice questions worth 1 mark, short-answer questions worth 2 marks, and longer questions worth 4 and 5 marks that test your ability to retell and explain facts. There are longer evaluation questions worth 12 marks that test your ability to analyse and evaluate different viewpoints.

Each examination question will test one of the two assessment objectives: the 1, 2, 4 and 5 mark questions test assessment objective 1 (AO1), and the 12 mark questions test assessment objective 2 (AO2). Each assessment objective represents 50 per cent of the total marks for a paper. The two assessment objectives are:

AO1: Demonstrate knowledge and understanding of religion and beliefs including:

- beliefs, practices and sources of authority
- influence on individuals, communities and societies
- similarities and differences within and/or between religions and beliefs.

AO2: Analyse and evaluate aspects of religion and belief, including their significance and influence.

For AO1 questions, the grid below gives guidance on how marks will be allocated:

Marks	Question type	Criteria
1 mark	Multiple choice	The correct answer chosen from four options
2 marks	Short answer (asking for two facts)	One mark for each of two correct points
4 marks	Asking for two ways in which beliefs influence Christians/Muslims/Jews today OR two contrasting beliefs of Christianity/Islam/Judaism OR two contrasting beliefs in contemporary British society	For each of the two ways/contrasts: • one mark for a simple explanation of a relevant and accurate way/contrast • two marks for a detailed explanation of a relevant and accurate way/contrast
5 marks	Asking for two Christian/Muslim/Jewish beliefs or teachings, or ways in which beliefs are shown in practice; may require reference to scripture or sacred writings	For each of the two beliefs/ways: • one mark for a simple explanation of a relevant and accurate belief/way • two marks for a detailed explanation of a relevant and accurate belief/way PLUS one mark for a relevant, accurate reference to scripture or sacred writing

The grid below gives you some guidance on different levels for the 12 mark evaluation question (testing AO2).

Levels	Criteria	Marks
4	A well-argued response, reasoned consideration of different points of view	10–12
	Logical chains of reasoning leading to judgement(s) supported by knowledge and understanding of relevant evidence and information	
3	Reasoned consideration of different points of view	7–9
	Logical chains of reasoning that draw on knowledge and understanding of relevant evidence and information	
2	Reasoned consideration of a point of view	4–6
	A logical chain of reasoning drawing on knowledge and understanding of relevant evidence and information	
	OR	
	Recognition of different points of view, each supported by relevant reasons/evidence	
1	Point of view with reason(s) stated in support	1–3
0	Nothing worthy of credit	0

You should remember that Christianity is the main religious tradition of Great Britain. When studying Islam or Judaism, there are specific topics for which you will need to be aware of the different interpretations and understandings between that religion and Christianity. You should also bear in mind non-religious views such as atheism and humanism, and understand the influence of beliefs, teachings and practices on individuals, communities and societies.

Spelling, punctuation and grammar (SPaG) is also important so it will be useful to practise the 12 mark extended writing questions. There are 5 marks available for SPaG: 1 mark for threshold performance, 2–3 marks for intermediate performance and 4–5 marks for high performance. You should aim to write correctly using a wide range of specialist religious terms.

Examination grades will be awarded on a scale of 9–1 rather than A* to G. Grade 9 will be the equivalent of a new grade for high performing students above the current A*. Grade 4 will be the same as a grade C pass. The aim of the new grading system is to show greater differentiation between higher and lower achieving students.

There are two accepted numberings of the psalms: the Hebrew numbering is normally used for translating the Bible, but the Greek numbering has traditionally been used in Catholic worship. To avoid confusion, both numbers will appear throughout this book, with the Hebrew first and the Greek in brackets.

Bible quotations in this book have been taken from the *New Revised Standard Version: Catholic Edition*, except for chapters 9–10 on Judaism, where quotes have been taken from the Jewish Publication Society's edition of the Tanach.

Quotations from sources of authority appear throughout the book; in longer quotes, certain phrases have been put in bold to help highlight key points in relation to the text.

An online version of this book is available for student access, with an added bank of tools for you to personalise the book.

Part 1: Catholic Christianity

1 Creation

1.1 Michelangelo's *Creation of Adam*

■ The meaning and significance of Michelangelo's *Creation of Adam*

Pictures allow artists to express ideas that can be hard to convey in words. They can inspire people and help them to understand their faith. One of the more common themes expressed in Christian art is the **creation**. Many artists have taken ideas from the Bible about creation and tried to convey these ideas in pictures rather than words. Some of the best-known examples of this are the paintings by **Michelangelo** in the Sistine Chapel in Rome. On the ceiling of the chapel, Michelangelo painted scenes from the book of **Genesis**. The most famous of these paintings is *Creation of Adam*.

The significance of this painting is that it focuses the viewer's attention on how dependent humanity is on God, yet at the same time shows that humanity is made in the image of God.

■ How does *Creation of Adam* reflect Catholic beliefs and teachings?

- In this painting Adam is shown as a perfect man, full of strength and potential. This reflects what is taught in Genesis: that God made everything 'very good' (Genesis 1:31). Adam is shown as the ideal man, but not yet fully alive. Adam's outstretched arm is almost touching the finger of God, but his fingers are still bent, waiting for God's life force to straighten them.
- This painting represents the moment when God makes Adam come to life. Michelangelo is showing that Adam depends on God for his life.
- God is powerful yet ancient. The white hair and beard reflect age but the body of God is still muscular. God looks much older than Adam. This evokes the idea that man is made in the image of God, though God is ancient while humanity is new. Adam and God are lying in similar positions, which also reinforces the idea that humanity is made in the image of God.
- The hands of Adam and God reaching out to each other reflect the longing for a close relationship between God and man. It is not just simply a passing on of life; it is the building up of a harmonious love, knowledge and appreciation of each other.

> **Objectives**
> - Understand the meaning and significance of Michelangelo's *Creation of Adam*.
> - Understand how this painting reflects Catholic beliefs about God as **creator**, and the creation of humanity in the image of God.

> **Key terms**
> - **creator:** the one who makes things and bring things about
> - **creation:** the act by which God brought the universe into being
> - **Michelangelo:** Michelangelo Buonarotti (1475–1564) was a famous Italian painter and sculptor
> - **Genesis:** the first book of the Bible, in which the stories of creation are found
> - **Creation of Adam:** part of the painting on the ceiling of the Sistine Chapel in the Vatican in Rome, which shows God giving life to Adam

> **Research activity**
> This painting (or certain sections of it) has been used on many occasions. Research some of these occasions and examine the impact of the painting in both religious and non-religious settings.

Chapter 1 Creation

- God is shown being carried through the air by a group of angels, reflecting his transcendence, while Adam is shown firmly on the ground. This is an attempt to convey the greatness and majesty of God.
- Humans have a unique place in God's creation, as they are created specially by God and are in close contact with him.
- One of the main messages of Michelangelo's paintings in the Sistine Chapel is that God is the creator of everything. Nothing comes into being without God.

Links

To learn about God's transcendence and what this term means see pages 14–15.

▲ Michelangelo's *Creation of Adam, painted on the ceiling of the Sistine Chapel around 1511*

Controversial aspects of this painting

Paintings are limited in what they can depict, and it can be difficult to present spiritual ideas in a physical way. Here are a few of the ways in which this painting does not reflect Catholic beliefs:

- Genesis 2 states that God made Adam out of dust, and brought him to life by breathing into his nostrils (Genesis 2:7). Nowhere in the Bible does it say that God touched Adam to give him life.
- God and Adam are depicted as nearly the same size, suggesting that man is equal with God, which does not reflect Catholic beliefs.
- Some people do not like the idea of the eternal God being shown as an old man.

Discussion activity

Can you think of any other reasons why this painting might not reflect Catholic teachings?

★ Study tip

Remember that words and images cannot convey the same idea. Some things are easier to put into words while others are easier to put into picture form. Don't expect the two forms of expression to do the same task.

Activities

1. Examine how Michelangelo's *Creation of Adam* reflects the creation stories in Genesis 1 and 2.
2. 'Michelangelo's *Creation of Adam* provides a good understanding of Catholic teaching about humanity.' Evaluate this statement. Be sure to include more than one point of view, and refer to Catholic beliefs and teachings in your answer.

Summary

You should now be able to interpret Michelangelo's Creation of Adam, and understand how this painting reflects Catholic beliefs about creation.

11

1.2 Other Christian art that depicts creation

Because one painting cannot express the whole truth, it can be helpful to consider and compare other images of creation. These images can be found in a variety of art forms, including paintings, mosaics, stained-glass windows and computer-generated imagery. Here are some examples:

■ A nineteenth-century stained-glass window depicting Adam and Eve

▲ A stained-glass window in the cathedral in Brussels, Belgium

This stained-glass window was painted by the Belgian artist Jean-Baptiste Capronnier in the second half of the nineteenth century, and can be found in the Cathedral of St Michael and St Gudula in Brussels, Belgium. It shows God blessing Adam and Eve after he made them and the animals.

- This image represents the Genesis 2 account of the creation of man and woman, while the Michelangelo painting could refer to either Genesis 1 or Genesis 2.
- The presence of the animals behind God, while Adam and Eve stand in front of God, reflects the relative importance of humanity compared with the rest of creation. This is one point that is not shown in Michelangelo's painting.
- There is a physical similarity between the humans and God, but God is a little bigger. This is similar to Michelangelo's depiction of God and Adam. However, in the stained-glass window, the way both Adam and Eve are standing reflects the idea that they are subservient to and dependent on God.
- The stained glass also shows the snake and a symbolic tree between God and the humans, which link to the story of the Fall in Genesis 3. This is not referred to in Michelangelo's painting.

Objectives

- Know at least one other work of art that shows a Christian understanding of creation.
- Understand what message this piece of art is trying to convey.
- Assess and evaluate the meaning and significance of Michelangelo's *Creation of Adam* compared with this piece of art.

Research activity

Search online to find a piece of art that you think best illustrates the idea of God the creator. Explain why you thought this image was the best one to choose.

Discussion activity

Examine the pictures shown on these pages and explain which one you find most informative, and which one is least informative, about the role of God the creator.

Activity

'It is pointless trying to show God the creator in art form.' Evaluate this statement. Be sure to include more than one point of view, and refer to Catholic beliefs and teachings in your answer.

Chapter 1   Creation

■ A twentieth-century mosaic depicting God's hand

This mosaic was created by the artist Hildreth Meière in the first half of the twentieth century, and can be found in St Bartholomew's Church in New York, USA. It depicts the hand of God at work in a powerful way.

- The lines going out from the hand to touch the edges of the universe, depicted by the circle round the edge of the mosaic, reflect the idea that God's influence and power touch all things.
- God's hand is relatively large compared to the size of the cloud, helping to illustrate God's greatness and power.
- This image conveys a greater sense of God as a creator than the Michelangelo painting. Michelangelo only deals with one point of creation, while the mosaic shows God always creating.
- The way God is presented is also different, and for some Christians more acceptable. Since God is infinite, some Christians maintain that God cannot and should not be depicted in the way Michelangelo draws him. The hand in the mosaic suggests the idea of God without actually showing the whole of him. However, some Christians are still uneasy about the depiction of the hand of God, as they think this suggests that God is like humans only in a much bigger form.

▲ *A mosaic by Hildreth Meière in a church in New York, USA*

■ A fifteenth-century fresco depicting the creation of the sun and moon

This fresco was painted by the artist John of Kastav in the fifteenth century, in the Holy Trinity Church in Hrastovlje, Slovenia. It depicts the creation of the sun and the moon; in Genesis this occurs on the fourth day of God's creation (Genesis 1:16).

- The presence of the land, water and trees in the fresco show the cumulative effect of the earlier days of creation. This is not suggested in *Creation of Adam*, as the focus of that painting is simply on humanity.
- In this fresco, God is holding a book. This reflects the idea that God created the universe purely through the power of his word, but also shows that the Bible is the word of God.
- God is shown in almost human form, reflecting the idea of humans being made in his image. This is similar to Michelangelo's painting.
- The halo round God's head illustrates his holiness.
- God has raised two fingers on his right hand to bless what he has made, which shows that all of his creation is blessed. This idea doesn't appear in Michelangelo's *Creation of Adam*.

▲ *A fresco by John of Kastav in a church in Slovenia*

Links

To read more about God's power to create through his word see page 14.

Summary

You should now be able to compare Michelangelo's *Creation of Adam* with another piece of art that represents God's act of creation.

⭐ Study tip

Make sure you can write in detail about one other Christian artwork that depicts the creation, and be able to contrast it with Michelangelo's *Creation of Adam*.

13

1.3 Creation and the nature of God in Genesis 1

■ God as transcendent

Genesis 1 is a poem that describes the creation of the universe, and shows the greatness of God as creator. God's power is shown in the effectiveness of his word. When God says 'Let there be …', that thing immediately comes into being. He does not require anything beyond his own word in order to create. God is completely beyond the created world. He is **transcendent**.

■ God as omnipotent

God is also **omnipotent** or all-powerful. He has the power to do whatever he wants; as seen in Genesis, he can even create things from nothing (*ex nihilo*). Everything that God made is 'good'. This reinforces the idea of God being omnipotent, as his power allows him to make everything exactly the way he wants it; nothing God makes has any imperfection in it.

Catholics do not think this poem is meant to be a scientific account of creation. It is meant to give a reason for creation rather than explain how it was done. Catholics do not interpret it literally or view it as a historical document. However, the poem does show that God creates in an orderly way. There is also symbolic logic in the order. For example, the sun, moon and stars – which many people at the time worshipped as gods – are said to have been created on the fourth day. This is a minor position in the sequence and shows that they are not gods.

In this version of the creation story, humans are the last thing created, as the end point of God's work. The importance of humanity is shown in the phrase: 'God created humankind in his image' (Genesis 1:27). This means that humans share qualities with God like love, knowledge and so on.

> **Objectives**
> - Know the scriptural basis for Catholic teachings about God and creation.
> - Understand what these teachings show about the nature of God as creator, transcendent and omnipotent.

> **Key terms**
> - **transcendent:** the idea that God is beyond and outside life on earth and the universe; a quality of God
> - **omnipotent:** almighty, having unlimited power; a quality of God

▲ A stained-glass window showing the seven days of creation

> **Activities**
>
> 1. Write out the main things created on each of the first six days of creation according to Genesis 1. Use two parallel columns, with days 1–3 in the first column and days 4–6 in the second column. Here is an example of the table you should draw:
>
> | Days 1–3 | Days 4–6 |
> |---|---|
> | | |
> | | |
> | | |
>
> Do you notice any parallels between the contents of the two columns? Why do you think the writer chose to present creation in this way? What message(s) do you think he was trying to get across?
>
> 2. 'The most important teaching of Genesis 1 is that humans are made in the image of God.' Evaluate this statement. Be sure to include more than one point of view, and refer to Catholic beliefs and teachings in your answer.

> **Links**
>
> To read more about different interpretations of the creation stories see pages 24–25.

Chapter 1 Creation

> **Discussion activity**
>
> Discuss whether you think Genesis 1 is an effective way to help people understand the role of God in creation.

Summary

You should now be able to explain the meaning of the words 'transcendent' and 'omnipotent', and understand what Genesis 1 shows about the nature of God and the process of creation.

⭐ **Study tip**

You need to be aware of the main points of Genesis 1, but you do not need to be able to write it out perfectly word for word.

> " In the beginning when God created the heavens and the earth, the earth was a formless void and darkness covered the face of the deep, while a wind from God swept over the face of the waters. **Then God said, 'Let there be light'; and there was light.** And God saw that the light was good; and God separated the light from the darkness. God called the light Day, and the darkness he called Night. And there was evening and there was morning, the first day.
>
> And God said, 'Let there be a dome in the midst of the waters, and let it separate the waters from the waters.' So God made the dome and separated the waters that were under the dome from the waters that were above the dome. And it was so. God called the dome Sky. And there was evening and there was morning, the second day.
>
> And God said, 'Let the waters under the sky be gathered together into one place, and let the dry land appear.' And it was so. God called the dry land Earth, and the waters that were gathered together he called Seas. And God saw that it was good. Then God said, 'Let the earth put forth vegetation: plants yielding seed, and fruit trees of every kind on earth that bear fruit with the seed in it.' And it was so. The earth brought forth vegetation: plants yielding seed of every kind, and trees of every kind bearing fruit with the seed in it. And God saw that it was good. And there was evening and there was morning, the third day.
>
> And God said, 'Let there be lights in the dome of the sky to separate the day from the night; and let them be for signs and for seasons and for days and years, and let them be lights in the dome of the sky to give light upon the earth.' And it was so. God made the two great lights – the greater light to rule the day and the lesser light to rule the night – and the stars. God set them in the dome of the sky to give light upon the earth, to rule over the day and over the night, and to separate the light from the darkness. And God saw that it was good. And there was evening and there was morning, the fourth day.
>
> And God said, 'Let the waters bring forth swarms of living creatures, and let birds fly above the earth across the dome of the sky.' So God created the great sea monsters and every living creature that moves, of every kind, with which the waters swarm, and every winged bird of every kind. And God saw that it was good. God blessed them, saying, 'Be fruitful and multiply and fill the waters in the seas, and let birds multiply on the earth.' And there was evening and there was morning, the fifth day.
>
> And God said, 'Let the earth bring forth living creatures of every kind: cattle and creeping things and wild animals of the earth of every kind.' And it was so. God made the wild animals of the earth of every kind, and the cattle of every kind, and everything that creeps upon the ground of every kind. And God saw that it was good.
>
> Then God said, 'Let us make humankind in our image, according to our likeness; and let them have dominion over the fish of the sea, and over the birds of the air, and over the cattle, and over all the wild animals of the earth, and over every creeping thing that creeps upon the earth.'
>
> **So God created humankind in his image,
> in the image of God he created them;
> male and female he created them.**
>
> God blessed them, and God said to them, 'Be fruitful and multiply, and fill the earth and subdue it; and have dominion over the fish of the sea and over the birds of the air and over every living thing that moves upon the earth.' God said, 'See, I have given you every plant yielding seed that is upon the face of all the earth, and every tree with seed in its fruit; you shall have them for food. And to every beast of the earth, and to every bird of the air, and to everything that creeps on the earth, everything that has the breath of life, I have given every green plant for food.' And it was so. **God saw everything that he had made, and indeed, it was very good.** And there was evening and there was morning, the sixth day.
>
> Thus the heavens and the earth were finished, and all their multitude. And on the seventh day God finished the work that he had done, and he rested on the seventh day from all the work that he had done. So God blessed the seventh day and hallowed it, because on it God rested from all the work that he had done in creation. "
>
> *Genesis* 1:1–2:3 (NRSV)

1.4 Creation and the nature of humans in Genesis 2

Genesis 2 is another creation story in the Bible, which was written earlier than the poem of Genesis 1.

In Genesis 2, God personally creates human beings, '**Adam**', from dust. This stresses how precious humanity is, which is emphasised even more when God breathes into man and he becomes a living being. In Hebrew the word for 'breath' is *ru'ach*, which is also translated as 'spirit'. Humans share the breath or Spirit of God.

All that humans need is provided for them. But God also gives humanity the gift of **free will**. God gives this gift when he tells Adam not to eat the fruit from the tree of the knowledge of good and evil. Even though he commands Adam not to eat from the tree, he does not actively prevent Adam from doing so. He gives Adam the choice (or free will) to decide for himself what he wants: either for God to provide everything for humanity, or for humanity to provide for itself.

The animals are made by God but presented to Adam to name. This naming gives each animal its nature. The fact that it is Adam who names the animals shows that humans have both authority and responsibility for them. None of the animals is a suitable helpmate for Adam, though, so God makes Adam fall into a deep sleep and from Adam's rib, God creates Eve. This shows that humanity is subdivided into two complementary parts. This gives sense to verse 24, 'Therefore a man leaves his father and his mother and clings to his wife, and they become one flesh'. When husband and wife join together they become one whole, perfected being.

■ The significance of beliefs about the nature of God and humans

For Catholics, the belief that God is transcendent means that human beings can only begin to appreciate what God is, as he is far beyond human understanding. Humans can see the power and wonder of God through all the things that he has created. The vastness of the universe reflects God's omnipotence, but the belief that God cares for every person shows that God is also intimate. Humans have been given their

▲ This stained-glass window shows Adam and Eve eating from the tree of knowledge and being banished from the Garden of Eden as a result

Objectives

- Know the scriptural basis for Catholic teachings about God and creation.
- Understand the concept of free will.
- Understand the relationship between men and women as given in Genesis 2.

Key terms

- **Adam:** the Hebrew word for humanity, which many people see as the name of the first man
- **free will:** belief that God gives people the opportunity to make decisions for themselves

Links

To read about how humans are created in the image of God see page 60.

Discussion activity

Discuss how the author of Genesis 2 shows that humans are important to God.

Chapter 1 Creation

distinct nature by God. The human qualities that reflect God's nature allow humans to have a close relationship with God, but they also require humans to care for all that God has created.

Activities

1. Explain how the creation stories in Genesis 1 and 2 show God as omnipotent.
2. 'God cannot be both the creator and transcendent.' Evaluate this statement. Be sure to include more than one point of view, and refer to Catholic beliefs and teachings in your answer. (To answer this, consider the differences between Genesis 1 and 2, and the idea that if God is 'transcendent' then he can create things out of nothing.)

Research activity

Search online for creation stories from other religions. Compare the messages of these stories with the messages of Genesis 1 and 2.

⭐ Study tip

Remember that Genesis 2 was written much earlier than Genesis 1. The two stories are not meant to be read as one account.

Summary

You should now be able to explain the meaning of the term 'free will', and understand what Genesis 2 shows about the nature of humans and the process of creation.

❝ In the day that the Lord God made the earth and the heavens, when no plant of the field was yet in the earth and no herb of the field had yet sprung up – for the Lord God had not caused it to rain upon the earth, and there was no one to till the ground; but a stream would rise from the earth, and water the whole face of the ground – **then the Lord God formed man from the dust of the ground, and breathed into his nostrils the breath of life; and the man became a living being.** And the Lord God planted a garden in Eden, in the east; and there he put the man whom he had formed. Out of the ground the Lord God made to grow every tree that is pleasant to the sight and good for food, the tree of life also in the midst of the garden, and the tree of the knowledge of good and evil.

A river flows out of Eden to water the garden, and from there it divides and becomes four branches. The name of the first is Pishon; it is the one that flows around the whole land of Havilah, where there is gold; and the gold of that land is good; bdellium and onyx stone are there. The name of the second river is Gihon; it is the one that flows around the whole land of Cush. The name of the third river is Tigris, which flows east of Assyria. And the fourth river is the Euphrates.

The Lord God took the man and put him in the garden of Eden to till it and keep it. And the Lord God commanded the man, "You may freely eat of every tree of the garden; but of the tree of the knowledge of good and evil you shall not eat, for in the day that you eat of it you shall die."

Then the Lord God said, "It is not good that the man should be alone; I will make him a helper as his partner." So out of the ground the Lord God formed every animal of the field and every bird of the air, and brought them to the man to see what he would call them; and whatever the man called every living creature, that was its name. The man gave names to all cattle, and to the birds of the air, and to every animal of the field; but for the man there was not found a helper as his partner. So the Lord God caused a deep sleep to fall upon the man, and he slept; then he took one of his ribs and closed up its place with flesh. And the rib that the Lord God had taken from the man he made into a woman and brought her to the man. Then the man said,

**"This at last is bone of my bones
    and flesh of my flesh;**
this one shall be called Woman,
    for out of Man this one was taken."

Therefore a man leaves his father and his mother and clings to his wife, and they become one flesh. And the man and his wife were both naked, and were not ashamed. ❞

Genesis 2:4–25 (NRSV)

1.5 The significance of the creation stories for Catholics

On the previous pages we learned what the creation stories can teach about the nature of God and humanity. Here we will learn about the significance of these beliefs for Catholics today.

■ Stewardship

The creation stories show that God is the creator of all things. This means that believers have a duty to respect all of God's creation. Catholics should do their best to ensure that no part of creation is destroyed or undervalued.

God made everything good. This means that all aspects of creation should be accepted as good. As God is omnipotent, all that he makes is an expression of himself and his care for his world. Humans have a duty to look after this world and support all that is contained within it.

Objectives
- Know the meaning of the terms stewardship, dignity and sanctity of life.
- Understand the importance of these concepts for a Catholic appreciation of human life.

Key terms
- **stewardship:** the idea that believers have a duty to look after the environment on behalf of God
- **dignity:** being worthy of honour and respect
- **sanctity of life:** all life is holy as it is created and loved by God; human life should not be misused or abused

▲ Can our current lifestyle allow us to pass on the world to the next generation in the same condition?

The command given to humans to subdue and have dominion over God's creation (Genesis 1:28) also includes the idea of **stewardship**. Catholics believe that humans have a duty to care for the earth, to protect it, and not to misuse creation in any way. It is the responsibility of each generation to inherit and then pass on to the next generation the gift of God's creation, leaving it as unspoiled as possible.

■ The dignity of human beings

The creation stories teach that humans are made in the image and likeness of God. All humans are equal because they all share in the qualities of God and are all loved into existence by God. This means that as everyone is a part of God's creation, no one should be mistreated in any way. This teaching stresses the **dignity** of each human person.

> **"** The earth was here before us and it has been given to us ... [there is] a relationship of mutual responsibility between human beings and nature ... **This responsibility for God's earth means that human beings ... must respect the laws of nature** and the delicate [balance] existing between the creatures of this world. **"**
>
> *Laudato Si 67–68*

18

Chapter 1   Creation

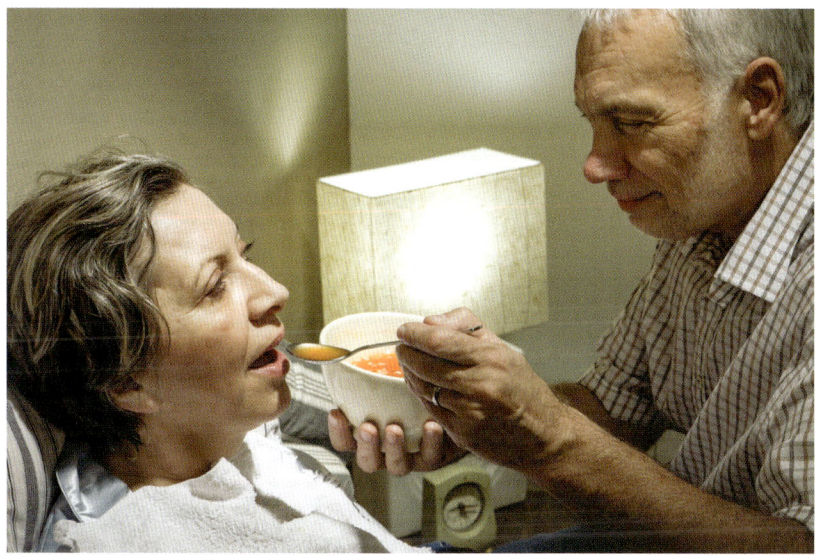
▲ Do some stages of life make it hard to treat people with dignity?

> **Every person, from the first moment of his life in the womb, has an inviolable dignity,** because from all eternity God willed, loved, created and redeemed that person and destined him for eternal happiness.
>
> *Youcat* 280

The creation stories also teach that human relationships are important to God. The role of sex is to unite a man and woman as one way of expressing their humanity. This is a sacred act which should not be undervalued.

Catholics believe that God gave humans their free will. Every human being is entitled to express their own beliefs freely and this should be respected. But along with this freedom comes the responsibility to respect your own dignity and the dignity of other people, as everyone is a child of God.

■ The sanctity of life

All creation is holy because it is blessed by God who 'saw that it was good'. This applies particularly to human life, which is sacred. Catholics should respect the **sanctity of life** as it is a gift from God. As God is the creator of all life, every stage of life from conception to death must be treated with care and respect.

Catholics believe that while the stories of creation contained in the Bible were written many centuries ago for people of a different type of culture and understanding, they pass on unchangeable or eternal truths about the nature and dignity of human beings. The truth cannot be changed, though it may be presented in revised and different ways to reflect changing times and tastes.

Discussion activity

Discuss whether you think the creation stories in the Bible are a good way of presenting the eternal truths about the nature of humanity.

Extension activity

Compare Catholic teachings about the sanctity of life with teachings from other religions. Note in which ways they are different and in which way similar.

★ Study tip

Try to focus on how the messages of the Genesis 1 and 2 stories link to the idea of stewardship and the sanctity of life.

Summary

You should now be able to explain the meanings of the terms stewardship, dignity and sanctity of life. You should also be able to relate Catholic beliefs and teachings to the creation stories.

Activities

1. Work in pairs. One person should examine the ways in which the creation stories in Genesis support the idea of the dignity of human beings, and the other person should do the same for the sanctity of life. Then compare your findings.
2. 'The most important gift God gave to humans was free will.' Evaluate this statement. Be sure to include more than one point of view, and refer to Catholic beliefs and teachings in your answer.

19

1.6 The origins and structure of the Bible

■ What is the Bible?

The word 'bible' comes from the Greek word *biblion* meaning 'book', and the **Bible** can be thought of as a collection of many small books. The Roman Catholic **Church** recognises 73 books in the Bible, written between approximately 1000 BCE and 100 CE. Because of this long period of writing, the individual books were written for different audiences and for different purposes. The Bible contains stories, prayers, poetry, prophecies, history, and advice about how to live.

The Bible is divided into two main sections: the Old Testament and the New Testament.

▲ *From left to right, Mark, Luke, Matthew and John: the writers of the four Gospels*

■ The Old Testament

The Old Testament deals with the ways that God related to the Jewish people throughout their history, before the coming of Jesus. It describes how God guided the Jews, protecting them and sending them messengers (prophets) to warn them when they were going wrong.

The Old Testament contains:

- the **Law** (Torah) – the first five books, which show how the Jews became the people of God. The Law also includes God's guidance

> **Objectives**
> - Examine what is included in the Bible.
> - Understand how Christians regard the different books of the Bible as sources of authority.

> **Key terms**
> - **Bible:** the sacred book of Christianity, containing the Old and New Testaments
> - **Church:** (1) the holy people of God, also called the Body of Christ, among whom Christ is present and active (2) a building in which Christians worship
> - **apostles:** 'one who is sent out'; the name given to those disciples who became leaders of the early Church

> ❝ **The Bible is not meant to convey precise historical information or scientific findings to us.** Moreover, the authors were children of their times. Their forms of expression are influenced by the sometimes inadequate cultural images of the world around them. Nevertheless, everything that man must know about God and the way of his salvation is found with infallible certainty in Sacred Scripture. ❞
> *Youcat* 15 (2011)

for how he wanted the Jews to live. This guidance includes the Ten Commandments.
- the **history books** – these show how God guided his people and how the people often refused to listen. These stories were included to help later generations avoid the same mistakes.
- the **wisdom books** – including prayers, psalms, books of advice and poems, which show people how to use God-given talents to do what is right, in order to be able to stay close to God.
- the **prophets** – containing the words of inspired figures who were sent by God to teach people about how God is active in the world, and to challenge people to stay faithful to God.

Somewhere between the middle of the second century BCE and the end of the first century CE, Jewish leaders accepted these books as part of their scriptures.

■ The New Testament

Jesus was a Jew and often referred to Old Testament writings in his teachings. The early Christians used the writings of the Old Testament to show how Jesus fulfilled God's promises. They also wrote their own books about Jesus' life and teachings, as well as letters discussing how Christians should apply these teachings to all aspects of life. Later on, Christians made a selection from these writings (using the criteria mentioned below) that became known as the New Testament.

The New Testament is based on the life and teachings of Jesus and the **apostles**. It can be divided into four sections:

- the **Gospels** (Matthew, Mark, Luke and John), which record the actions and teachings of Jesus.
- the **Acts of the Apostles** (a continuation of the Gospel of Luke), which tell of some of the events in the early Church up to about 60 CE.
- the **Epistles** (letters), which show Christians how to live by Jesus' teachings and what it means to be a Christian.
- the **Book of Revelation**, an apocalyptic book written by John, featuring his own mystical visions, which some Christians believe describe the end of the world.

These books were not the only early Christian writings. They were accepted into the New Testament, however, because they passed four important criteria:

- The authority behind the material had to be one of the apostles. (Mark was accepted as the scribe of Peter, and Luke was a companion of Paul.)
- They were written early on (mostly before the end of the first century).
- They matched other presentations of Christian beliefs.
- They were accepted by all Christian Churches.

These criteria explain why Christians trust what is contained in the New Testament. Other documents, such as *The Gospel of Thomas*, *The Gospel of Barnabas* and *The Gospel of Jude* were rejected because the early Christians considered these documents to be a distortion of the teachings of Jesus.

Activities

1. What types of books are contained in the Old Testament? Give two examples of each type of book.
2. 'The Old Testament books contain nothing that Christians need.' Evaluate this statement. Be sure to include more than one point of view, and refer to Catholic beliefs and teachings in your answer.
3. a) Which books were accepted as part of the New Testament?
   b) Explain why these books were accepted but others were not.

Extension activity

Explain ways in which Christians may use the Old Testament to help them understand the Christian faith. Find three examples from the Old Testament that help Christians in this way.

Discussion activity

Discuss whether everything that is contained in both the Old and the New Testaments should be accepted equally by Christians.

★ Study tip

You do not need to know all the books of the Bible, but you should be aware of the different types of writings contained in the Bible.

Summary

You should now be able to describe the main sections of the Bible, explain how they differ, and understand why Christians accept the Bible as a source of authority.

1.7 Inspiration and the Bible as the word of God

The Bible as the word of God

All Christians accept that through the Bible God speaks to his people, and so the Bible is called 'the word of God'. The way God speaks is not thought of as a voice coming from the skies but as gentle stirrings within the human heart, especially as the words of the Bible are read. This is the **Holy Spirit**, inspiring believers to accept the message of God and share it with other people. Christians should be guided by the teachings contained in the Bible.

The Hebrew word for 'spirit' is *ru'ach*, which is also translated as 'breath' (see Genesis 2:7). When God breathed into Adam and gave him life, God's own Spirit was shared with human beings. God sends his Spirit to guide people. This is called **inspiration**. The term can be used to refer to the guidance that God gave to the writers of the Bible.

Many people see God working through the events of every day and throughout history. The books of the Bible that record historical events help other people to respond to God's actions and words, in order to learn from God. The history books and the wisdom books in the Old Testament are seen as important because God speaks through the words, and people listen and act on them.

The prophets and the word of God

The prophets were inspired to see God's work in a special way. They saw their task as encouraging everybody to stay faithful to God. As they warned and guided people, they passed on God's word and message.

The Gospels and the word of God

Christians believe that Jesus is the Word of God made flesh. In Jesus, God speaks directly to all people. The Gospels present the teachings and actions of Jesus, the Word-made-flesh, which means that the Gospels are in a very special way the word of God.

The Epistles and the word of God

The Epistles (or letters) are the writings of the apostles, the early witnesses to Jesus' life. They were written to help Christians apply the principles of Jesus' teachings to their everyday lives. The apostles were filled with the Holy Spirit, and therefore inspired to preach and teach God's word.

> ❝ Since everything asserted by the inspired authors or sacred writers must be held to be asserted by the Holy Spirit, it follows that **the books of Scripture must be acknowledged as teaching solidly, faithfully and without error that truth** which God wanted put into sacred writings for the sake of salvation. ❞
>
> *Dei Verbum* 11

Objectives

- Examine what it means to say that the Bible is the word of God.
- Evaluate to what extent the Bible should be a Catholic's only guide.

Key terms

- **Holy Spirit:** the Third Person of the Trinity whom Christians believe is the inspiring presence of God in the world
- **inspiration:** the guidance that God gives to people
- **Magisterium:** the teaching authority of the Catholic Church, exercised by the Pope and the bishops

⭐ Study tip

Think about how much you find out about another person from what they say and the way they say it.

▲ *Paul preaching the word of God to a crowd in Athens*

Chapter 1   Creation

The teachings of the Magisterium and the Bible

The Holy Spirit is believed to be constantly working in the Catholic Church. It was with the guidance of the Holy Spirit that the Church decided which books were to be accepted as part of the Bible, which is regarded as the true word of God. The Bible is interpreted in light of the Church's teachings.

The successors of the apostles – the Pope and the bishops – exercise the teaching authority of the Church. This authority is known as the **Magisterium**. It is through the Magisterium that the true message of the Bible is to be interpreted.

▲ *How do you feel when you walk past someone preaching on the street?*

> **Sacred Scripture is the word of God** inasmuch as it is consigned to writing under the inspiration of the divine Spirit, **while sacred tradition takes the word of God** entrusted by Christ the Lord and the Holy Spirit to the Apostles, and **hands it on to their successors in its full purity,** so that led by the light of the Spirit of truth, they may in proclaiming it preserve this word of God faithfully, explain it, and make it more widely known. Consequently it is not from Sacred Scripture alone that the Church draws her certainty about everything which has been revealed.
>
> *Dei Verbum* 9

> Your word is a lamp to my feet and a light to my path.
>
> *Psalms* 119(118):105 (NRSV)

God spoke through the Holy Spirit's inspiration of the Bible, so the Bible is the word of God. However, the Holy Spirit also guides the Church and speaks through the Magisterium. The Magisterium makes the word of God relevant to the modern world, applying the eternal truths that come from God, including the Bible, to the needs of the present day. Believers can trust the teachings of the Magisterium because of the inspiration of the same Holy Spirit who inspired the Bible.

Activities

1. Explain how God can speak to believers.
2. Explain why Christians pay special attention to the Gospels.
3. 'Everything a Christian needs is contained in the Bible.' Evaluate this statement. Be sure to include more than one point of view, and refer to Catholic beliefs and teachings in your answer.
4. Explain why for Catholics the Magisterium is important for the interpretation of the Bible.

Extension activity

'Only the Gospels are important for Christians.' Do you agree? Give reasons for your answer, showing that you have considered more than one point of view.

Research activity

Find an example of a famous speech that has inspired people. Examples might include speeches by Winston Churchill or Martin Luther King. Why was the speech so effective and what did it inspire people to do?

Summary

You should now understand in what ways the Bible is considered to be the word of God. You should also understand how the Catholic Church bases its teachings on the Bible.

1.8 Interpreting the Genesis creation stories

Catholic interpretations of the Genesis creation stories

Many Christians accept Genesis 1:1–2:4 and 2:5–2:27 as two creation stories, written as myths. A **myth** is a simple story that tries to convey a deep or complex truth. Myths are not meant to be taken literally. The intention is that people remember and reflect on the underlying truths presented. The message that the story conveys is what is of greatest importance.

▲ *Many Christians think that God was necessary to create something out of nothing, so it is possible to believe in God and the theory that the universe started with the Big Bang*

People believe that the creation story in Genesis 2 was written down about 950 BCE. The later creation story in Genesis 1 is a poem from about 450 BCE. In the message of the two stories, there is no contradiction:

1. God made everything.
2. Everything that God made was good.
3. Humans are the high point of God's creation.

The Catholic Church teaches that the creation stories should not be interpreted literally. It accepts that the stories come from different times, and reflect the thoughts and attitudes of the societies in which they originated. This should be considered when interpreting the stories today.

> ❝ Since God speaks in **Sacred Scripture** through men in human fashion, **the interpreter of Sacred Scripture … should carefully investigate what meaning the sacred writers really intended,** and what God wanted to manifest by means of their words. To search out the intention of the sacred writers, attention should be given, among other things, to 'literary forms'. ❞
>
> *Dei Verbum* 12

Objective
- Understand different Christian opinions about how important Genesis 1 and 2 are as accounts of creation.

Key terms
- **myth:** a story that intends to convey a deep truth or message, but not in a literal way
- **Sacred Scripture:** the holy writings of a religion that are believed to be inspired by God
- **fundamentalist:** someone who believes the Bible is a factual record that describes events exactly as they happened; fundamentalists believe that the Bible is divinely inspired and without error

⭐ Study tip
Remember that people use stories as a way of presenting complicated ideas in a simple way. Think of how a joke or anecdote can sometimes help people to understand something more easily than a detailed explanation.

Extension activity
Find a complicated piece of information that is difficult to understand, such as a scientific theory, mathematical formula or complex poem. What different ways could you use to present this information to help other people to understand it? Think about how the creation stories try to present complex ideas in simple ways: could you also use a story to make your information easier to understand?

Chapter 1 Creation

As the Bible is not to be interpreted literally, Catholics are able to accept both the creation stories and the theory of evolution. Pope Francis supported this view when he said:

> When we read in Genesis the account of Creation, we risk imagining God as a magus (magician), with a magic wand able to make everything. But that is not so … **Creation continued for … millennia and millennia, until it became which we know today, precisely because God is not a … conjurer, but the Creator who gives being to all things.** The beginning of the world is not the work of chaos … but derives directly from a supreme Origin that creates out of love. **The Big Bang … does not contradict the divine act of creating, but rather requires it.** The evolution of nature does not contrast with the notion of Creation, as evolution presupposes the creation of beings that evolve.
>
> Pope Francis, 27 October 2014

Fundamentalist interpretations of the Genesis creation stories

There are certain Christians who do not accept that the Bible should be interpreted in this way. They are known as **fundamentalists**.

Among their main beliefs are:
1. The Bible is the word of God and so must be accurate in all respects.
2. God has informed humanity of his truth.
3. Since God loves all humans, he will not mislead people by giving incorrect information.
4. Humans have no right to prefer their own interpretations to the actual words of God.

Some fundamentalists, called literalists, believe that every word in the Bible is accurate. Some believe that the world is only a few thousand years old. Some would support Anglican Archbishop Ussher who, in the seventeenth century, said that the first day of creation was Sunday 23 October 4004 BCE. While few people would go as far as that, many fundamentalists believe that the world is much younger than scientists claim.

Other fundamentalists are happy to accept that the world and universe might be as old as scientists suggest. These Christians still believe in the order of creation found in Genesis, but are willing to accept that the word 'day' does not refer to a 24-hour period.

Activities
1. Explain the purpose of myths in religious writings.
2. 'The fundamentalist approach is the only meaningful way to appreciate the Genesis creation stories.' Evaluate this statement. Be sure to include more than one point of view, and refer to Catholic beliefs and teachings in your answer.

▲ Some Christians believe that humanity began when God created Adam and Eve

> **The right way to read Sacred Scriptures is to read it prayerfully,** in other words, with the help of the Holy Spirit, under whose influence it came into being. It is God's Word and contains God's essential communication to us.
>
> *Youcat* 16

Discussion activity

Discuss why some Christians might be reluctant to accept both Genesis 1 and Genesis 2 as two accounts of the same act of creation.

Summary

You should now understand how and why Catholics and other Christians interpret the creation stories differently.

25

1.9 Natural law and Catholic attitudes towards science

Natural law

Catholic teaching states that God made everything good. Everything that exists depends on God for its existence. Human beings are one part of this whole, beautiful, good creation. Humans find their fulfilment by becoming the people God wants them to be, by living harmoniously with God, other people and all of creation. This fulfilment comes from following the **natural law**.

The basic natural law is 'do good and avoid evil'. Catholics believe this principle applies to all humans simply because they are created in the image and likeness of God (Genesis 1:27). Humans have an instinctive (or natural) knowledge of what it is to be good and fully human, because each person has been made by God. Natural law implies that people intuitively know what is the right thing to do, and they should not need rules to tell them what is right.

Objectives

- Understand the importance of natural law for Catholics.
- Understand how the Catholic Church values the role of science and scientific research.

Key terms

- **natural law:** moral principles and values that are considered to be inherent to all humans
- **Magisterium:** the teaching authority of the Catholic Church, exercised by the Pope and the bishops
- **Second Vatican Council:** a series of important gatherings of all the Catholic bishops between 1962 and 1965, which updated many Catholic teachings

▲ You buy something in a shop and you're given too much change. Does natural law mean that you know what is the right thing to do in this situation?

> **If people are to do good and avoid evil, certainty about what is good and evil must be inscribed within them.** In fact there is such a moral law that is, so to speak, "natural" to men and can be known in principle by every person by reason.
>
> *Youcat* 333

Catholic teachings often refer to natural law. As all life comes from God, every life is an expression of God's love, so every life is holy. The technical phrase for this is the 'sanctity of life'. Humans have a duty to respect the sanctity of all life, from the moment that life begins to its natural end.

Links

To read more about the sanctity of life see page 19.

Chapter 1 Creation

■ The Catholic Church and science

Members of the Catholic Church have always been involved in scientific developments. A few famous Catholic scientists include:

- St Albert the Great, a lecturer in theology and an expert in various scientific fields. He is the patron saint of scientists.
- Jean Baptiste Lamarck, who devised an early theory of evolution, called Lamarckism.
- Friar Gregor Mendel, who pioneered genetics.
- Georges Lemaitre, who devised a Big Bang model.

During the **Second Vatican Council** (1962–1965), the **Magisterium** stressed the need for science and religion to be mutually supportive. Catholics believe that scientists should use their God-given talents to help people understand the nature and purpose of God's creation. Religion and science might examine the same issue and come up with slightly different responses. This is not because they are contradicting each other but because they are asking slightly different questions. It is sometimes said that science explains the *how* of things and religion explains the *why*.

▲ *Gregor Mendel experimented with pea plants to show how certain characteristics can be inherited from one generation to the next*

> **If methodical investigation** within every branch of learning **is carried out in a genuinely scientific manner** and in accord with moral norms, **it never truly conflicts with faith,** for earthly matters and the concerns of faith derive from the same God.
>
> *Gaudium et Spes* 36

The bishops in the Second Vatican Council also insisted that religious viewpoints must not be disregarded when they said:

> For their part, however, **all believers of whatever religion always hear His revealing voice in the discourse of creatures.** When God is forgotten, however, the creature itself grows unintelligible.
>
> *Gaudium et Spes* 36

Activities

1. Explain what is meant by 'natural law'. Suggest two examples of how natural law might work in modern life.
2. 'Catholics should not expect every person to live according to natural law.' Evaluate this statement. Be sure to include more than one point of view, and refer to Catholic beliefs and teachings in your answer.

Summary

You should now be able to explain natural law and understand why it is important for Catholics. You should also understand Catholic attitudes about how science and religion can work together.

Research activity

Investigate one scientific development that resulted from the work of a Catholic scientist.

Discussion activity

Discuss whether it is important that science and religion work together. Refer to Catholic teachings in your discussion.

Extension activity

Find out about the life and work of St Albert the Great.

★ Study tip

Remember that science is built on testing ideas, some of which are wrong but take time to be proved they are wrong before they are discarded. Many Christians believe religion and science do not have to contradict each other when the truth is found.

27

1.10 Caring for the environment

Catholic teachings about creation and the environment

Catholics believe that the whole universe was created by God, and is sustained by God in a great act of out-flowing love. The whole of creation is God's gift and is holy because it comes from God. There is nothing in creation that should be rejected or neglected.

Pope Francis described the Catholic understanding of the word 'creation' like this:

> In the Judaeo-Christian tradition, **the word 'creation' has a broader meaning than 'nature', for it has to do with God's loving plan in which every creature has its own value and significance.** Nature is usually seen as a system which can be studied, understood and controlled, whereas creation can only be understood as a gift from the outstretched hand of the Father of all, and as a reality illuminated by the love which calls us together into universal communion.
>
> *Laudato Si* 76

When Jesus was asked which was the greatest commandment, he replied:

> The first is, 'Hear, O Israel: the Lord our God, the Lord is one; **you shall love the Lord your God with all your heart,** and with all your soul, and with all your mind, and with all your strength.' The second is this, **'You shall love your neighbour as yourself.'** There is no other commandment greater than these.
>
> *Mark* 12:29–31 (NRSV)

▲ Reducing pollution is one of the biggest environmental challenges facing the world today

Objectives
- Know of Jesus' commandments to love God and your neighbour.
- Understand how caring for the environment is a response to these commandments.
- Understand the importance of protecting the environment.

Key terms
- **environment:** the natural world; the surroundings in which someone lives
- **natural resources:** materials found in nature – such as oil and trees – that can be used by people to make more complex products
- **hypocrites:** people who tell others how they should live but who do not live by these standards themselves

> Once we start to think about the kind of world we are leaving to future generations, we look at things differently; we realize that **the world is a gift which we have freely received and must share with others.** Since the world has been given to us, we can no longer view reality in a purely utilitarian way, in which efficiency and productivity are entirely geared to our individual benefit.
>
> *Laudato Si* 159

28

Chapter 1   Creation

■ How Catholics care for the environment

One of the ways in which Christians show their love of God is by valuing what God has created. They do this by taking care of the world and not abusing the **environment** in any way. There is a delicate balance within creation. If one element of nature is damaged, this may often affect other elements too. Just as John Donne once wrote that 'No man is an island', no part of nature can be isolated from the rest. Respect for God's creation involves protecting the whole of creation.

The second commandment is to love your neighbour. One of the most important ways in which believers can do this is by caring for the environment in which their neighbour lives. If one person does not care about issues like pollution, littering and so on, they are not just affecting their own life but the lives of everyone else as well, including future generations.

All Catholics should be aware of how their actions today might affect the world in centuries to come. An example of this is being aware of how pollution or the exploitation of limited **natural resources** will damage the lifestyles of future generations.

However, just thinking about these issues is not enough. If the thinking does not lead to constructive action to improve the current situation, then such thinking is pointless. Catholics must not allow themselves to become **hypocrites** in this regard. Words should turn into action immediately. No one should expect other people to take action to care for the environment without doing the same thing themselves.

Using solar panels to power the Vatican

In 2008, the Vatican installed thousands of solar panels on the roof of one of its main halls. This was done in such a way that there was no obvious change to the skyline of the Vatican. The solar panels help to light and regulate the temperature of a number of buildings in the Vatican. They have reduced the Vatican's carbon emissions by about 200 tonnes each year.

▲ More than 2000 solar panels were installed on the roof of the Vatican in 2008

Research activity

Find three other examples of how Catholics care for the environment today.

Summary

You should now understand how Catholic teachings about the creation and the commandment to love your neighbour influence Catholic attitudes about caring for the environment.

Activities

1. Explain why the Catholic Church teaches that the environment should be respected.
2. 'The best way for Catholics to show love for their neighbour is to protect the environment.' Evaluate this statement. Be sure to include more than one point of view, and refer to Catholic beliefs and teachings in your answer.

Extension activity

Devise a small group project that could help to care for your local environment. What would you need to do to carry out the project, and how would it help?

> ❝ [God] covers the heavens with clouds, prepares rain for the earth, makes grass grow on the hills. He gives to the animals their food, and to the young ravens when they cry. ❞
> *Psalms* 147(146):8–9 (NRSV)

⭐ Study tip

Many of the Church's teachings are issued in documents that are named after the introductory words. You only need to know the names of the four major documents of Vatican II: *Gaudium et Spes*, *Lumen Gentium*, *Dei Verbum* and *Sacrosanctum Concilium*.

29

1.11 The meaning of stewardship

Christians are commanded by God to have dominion over creation (Genesis 1:28) but also to care for it. This latter command is found in Genesis 2:15 where it says: 'The Lord God took the man and put him in the garden of Eden to till it and keep it.' The phrase 'till it and keep it' leads to the idea of **stewardship**. Humans have a responsibility to take care of the whole earth, and not exploit it for their own ends.

▲ *This is just one example of how Catholics can be good stewards*

Pope Francis talks about the challenges of stewardship when he says:

> ❝ If we acknowledge the value and the fragility of nature and, at the same time, our God-given abilities, we can finally leave behind the modern myth of unlimited material progress. **A fragile world, entrusted by God to human care, challenges us to devise intelligent ways of directing, developing and limiting our power.** ❞
>
> *Laudato Si 78*

Christians must accept their **interdependence** with the rest of creation if they are to make meaningful efforts not only to change their own attitudes and actions, but to inspire other people to contribute to protecting the world as well.

There are many practical steps that Catholics can take to change their own lifestyles and challenge the attitudes of other people. Here are just a few examples.

At a local level, Catholics can:
- try to reduce the amount of unnecessary rubbish they produce in their homes

Objectives
- Understand the concept of stewardship.
- Give examples of how Catholics can be good stewards at local, national and global levels.

Key terms
- **stewardship:** the idea that believers have a duty to look after the environment on behalf of God
- **interdependence:** relying or depending on each other, as a change to one thing affects other things as well

> ❝ Like good stewards of the manifold grace of God, serve one another with whatever gift each of you has received. ❞
>
> *1 Peter* 4:10 (NRSV)

> ❝ God wills the interdependence of creatures. The sun and the moon, the cedar and the little flower, the eagle and the sparrow: the spectacle of their countless diversities and inequalities tells us that **no creature is self-sufficient. Creatures exist only in dependence on each other, to complete each other,** in the service of each other. ❞
>
> *Catechism of the Catholic Church* 340

Chapter 1 Creation

- recycle more waste
- use public transport, or walk or cycle more often
- take part in local environmental campaigns or projects.

At a national level, Catholics can:

- put pressure on politicians to support laws that protect the environment and endangered species
- support and buy products from environment-friendly businesses
- put pressure on companies to ensure that environment-friendly policies are followed, such as replanting trees whenever they are cut down to make products.

At a global level, Catholics can:

- put pressure on governments to support and implement the policies accepted at meetings such as Rio+20 (a conference organised by the United Nations in 2012, held in Rio de Janeiro, Brazil, to work out how to tackle environmental issues)
- boycott or help to expose multinational companies that threaten the environment through their drive to make a profit.

Many people feel that there is no point in taking any individual action to help save the environment, as the actions of one person cannot make much of a difference. However, the whole world is made up of single individuals, and as long as individuals are working towards the same goals, progress will be made.

▲ Deforestation is one major environmental problem that needs to be tackled at a global level

> **❝** As the bishops of Southern Africa have stated: **'Everyone's talents and involvement are needed to redress the damage caused by human abuse of God's creation'.** All of us can cooperate as instruments of God for the care of creation, each according to his or her own culture, experience, involvements and talents. **❞**
>
> Pope Francis quoting the bishops of South Africa, *Laudato Si* 14

An environment-friendly church

In 2011, the Catholic church of the Sacred Heart of Jesus and St Peter the Apostle in Hampshire, England, was opened. It includes a rain-water harvesting system and solar panels that help to heat and light the church. In this very practical way, the church is showing how carbon footprints can be reduced.

Activities

1. Explain what is meant by the term stewardship in reference to creation.
2. 'For Catholics, supporting global action on the environment is more important than supporting local and national efforts.' Evaluate this statement. Be sure to include more than one point of view, and refer to Catholic beliefs and teachings in your answer.

Discussion activity

Discuss whether it is possible to impose environment-friendly policies on everybody. Refer to Catholic teachings in the discussion.

Extension activity

Research what happened at Rio+20. Find out what the outcomes of the conference were, and its effects on world attitudes and actions. Evaluate how useful Rio+20 was.

⭐ Study tip

It is often easier to examine stewardship through practical examples, rather than just talking about it in the abstract.

Summary

You should now understand why the concept of stewardship is important to Catholics, and be able to give examples of how Catholics can be good stewards.

31

1.12 CAFOD and sustainability

■ What is sustainability and why is it important?

Sustainability is the ability of the whole world to carry on working in the right balance. It is the acceptance that humans need a healthy, self-perpetuating environment for all life to prosper. Unless people recognise that ecology, economics, politics and culture are all linked together, many believe there is a strong chance that the delicate harmony that allows for a wide variety of life in the world will be destroyed.

Most international organisations, like the United Nations, now accept that humans cannot simply use and abuse the world for their own immediate advantage. Pollution, deforestation and overpopulation are just a few of the problems that have contributed to an imbalance in the world's ecology.

> **Objectives**
> - Know why sustainability is important to many people.
> - Understand how CAFOD supports sustainable projects.

> **Key term**
> - **sustainability:** only using natural resources at a rate at which they can be replaced

 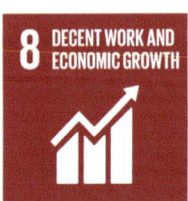    

▲ The sustainable development goals are a set of goals that the United Nations wants all countries to work towards achieving by 2030 in order to create a sustainable world

Sustainability projects aim to redress this imbalance and allow all aspects of life to prosper. The hope is that such projects will help to:
- reverse some of the damage that has already been done to the environment
- reduce poverty, by allowing people to live in a more balanced way that enables everyone to share in what nature provides
- reduce tension in the world as there is less need to fight over resources, which leads to a greater sense of security.

Chapter 1 Creation

■ The influence of Catholic teachings

Christians believe that it is only through caring for all aspects of creation, in recognition that God's creation is an integrated whole, that people will fulfil their duty as stewards of creation.

Pope Francis calls for a 'bottom-up' approach to caring for the world that puts the poorest and their needs at the centre of world politics and economics. Improving the lives of the poorest in the world, to create a better balance between everyone, will help to ensure sustainability.

Pope Francis also believes there is a need in the world for people to listen to each other. This includes a recognition that developing countries are often good sources of sustainable techniques, such as farming methods that don't exhaust the soil, or fishing methods that don't deplete the number of fish in the sea.

■ CAFOD's work on sustainability

CAFOD is the official aid agency for the Catholic Church in England and Wales. The main aim of CAFOD is to work with the poorest people to achieve a more just world. CAFOD supports sustainability by:

- encouraging people in England and Wales to live more simply, so that natural resources are not used up so quickly
- supporting and setting up projects which recognise that humans, resources and the environment are all important and interrelated; CAFOD helps all of its partners to ensure that their projects protect the environment
- working with other international organisations to ensure that sustainability is one of the leading approaches to national and international politics and trade
- helping to found the Beyond 2015 campaign, which supported the creation of the UN Sustainable Development Goals in 2015; these seek to protect the environment and improve people's quality of life (particularly those living in poverty) by 2030, partly through the use of sustainable projects around the world
- working with groups like MONLAR in Sri Lanka, which helps farmers to use sustainable techniques that are economical yet effective (such as the use of natural fertilisers).

▲ One of MONLAR's goals is to help farmers to adopt sustainable farming methods

> **We recognise the intimate relationship between protecting and sustaining the environment and promoting human development.** We aim to take proper account of ecological sustainability in our work and in our lifestyle, believing we are enriched by living simply.
>
> CAFOD

Activities

1. Explain the importance of sustainability for the world.
2. 'There is no need for Catholics to support sustainability programmes.' Evaluate this statement. Be sure to include more than one point of view, and refer to Catholic beliefs and teachings in your answer.

Research activity

Research one project of sustainability that was either started by CAFOD or is supported by CAFOD. How effective do you think this project is?

★ Study tip

This topic is more easily understood by looking at specific projects that help to improve sustainability, such as some of the projects that CAFOD supports.

Summary
You should now know why sustainability is important to many Catholics. You should also know how CAFOD supports sustainability.

33

1 Assessment guidance

Creation – summary

You should now be able to:

- ✔ explain what Michelangelo's *Creation of Adam* shows about humanity being created in the image of God, and be able to contrast it with another work of art that depicts creation
- ✔ explain what Genesis 1 and 2 show about God as creator, transcendent and omnipotent, and understand the importance of these beliefs
- ✔ explain the significance of humans being made in the image of God, and what this shows about free will, stewardship, human dignity and the sanctity of life
- ✔ explain how the Bible was written, and describe the types of writings that it contains
- ✔ explain the significance of inspiration and of the Bible as the revealed word of God
- ✔ explain different Christian interpretations of the Genesis creation stories
- ✔ explain how the idea of natural law is based on belief in the goodness of creation, and how natural law influences Catholic understanding of the sanctity of life
- ✔ explain how Catholics believe science and religion can work together
- ✔ explain how caring for the environment is a way of 'loving the neighbour'
- ✔ explain how Catholics show the idea of stewardship at work at different levels
- ✔ explain how CAFOD's work on sustainability shows Catholic beliefs about the goodness of creation.

Sample student answer – the 4 mark question

1. Write an answer to the following question:

   Explain two ways in which Michelangelo's *Creation of Adam* expresses Catholic beliefs about human beings. **[4 marks]**

2. Read the following sample student answer:

   "Michelangelo shows that humans reflect God's image because God and Adam are painted to look similar. Catholics believe that humans reflect the image and likeness of God. Michelangelo suggests that the life force of human beings comes from God as the hands of God and Adam almost meet. This means that humans are special."

3. With a partner, discuss the sample answer. Is the focus of the answer correct? Is anything missing from the answer? How do you think it could be improved?

4. What mark (out of 4) would you give this answer? Look at the mark scheme in the Introduction (AO1). What are the reasons for the mark you have given?

5. Now swap your answer with your partner's and mark each other's responses. What mark (out of 4) would you give the response? Refer to the mark scheme and give reasons for the mark you award.

Sample student answer – the 5 mark question

1. Write an answer to the following question:

   Explain two ways in which, for Catholics, science and religion can be seen to be in harmony. Refer to Christian beliefs in your answer. **[5 marks]**

2. Read the following sample student answer:

   "Catholics do not believe that the Bible has to be taken as the literal truth. God gave human beings intelligence that they can use to discover his creation. Science uses this gift from God to understand how God's creation works. Humans also use this intelligence to appreciate why the early stories of creation came about. Pope Francis teaches that the Big Bang does not contradict the divine act of creating but rather requires it. Science and the Bible are totally in harmony, if the Bible is read in the correct way."

3. With a partner, discuss the sample answer. What are its good points and are there any weaknesses? How do you think the answer could be improved?

4. What mark (out of 5) would you give this answer? Look at the mark scheme in the Introduction (AO1). What are the reasons for the mark you have given?

5. Now swap your answer with your partner's and mark each other's responses. What mark (out of 5) would you give the response? Refer to the mark scheme and give reasons for the mark you award.

Practice questions

1. What does stewardship mean for Catholics?
   A) God told humans to look after the world
   B) Catholics can use all the resources they want as God will provide more
   C) The world will end soon so there is no need to worry about it
   D) Adam and Eve were made in the image of God **[1 mark]**

2. Give two ways in which CAFOD supports sustainability. **[2 marks]**

3. Explain two ways in which the idea of stewardship influences the work of CAFOD. **[4 marks]**

4. Explain two beliefs about the nature of God that are expressed in the creation stories of Genesis 1 and 2. Refer to Christian beliefs in your answer. **[5 marks]**

5. 'The teachings about the nature of God expressed in Genesis 1 and 2 have no relevance for Catholics in the 21st century.'

   Evaluate this statement. In your answer you should:
   - give developed arguments to support this statement
   - give developed arguments to support a different point of view
   - refer to Catholic teaching
   - reach a justified conclusion. **[12 marks]**

> **Study tip**
>
> You should aim to develop contrasting viewpoints. You might discuss how some people think that what these ancient documents have to say about God is only a reflection of the time and culture in which they were written. Others might argue that these stories present eternal truths about God as creator, transcendent and omnipotent. You should aim to refer to Catholic teaching in your answer: for example, you could refer to passages from the Bible (especially Genesis 1 and 2), religious writings or the teachings of the popes.

2 Incarnation

2.1 Jesus as God incarnate

■ The meaning of incarnation

'Incarnate' means being made flesh. The **doctrine** of the **incarnation** teaches that God took on the full limitations of the human condition when he became Jesus. Jesus went through the whole cycle of a human life: he was conceived, born naturally, grew up, learned, worked, hungered and feasted, felt fear and loss, suffered and died. Jesus was truly man. This shows that God loves the human race so much that he was prepared to share in it to the fullest extent. God in Jesus knows all the trials, stresses and issues of being human. He can empathise with the human race. This helps Christians to value God's love.

■ The annunciation

> In the sixth month the angel Gabriel was sent by God to a town in Galilee called Nazareth, to a virgin engaged to a man whose name was Joseph, of the house of David. The virgin's name was Mary. And he came to her and said, 'Greetings, favoured one! The Lord is with you.' But she was much perplexed by his words and pondered what sort of greeting this might be. The angel said to her, 'Do not be afraid, Mary, for you have found favour with God. **And now, you will conceive in your womb and bear a son, and you will name him Jesus. He will be great, and will be called the Son of the Most High,** and the Lord God will give to him the throne of his ancestor David. He will reign over the house of Jacob forever, and of his kingdom there will be no end.' Mary said to the angel, 'How can this be, since I am a virgin?' The angel said to her, 'The Holy Spirit will come upon you, and the power of the Most High will overshadow you; therefore the child to be born will be holy; he will be called Son of God. And now, your relative Elizabeth in her old age has also conceived a son; and this is the sixth month for her who was said to be barren. For nothing will be impossible with God.' **Then Mary said, 'Here am I, the servant of the Lord; let it be with me according to your word.'** Then the angel departed from her.
>
> Luke 1:26–38 (NRSV)

The **angel** Gabriel came to announce God's plan of sending his Son into the world. The message is given to a young virgin. Mary has found favour with God, but the message is not just for her; it is a message for all Jewish people, as God is fulfilling all the promises that he made to Abraham and his descendants.

Objectives

- Know what the term incarnation means.
- Understand what the incarnation shows about God's love.

Key terms

- **doctrine:** official Church teaching
- **incarnation:** God taking on the human condition in Jesus
- **annunciation:** when the angel Gabriel asked Mary to accept the role of the mother of the Son of God
- **angel:** a spiritual being believed to act as a messenger of God
- **grace:** God's free gift of his unconditional love to the believer

▲ A modern stained-glass window showing the annunciation

Chapter 2 Incarnation

The name chosen for the child is Jesus, which in Hebrew means 'saviour'. Jesus is Son of 'the Most High', which is another way of referring to God. The statement that the child will reign over the house of Israel forever shows that in him all of God's promises to the Jewish people, and to the world, will be fulfilled.

> **"** You have heard, O Virgin, that you will conceive and bear a son … We too are waiting, O Lady, for your word of compassion … **In your brief response we are to be remade. "**
>
> St Bernard of Clairvaux

▲ *A fifteenth-century painting of the annunciation*

Mary's question: 'How can this be, since I am a virgin?' is not a rejection of God's wishes but a request for information. The response, 'The Holy Spirit will come upon you, and the power of the Most High will overshadow you,' means that Jesus is a unique gift from God. The power of God, his free gift or **grace** to the people, works through Mary to bring the Son of God into the world.

However, this gift had to be freely accepted. God's wishes couldn't come about without both human involvement and human consent. Mary had the choice to accept the role of mother of Jesus or to reject it. Mary's words, 'Here am I, the servant of the Lord; let it be with me according to your word,' show her willing but humble acceptance of the role God wants her to play.

Discussion activity

Discuss whether you think Mary was sensible when she agreed to become the mother of the Son of God.

★ Study tip

You need to know Luke 1:26–38 well as it is central to Christian understanding of the incarnation.

Summary

You should now understand the meaning and significance of the term incarnation. You should also be able to explain the importance of Luke's story about the annunciation.

Activities

1. Explain what the word 'incarnate' means.
2. 'The incarnation is God's great act of love for the human race.' Evaluate this statement. Be sure to include more than one point of view, and refer to Catholic beliefs and teachings in your answer.

2.2 God's message to Joseph

■ The role of Joseph in Jesus' birth

In Luke's Gospel, discussed on the previous page, the story of the annunciation focuses on Mary. But in Matthew's Gospel, the focus is more on the role of Joseph. Matthew's Gospel starts with a **genealogy**, a list of fathers and sons from Abraham to Joseph. When the list reaches Joseph, however, the wording changes. It moves from: 'Matthan the father of Jacob, Jacob the father of Joseph' to 'Joseph the *husband* of Mary, of whom Jesus was born'. This is the first indication that Jesus was not simply of human parentage. This story about Joseph is stressing that Jesus was born of a virgin, conceived by the power of God.

▲ *Joseph with Jesus as a child*

> **Objectives**
> - Know Matthew's account of the message to Joseph.
> - Understand the importance of the virgin birth.
> - Compare Matthew's and Luke's accounts.

> **Key terms**
> - **genealogy:** a list of the generations in a family, which shows how people are related to each other
> - **Emmanuel:** a Jewish name meaning 'God is with us'
> - **virgin birth:** the belief that Jesus was fully human but did not have a human father

> ❝ Now the birth of Jesus the Messiah took place in this way. When his mother Mary had been engaged to Joseph, but before they lived together, she was found to be with child from the Holy Spirit. Her husband Joseph, being a righteous man and unwilling to expose her to public disgrace, planned to dismiss her quietly. But just when he had resolved to do this, an angel of the Lord appeared to him in a dream and said, 'Joseph, son of David, do not be afraid to take Mary as your wife, **for the child conceived in her is from the Holy Spirit. She will bear a son, and you are to name him Jesus, for he will save his people from their sins.'** All this took place to fulfil what had been spoken by the Lord through the prophet:
>
> 'Look, the virgin shall conceive and bear a son, and they shall name him **Emmanuel**',
>
> which means, 'God is with us.' When Joseph awoke from sleep, he did as the angel of the Lord commanded him; he took her as his wife. ❞
>
> *Matthew* 1:18–24 (NRSV)

Chapter 2 Incarnation

Joseph is shown as someone who is willing to obey God's plan, no matter what it costs. When he first hears about Mary's pregnancy he wishes to make the situation easier for her by not exposing her publicly. Then he is informed by God's messenger that the child is of God, and the child will be 'God with us'. For Jews it is the father's privilege to choose the name for his son, but here God has chosen the name: Jesus, 'God saves'.

Jesus is shown here as the Son of God, who is God present with his people as the one who saves. Jesus is also the fulfilment of the promises God made to his people through the prophets. The **virgin birth** stresses that while Jesus was fully human, getting his humanity from Mary, he was also fully God, 'conceived by the Holy Spirit'.

> ❝ St Joseph was chosen among all men, to be the protector and guardian of the Virgin Mother of God; the defender and foster-father of the Infant-God, and the only co-operator upon earth, the one confidant of the secret of God in the work of the redemption of mankind. ❞
>
> St Bernard of Clairvaux

■ Comparing Matthew's and Luke's accounts

Matthew wrote his account for Jewish Christians. Women had limited roles in Judaism at the time Matthew was writing, and no woman's evidence was accepted as having any value. This is probably why Matthew focused on Joseph's role in Jesus' birth. In contrast, Luke was writing for non-Jewish Christians for whom the value of women was higher. This meant that he could write about Mary's role in Jesus' birth.

Despite these differences, the message of both accounts is the same:
- Mary was a virgin.
- God worked through human beings to enable his plan for humanity to come about.
- Jesus was conceived by the power of the Holy Spirit.
- An angel announced Jesus' birth.

▲ Catholics believe that the holy family of Jesus, Mary and Joseph is the model for all families

Discussion activity
Discuss how easy you think it was for Joseph to accept God's will.

⭐ Study tip
Remember that Matthew and Luke wrote their accounts independently but they were trying to get the same message across.

Activities
1. Explain why the virgin birth is important to Catholics.
2. 'Matthew's account of the virgin birth is easier to understand than Luke's story of the annunciation.' Evaluate this statement. Be sure to include more than one point of view, and refer to Catholic beliefs and teachings in your answer.

Summary

You should now understand the meaning and significance of the virgin birth, and be able to explain the main points of Matthew's story about God's message to Joseph.

2.3 Jesus, the Word of God

> In the beginning was the Word, and the Word was with God, and **the Word was God.** He was in the beginning with God. All things came into being through him, and without him not one thing came into being. What has come into being in him was life, and the life was the light of all people.
>
> And **the Word became flesh and lived among us,** and we have seen his glory, the glory as of a father's only son, full of grace and truth.
>
> *John 1:1–4, 14 (NRSV)*

▲ *John writing his Gospel*

Objectives

- Know what John says about the Word of God.
- Understand how Jesus is the Word made flesh.

Key terms

- **Word of God:** the Second Person of the Trinity, God the Son, who became flesh in Jesus
- **eternal:** without beginning or end
- **co-exist:** live together in harmony
- **dynamic:** full of energy and creativeness

John's Gospel starts with an explanation of Jesus as the **Word of God** made flesh.

John deliberately echoes the beginning of the book of Genesis, the first account of creation, which states: 'In the beginning [when] God created … God said …' (Genesis 1:1–3). John parallels this verse with 'In the beginning was the Word'.

⭐ Study tip

It might be helpful before you start thinking about the Word of God to think about what happens when you say something. What is the relationship between yourself and the words you speak?

Links

For more on the importance of God's word in the creation stories see pages 14–15.

In the beginning was the Word

With the phrase 'In the beginning was the Word', John is showing that the Word existed before all things. While the other Gospels show what happened when the Word became human (as Jesus), John is stressing the further dimension that the Word is an **eternal** being.

The Word was God

A word comes from within a person and is an expression of what is inside that person. In the same way, the Word of God is inside God and is God's self-expression. That is why it is true to say that 'the Word was God'.

> **In Jesus Christ, God himself came to earth.** He is God's last Word. By listening to him, all men of all times can know who God is and what is necessary for their salvation.
>
> *Youcat 10*

Chapter 2 Incarnation

The Word was with God

The phrase 'the Word was with God' indicates that while the Word and God are united and **co-exist**, there is also a distinction between them.

The Word of God is how God expresses his power. It goes forth from God, and is **dynamic** and creative. Everything that exists depends on the Word of God. The Word gives life, light and guidance to people, particularly to those who accept him.

> **Links**
>
> 'The Word was with God' is one of the important phrases that help Christians to understand the nature of the Trinity. To learn more about the Trinity see pages 70–71.

The Word became flesh

Verse 14 is the great statement of the incarnation: 'the Word became flesh and lived among us'. The Word, the self-expression of God, took on human nature, coming down to earth to live as a full human being.

The Word as an expression of love

The Word is the expression of God's love for humans. The word 'grace' means 'free gift', and Jesus is God's free gift to the human race, to help humans learn to respond fully to the love of God. Jesus came to bring people to the truth. It was an offering for people to accept or reject. Christians believe that God does not force people to choose him; instead he stretches out his hands and hopes people will accept his grace.

▲ Christians believe that Mary gave birth to Jesus, the Word of God made flesh, and therefore she is the Mother of God

> **Links**
>
> For more on the meaning of incarnation see pages 36–37.

> **Activities**
>
> 1 Explain the relationship between the Word and God.
> 2 'The teaching that God's Word became flesh shows that humans are very important to God.' Evaluate this statement. Be sure to include more than one point of view, and refer to Catholic beliefs and teachings in your answer.

> **Extension activity**
>
> Look up passages from the Bible that refer to God's word and wisdom (for example Genesis 1:1–18, Wisdom 7:25–26, Ecclesiasticus 24:2–11 and Hebrews 4:12–13). What similarities are there between these passages and John 1:1–4?

> **Summary**
>
> You should now know what John says about the Word of God, and understand how Jesus is the Word of God made flesh.

2.4 Jesus as both fully human and fully God

■ Jesus as the Son of Man

Throughout the Gospels, the **evangelists** showed how Jesus experienced all the joys and trials of what it means to be human. Jesus was tempted (Matthew 4:1–11), he ate and drank with all types of people (Luke 5:29–32), he pitied the widow (Luke 7:11–17), he wept when his friend had died (John 11:28–36), he was troubled (Mark 14:32–42), and he suffered and died in agony (Mark 15:33–36). Jesus was fully human.

Sometimes Jesus talked about himself using the phrase 'the **Son of Man**'. This phrase is used in two different ways in the Old Testament:

- It is used in a general way to refer to the speaker, just like some people in England use the word 'one' instead of 'I'. This is how the phrase is used in the prophecies of Ezekiel.
- It is sometimes used about a human who is taken up into the heavenly court and given power over all the world. This is particularly the case in Daniel 7:13.

Sometimes when Jesus used the phrase 'Son of Man', it is not clear whether he was referring to himself as a normal person (this might be the case in Luke 9:44) or as someone who has special authority from God (perhaps this is the case in Luke 5:24 and Mark 2:28). However, when Jesus talked about himself and the suffering that he would have to endure, he used the phrase 'Son of Man'. If Jesus were not fully human, the pain and suffering that he predicted would not have bothered him. He warned his disciples about his coming suffering and death. This was not a future he looked forward to with pleasure, but he trusted in God's promises that those who are faithful to God would be raised up to heaven.

▲ *A statue of Jesus weeping in Oklahoma, which relates to the Bible verse where Jesus cried after his friend died. This statue also remembers the victims of the Oklahoma bombing in 1995, when 168 people were killed in the blast.*

> **❝** Then he began to teach them that the Son of Man must undergo great suffering, and be rejected by the elders, the chief priests, and the scribes, and be killed, and after three days rise again. **❞**
>
> *Mark* 8:31 (NRSV)

Objectives

- Know passages in the Bible which show that Jesus is fully God and fully man.
- Understand how Jesus being fully human affected his life on earth.
- Understand the meanings of the titles Son of God and Son of Man.

■ Jesus as the Son of God

When Jesus was arrested and stood before the **Sanhedrin**, he was at first silent as he followed Jewish law. According to Jewish law, no accused person on trial could be asked a direct question and nothing that the accused said during the trial could be taken as evidence. The high priest, however, asked Jesus a question that he had to answer:

> But he was silent and did not answer. Again the high priest asked him, **'Are you the Messiah, the Son of the Blessed One?' Jesus said, 'I am;** and you will see the Son of Man seated at the right hand of the Power, and coming with the clouds of heaven.'
>
> *Mark* 14:61–62 (NRSV)

Jesus was asked directly if he was the Son of God ('the Son of the Blessed One'). To this Jesus replied, 'I am'. The words 'I am' are a translation of the phrase that God used to reveal himself to Moses (Exodus 3:14). In this reply Jesus acknowledged that he was the Son of God, and had a share in God's power. But he also called himself the Son of Man, emphasising his humanity as well as his divinity.

In the resurrection, Jesus was raised to new life and sat at God's right hand. This means that he took his place as God. Nobody can become God, as God by definition has no beginning or end. The resurrection proves that Jesus always was God, but that during his life on earth he limited himself to the condition of a human being, with all that that involved.

> **In Jesus, God really became one of us and thus our brother;** nevertheless, he did not cease to be God at the same time and thus our Lord.
>
> *Youcat* 77

Key terms

- **evangelists:** the writers of the Gospels (Matthew, Mark, Luke and John)
- **Son of Man:** a title that could refer to either just a human being, or a human who is given power by God
- **Sanhedrin:** the Jewish Council that looked after all aspects of Jewish life and religion at the time of Jesus

▲ *Jesus on trial before the Sanhedrin*

Research activity

Look up all the biblical references that appear on these two pages and summarise what each one shows about Jesus.

Activities

1. Explain why Jesus used the title 'Son of Man' when talking about himself.
2. 'Jesus could not have been anything other than a human being.' Evaluate this statement. Be sure to include more than one point of view, and refer to Catholic beliefs and teachings in your answer.

> [Jesus] worked with human hands, he thought with a human mind, acted by human choice and loved with a human heart.
>
> *Gaudium et Spes* 22

⭐ Study tip

Be careful with the terms Son of Man and Son of God. In the context of Jesus' teachings and the Gospels, it is wrong to say that 'Son of Man' is just talking about Jesus as a human being, as sometimes the term is meant to imply that Jesus has a share in God's power.

Summary

You should now understand why Jesus can be described as both Son of Man and Son of God, and what these titles show about his nature.

2.5 Christian symbols

The power of symbols

A symbol is a sign or design that represents something else. Symbols are useful in religion as many religious ideas cannot easily be put into words. It can sometimes be difficult to portray complex, abstract truths about God and religious beliefs using limited, specific words.

One way to avoid the problems connected with expressing ideas through words is to use a representational symbol. Symbols are only intended to convey a vague idea of what they are pointing to. They direct the mind to something beyond themselves: something that cannot be fully explained but which may be sensed in an abstract way.

Christianity has used many symbols during its existence. Catholicism values these symbols and uses them a lot in church design and the liturgical vestments (the robes worn by the clergy). Three of the most common symbols are the **Ichthus (fish)**, **Alpha and Omega**, and **Chi-Rho**.

Ichthus (fish)

In the early days of Christianity, when people could be persecuted for their faith, Christians used to quickly draw and erase the outline of a fish to show that they were a Christian, or to indicate where Christian prayer meetings were being held. The outer shape is very easy to draw, even with your foot on a dusty road, and only fellow Christians would recognise the symbolism.

The Greek word *ichthus* means 'fish', but Christians also use it as a type of acronym, where each of the letters represent one word of a Greek saying about Jesus:

- I is the first letter of the Greek word *Iesous*, which means Jesus
- Ch is the first letter of *Christos*, which means Christ
- Th is the first letter of *Theou*, which means God
- U is the first letter of *(H)uios*, which means Son
- S is the first letter of *Soter*, which means Saviour

Or: Jesus Christ, Son of God, Saviour. Only a Christian would make this declaration of faith about Jesus, and so the fish symbol came to be used regularly among Christian believers.

Alpha and Omega

Alpha (A) is the first letter of the Greek alphabet, while Omega (Ω) is the last letter. The use of these two letters indicates that God and Jesus are involved in everything from beginning to end.

The use of Alpha and Omega to talk about God and Jesus goes back to at least the Book of Revelation, written towards the end of the first century:

> ### Objectives
> - Know the meaning of the symbols Ichthus, Alpha and Omega, and Chi-Rho.
> - Understand the purpose and use of these symbols.

> ### Key terms
> - **Ichthus (fish):** a symbol of a fish, based on a Greek acronym that translates as 'Jesus Christ, Son of God, Saviour'
> - **Alpha and Omega:** a symbol made from the first and last letters of the Greek alphabet, which are used to show that God and Jesus are eternal – the beginning and end of all things
> - **Chi-Rho:** a symbol to represent Jesus, made up of the first two letters of his name in Greek

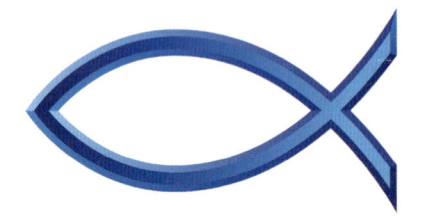

▲ The Ichthus symbol

Chapter 2 Incarnation

> ❝ 'I am the Alpha and the Omega,' says the Lord God, who is and who was and who is to come, the Almighty. ❞
>
> *Revelation* 1:8 (NRSV)

> ❝ Then he said to me, 'It is done! I am the Alpha and the Omega, the beginning and the end.' ❞
>
> *Revelation* 21:6 (NRSV)

The Alpha and Omega symbol can be used to refer to both God and Jesus. The symbol is used in many places in churches, vestments and drawings, but it has a special place on the Paschal candle (the large candle that is lit at the Easter Vigil to represent the Risen Christ).

■ Chi-Rho

The Chi-Rho is a monogram that was first used by the early Christians and is still widely used today. It is formed from the first two letters of the Greek word for Christ, when it is written in capitals (ΧΡΙΣΤΟΣ):

- The letter chi = X
- The letter rho = P

While the design does not technically form a cross shape, for Christians it is a reminder of the death of Jesus. It is an affirmation that Jesus is the Messiah, the anointed one of God who was sent to save the world through his redeeming death. As such it has a great power to inspire believers. Many Christians wear the Chi-Rho as an alternative to a cross or crucifix as an expression of their faith.

Activities

1. Explain why Christians use symbols as expressions of their faith.
2. 'The Ichthus, the Chi-Rho and the Alpha and Omega symbols have no value for Christians in the twenty-first century.' Evaluate this statement. Be sure to include more than one point of view, and refer to Catholic beliefs and teachings in your answer.

Research activity

Search online and examine as many different Christian symbols as you can find. Do you think any of them are better than the Ichthus, the Chi-Rho and the Alpha and Omega? Explain your answer.

Extension activity

Examine sources that discuss the importance of these three symbols, both for early Christians and for Christians today.

▲ The Alpha and Omega symbols

Links

Read more about the importance of the Paschal candle on pages 142–143.

▲ The Chi-Rho symbol

★ Study tip

To help you understand the importance of these symbols, visit a number of Catholic churches and see how often and where these symbols appear in the church.

Summary

You should now know the meaning of the Ichthus, Alpha and Omega, and Chi-Rho symbols. You should also know why they are important to Christians.

2.6 How the incarnation affects Catholic attitudes towards religious art

■ Reasons against religious art

Some religions are reluctant to portray God and some forbid it. In both Judaism and Islam, for example, it is an offence to show God in any form. There are a number of reasons for this:

- God is infinite. It is not possible to show the infinite using finite (limited) means like art and sculptures.
- Jews and some Christian groups (such as Baptists and Methodists) believe that the second commandment forbids people to make any form of statue or artistic representation of God: 'You shall not make for yourself an idol, whether in the form of anything that is in heaven above, or that is on the earth beneath, or that is in the water under the earth. You shall not bow down to them or worship them' (Exodus 20:4–5 (NRSV)).
- When someone prays in front of a statue or picture, even though they are only using the image as a stimulus for prayer to God, other people can get the impression that the statue or image is actually being worshipped as a god.
- Sometimes statues and images may give people wrong ideas about God, particularly when they are young. A common example of this is when people ask: 'Why is God an old man with a beard?' They mistake the image for the real thing.

▲ Statues like Michelangelo's *La Pieta*, which shows Mary holding the dead body of Jesus after the crucifixion, can help Christians relate to important teachings of the Christian faith

Objectives

- Understand why some Christians reject the use of religious art and imagery.
- Understand how the incarnation has influenced Catholic attitudes to religious art.

Statues in a church

Marianne, an 82-year-old Catholic, says: 'I like statues as a reminder of Our Lord and Our Lady. Statues help us to pray and to remember. A church needs them to bring the church to life. I used to go into a Methodist chapel but to me it just seemed like a bare room. Without statues, a church would have nothing spiritual to it.'

> **'Whoever venerates an image venerates the person portrayed in it.'** The honour paid to sacred images is a 'respectful veneration', not the adoration due to God alone.
>
> *Catechism of the Catholic Church* 2132

■ The influence of the incarnation

For Catholics, the incarnation – when God took on the human condition in Jesus – has provided a unique opportunity to portray God:

- God has taken on the limitations of human nature. It is therefore acceptable to reflect God in this limited form. As Jesus was a full human being, he can be shown in a human form. As Jesus is also God, it is acceptable to use human images to depict God.
- While we do not have any evidence of what Jesus looked like, we know that he was a man with all the human qualities. Any representation of Jesus that captures these qualities has value.
- God became man for all people in the world. In fact Jesus was a Jew, but since Christians believe that all people are affected by the salvation that Jesus gave through his death and resurrection, they think it is reasonable to show Jesus as a member of any ethnicity.
- Artistic representations can help people focus on spiritual ideas and aspects of God's work. As a focus for prayer and inspiration, they have a very positive role in religious life.

Links

To read more about the incarnation see page 36.

▲ This huge mosaic of Jesus, in Monreale Cathedral in Italy, dates from the twelfth century

> **"** Very rightly the fine arts are considered to rank among the noblest activities of man's genius, and this applies especially to religious art and to its highest achievement, which is sacred art. These arts, by their very nature, are oriented toward the infinite beauty of God which they attempt in some way to portray by the work of human hands; **they achieve their purpose** of redounding to God's praise and glory in proportion **as they are directed the more exclusively to the single aim of turning men's minds devoutly toward God. "**
>
> *Sacrosanctum Concilium* 122

Activities

1. Explain why some Christians are against the practice of depicting God in art.
2. 'The incarnation has given Christians the right to use statues and art forms to show God at work.' Evaluate this statement. Be sure to include more than one point of view, and refer to Catholic beliefs and teachings in your answer.

⭐ Study tip

Think back to the type of picture you drew of your parents when you were four years old. In what ways was this a good and a bad picture? In many ways, the same thoughts apply to ideas about drawings of God and Jesus.

Discussion activity

Discuss whether it is helpful to believers to try to depict God in an artistic way.

Summary

You should now know why some Christians don't agree with the artistic portrayal of God. You should also understand how belief in the incarnation affects Catholic attitudes towards religious art.

2.7 Interpreting statues of Jesus

There are many different statues of Jesus that can help Catholics to focus their minds on his various qualities. We will discuss three of them below.

■ Christ the Redeemer in Rio de Janeiro

▲ *Christ the Redeemer in Rio de Janeiro*

This famous statue, completed in 1931, sits on top of a mountain overlooking the city of Rio de Janeiro in Brazil. It was paid for largely by the Catholic population of Rio de Janeiro. It challenged the perceived 'godlessness' of society at the time, by reminding people of the continuing love of God. The outstretched arms are a reminder of the cross on which Jesus accepted death, and are a symbol of Jesus' love and obedience to God the Father. They also show that Jesus' love takes in all people; there is nobody excluded from the love of God shown in Jesus Christ.

■ The Sacred Heart

A **Sacred Heart** statue is a statue of Jesus that usually features some or all of the following:
- holes in his hands (from where he was nailed to the cross)
- one of his hands pointing to the heart that is shown on his breast
- an expression of peace and love
- a crown of thorns surrounding the heart, to represent the crown that was placed on Jesus' head when he was mocked by soldiers at his crucifixion
- a piercing through the heart, to echo the words from John's Gospel: 'one of the soldiers pierced his side with a spear' (John 19:34)
- flames coming from the heart, as a symbol of the burning love that Jesus has for all people.

Objectives
- Know the symbolism of one statue of Jesus.
- Understand why some Christians have different attitudes towards images of Jesus.

Key terms
- **Sacred Heart:** a representation of Jesus that focuses on his burning love for everybody
- **crucifix:** a representation of Jesus on the cross on which he died

> [Jesus] is the image of the invisible God.
> *Colossians* 1:15 (NRSV)

▲ *An example of a Sacred Heart statue*

Chapter 2 Incarnation

As the heart is used by many cultures to show a person's love, Sacred Heart statues reflect the total, self-giving human love that Jesus has for all people. The statues are intended to remind people of the words of Jesus: 'I am gentle and humble in heart, and you will find rest for your souls' (Matthew 11:29).

The final proof of Jesus' love was when he accepted death on the cross to save all people. This is why the symbols of Jesus' suffering (the crown of thorns, the nail marks and the piercing) are shown on this statue.

■ The crucifix

One of the most common representations of Jesus is the **crucifix**. The crucifix is a reminder of the pain and suffering that Jesus went through as he died. Jesus' death was redemptive, which means that through his willing obedience to God, Jesus freed all people from the power of sin and death. When Catholics look at the crucifix, they remember the love of God poured out in Jesus. This loving obedience to the will of God cancelled the sin of all humans, giving everybody the chance of eternal life with God.

There are a variety of forms of the crucifix. Some focus on the intense agony that Jesus went through, sometimes depicting his dead body. Sometimes Jesus is dressed in a priest's vestments, showing that he is offering the sacrifice of his life to God for the sake of humanity. Sometimes Jesus is dressed in kingly robes, wearing a crown, showing that through his suffering and death, Jesus gained eternal victory over sin and death.

■ Different Christian attitudes to sculptures, statues and images of Jesus

- Some Christians believe that it is wrong to depict Jesus in art, as the second commandment forbids using images in worship.
- Some think that it is not at all possible to know what Jesus looked like, so it is wrong to try to depict him in any physical way.
- Jesus, as God the Son, is infinite. Some Christians think it is therefore wrong to use the humanity of Jesus as a basis for any depiction, as it could destroy people's understanding of the divinity of Jesus.
- However, some Christians believe that a statue of Jesus can help people to concentrate on aspects of Jesus' teachings and life.

▲ Statues can help to provide focus and inspiration for prayer; here a girl prays in front of a crucifix, in a graveyard in Bangladesh

Activities

1 'Christians should not depict Jesus in art forms.' Evaluate this statement. Be sure to include more than one point of view, and refer to Catholic beliefs and teachings in your answer.

2 'Since people have different tastes and ideas, Jesus can be depicted in any way a person wants.' Evaluate this statement. Be sure to include more than one point of view, and refer to Catholic beliefs and teachings in your answer.

Discussion activity

Discuss the merits of one sculpture or statue of Jesus.

Research activity

Search online and elsewhere for different images of Jesus. Choose one that most appeals to you and examine its symbolism and significance.

★ Study tip

Make sure that you know about one statue or sculpture of Jesus, and understand what it is trying to convey about Jesus. You could pick one of the statues on these pages or choose your own.

Summary

You should now be able to describe a statue of Jesus and explain its meaning and significance. You should also be aware of different Christian attitudes to the depiction of Jesus.

2.8 The moral teachings of Jesus

Throughout his teachings, Jesus led his followers to a new understanding of the **law**. Jesus said: 'Do not think that I have come to abolish the law or the prophets; I have come not to abolish but to fulfil' (Matthew 5:17). Jesus showed his followers a deeper appreciation of the call to love God, not just through observing the commandments but also through a change of attitude, which in turn affects people's actions.

The Beatitudes

In the **Sermon on the Mount**, Jesus is the new lawgiver, building upon the law given to Moses in the Old Testament. Jesus opens his sermon with a call to people to change their attitudes. This part of the sermon is known as the Beatitudes:

> When Jesus saw the crowds, he went up the mountain; and after he sat down, his disciples came to him. Then he began to speak, and taught them, saying:
>
> **'Blessed are the poor in spirit, for theirs is the kingdom of heaven.**
>
> 'Blessed are those who mourn, for they will be comforted.
>
> 'Blessed are the meek, for they will inherit the earth.
>
> 'Blessed are those who hunger and thirst for righteousness, for they will be filled.
>
> 'Blessed are the merciful, for they will receive mercy.
>
> 'Blessed are the pure in heart, for they will see God.
>
> 'Blessed are the peacemakers, for they will be called children of God.
>
> 'Blessed are those who are persecuted for righteousness' sake, for theirs is the kingdom of heaven.
>
> 'Blessed are you when people revile you and persecute you and utter all kinds of evil against you falsely on my account. Rejoice and be glad, for your reward is great in heaven, for in the same way they persecuted the prophets who were before you.
>
> Matthew 5:1–12 (NRSV)

The old law was given so that people could know how to respond to **God's will**. Jesus transforms this law by focusing on what people's attitudes should be. If people have the right attitude towards God, themselves and their fellow human beings, they will do the right thing and will therefore be pleasing to God.

Christians believe that Jesus took the old law and made it more perfect. People are not just to avoid murder, they are to avoid being angry with their neighbour. Instead of not committing adultery, no lustful thought is to be allowed to develop, as this is the first step to adultery. These rules might appear to be challenging to follow, but the basic point is that if you are careful over the smaller issues, the bigger temptations will

Objectives

- Know what Jesus taught in the Beatitudes and the Parable of the Sheep and the Goats.
- Understand how Jesus fulfils the law but also sets a higher standard for his followers.

Key terms

- **law:** the commandments and rules laid down in the Old Testament
- **Sermon on the Mount:** Jesus' teachings found in Matthew 5–7, which give Christians a set of rules and values to apply in their lives
- **God's will:** the things that God wants people to do

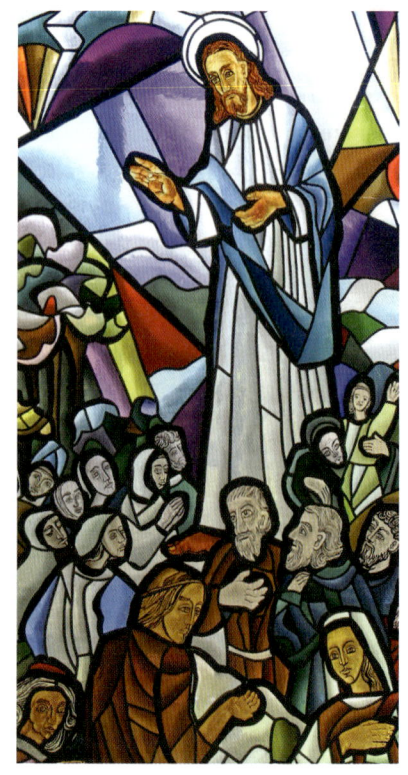

▲ Jesus' Sermon on the Mount

Chapter 2 Incarnation

not develop. This is not making Jesus' followers cold and inhuman, but allowing them to experience the quiet peace that comes from being in control of their own lives.

■ The Parable of the Sheep and the Goats

Jesus believed that having the right attitude would allow his followers to care for other people. Jesus shows the need for this in the Parable of the Sheep and the Goats:

> ❝ Those who yearn for the Kingdom of God look to Jesus' list of priorities: the Beatitudes. ❞
>
> *Youcat* 284

> ❝ When the Son of Man comes in his glory, and all the angels with him, then he will sit on the throne of his glory. All the nations will be gathered before him, and he will separate people one from another as a shepherd separates the sheep from the goats, and he will put the sheep at his right hand and the goats at the left. Then the king will say to those at his right hand, 'Come, you that are blessed by my Father, inherit the kingdom prepared for you from the foundation of the world; for I was hungry and you gave me food, I was thirsty and you gave me something to drink, I was a stranger and you welcomed me, I was naked and you gave me clothing, I was sick and you took care of me, I was in prison and you visited me.' Then the righteous will answer him, 'Lord, when was it that we saw you hungry and gave you food …?' … And the king will answer them, **'Truly I tell you, just as you did it to one of the least of these who are members of my family, you did it to me.'** Then he will say to those at his left hand, 'You that are accursed, depart from me into the eternal fire prepared for the devil and his angels; for I was hungry and you gave me no food …' Then they also will answer, 'Lord, when was it that we saw you hungry or thirsty or a stranger or naked or sick or in prison, and did not take care of you?' Then he will answer them, 'Truly I tell you, just as you did not do it to one of the least of these, you did not do it to me.' And these will go away into eternal punishment, but the righteous into eternal life. ❞
>
> Matthew 25:31–46 (NRSV)

In this parable, Jesus tells his followers that they must care for people who are in need. Jesus identifies himself as one of these people. He says that anyone who claims they are following him, but who ignores the needs of other people, will be damned, while anyone who cares for those in need will be rewarded and taken into heaven.

Activities

1. Explain how Jesus fulfilled the law and then developed it further.
2. 'It is impossible for Jesus' followers to live by the Beatitudes today.' Evaluate this statement. Be sure to include more than one point of view, and refer to Catholic beliefs and teachings in your answer.

Extension activity

Examine the whole Sermon on the Mount (Matthew 5–7). Identify which teachings you think are very practical and which may be more difficult to put into practice.

⭐ Study tip

The two passages from *Matthew* are worth knowing in full as they help to explain a lot of Jesus' ideas and Church teachings.

Summary

You should now know what Jesus taught in the Beatitudes and the Parable of the Sheep and the Goats. You should understand how Jesus fulfilled the law but also developed it further.

2.9 Tradition and St Irenaeus' writings about Jesus

■ The importance of tradition

For Catholics, **tradition** is part of the 2000-year heritage that has helped Christians to understand more fully what God has revealed. During this time there have been prominent teachers whose work has been accepted by Catholics, who believe that the Holy Spirit has inspired these thinkers. The fact that their teachings have been accepted down the ages, and have become part of Catholic tradition, reassures Catholics that what they said is in accordance with the will of God.

■ St Irenaeus' teachings about Jesus

From the earliest days of Christianity, there has been a strong belief that the incarnation of Jesus was not just something to do with showing God's love. It also showed the importance of the human race. St Irenaeus, who died at the start of the third century BCE, showed how Jesus, the incarnate Word, is a meeting point between God and humanity.

> From the beginning the Son is the one who teaches us about the Father; he is with the Father from the beginning. He was to reveal to the human race visions of prophecy, the diversity of spiritual gifts, his own ways of ministry, the glorification of the Father, all in due order and harmony, at the appointed time and for our instruction. Where there is order, there is also harmony; where there is harmony, there is also correct timing; where there is correct timing, there is also advantage.
>
> The Word became the steward of the Father's grace for the advantage of men, for whose benefit he made such wonderful arrangements. **He revealed God to men and presented men to God.** He safeguarded the invisibility of the Father to prevent man from treating God with contempt and to set before him a constant goal toward which to make progress. On the other hand, he revealed God to men and made him visible in many ways to prevent man from being totally separated from God and so cease to be. **Life in man is the glory of God; the life of man is the vision of God.** If the revelation of God through creation gives life to all who live upon the earth, much more does the manifestation of the Father through the Word give life to those who see God.
>
> St Irenaeus, *Adversus haereses* 4:20:7

Objectives
- Know why tradition is important to Catholics.
- Understand how Jesus, the Word of God, shows both the fullness of God and the fullness of man.

Key term
- **tradition:** that which has been handed on or passed down; things which have value because they have 'stood the test of time'

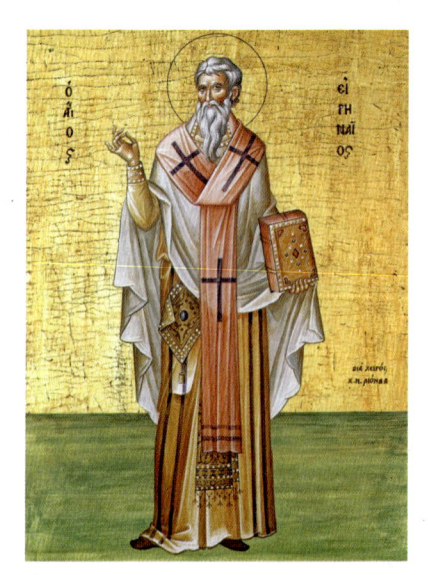

▲ *St Irenaeus was a leading Christian theologian in the second century CE*

In this passage, St Irenaeus teaches:
- The Son (Jesus) was with the Father (God) from the beginning. This echoes John 1:1–3.
- The Son, as the Word of God, was the one who spoke through the Old Testament prophets and who inspired people through visions and dreams.

Chapter 2 Incarnation

- It is through the Word (Jesus) that humans receive God's free gift: his grace.
- The Word (Jesus) shows people what the Father is like. God is beyond human sight: he is invisible because God is unlimited and humans can only see limited things. But people can get to know God in and through Jesus. This is also shown in the words of Jesus himself: 'Whoever has seen me has seen the Father' (John 14:9), and St Paul's statement about Jesus: 'He is the image of the invisible God' (Colossians 1:15).
- The qualities that humans value in Jesus are also the qualities that are found in God. This means that humans can get a true, though limited, understanding of the nature of God through the life and actions of Jesus. God is not hidden from humans.
- These qualities also appear in most people, unless the individual has deliberately blocked them or damaged them. The difference is that in Jesus these qualities are shown in their purest form. Jesus is not only truly God; he is truly human, showing human qualities in their most perfect state.
- Jesus is the perfect human being. He is totally open to the working of God in his life. He sets the example that all people are called to follow. He is the one who is fully alive and so it is true to say of Jesus, as of all people who are open to God, 'Life in man is the glory of God'.

▲ Jesus displaying human qualities of humility and love as he washes the feet of his disciples before the Last Supper

Activities

1. Explain why tradition is important to Catholics
2. Explain three of the ways in which Jesus 'revealed God to men and presented men to God'.
3. 'People cannot get to know God just by looking at Jesus.' Evaluate this statement. Be sure to include more than one point of view, and refer to Catholic beliefs and teachings in your answer.

Links

For an explanation of the incarnation read pages 36–37. For more about Jesus as the Word of God see pages 40–41. For more on how Jesus is both fully human and fully God read pages 42–43.

Extension activity

Look up references in the writings of prominent Catholic teachers (such as Athanasius and Cyril of Alexandria) about Jesus being the meeting point between God and humans.

Summary

You should now know why tradition is important for Catholics. You should also understand how St Irenaeus' teachings show that Jesus is the meeting point between God and humanity.

⭐ Study tip

Think about what people mean when they say 'You are the spitting image of your mother (or father).' Use that as your starting point to think about how Jesus reveals the Father.

2.10 Different understandings of the incarnation

■ Jesus as fully God and fully man

Christianity has long been concerned with how to present Jesus as both fully God and fully man:

- When the focus is too much on Jesus as God, there is a tendency to slip into the mistaken belief or **heresy** that Jesus only *appeared* to be human; that he was basically God in disguise.
- When the focus is too much on Jesus as man, there is a tendency to slip into the heresy that Jesus was not really God, just a very good human being.

The Catholic Church teaches that both of these positions are wrong. However, it can sometimes be difficult in one document to present the belief that Jesus is both fully God and fully man, keeping the right balance between the two.

Here are extracts from two documents issued by the **Magisterium** in the last 60 years that show how Jesus is both fully God and fully human.

■ Dei Verbum 4

> … Then, after speaking in many and varied ways through the prophets, 'now at last in these days God has spoken to us in His Son' (Hebrews 1:1–2). For He sent His Son, the eternal Word, who enlightens all men, so that He might dwell among men and tell them of the innermost being of God (see John 1:1–18). Jesus Christ, therefore, **the Word made flesh, was sent as 'a man to men.'** He 'speaks the words of God' (John 3:34), and completes the work of salvation which His Father gave Him to do (see John 5:36; John 17:4). To see Jesus is to see His Father (John 14:9) … Moreover He confirmed … that **God is with us to free us from the darkness of sin and death, and to raise us up to life eternal.**
>
> *Dei Verbum* 4

This passage shows that:

- God is revealed in Jesus, and speaks through Jesus. As 'God with us', Jesus defeats sin and brings **salvation** to all people.
- At the same time, Jesus is also sent as a man to be among his people; this stresses his human nature.

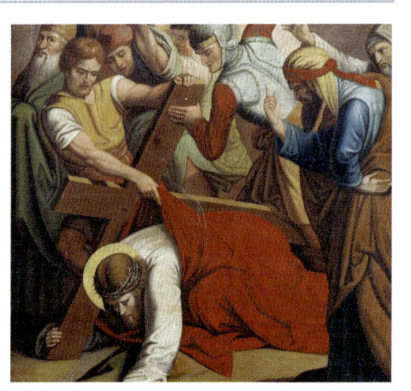

▲ As a human Jesus had to face extreme suffering: something that is common to humanity around the world

Objectives

- Understand recent documents from the Magisterium that show how Jesus is both fully God and fully man.
- Appreciate the importance of these teachings about Jesus' humanity and his divinity.

Key terms

- **heresy:** a belief that goes against the accepted teaching of the Church
- **Magisterium:** the teaching authority of the Catholic Church, exercised by the Pope and the bishops
- **salvation:** freedom from sin, and from the eternal separation from God that is brought about by sin
- **apostolic exhortation:** a letter or document from the Pope encouraging Catholics in their religion

Activities

1. Explain what a heresy is and give an example of one.
2. 'The best explanation of the incarnation is the phrase "the eternal Word became small – small enough to fit into a manger".' Evaluate this statement. Be sure to include more than one point of view, and refer to Catholic beliefs and teachings in your answer.

Verbum Domini 12

> **'The Son himself is the Word, the Logos: the eternal word became small – small enough to fit into a manger.** He became a child, so that the word could be grasped by us'. Now the word is not simply audible; not only does it have a *voice*, now the word has a *face*, one which we can see: that of Jesus of Nazareth.
>
> … In his perfect humanity (Jesus) does the will of the Father at all times; Jesus hears his voice and obeys it with his entire being; he knows the Father and he keeps his word (cf. *Jn* 8:55); … Jesus thus shows that he is the divine *Logos* which is given to us, but at the same time **the new Adam, the true man, who unfailingly does not his own will but that of the Father** …
>
> Jesus' mission is ultimately fulfilled in the paschal mystery: here we find ourselves before the 'word of the cross' (*1 Corinthians* 1:18). The word is muted; it becomes mortal silence, for it has 'spoken' exhaustively, holding back nothing of what it had to tell us …
>
> In the most luminous mystery of the resurrection, this silence of the word is shown in its authentic and definitive meaning. Christ, the incarnate, crucified and risen Word of God, is Lord of all things; he is the victor, the *Pantocrator* (the Ruler of all things) and so all things are gathered up forever in him (cf. *Eph* 1:10).
>
> *Verbum Domini* 12

▲ When Jesus ascended to heaven his divine nature became truly apparent to his followers

In this **apostolic exhortation**, Pope Benedict XVI shows how:
- The incarnation meant that the Word of God deliberately limited himself so that humans could make sense of God's love. This is most forcibly asserted in the phrase 'the eternal word became small – small enough to fit into a manger'.
- As a human being, Jesus was fully in tune with the will of God: he always chose to do God's will, no matter what it cost him.
- It was through the very human act of dying that Jesus gave himself into God's hands. This led to the resurrection and the glorification of Jesus as the Christ.

The benefits of Jesus as man and God

Francis, a 62-year-old vicar, says: 'As far as I am concerned, if Jesus was not a full human being, if he only pretended to be human, he can do nothing for me because he doesn't know me or where I am. But he has to be God as well as man otherwise I would still be stuck in my sins.'

Summary
You should now appreciate the difficulties in presenting Jesus as both fully God and fully human, and understand how different documents from the Magisterium have achieved this.

Discussion activity
Discuss whether you think it is possible for a person to understand the belief that Jesus is both fully God and fully man.

Research activity
Look up three of the biblical references that appear in the quotations above and explain how they support the documents.

⭐ Study tip
It is very easy to focus too much on either Jesus as God or Jesus as human. Remember that Jesus is both fully God *and* fully human.

2.11 Grace and the sacramental nature of reality

■ The meaning of grace

The term 'grace' comes from the Latin word 'gratis' which mean 'free'. Christians believe it is the free gift of God himself to all people. **Grace** is the life-force of the Trinity, the mutual love of the Father for the Son in the Holy Spirit. This love that unites the three Persons of the Trinity is dynamic: it makes things happen. It is also creative: it pours out from the Trinity and gives life to all things. It is poured into people's hearts to allow them to share in **the divine life**. The believer has the ability to reject or to ignore this gift, but it always available to those who choose to accept it.

Christians believe that no person can deserve or earn God's grace. Grace is God's free self-communication to humanity. The incarnation is the ultimate sign of God's love, since he freely gave his Son to the human race as a sign and pledge of his eternal acceptance of humanity. Grace is also the inward call of God to respond to God's love, by doing God's will and being close to God at all times.

▲ *A sixteenth-century painting showing the three Persons of the Trinity*

> **Objectives**
> - Understand the meaning of the term 'grace'.
> - Understand how reality can be thought of as 'sacramental'.
> - Understand how each of these ideas affects Catholic understanding of God's creation.

> **Key terms**
> - **grace:** God's free gift of his unconditional love to the believer
> - **the divine life:** the shared love of the Father and the Son in the Holy Spirit
> - **sinful:** when humans turn away from God and do what they want, rather than what God wants
> - **sacrament:** rites and rituals through which the believer receives a special gift of grace; for Catholics, Anglicans and many Protestants, sacraments are 'outward signs' of 'inward grace'

> ❝ **Grace is favour, the free and undeserved help that God gives us** to respond to his call to become children of God, adoptive sons, partakers of the divine nature and of eternal life. ❞
> *Catechism of the Catholic Church* 1996

Chapter 2 Incarnation

> God's grace is freely bestowed on a person, and it seeks and summons him to respond in complete freedom. Grace does not compel. **God's love wants our free assent.**
>
> *Youcat* 340

Humans are **sinful**, yet God's grace is poured into the human heart to call each person to a deeper relationship with God. Each of the **sacraments** is a moment of grace: a time when a person may receive this gift of God in a more complete manner. Grace enables people to become aware of what God wants for each of them. It also strengthens individuals to do what God wants.

Grace and the incarnation

For Christians, Jesus gave the perfect example in the incarnation of how to live according to God's will and love.

The incarnation makes people aware of the presence of God among humans. Even though Jesus is no longer present as a human being on Earth, his Spirit is still fully active. The Spirit continues to work in the hearts and minds of believers, sharing the life and love of God with all people, directly through grace and in the loving actions performed by other people.

Christians believe that the gift of the incarnation and the gift of grace are two aspects of God's gift of love to the human race.

■ The sacramental nature of reality

For Christians, the incarnation, death and resurrection of Jesus are the transforming events in all of creation. The whole of Christian life is based around the idea that God became man, died and rose for all human beings.

In the incarnation, God and man are united and the whole of creation is made holy. This holiness is an enduring reality. This reality includes and goes beyond creation in all its aspects, as it covers both the physical and spiritual dimensions. Jesus promised: 'I am with you always, to the end of the age' (Matthew 28:20). This promised presence of Christ is seen in those things that he has established, noticeably the Church and the sacraments.

A sacrament is 'an outward sign of inward grace, ordained by Jesus Christ, by which grace is given to our souls' (*A Catechism of Christian Doctrine*). The whole of creation is infused with the presence of God, not just because God created it but because God's presence in Jesus has touched it and made it holy. Just as Jesus is the sacrament – or sign – of God's presence here on earth, so the whole of reality can be seen as a sacrament of God's love. Before the incarnation, humans could only appreciate God as a distant, though caring, being. Since Jesus has lived on earth, Christians are able to see God as a living and active presence.

▲ *Christians believe that the incarnation is the ultimate sign of God's love*

Activities

1. Explain what is meant by grace.
2. Explain how grace might affect a believer's actions and attitudes.
3. Explain what is meant by the 'sacramental' nature of reality.
4. 'The incarnation has changed human understanding of the value of the creation.' Evaluate this statement. Be sure to include more than one point of view, and refer to Catholic beliefs and teachings in your answer.

⭐ Study tip

To understand grace, think of the things your parents, relatives or friends do for you, not because you deserve them but just to show they care. Catholics think that God's grace is a thousand times more loving than even these people's love.

Summary

You should now understand the meaning of the term grace. You should also understand why Catholics see reality as sacramental.

57

2.12 The seven sacraments

There are seven **sacraments** in the Roman Catholic Church: baptism, confirmation, the Eucharist, marriage, ordination, reconciliation and the sacrament of the sick.

According to the Catholic Church, a sacrament is 'an outward sign of inward grace, ordained by God, by which grace is given to the soul.'

What this means is that each sacrament not only symbolises the giving of grace, but through the process of the sacrament, grace is actually given to the believer. Grace is the life of God freely given, which increases in the believer every time a sacrament is received.

In the definition above, 'ordained by God' means that the sacrament originates in the work and teaching of Jesus.

The table below gives the actions, words, and symbolism or effects of the seven sacraments.

> **Objectives**
> - Know the names and effects of the seven sacraments.
> - Understand how the sacraments sanctify life.

Sacrament	Action	Symbolism/effect	Words
Baptism	the pouring of water	the cleansing of sins	'I baptise you in the name of the Father and of the Son and of the Holy Spirit.'
Confirmation	the anointing of the forehead with chrism (holy oil)	receiving the gifts of the Holy Spirit	'Be sealed with the gift of the Holy Spirit.'
Eucharist	the receiving of the consecrated Bread and Wine, the Body and Blood of Christ	receiving the fullness of Christ	'This is my body. This is my blood.'
Marriage	the consent	each partner accepting the other person as husband/wife for life	'Will you, [full name], take [full name] here present as your lawful wedded husband /wife according to the rites of our Holy Mother the Church?' 'I will.'
Ordination	the **laying on of hands** and the anointing of the hands with chrism	conferring the dignity of the priesthood	'Almighty Father, grant to this servant of yours the dignity of the priesthood.'
Reconciliation	the laying on of hands	the passing on of God's power of forgiveness	'I absolve you from your sins in the name of the Father and of the Son and of the Holy Spirit.'
Sacrament of the sick	the anointing of the head and hands (the senses) with the oil of the sick	strengthening and forgiveness	'Through this holy anointing may the Lord in his love and mercy help you with the grace of the Holy Spirit. May the Lord who frees you from sin save you and raise you up. Amen.'

Chapter 2 Incarnation

▲ *Baptism*

▲ *Confirmation*

▲ *Eucharist*

▲ *Marriage*

▲ *Sacrament of the sick*

▲ *Ordination*

▲ *Reconciliation*

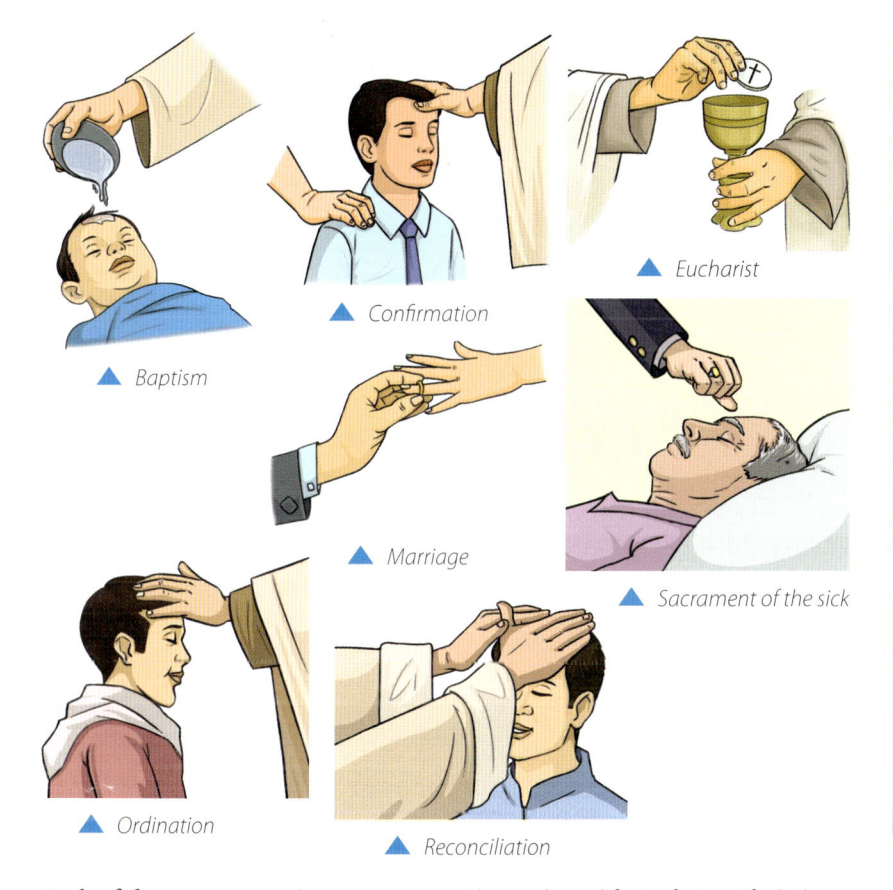

Each of the sacraments is seen as a meeting point with God. For Christians they are an opportunity to welcome Christ into their lives at important moments, sometimes as a one-off event and sometimes as a regular event.

The sacraments help to build up the holiness of the individual. They **sanctify** the life of the believer, helping to make the person a stronger **witness** to the love and presence of God. Each of the sacraments strengthens the relationship with God in a different way:

- In **Baptism** a person becomes a child of God.
- In **Confirmation** the faith is strengthened and the power of the Holy Spirit is renewed in the believer's life.
- Through the **Eucharist** the life of Christ is received, enabling the believer to continue growing in God's love.
- In **Marriage** the couple accept that their love for each other is the love of God active in their lives.
- In **Ordination** the priest commits himself to God and to the Church. He is given the power to consecrate at Mass, to preach and to forgive sins.
- In **Reconciliation** the believer rejects those areas of life that have damaged the relationship with God and this relationship is restored.
- In the **Sacrament of the sick** the sick are made aware of the strength and love of Christ with them in their time of need.

The Eucharist, reconciliation and the sacrament of the sick can be received regularly. Baptism, confirmation and ordination can only be received once. For Catholics, marriage cannot be received a second time while your partner is still alive.

Key terms

- **sacrament:** rites and rituals through which the believer receives a special gift of grace; for Catholics, Anglicans and many Protestants, sacraments are 'outward signs' of 'inward grace'
- **laying on of hands:** a symbolic gesture that passes on the power of the Holy Spirit
- **sanctify/sanctification:** being made holy
- **witness:** when someone shows their faith in their words and actions

Research activity

Choose one of the seven sacraments and interview a person who has recently received that sacrament. Ask the person how they felt both before and after receiving the sacrament.

Activities

1. Name the seven sacraments.
2. Write about the central action of each of the seven sacraments.
3. 'Catholics need the sacraments as constant reminders that God has made them holy.' Evaluate this statement. Be sure to include more than one point of view, and refer to Catholic beliefs and teachings in your answer.

★ Study tip

You may find it helps to remember the symbol of each sacrament, as they reflect what the sacrament is doing for the believer.

Summary

You should now know the names and purposes of the seven sacraments. You should also understand how they help to sanctify Catholic lives.

2.13 *Imago dei* and abortion

The concept of *imago dei*

Genesis 1:27 says: 'God created humankind in his image, in the image of God he created them; male and female he created them.' The Latin phrase for the 'image of God' is '***imago dei***'. This Latin term is often used in debates about the nature of human beings. Catholic teachings stress that because all humans are made in *imago dei*, all humans are holy and should be respected and protected.

Shortly after the annunciation (Luke 1:26–38), when Mary had conceived Jesus, she went to visit her cousin Elizabeth. At this point Elizabeth was a little over six months pregnant with John the Baptist. As Mary reached Elizabeth's house and greeted her, the Gospel says: 'When Elizabeth heard Mary's greeting, the child leapt in her womb. And Elizabeth was filled with the Holy Spirit and exclaimed with a loud cry, 'Blessed are you among women, and blessed is the fruit of your womb. And why has this happened to me, that the mother of my Lord comes to me? For as soon as I heard the sound of your greeting, the child in my womb leapt for joy.' (Luke 1:41–42 (NRSV)).

▲ *A march in Ireland – a largely Catholic country – against abortion*

For Catholics, these verses are clear proof that Jesus was truly present in his mother's womb from the moment of his conception. Catholic teaching says that the same fact applies to all humans.

For Catholics, human life begins at the moment of **conception**. From this moment the whole person is present. All that happens afterwards is that the baby develops following its natural course. There is never a moment when anything extra is added to change the nature of what is developing in the womb. The relationship between the foetus from conception to birth is just the same as the relationship between a 4-year-old girl and the 84-year-old grandmother she becomes.

> **Objectives**
> - Understand the concept of *imago dei*.
> - Understand how *imago dei* affects Catholic teaching on protecting the unborn.

> **Key terms**
> - ***imago dei:*** 'the image of God', the Latin term used to show that God made humans in his image and likeness
> - **conception:** when the male sperm fertilises the female ovum, seen by Catholics as the start of life
> - **abortion:** the removal of a foetus from the womb to end a pregnancy, usually before the foetus is 24-weeks-old

> **Activities**
> 1. Explain the term *imago dei*.
> 2. 'Since all humans are in *imago dei*, no abortion should be allowed.' Evaluate this statement. Be sure to include more than one point of view, and refer to Catholic beliefs and teachings in your answer.

> 66 Man's life comes from God; it is his gift, his image and imprint, a sharing in his breath of life. **God therefore is the sole Lord of this life:** man cannot do with it as he wills. 99
>
> *Evangelium Vitae* 39

Chapter 2 Incarnation

Development and changes take place, but it is the same person who is being developed and changed. This means that it is one person who is conceived, develops and eventually dies. This person is in *imago dei* at every step of the way.

Catholic views about abortion

> From the moment of its conception life must be guarded with the greatest care while **abortion** and infanticide are unspeakable crimes.
>
> *Gaudium et Spes* 51

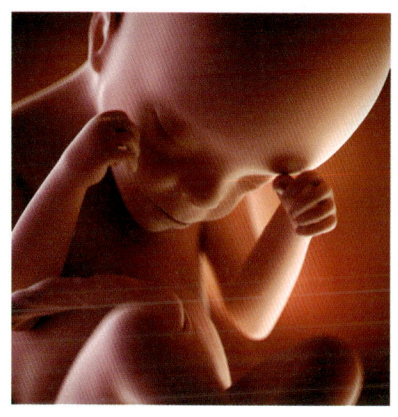

▲ A computer-generated model of a 24-week-old foetus. In most cases, abortion is legal in England up to 24 weeks

Ruth's experience of pregnancy

Ruth tells us: 'When my second child was born by caesarean section, the doctor told me that if I had another child within a year, there would be problems both for me and for the child. As it happens, I became pregnant three months later. I decided not to go to see the doctor as I knew he would put pressure on me to have an abortion. I believe all my children are gifts from God and are all special and unique. I only went to the doctor after the time for legal abortions had passed. In fact, my third pregnancy was the simplest. The child was born perfectly healthy in the natural way with no problems at all.'

Many Catholics feel it is their duty not only to ensure that their own children are allowed to live full lives, but that the same applies to all children. Many belong to pro-life organisations like SPUC (the Society for the Protection of Unborn Children) and Life. Pro-life organisations campaign to reduce the abortion limit – the point at which an abortion becomes illegal during a pregnancy – or to ban abortion completely.

Many Catholics also support organisations and individuals that care for women who have decided not to abort their child but who are having problems, possibly financial or emotional, during pregnancy and in the early years after the child is born.

Catholics also believe that children with severe disabilities are loved by God and should be cared for as well as possible throughout their natural lives. *Imago dei* does not mean that everybody looks perfect; it means that every person has divine qualities that must not be destroyed.

> I feel the greatest destroyer of peace today is abortion, because it is a war against the child, a direct killing of the innocent child, murder by the mother herself; and if we can accept that a mother can kill even her own child, how can we tell other people not to kill one another?
>
> Mother Teresa

Research activity

Research a pro-life organisation. Find out what their main aims are and what they are doing to achieve those aims.

⭐ Study tip

Try to keep an open mind about the arguments for and against abortion, otherwise you may miss essential points of the debate.

Summary

You should now be able to explain the concept of *imago dei*, and understand how this influences Catholic teachings about abortion.

Discussion activity

1. Discuss the value of the teachings about *imago dei* for the debate on whether abortion should be allowed or not.
2. Discuss Ruth's case study. What are the main issues that the parents and doctor would have to consider in a situation such as this? What are the risks involved? Make sure you include reference to religious teachings in your discussion.

2 Assessment guidance

Incarnation – summary

You should now be able to:

- ✔ explain what the Bible teaches about Jesus as the incarnate Son and divine Word, fully God and fully man, Son of God and Son of Man
- ✔ explain why Christians use the symbols Ichthus, Alpha and Omega, and Chi-Rho
- ✔ explain how the belief that God became man has influenced Catholic attitudes to religious art
- ✔ explain what one sculpture or statue of Jesus teaches about Jesus, and explain different Christian attitudes to religious sculptures, statues and images of Jesus
- ✔ explain how Jesus fulfils the law, and how he shows people how to live through his actions, attitudes and teachings
- ✔ explain what St Irenaeus meant when he wrote 'the glory of God is a human being, fully alive'
- ✔ explain how the incarnation is talked about in *Dei Verbum* 4 and *Verbum Domini* 12
- ✔ explain what the belief that Jesus is God incarnate teaches about grace and the sacramental nature of reality
- ✔ explain how the seven sacraments help make life holy for Catholics
- ✔ explain how the idea of humans being *imago dei* influences Catholic beliefs about the protection of the unborn.

Sample student answer – the 12 mark question

1. Write an answer to the following question:

   'Catholics should only use symbols to represent Jesus, not statues or images.'

   Evaluate this statement. In your answer you should:
   - give developed arguments to support this statement
   - give developed arguments to support a different point of view
   - refer to Catholic teaching
   - reach a justified conclusion.

   [12 marks]

2. Read the following sample student answer:

   "Nobody knows what Jesus looked like. There is no description of him or any suggestions about his physical features anywhere in the Bible. Because of this, it is wrong to depict Jesus in any physical way. In the Bible God tells people not to make images of anything or not to worship images. Since statues of Jesus are images, making them would be disobeying God's law.

   Symbols like the Chi-Rho are based on the name of Jesus, so are simple yet effective ways of referring to Jesus in a picture form. The Ichthus is also very good as it shows the belief not just in Jesus but also in him being Son of God and saviour. This symbol includes a lot more than any painting or statue could do. It is also a very useful way of helping to teach people about Jesus and a good reminder of what the faith means.

   However, the Catholic Church believes that, since God took on human nature in the person of Jesus, God is happy to be seen in a limited form. Statues and images are limited, so they should not be worshipped. But there is nothing wrong with making a statue that represents Jesus, even though it cannot show anything directly about Jesus. We know that Jesus was human, that he was male and that he was a Jew. Statues that suggest these points should be acceptable, even though they are really just a symbolic representation of an idea, not of an individual.

Statues help Catholics focus on the person of Jesus. They help them to pray and to meditate and in this way come closer to God. The physical presence of a statue can be a stimulus for prayer. Also, the depictions of Jesus, with his pierced heart or as the Good Shepherd, help believers to remember important teachings about the love and care that Jesus shows to his followers.

Symbols might be good at summarising ideas, but people have got to know and understand what the symbols mean. Symbols are only effective when a person understands the key, whereas a statue can help simply by being a physical expression of a deep truth. Statues do not go against God's teachings about worshipping images because Catholics do not worship statues. God limited himself so we could make direct contact with him. What is wrong with passing on this limited representation through statues?"

3. With a partner, discuss the sample answer. Consider the following questions:
- Does the response answer the question?
- Does the answer refer to Christian teachings and if so what are they?
- Is there an argument to support the statement and how well developed is it?
- Is a different point of view offered and how developed is that argument?
- Has the student written a clear conclusion after weighing up both sides of the argument?
- What is good about this answer?
- How do you think it could be improved?

4. What mark (out of 12) would you give this answer? Look at the mark scheme in the Introduction (AO2). What are the reasons for the mark you have given?

Practice questions

1 What does it mean to say that Jesus is the 'divine Word'?
 A) Everything that Jesus said and taught was wrong
 B) Nobody can describe Jesus as nobody knows what he looked like
 C) Jesus is the physical expression of what God has said
 D) Jesus is a made-up character who is not real [1 mark]

2 Give two teachings from the Bible which show that Jesus is the incarnate Son. [2 marks]

> ⭐ **Study tip**
>
> This question only requires you to briefly describe the two teachings. Do not waste time by explaining in detail how these teachings show that Jesus is the incarnate Son.

3 Explain two ways in which the belief that humans are *imago dei* influences Catholic understandings about abortion. [4 marks]

4 Explain two ways in which Jesus is the fulfillment of the law. Refer to Christian beliefs in your answer. [5 marks]

5 'It is impossible for Christians to follow Jesus' example and moral teachings.'
Evaluate this statement. In your answer you should:
- give developed arguments to support this statement
- give developed arguments to support a different point of view
- refer to Christian teaching
- reach a justified conclusion. [12 marks]

3 The Triune God

3.1 Psalms and the use of music in worship

The value of music in worship

Musical tastes vary greatly and few people will be in agreement about how music can best be used in any public setting. The Catholic Church has always used music in its **praise** of God. Over the centuries many composers have written music for the **Mass** or other services.

> ❝ Sacred music is to be considered the more holy in proportion as it is more closely connected with the liturgical action, whether it adds delight to prayer, fosters unity of minds, or confers greater solemnity upon the sacred rites. ❞
>
> *Sacrosanctum Concilium* 112

The bishops at the Second Vatican Council stressed that music:
- unites people in praise
- increases the beauty of worship
- helps people to feel more involved in their prayer.

In the fourth century CE, St Augustine of Hippo said, 'For he who sings praise, does not only praise, but also praises joyfully.'

> ❝ Sacred song united to the words … forms a necessary or integral part of the solemn liturgy. ❞
>
> *Sacrosanctum Concilium* 112

Music has always helped people to get more involved in worship. Singing is a physical activity as well as an emotional one. Music has inspired people to become fully involved in the praise of God.

▲ The Sistine Chapel Choir is one of the oldest religious choirs in the world

Objectives
- Understand why music is important in worship.
- Understand the role of the psalms in Church worship.

Key terms
- **praise:** an expression of respect, honour and thanks to God
- **Mass:** a ceremony, also called Eucharist, in which the sacrificial death and resurrection of Jesus is celebrated using bread and wine
- **Psalms:** a book in the Old Testament containing pieces of poetry that are sometimes set to music
- **Divine Office:** a collection of psalms and readings that every priest, monk and nun has to say at least four times a day

Activities
1. Explain why the Catholic Church supports the use of sacred music.
2. 'It is good to join in the singing at church.' Evaluate this statement. Be sure to include more than one point of view, and refer to Catholic beliefs and teachings in your answer.
3. Explain the role of the psalms in Church worship.

Why sing in church?

Father Bernard says: 'I encourage all my congregation to sing the hymns at Mass. Singing and music changes the Mass from something people follow to something that they actively engage in. Because people give more to the Mass when they sing, they feel more inspired by what happens in it. They feel closer to God. Some people tell me that they do not feel comfortable singing because they have bad voices. My answer to them is simple: it was God who gave them that particular voice with all its failings. Let God be the one who benefits or suffers from it. If God does not like the sound made by the voice, he has the power to change it!'

The psalms

The Old Testament contains the book of **Psalms**. These are 150 pieces of poetry that were originally written down to be sung during Jewish prayer. The Catholic Church uses these psalms every day; they form the backbone of the **Divine Office** that every priest, monk and nun has to recite. Wherever possible, when priests, monks and nuns recite the Divine Office together, they sing it.

The psalms are centred around the praise of God, though they touch on all aspects of life: sickness, seeking forgiveness, praying for the harvest and so on. The psalms acknowledge that everything people have comes from God, and without God they are nothing.

▲ *People of all voices can join in with singing the praise of God*

Singing for joy is one of the recurring themes of the psalms. Joy comes from knowing that God is with his people, guiding them and protecting them.

> ❝ O sing to the Lord a new song;
> sing to the Lord, all the earth.
> Sing to the Lord, bless his name;
> tell of his salvation from day to day.
> Declare his glory among the nations,
> his marvellous works among all the peoples. ❞
>
> *Psalms* 96(95):1–3 (NRSV)

Psalms are also used during Mass between the first and second reading. They are often the source of antiphons (short extracts that are said in order to help people to focus), which occur at the beginning and end of Mass.

Psalms form the basis and inspiration of many hymns used in church, for example:

- 'The Lord's my Shepherd' is based on Psalm 23(22)
- 'All People That on Earth do Dwell' is based on Psalm 100(99)
- 'Sing to the Mountains, Sing to the Sea' is based on Psalm 118(117).

Extension activity

Select two of the psalms at random and compare them. In what ways do you think they might be helpful as a source of prayer?

⭐ Study tip

To help you consider the role and power of music, think about how football crowds and party gatherings use singing to bring people together.

Summary

You should now understand why music is an important part of Catholic worship, and know how the psalms are used in church worship.

3.2 Music in the liturgy

'Liturgy' refers to the practices and rituals that happen during the communal worship of God. Music helps to enliven the liturgy and allows people to take part in it in a meaningful way.

These two pages will introduce some of the different types of music that play a part in the Catholic liturgy.

■ Plainchant

Plainchant (or Gregorian chant) is an ancient form of music that is usually unaccompanied and sung to a limited range of notes. Most plainchant tunes date back to between the ninth and thirteenth centuries. Plainchant is used in monasteries to sing the Divine Office in Latin. It is also used in churches, especially when the Latin parts of the Mass are sung.

> The Church acknowledges Gregorian chant as specially suited to the Roman liturgy: therefore, other things being equal, it should be given pride of place in liturgical services.
>
> *Sacrosanctum Concilium* 116

■ Traditional hymns

When people talk about traditional hymns, they normally mean hymns that have been used by generations of believers. Until the mid-1960s in the Catholic liturgy, traditional hymns were only used in devotional services like Benediction, Processions and for the Christmas season.

Traditional hymns that are still in use, like 'Soul of my Saviour', have passed the test of time: their ability to help believers raise their minds and hearts to God has not been limited to one period of time. These hymns are still used alongside more modern hymns to help people of all ages to feel involved in the Mass.

Most of these hymns were written to be accompanied by an organ.

■ Contemporary worship songs

The Mass is the name given to the celebration of the Eucharist when Catholics re-enact the Last Supper. In the 1960s, the Second Vatican Council allowed the Mass to be said in a country's own language rather than in Latin. This meant that people could be more personally involved in the Mass, particularly by joining in with the singing.

This led to a desire to have more contemporary music to encourage people to sing. Because of this, there has been a vast increase in the number of hymns and songs produced for use in worship in Catholic

Objectives

- Know about different styles of religious music including plainchant, traditional hymns, contemporary worship songs and mass settings.
- Understand how these different styles of music are used in worship.

Key terms

- **liturgy:** the practices and rituals that make up the communal worship of God
- **plainchant:** an ancient form of song, usually unaccompanied, which uses a limited range of notes
- **traditional hymns:** religious songs that have been used by believers over generations
- **contemporary worship songs:** religious songs that have been written recently for the praise of God, often using modern instruments
- **Mass settings:** music that enables people to sing certain parts of the Mass

▲ An example of plainchant, written in an early form of music notation

liturgies. These **contemporary worship songs** often use musical instruments that are more modern, like guitars and drums, rather than the organ. The tunes have often been more upbeat than the traditional hymns, though there have also been many very reflective songs produced.

Many people believe that God should be worshipped in a way that reflects the feelings of the people present, using forms and styles of worship and music that both speak to them and reflect what they want to say to God. Some people think that this type of music is disrespectful, as they feel that upbeat music can distract people rather than helping them to focus on God. However, many welcome it and see it as a way in which the Church is responding to the needs of Catholics in the twenty-first century.

■ Mass settings

There are parts of the Mass that should be sung rather than said. In order of importance, these are: the Alleluia, the Eucharistic Acclamations (the Sanctus, the Mystery of Faith and the Great Amen), the 'Lord have mercy' ('Kyrie eleison'), the 'Glory to God' ('Gloria'), and the 'Lamb of God' ('Agnus Dei').

Over the centuries, there have been many composers who have written choral music for these parts of the Mass, including Mozart and Beethoven. However, for many people these are seen as pieces for musical performance rather than for the celebration of the Mass. They are usually intended for performance by a choir of trained singers rather than a congregation.

Since the 1960s (when it was no longer required that the Mass be said or sung in Latin) many musical settings have been composed that are more accessible, to encourage the whole congregation to join in. These **Mass settings** often use simple melodies to reflect a style of music that is both contemporary yet suited to public worship, and easy to join in with. These settings help to make the Mass appeal to the whole congregation, including younger members of the church.

Research activity

Interview two or three Catholics and ask them what type of religious music they prefer for the Mass, and why.

> **Where words are not enough to praise God, music comes to our aid** … Music in a worship service should make prayer more beautiful and more fervent, move more deeply the hearts of all in attendance and bring them closer to God, and prepare for God a feast of melody.
>
> *Youcat* 183

▲ Many churches use organs to accompany singing

Activities

1. 'Plainchant should not be used in Catholic churches today.' Evaluate this statement. Be sure to include more than one point of view, and refer to Catholic beliefs and teachings in your answer.
2. Compare a traditional hymn with a contemporary worship song, and explain the strengths and weaknesses of each type of song in terms of how suitable they are for Catholic worship today.

Discussion activity

Discuss whether it is better to have music in the Mass or for the Mass to just be spoken.

Summary

You should now know about the different purposes of plainchant, traditional hymns, contemporary worship songs and Mass settings, and how they are used in the Catholic liturgy.

⭐ Study tip

Think of how different styles of music appeal to different people and how some forms of music just feel more 'right' in particular situations.

3.3 Acclamations used in the Mass

The word 'Eucharist' means 'to give thanks'. In celebrating the **Eucharist**, Christians are giving thanks to God for all his love and kindness.

While the whole Eucharist is a hymn of praise to God, there are specific parts within the Mass that highlight celebration. These parts are sometimes called **acclamations**.

■ The Gloria

The **Gloria** is based on the hymn of the angels.

> " Glory to God in the highest heaven, and on earth peace among those whom he favours! "
>
> *Luke* 2:14 (NRSV)

The Gloria is a great hymn of praise to God. For this reason, many of the musical versions of it use more complex arrangements of voices to try to convey the feeling of thankfulness to God for all his care and love. The Gloria is not said during the seasons of Advent and Lent, which are the more penitential (sorrowful) periods during the Church's year when the Church prepares to celebrate the coming of Christ (Advent) and remembers Jesus' suffering (Lent).

There are many different musical versions of the Gloria. The most common plainchant version is from the *Missa de Angelis (Missa VIII)*. A more contemporary example is the Mass of Saint Ann by Ed Bolduc.

■ Alleluia

'**Alleluia**' is a Hebrew word that means 'praise God'. At the Easter Vigil (the ceremony on Holy Saturday when Christians celebrate the resurrection), Alleluia is sung three times to announce the resurrection. It is a hymn of joy, triumph and praise of God. Like the Gloria, Alleluia should never be used during Lent, as Lent is a penitential season that prepares for the celebration of the suffering, death and resurrection of Jesus.

At every Mass, except during Lent, the **Gospel** is introduced by an Alleluia and a short verse from the Bible. These should be sung to greet the presence of Christ the Word of God, as the Gospel is proclaimed. During Lent, the Gospel acclamation is introduced by a phrase such as 'Glory and praise to you, Lord Jesus'.

▲ *Alleluia is sung during the Easter Vigil to announce the resurrection*

Objectives

- Know about the different Eucharistic acclamations.
- Understand the importance of the Eucharistic acclamations for Catholics.
- Appreciate how words and music praise God's love.

Key terms

- **Eucharist:** meaning 'thanksgiving', it is especially used about the Mass as a thanksgiving sacrifice to God
- **acclamation:** praising with great enthusiasm
- **Gloria:** a hymn of praise of God's glory and goodness, which is sung early in the Mass
- **Alleluia:** meaning 'Praise God', it is the Easter proclamation (the announcement of the resurrection) and is used before the reading of the Gospel at Mass
- **Gospel:** a reading from one of the four Gospels (Matthew, Mark, Luke and John), which tells of the life and teachings of Jesus
- **Sanctus:** a hymn of praise to the three-fold Holy God, which is used before the Eucharistic Prayer in Mass
- **Eucharistic Prayer:** the prayer of thanksgiving that is the central part of the Mass, during which Jesus' words from the Last Supper are said over the bread and wine
- **consecration:** when the bread and wine are blessed and become the Body and Blood of Christ
- **Mystery of Faith:** the acclamation after the consecration, when people acknowledge what Christ has done for them

There are many tuneful variations of Alleluia, with one of the simpler plainsong versions being the most commonly used.

■ Eucharistic acclamations

Sanctus

The word '**Sanctus**' is Latin for 'holy'. It is the first word of the hymn sung just before the **Eucharistic Prayer** at every Mass. The Sanctus is based on the vision of Isaiah in the Temple (see Isaiah 6:1–3), when the angels cried out: 'Holy, holy, holy is the Lord of hosts; the whole earth is full of his glory'. The three-fold repetition of 'holy' is showing that God is completely holy. For Christians, the idea of the three Persons in one God (the Trinity) being thrice holy adds another dimension to this great hymn of praise.

The Sanctus can be sung in a reflective manner, showing the peace and harmony of the heavenly court, where angels and people are together in the presence of God. Some of the plainchant versions follow this approach. The Sanctus can also be sung as a jubilant hymn of praise to God. The Sanctus from the *Missa Luba* is an example of this; it sets the Latin words of the Mass to music from the Democratic Republic of Congo in Africa. This helps to show the power of words and music to bring together different cultures. It can also be sung with increasing intensity to show the praise of God, as in Gounod's Mass of St Cecilia.

▲ *At the birth of Jesus, angels sang the praises of God*

The Mystery of Faith

Immediately after the **consecration**, when the bread and wine have become the Body and Blood of Christ, people acclaim the **Mystery of Faith**. In these words, everyone proclaims that they accept that the consecration has made present the whole saving event of Christ's life, death and resurrection. It is through this event that God has shown the depth of his love for all people. In response to God's love, this acclamation should be as powerful and wholehearted as it can possibly be.

Activities

1. Explain the importance of Alleluia.
2. 'The most important acclamation in the Mass is the Sanctus.' Evaluate this statement. Be sure to include more than one point of view, and refer to Catholic beliefs and teachings in your answer.

Research activity

Listen to three musical versions of either the Sanctus or the Gloria. Which do you think best praises God? Explain your answer.

Discussion activity

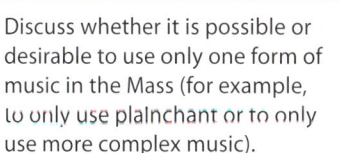

Discuss whether it is possible or desirable to use only one form of music in the Mass (for example, to only use plainchant or to only use more complex music).

★ Study tip

The best way to appreciate and understand the Eucharistic acclamations would be to listen to, and possibly sing, some different versions of them.

Summary

You should now be able to describe the different characteristics and purposes of the Eucharistic acclamations.

3.4 The Triune God explained in the Bible

■ The concept of the Triune God

To refer to the belief of three Persons in one God, two terms are used:

1. The **Triune God** stresses the fact that within the one God there is a three-ness.
2. The **Trinity** focuses on the distinctive qualities of each of the three Persons: Father, Son and Holy Spirit.

The terms Trinity and Triune God reinforce each other. They help believers to see that God is dynamic (full of power and life) and that God is relational (exists as a community of Persons).

■ The Old Testament: Deuteronomy 6:4

The great Jewish statement of faith is called the **Shema** in Hebrew. It begins with a passage from Deuteronomy:

> Hear, O Israel: **The Lord is our God, the Lord alone.** You shall love the Lord your God with all your heart, and with all your soul, and with all your might.
>
> *Deuteronomy 6:4–5 (NRSV)*

Like Christians, Jews believe there is only one God. However, unlike Christians they do not accept the belief that God exists as three distinct Persons. This passage from Deuteronomy states the oneness of God. It is also important to Jews as it tells people to love God completely.

Jesus used this passage of scripture when he was asked which was the most important commandment (see Mark 12:28–31). Christians also accept that God is one, 'the Lord alone'. However, through the teachings of Jesus, Christians have also come to believe that there are three Persons in this one God.

■ The New Testament: Matthew 3:16–17

For Christians, the belief in one God is essential to their faith. Since God is infinite (without limit in any dimensions), there can only be one God.

However, Christians also believe that God has revealed himself in three Persons: the Father, Son and Holy Spirit. It can be difficult for people to really understand what this means about God: Christians view it as a **mystery**.

One of the great scenes in the New Testament in which the Trinity is revealed comes at the baptism of Jesus:

Objectives

- Know passages in the Bible that show the scriptural origins of belief in the Trinity.
- Understand the implications of belief in the Trinity for the believer.

Key terms

- **Triune God:** within the one God there is a three-ness
- **Trinity:** the belief that there are three Persons in one God; the Father, the Son and the Holy Spirit are separate, but are also one being
- **Shema:** a Jewish prayer affirming belief in the one God, found in the Torah
- **mystery:** a belief that cannot be fully understood by the human mind

▲ *A statue representing the Trinity*

> And when Jesus had been baptised, just as he came up from the water, suddenly the heavens were opened to him and he saw the Spirit of God descending like a dove and alighting on him. And a voice from heaven said, 'This is my Son, the Beloved, with whom I am well pleased.'
>
> *Matthew* 3:16–17 (NRSV)

In this passage:

- The Spirit of God is shown as a dove, free to go where it wills. The Spirit comes down on Jesus and stays with him, reflecting the intimate relationship between Jesus and the Spirit.
- Jesus is called by God the Father 'my Son, the Beloved'. This is a statement of an eternal fact. This means that the Son of God has always existed and became man in Jesus at a specific time in history. The Son and the Father are one (as stated in John 10:30).
- The Father is unseen but makes his presence felt through his Word. The Father loves the Son. The Holy Spirit is the bond of love between the Father and the Son.

The New Testament: Galatians 4:6

St Paul sums up the importance of a Christian's life in relationship to the Trinity in the following passage:

> And because you are children, God has sent the Spirit of his Son into our hearts, crying, 'Abba! Father!'
>
> *Galatians* 4:6 (NRSV)

When a Christian is baptised, they become a child of God, and a brother or sister to Jesus Christ. God the Father pours out the same Holy Spirit that unites God the Son with God the Father. This fills the person with grace, and with the life and power of the dynamic, living God.

> We know that God is triune from Jesus Christ: He, the Son, speaks about his *Father in heaven* …, He prays to him and sends us the *Holy Spirit*, who is the love of the Father and the Son.
>
> *Youcat* 35

Activities

1. Explain the importance of Deuteronomy 6:4 for Jews and for Christians.
2. Explain how Matthew's account of the baptism of Jesus (Matthew 3:16–17) shows the Trinity.
3. 'The religious life of a Christian depends totally on belief in the Triune God.' Evaluate this statement. Be sure to include more than one point of view, and refer to Catholic beliefs and teachings in your answer.

▲ A painting of Jesus' baptism, showing the Holy Spirit descending like a dove

Link

For a more in-depth analysis of Galatians 4:6 see page 77.

Extension activity

Look up the following passages in the New Testament: John 16:13–15, Galatians 4:4–7, Romans 8:14–17, and 1 John 4:13–17. Show how each one is connected to belief in the Trinity.

★ Study tip

The idea of the Trinity is not easy to put into words in a way that is both understandable and accurate. If you start with an equilateral triangle – with three equal sides and angles forming one shape – you might get the right idea about God as Trinity.

Summary

You should now understand the concept of the Triune God. You should also know about the Bible passages that help Christians to understand this concept.

3.5 The Trinity in the Nicene Creed and Genesis 1

The Nicene Creed

The Nicene Creed is a statement of faith that presents what Catholics believe:

> **I believe in one God, the Father almighty,** maker of heaven and earth, of all things visible and invisible. I believe in one Lord Jesus Christ, **the Only Begotten Son of God,** born of the Father before all ages. God from God, Light from Light, true God from true God, begotten, not made, consubstantial with the Father; through him all things were made. For us men and for our salvation he came down from heaven, and by the Holy Spirit was incarnate of the Virgin Mary, and became man. For our sake he was crucified under Pontius Pilate, he suffered death and was buried, and rose again on the third day in accordance with the Scriptures. He ascended into heaven and is seated at the right hand of the Father. He will come again in glory to judge the living and the dead and his kingdom will have no end. I believe in **the Holy Spirit, the Lord, the giver of life,** who proceeds from the Father and the Son, who with the Father and the Son is adored and glorified, who has spoken through the prophets. I believe in one, holy, catholic, and apostolic Church. I confess one Baptism for the forgiveness of sins and I look forward to the resurrection of the dead and the life of the world to come. Amen.

This **creed** teaches the following about each Person of the Trinity:

God the Father

- God the Father is the almighty creator of all things, and the source of all life.

God the Son

- Christ is the 'only begotten Son of God'. This means that the Son shares in the same nature as the Father in a unique way. God the Son was 'born before all ages'. This means there was never a point when the Son did not exist.
- The Son is true God, '**consubstantial** with the Father'. This stresses the fact that there is no distinction in nature between the Father and the Son.
- The Son took on the limitations of human nature. 'By the Holy Spirit was incarnate of the Virgin Mary' stresses the fact that God the Son, in Jesus, did not have an earthly father (but did have a human mother).
- God the Son became human out of love for people, to save humans from the eternal separation from God that is caused by sin. He suffered and died as a human being, fulfilling God's promises in the Old Testament.

Objectives

- Know what the Nicene Creed teaches about the nature of God.
- Understand what Genesis 1:1–3 says about the Triune God.

Key terms

- **creed:** a statement of faith
- **consubstantial:** literally 'of one being', showing that the Father, Son and Spirit are not separate entities but one God

Link

Read about the origins of the Nicene Creed on page 81.

▲ The Trinity is often depicted in art as God the Father (an old man with symbols of power), the Son (a younger man sitting on the Father's right) and the Holy Spirit (as a dove)

Chapter 3   The Triune God

- Jesus rose from the dead and ascended into heaven, where he takes his place as Son of God, as Judge and as Lord of all. Jesus did not become God at the resurrection. He had *always* been God but he limited himself to a human nature while on earth.

God the Holy Spirit

- The Spirit or breath of God gives life to all things.
- The Spirit comes from both the Father and the Son, uniting them in love.
- The Spirit is equal in majesty, power and worship to the Father and the Son.
- The Spirit inspires people to let them know the will of God.

■ Genesis 1:1–3

Belief in the Triune nature of God has given Christians a deeper insight into the first verses of the Bible:

> In the beginning when God created the heavens and the earth, the earth was a formless void and darkness covered the face of the deep, while a wind from God swept over the face of the waters. Then God said, 'Let there be light'; and there was light.
>
> *Genesis* 1:1–3 (NRSV)

This passage shows God to be the creator, but it also reveals how the Trinity shared in the act of creation:

- The word 'God' is referring to the Father. The Father is the creator, but he is not alone in his creative act.
- The Hebrew word *ru'ach* is here translated as 'a wind from God', but it could also be translated as 'breath' or 'spirit'. The presence of the Holy Spirit was involved in the act of creation.
- God created by his word. God the Son is the Word of God, the creative power coming forth from the Father, but distinct from the Father and the Spirit.

God the Father, through God the Son (the Word of God), creates the universe through the power of the Holy Spirit.

▲ This illustration shows how the three Persons relate to each other: the Father (Pater), Son (Filius) and Holy Spirit (abbreviated to Spus Sctus for Spiritus Sanctus). 'Est' means 'is' and 'non est' means 'is not'.

Link

To read more about the Genesis creation stories see pages 14–17.

Link

To read more about how Jesus is the Word of God see pages 40–41.

Activities

1. Explain what the Nicene Creed teaches about each of the Persons of the Trinity.
2. 'The words of the Nicene Creed cannot help Christians to fully understand the nature of God.' Evaluate this statement. Be sure to include more than one point of view, and refer to Catholic beliefs and teachings in your answer.

Extension activity

Write a poem that expresses belief in God as Trinity.

⭐ Study tip

Remember that the Nicene Creed was written as a statement of faith that expresses what all Catholics should believe about God. Sometimes the phrasing might not be easy to understand but the main ideas are very important.

Summary

You should now understand what the Nicene Creed teaches about each Person of the Trinity, and understand how the Triune God created the universe.

3.6 The influence of the Trinity on Christians today

How belief in the Trinity influences Christians

The life of the Trinity flows from the love of the Father and the Son for each other, which is the Holy Spirit. Christians believe this love flows outward into the lives and hearts of all believers as grace. Just as the life of the Trinity is shared with Christians, so Christians are called to pass on this love to others. They believe love is meaningless if it is not shared.

Pope Benedict XVI wrote in 2005:

> **'If you see charity [love], you see the Trinity',** wrote Saint Augustine … we have been able to focus our attention on the Pierced one (cf. *Jn* 19:37, *Zech* 12:10), recognizing the plan of the Father who, moved by love (cf. *Jn* 3:16), sent his only-begotten Son into the world to redeem man. By dying on the Cross … Jesus 'gave up his Spirit' (*Jn* 19:30) …
>
> The Spirit is … the energy which transforms the heart of the ecclesial community, so that it becomes a witness before the world to the love of the Father, who wishes to make humanity a single family in his Son. **The entire activity of the Church is an expression of a love that seeks the integral good of man:** it seeks his evangelization through Word and Sacrament, an undertaking that is often heroic in the way it is acted out in history; and it seeks to promote man in the various arenas of life and human activity. Love is therefore the service that the Church carries out in order to attend constantly to man's sufferings and his needs, including material needs.
>
> *Deus Caritas Est* 19

In all its activities, the Church bears **witness** to the love of the Trinity, as the life of the Trinity flows through these actions.

There are two main aspects of the Church's witness: mission and evangelism.

Objectives

- Understand how Christians are called to share the life of the Trinity.
- Understand how Christians use mission and evangelism to share the love of God.

Key terms

- **witness:** when someone shows their faith in their words and actions
- **mission:** 'sending out' people with a job or function to perform
- **evangelism:** preaching the good news about Jesus to other people
- **preach:** publicly announcing a religious message
- **Gospel:** the good news of the teaching of Jesus and the message that God loves all people

▲ *A Christian missionary showing God's love through her actions*

Chapter 3 The Triune God

■ Mission

'**Mission**' comes from the word 'to send out'. The Church sends people out to care for the needs of other people in many ways. For example, there are many Catholic charity organisations whose mission it is to help poor people develop better lifestyles, by providing education, medical care, guidance on farming techniques, help to access water supplies and irrigation methods, and so on.

> For those who do not love a brother or sister whom they have seen, cannot love God whom they have not seen. The commandment we have from him is this: **those who love God must love their brothers and sisters also.**
>
> 1 John 4:20–21 (NRSV)

This care is given because missionaries believe they should love others as they love God, and as God loves them. They believe they show the love of God in their actions. They follow the spirit of St Francis whose guidance can be summed up in the phrase: 'Preach the Gospel at all times. Use words if you have to.'

■ Evangelism

There are two different ways to influence other people: by letting them see how you are doing good things through your actions, and by talking to them about what you are doing and why. These approaches overlap but the first (using actions) is more to do with mission and the second (using words) is more to do with evangelism.

'**Evangelism**' means **preaching** the **Gospel** by words. For some Christians, their knowledge and experience of the love of God is so great that they want to share it with other people. One of the driving forces of Christianity has been the power of the Spirit speaking through preachers, to influence the lives and attitudes of other people.

Jesus sent out his disciples to places that he could not visit himself, to help others hear his message. Jesus' last instructions to his followers were:

> 'All authority in heaven and on earth has been given to me. Go therefore and make disciples of all nations, **baptizing them in the name of the Father and of the Son and of the Holy Spirit,** and teaching them to obey everything that I have commanded you. And remember, I am with you always, to the end of the age.'
>
> Matthew 28:18–20 (NRSV)

Christians pass on the Gospel because they want to help others experience the joy, peace and love of being a believer. It is done as an expression of deep love and sometimes it is at great personal cost. Many evangelists have to face ridicule and sometimes persecution – even up to the point of death – as people try to stop them preaching.

▲ *A Christian evangelist preaching from the Bible*

Research activity

Research a Catholic missionary society, examining its aims and actions.

Discussion activity

Discuss whether it is better to show the love of the Trinity in preaching or in actions.

Activities

1. Explain why many Christians support missionary activities.
2. 'People cannot show the love of the Trinity through preaching.' Evaluate this statement. Be sure to include more than one point of view, and refer to Catholic beliefs and teachings in your answer.

⭐ Study tip

To help understand the difference between mission and evangelism think about your own life. Do you listen to what people tell you to do or do you follow their example?

Summary

You should now understand how Christian belief in the Trinity inspires mission and evangelism.

3.7 The Trinity in the Bible

For Christians, the Bible is the word of God. This means that God inspired the authors who wrote the Bible, who spoke to the people of their own times in ways that were appropriate to them. The message came from God, so the message of the books in the Bible must be respected. The Catholic Church maintains that all its teachings must be in accordance with the Bible. This means that its teachings are consistent and do not contradict the words of the Bible.

The words 'Triune God' and 'Trinity' do not appear in the Bible. However, the justification for these beliefs is clearly found in the New Testament, where there are many references to the Father, the Son and the Spirit. Even when the words 'Triune God' and 'Trinity' are not explicitly used, there is clear reference throughout the New Testament to the work of the Trinity.

Two examples of this are in the accounts of the baptism of Jesus and in Paul's letter to the Galatians.

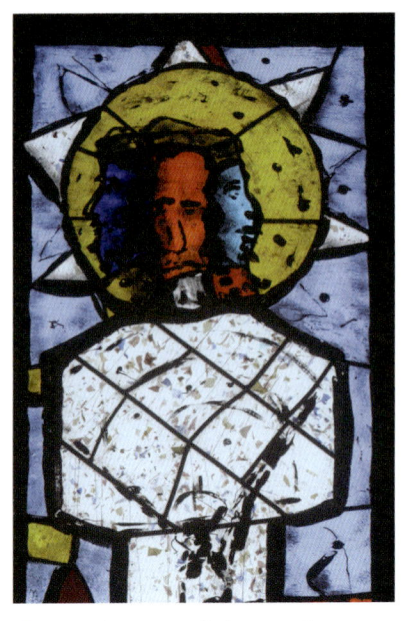

▲ *A modern stained-glass window showing the Holy Trinity*

Objectives

- Understand how the Bible refers to the Trinity.
- Know the accounts of the baptism of Jesus and Paul's letter to the Galatians.

Key terms

- **epistles:** the letters written by the apostles to the early churches
- **Aramaic:** the language that Jesus spoke

> Therefore, like the Christian religion itself, all the preaching of the Church must be nourished and regulated by Sacred Scripture.
>
> *Dei Verbum* 21

> The Triune God in himself is 'social', a communion, an eternal exchange of love.
>
> *Youcat* 122

■ The baptism of Jesus

On page 70, we came across Matthew's account of the baptism of Jesus. This is very similar to Mark's account in his own Gospel.

It is generally accepted that Mark's Gospel was the first one to be written, and Matthew used Mark's Gospel as one of his main sources. Mark probably wrote his Gospel in about 65 CE, and Matthew wrote his about 15 years later.

The fact that Matthew left Mark's account of the baptism almost intact indicates that the early Christians understood the role of the Father, Son and Spirit as separate yet united. Matthew did not feel the need to add any explanation to his account.

> In those days Jesus came from Nazareth of Galilee and was baptized by John in the Jordan. And just as he was coming up out of the water, he saw the heavens torn apart and the Spirit descending like a dove on him. And a voice came from heaven, 'You are my Son, the Beloved; with you I am well pleased.'
>
> *Mark* 1:9–11 (NRSV)

Chapter 3   The Triune God

In this passage, the Spirit descends on Jesus and remains with him. The voice of the Father proclaims Jesus as his Son.

The work and teachings of Jesus started with his baptism. At this baptism the Father, Son and Spirit were present, showing that the work done by Jesus was the work of God. This means that, just as the Trinity was involved in the creation, the Trinity was involved in the salvation brought about through the life, death and resurrection of Jesus.

■ Paul's letter to the Galatians

Paul wrote his **epistles** to the various churches that he had visited and preached to. He wrote these letters from about 51 CE (about 20 years after the death and resurrection of Jesus) up to his death, which probably took place about 67 CE. His letter to the Galatians was probably written about 57 CE.

Throughout his writings, Paul made constant reference to the Father, Son and Spirit. Paul showed how the relationship between the Father, Son and Sprit was not just dealing with how the three Persons of the Trinity are linked together; he showed how this relationship also applied to all believers. This is made clear in Galatians 4:6–7:

> And because you are children, God has sent the Spirit of his Son into our hearts, crying, 'Abba! Father!' So you are no longer a slave but a child, and if a child then also an heir, through God.
>
> *Galatians* 4:6–7 (NRSV)

This passage shows that:
- Jesus took on human nature so that all people might come close to God the Father, as God's children.
- As God's children, believers can use the title for God that Jesus used: 'Abba', which is the **Aramaic** word for 'Father'. This shows that the believer has an intimate relationship with God.
- It is the Spirit of God that gives the believer the strength and conviction to accept this relationship with God the Father.
- The Spirit is the same Spirit that filled Jesus, showing how the relationship between the Father, Son and Spirit is also shared with the believer.

▲ *The Holy Trinity is often represented by a symbol that contains three distinct yet interlinked sections, such as this one*

Extension activity

Look at two of Paul's letters (possibly Philippians, Galatians or Colossians). Make a note of how often Paul refers to the Father, Son and Spirit. What does this show about Paul's understanding of God?

★ Study tip

You are not expected to know the whole Bible but there are useful sections, like the ones mentioned in this spread, that you should know and understand.

Activities

1. Explain why it is important that all Catholic beliefs are in accordance with the Bible.
2. 'Christians can feel encouraged by calling God "Father".' Evaluate this statement. Be sure to include more than one point of view, and refer to Catholic beliefs and teachings in your answer.

Summary

You should now understand how the Bible talks about and explains the three Persons of the Trinity, particularly in the accounts of Jesus' baptism and Paul's letter to the Galatians.

77

3.8 The Trinity and God's love

Christians have always believed that there are three Persons in one God. The Persons are distinct, yet they are of one nature. In this context, 'Person' is talking about *who* God is, while 'nature' is talking about *what* God is. **Theologians** have tried to communicate the idea of the Trinity in different ways, but they always try to show that God is interactive and **relational**.

Throughout the centuries, Christians have tried to gain better insights into the mystery of the Trinity. Two theologians are introduced here to give some insight into ways of understanding the Trinity.

▲ *The Holy Spirit is often represented as a dove, able to go where he wills*

> **Objectives**
> - Know what St Augustine said about the Trinity and love.
> - Understand what Catherine LaCugna meant by the idea of the Trinity as a relationship.

> **Key terms**
> - **theologian:** a person who studies things related to God and religion
> - **relational:** having a personal, direct link with another person or with other people
> - **immanent theology:** the study of the internal life of God
> - **self-revelation:** the idea that humans can only know God through what God has chosen to show about himself

■ St Augustine of Hippo

St Augustine lived from 354 CE to 430 CE. He was the bishop of Hippo in North Africa for 34 years. He was an active member of the Church and a great theologian. One of his most important works is *On the Trinity*.

One of St Augustine's starting points for understanding the Trinity is 1 John 4:16, which states that 'God is love'. St Augustine argues that in order to have love there must be three things: a lover, the person they love, and the love that unites them. However, as these three are all reflections of one thing, they are actually three parts of one nature.

To express this in terms of grammar: God is the subject, the object and the verb of love. In other words: 'Love loves the beloved'. If we put the names of the Trinity in this sentence, replacing 'loves' with 'Holy Spirit', it can be read: 'The Father loves (which is the Holy Spirit) the Son' and 'The Son loves (which is the Holy Spirit) the Father'. Love cannot exist on its own: it needs someone to give it and someone to receive it. Love needs to be in three parts, just as in the life of the Trinity there are three Persons united together in love.

For St Augustine, this love of God is not just contained within God. It pours outward into the hearts and lives of believers as the Holy Spirit, the gift of love to all people. Love is always sharing, self-giving and creative.

> ❝ True love is: **a trinity of lover, beloved and the love that binds** them together into one. ❞
>
> *On the Trinity*

> ❝ Love ... which is of God and is God, is specially the Holy Spirit, by whom the love of God is shed abroad in our hearts, by which love the whole Trinity dwells in us. ❞
>
> *On the Trinity*

Catherine LaCugna

Catherine LaCugna (1952–1997) was an American Catholic theologian who died of cancer at the age of 44. She is famous for re-examining Christian understanding of the Trinity. She claimed that for too long people had focused on the inner life and nature of the Godhead (the whole being of God, or all that God is): a type of study sometimes called **immanent theology**. For LaCugna, everything that can be known about God is based on God's **self-revelation**. It is only possible to experience and understand what God is through his actions in people's lives.

LaCugna thought the whole action and being of God is relational. The Father begets the Son. This means that the Son comes from the Father. But the Son did not just suddenly come into being; he has always been a part of God, without beginning or end. This means that the Son is continually, eternally coming from God. This is known as eternal generation. The Holy Spirit is the bond that eternally unites the Father and the Son. This continual creative act flows outwards into the whole of creation.

Christ came to earth to bring redemption: to bring people back to a relationship with the Father. The Holy Spirit completes the task of bringing the world into union with Christ. Christ brings all things back to the Father. The act of his incarnation and redemption shows how the Son, as love, comes out from God to save human beings. The Holy Spirit guides believers to complete the work of redemption. Once the task is fulfilled all things are brought back to God, so that God may be 'all in all'.

LaCugna once wrote:

> The doctrine of the Trinity, which is the specifically Christian way of speaking about God, summarizes what it means to participate in the life of God through Jesus Christ in the Spirit. **The mystery of God is revealed in Christ and the Spirit as the mystery of love,** the mystery of persons in communion who embrace death, sin, and all forms of alienation for the sake of life.
>
> *God for Us: The Trinity and Catholic Life*

Comparing St Augustine and LaCugna's views

Both St Augustine and LaCugna stress the role of love in the life of the Trinity. They both recognise the importance of the eternal relationship between the Father, Son and Spirit. Where they differ is a matter of emphasis:

- LaCugna stresses that humans can know the Trinity through what the Trinity reveals: its *outward* effects. This revelation allows humans too to share in the life of the Trinity.
- St Augustine focuses more of the relationship *within* the Trinity. He acknowledges that this flows outwards into the lives of believers, but believes it is the inner relationship of the Trinity that is essential.

▲ *St Augustine was an influential theologian, philosopher and writer*

Activities

1. Explain why St Augustine compared the Trinity to love.
2. 'Humans cannot have a relationship with the Trinity.' Evaluate this statement. Be sure to include more than one point of view, and refer to Catholic beliefs and teachings in your answer.

Discussion activity

Discuss whether St Augustine's ideas or Catherine LaCugna's ideas give you a better understanding of the Trinity.

⭐ Study tip

To help understand the ideas on this page, think of yourself. You are aware of what drives you and how you feel about yourself (immanent). But equally important is the way you relate to your parents, siblings, friends and others (relational).

Summary

You should now understand the views of St Augustine and Catherine LaCugna on the Trinity, and what this tells Christians about the nature of God's love.

3.9 The authority of the Magisterium and its views on the Trinity

■ The authority of the Magisterium

The teaching authority of the Church stems from the fact that when the apostles went to a new area to preach, they chose individual believers to lead the Church in that area. This choice (or designation) was performed by the **laying on of hands**. When bishops were designated, the laying on of hands also passed on the **apostolic authority**. This means that the bishops were appointed successors to the apostles.

Peter, whom Jesus chose to lead the apostles, died in Rome. Since the death of Peter there has been an unbroken (although sometimes disputed) succession of Bishops of Rome. The Bishop of Rome, who for many centuries has been called 'the Pope', is accepted by Catholics as the Head of the Church.

Catholics believe that the Holy Spirit guides the whole Church in the truth, and that this truth is clearly expressed in the **magisterial teachings**. When the bishops of the Church gather together to discuss a teaching, their decision is accepted as binding for all believers. Official declarations of faith by the Pope and also by **Councils** are accepted as infallible (without error) as Catholics believe that it is the Holy Spirit guiding the Church.

> ❝ Through those who were appointed bishops by the apostles, and through their successors down in our own time, the apostolic tradition is manifested and preserved. ❞
>
> *Lumen Gentium* 20

▲ Authority in the Catholic Church is shared and passed on by the laying on of hands

Objectives

- Understand the importance of the Magisterium for beliefs about the Trinity.
- Understand the teachings of the Councils of Nicea and Constantinople.

Key terms

- **laying on of hands:** a symbolic gesture that passes on the power of the Holy Spirit
- **apostolic authority:** the authority of the apostles, as leaders of the early Church, that is passed on to the bishops
- **magisterial teachings:** the decisions of the Magisterium that should be accepted by Catholics
- **Council:** a gathering of bishops to make decisions about important issues for the Church
- **heresy:** a belief that goes against the accepted teaching of the Church

Councils of Nicea (325 CE) and Constantinople (381 CE)

Since the second century CE, thinkers and theologians have been asking questions about the nature of Jesus as Son of God, and his relationship with the Father and the Holy Spirit. Sometimes these thinkers' ideas have been rejected by the majority of believers very quickly. However, sometimes they have led to major disputes.

One of the most important debates took place at the beginning of the fourth century CE, about a **heresy** called Arianism. The priest Arius taught that only God the Father was eternal. He said that the Son had a beginning before time began, and so 'there was when he was not'.

The bishops of the Church met at a Council in the Turkish town of Nicea in 325 CE to discuss this idea, which they decided to reject.

> ⭐ **Study tip**
>
> You will not be expected to know the names of the heresies, but it useful to have some idea of what the debates were about.

The main teachings of the Council of Nicea were:

- The Son is eternally begotten from the Father. This means the Son has no beginning or end but is eternal.
- The Father and Son have always existed together: co-eternal, co-equal, of one nature.

After the Council of Nicea, there were further disputes about the nature of the Holy Spirit. A second council was called in Constantinople in 381 CE. Here, teachings that implied that Jesus was not fully human were rejected. The position of the Holy Spirit as the Third Person of the Trinity was also affirmed. The bishops declared that:

- the Holy Spirit is the Lord, the Giver of Life
- he proceeds from the Father
- he with the Father and the Son is worshipped and glorified
- he spoke through the prophets.

▲ *The Council of Nicea was attended by 318 bishops and Emperor Constantine*

The bishops at Nicea devised a creed – a statement of the Catholic faith that all believers accept. This creed was amended at Constantinople. The Nicene Constantinopolitan Creed is still used as the basis of Catholic faith, and is the creed recited at Mass.

> 🔍 **Research activity**
>
> Research the decisions of the Council of Nicea. How can they be seen as reactions to the teachings of Arius?

Activities

1. Explain the importance of the Magisterium for beliefs about the Trinity.
2. 'The teaching of the early Councils should not affect Christians in the twenty-first century.' Evaluate this statement. Be sure to include more than one point of view, and refer to Catholic beliefs and teachings in your answer.

Summary
You should now understand where the authority of the Magisterium comes from. You should also know what the bishops talked about at the Councils of Nicea and Constantinople.

> 💬 The apostles were enriched by Christ with a special outpouring of the Holy Spirit ... and **they passed on this spiritual gift to their helpers by the imposition of hands.**
>
> *Lumen Gentium* 21

3.10 Baptism

■ The origins of baptism

Jesus ordered his disciples to 'Go and make disciples of all nations, baptising them in the name of the Father and of the Son and of the Holy Spirit,' (Matthew 28:19). This wording was used at **baptisms** in the earliest days of the Church and is still used at every Catholic baptism today.

Baptism, the immersion in water to show a new stage of life, has been used in many different contexts. Jesus himself was baptised by John the Baptist (see Mark 1:9).

■ The symbolism of baptism

Christian baptism symbolises more than just starting a new stage of life. It also symbolises joining in with Jesus' death and resurrection:

> ❝ Do you not know that all of us who have been baptized into Christ Jesus were baptized into his death? Therefore we have been buried with him by baptism into death, so that, **just as Christ was raised from the dead by the glory of the Father, so we too might walk in newness of life.** ❞
>
> *Romans* 6:3–4 (NRSV)

The symbolism of baptism is best seen when the person is **totally immersed**. In the early Church, adults who wanted to be baptised would enter the water with the priest and would be totally submerged under the water. The water was called 'the waters of the tomb'. Going down into the water symbolised joining Christ in the tomb: the result of Jesus giving up his life to the will of God. The believer commits their life to God in the same way. Water is therefore the symbol of both death and life: the person being baptised would join Jesus in the tomb but would then rise up into a new life of the Spirit.

Today, the sprinkling of water on a baby's head is only a symbolic gesture, but the meaning is the same. In the Catholic Church, this sprinkling of water on the head is used in all baptisms. In contrast a number of Reformed Churches, like the Baptists, only have baptism by total immersion.

Water is one of the symbols of the Holy Spirit. It is the Holy Spirit that calls a person into faith and who sustains that faith and commitment, which is expressed in baptism. The believer is filled with the Holy Spirit: the same Spirit that worked in Jesus during his life on earth.

■ The importance of baptism

All Christians, except the Quakers and the Salvation Army, accept baptism as the entry sign or **sign of initiation** into belief in Christ,

Objectives

- Understand the symbolism of baptism.
- Understand how baptism allows the believer to join in the life of the Trinity.

Key terms

- **baptism:** the sacrament in which a person becomes a child of God and a Christian
- **totally immersed:** being under the water at a baptism so the whole body and head are covered
- **sign of initiation:** an action to show that a person has become a formal member of the Church

⭐ Study tip

To understand the importance of baptism, start by thinking about how essential water is for life, and how it has the power to both give life and to kill.

▲ *A baby is baptised by pouring water over its head*

Chapter 3   The Triune God

▲ In some Christian traditions, adults are baptised by total immersion

Link

For links with Easter and the Paschal candle see pages 142–143.

no matter which Christian actually baptises the new believer or at what stage in life baptism happens. Through baptism, the believer becomes a member of the Church (the Body of Christ), and a child of God. In baptism a person is cleansed of all sin. This is the defeat of evil in the person's life, and they are given the strength of the Holy Spirit to resist further evil.

Baptism takes place 'In the name of the Father and of the Son and of the Holy Spirit.' For Jesus, as he was a Jew, and for many other people as well, the name of a person is not simply an identification tag: it symbolises all that a person is. The act of the parents choosing their child's name symbolises their power and the responsibility they have for their child, but the name is also giving the child their identity and individuality.

When a person is baptised in the name of God, they are made a sharer in the life of the Father, Son and Spirit. In this way, grace enters the person's life and they are given a new meaning and purpose in life. As a child of God, they are called to live in the Spirit; to fulfil all that God the Father has made them to be; to join in Christ's death and the defeat of evil (Christ's redeeming death); and to enter the life of the resurrection, both by living the life of grace in the struggle against sin and by sharing in Christ's victory over death. The waters of baptism are a pledge that when the believer's earthly journey is over they will join in eternal life with God in heaven.

> ❝ Baptism is the way out of the kingdom of death into life, the gateway to the Church, and the beginning of a lasting communion with God. ❞
>
> *Youcat* 194

Research activity

Research the use of total immersion in baptism, possibly by interviewing somebody who has been baptised in a Baptist church or another church that baptises people in this way.

Discussion activity

Discuss at what point in their life a person should be baptised.

Activities

1. Explain how baptism shows that a person has entered the life of the Trinity.
2. 'Baptism is essential for a person to be a Christian.' Evaluate this statement. Be sure to include more than one point of view, and refer to Catholic beliefs and teachings in your answer.

Summary

You should now understand why baptism is important to Christians, and know what it symbolises.

3.11 Traditional and spontaneous prayer

Prayer is often referred to as 'raising the heart and mind to God'. Prayer is basically a conversation where the believer opens him- or herself up to the presence of God. This conversation demands listening as well as talking.

Experiencing prayer

A priest often went into a Roman Catholic church at about 4 pm and would see an old man in scruffy clothes sitting at the back of the church, looking at the tabernacle. On one occasion, the priest went up to the man and asked what he was doing. The man replied: 'I just like to come in and sit here. I look at him and he looks at me.' Months later, the priest went to visit the local hospital and the nurse asked him to have a word with an old man who never had any visitors. The priest found that it was the old man from the church. The priest said that he understood that the old man never had any visitors. The old man was a little surprised at this and he said: 'Every day at 4 pm he comes in and he sits there. And he looks at me and I look at him.'

Catholics believe the highest form of prayer is Jesus offering himself to the Father on the cross: the sacrifice of Calvary. At every Mass, Catholics offer up the sacrifice of Calvary and join their prayers with this sacrifice. All Christian prayer is offered up to God the Father in the name of Jesus, through Jesus' offering of himself to God the Father. As the priest says at the end of the Eucharistic Prayer in Mass: 'Through him (Jesus), with him and in him, in the unity of the Holy Spirit, all glory and honour is yours, Almighty Father, for ever and ever.'

Christians do not pray on their own, even when they are physically alone. There is nearly always a Mass being offered somewhere in the world. Since all prayers are joined to Jesus' prayer, all prayers are one. There is a constant stream of prayer and praise being offered up to God.

St Paul reminds believers that the desire to pray comes from the Holy Spirit. The Holy Spirit also stirs up the hearts and minds of believers as they pray, so that their prayers are sincere and pleasing to God. All prayer is offered to the Father, with the Son, in the Holy Spirit.

■ Traditional prayer

Many Catholics like to make use of **traditional prayers**. These are prayers that have been passed down over generations, some of which are used regularly like the Our Father and Hail Mary. Traditional prayers already have the words laid out, so people do not have to think of their own words to use. People want the words to create a feeling of ease so

Objectives

- Understand the importance of prayer as a raising of the heart and mind to God.
- Understand the different purposes of traditional and spontaneous prayer.

Key terms

- **prayer:** the raising of the heart and mind to God
- **traditional prayer:** forms of prayer that have been used by generations of believers
- **spontaneous prayer:** prayer that does not have a set structure, where the words are made up on the spur of the moment

▲ Praying the rosary. The beads are used to help count the prayers so the correct number are said.

> " Prayer is turning the heart toward God. When a person prays, he enters into a living relationship with God. "
>
> *Youcat* 469

Chapter 3 The Triune God

that they can become open to the presence of God, rather than being distracted by the words.

For this reason many people like to use the rosary. This is a repetitive prayer of one 'Our Father', ten 'Hail Marys' and one 'Glory be to the Father', usually repeated five times in total. Saying the rosary, with the simple repetition of the same words, allows the mind to go deeper than the words.

Another strength of traditional prayers is that when people are upset, they can use familiar words and phrases. The phrasing feels right and this can bring comfort to people who really want to focus on God. These prayers can also be very useful at those times when people do not feel like praying but recognise that prayer is the thing that they most need. On such occasions the use of something that is immediately available and comforting can bring strength and support.

> The Spirit helps us in our weakness; for we do not know how to pray as we ought, but that very Spirit intercedes with sighs too deep for words.
>
> Romans 8:26 (NRSV)

■ Spontaneous prayer

Spontaneous prayer is done suddenly or without any set format, and involves choosing your own words to say. People who use spontaneous prayer believe that the Spirit guides them in what to say. They may want to offer their own prayers and have particular concerns that they want to share with God.

▲ Christians often use a reading as a source for meditation and prayer

Sometimes people can speak in tongues, called glossolalia. This is when the person is so totally taken over by the Spirit that they do not know what they are saying, they are just aware of the desire to praise and thank God.

Christians believe that spontaneous prayer comes from the heart and reflects how the person is feeling at that moment. Some people think this form of prayer is more sincere than traditional prayer as it reflects the person's individual relationship with God.

Activities

1 Explain the strengths and weaknesses of both traditional and spontaneous prayer.
2 'The only prayer that has any importance is the prayer that Jesus offered.' Evaluate this statement. Be sure to include more than one point of view, and refer to Catholic beliefs and teachings in your answer.

Research activity

Research the life story of a saint, and find out how important and how hard prayer was for them.

⭐ Study tip

To get a feel for what prayer is about, try to sit for five minutes in total silence and either think about God or reflect on something that you need help with, either for yourself or for another person.

Summary

You should now understand why prayer is important to Christians, and know what the differences are between traditional and spontaneous prayer.

3.12 Prayer and posture

In prayer, believers not only open their hearts and minds to God, they also give God time, part of their lives that they can never get back. This fact shows how important God is to believers.

Prayer is not just a mental exercise. The whole person is involved in some way. Physical **postures** can both assist prayer and show the intention behind that particular moment of prayer. No posture has an exclusive meaning but many postures suggest a specific focus.

Kneeling

Kneeling shows that the person is submissive to the will of God. It is a posture which acknowledges that God is in the position of authority and that the person praying is humble before God. It also is a position that is asking for forgiveness and pardon for what the person has done wrong, knowing that they do not deserve forgiveness but that God in his mercy is all-loving and forgiving.

Genuflecting

Genuflecting literally means 'bending the knee'. It is going down on one knee as a sign of respect. Catholics genuflect as they enter church or as they pass the tabernacle, as an acknowledgement of Christ's presence.

Prostrating

To **prostrate** is to lie flat with your face on the ground. For believers it is a position of total humility and self-giving to God. It shows the belief that everything comes from God and people are nothing without God. It is a position where a person pleads for help and mercy. It also symbolises that the person has given themselves up to God: they will no longer do what they themselves want but only what God wants them to do.

Objectives

- Know different postures of prayer used in Christian worship.
- Understand the symbolism of these postures.

Key terms

- **postures:** particular positions of the body
- **kneeling:** being on both knees as a sign of humility
- **genuflecting:** going down on one knee as a sign of respect
- **prostration:** lying flat as a sign of total submission
- **bowing:** bending from the waist as a sign of respect

Activities

1. Choose three of the postures mentioned here and explain the strengths and weaknesses of each posture.
2. 'Postures for prayer do not matter. What is important is that people pray.' Evaluate this statement. Be sure to include more than one point of view, and refer to Catholic beliefs and teachings in your answer.

Discussion activity

Discuss which posture you think is most helpful for prayer.

Chapter 3 The Triune God

Standing

Standing for prayer can show respect for the authority of God and acceptance that God has permitted the person to be there. It also shows respect for God's word, which is why Catholics stand for the Gospel reading at Mass. Standing is a position from which other actions can easily flow. It show readiness to act on behalf of God, to make God's will a reality in the person's life.

Bowing

To **bow** is to lower the upper part of the body. Different cultures use different degrees of bowing, but they all show respect for the person or God to whom you are bowing. It shows that the believer reveres God and acknowledges God to be great. In this way, bowing is a sign of praise to God.

Sitting

People often sit to have a conversation as it is a more comfortable position. It allows people to focus more on what is being said. Sitting in the presence of God shows that the believer is prepared to listen to God from a position in which no physical discomfort will distract them. Many people sit when they meditate as it is one position that allows them to be still for long periods.

Standing with arms stretched out in front

This is a position of pleading. The person is begging God to help. It shows that they are willing to accept whatever God sends them, as their hands and arms are open.

Standing with arms raised above the head

This position is one that shows praise of the greatness of God. It focuses on God 'above', in heaven, where God's glory is revealed and from where God's love and power descends. The person in this position is defenceless and totally open to God.

Walking

This can show that the person wants God to be with them in all the events of the day, in every step that they take. Christians believe that prayer should be an on-going action; it does not have to be confined to specific moments or places.

With joined hands

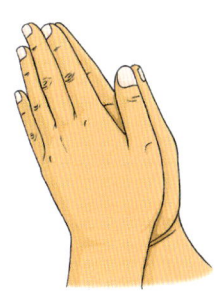

Joined hands is a sign of asking. The person is making a request for help from God, acknowledging their dependence on God.

With open hands

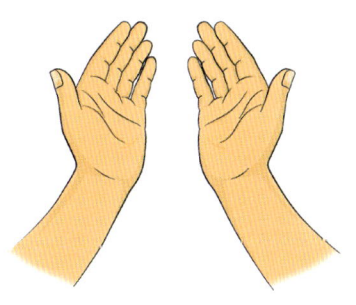

Open hands is a sign of praise and acceptance of all that God will send.

★ Study tip

Try each of the postures mentioned here and think about how each posture feels. This might help you understand the use of these postures in prayer.

> **Summary**
> You should now be able to describe different postures that are used in prayer, and explain their significance.

87

3 Assessment guidance

The Triune God – summary

You should now be able to:

✔ explain how different styles of music are used in Catholic worship
✔ explain why acclamations used in the Mass like the Gloria, Alleluia, Sanctus and Mystery of Faith are important for Catholics
✔ explain how the idea of the Triune God is shown in the Bible, and explain why the Nicene Creed is important for an understanding of the Trinity
✔ explain how Catholics see the Trinity at work in Genesis 1:1–3
✔ explain how mission and evangelism are examples of the Spirit at work in the Catholic Church today
✔ explain what St Augustine and Catherine LaCugna say about God's love
✔ explain the importance of the Councils of Nicea and Constantinople, especially for teachings about the Trinity
✔ explain the importance of baptism as a sign of joining and sharing in the life of the Trinity
✔ explain how prayer, both traditional and spontaneous, helps Catholics to raise their hearts and minds to God
✔ explain how prayer and posture work together in worship.

Sample student answer – the 4 mark question

1. Write an answer to the following question:

   Explain ways in which two Eucharistic acclamations influence Catholic understanding of the glory of God. **[4 marks]**

2. Read the following sample student answer:

   "The Sanctus is a hymn of praise that uses the words sung by the angels in Isaiah's vision. The words of this hymn talk about God being totally holy, as the word 'holy' is repeated three times. This means that God is greater than any other being, and is the only one who is worthy of worship. The singing of these words helps a Catholic to raise their heart and mind to God in praise and thanksgiving."

3. With a partner, discuss the sample answer. Is the focus of the answer correct? Is anything missing from the answer? How do you think it could be improved?

4. What mark (out of 4) would you give this answer? Look at the mark scheme in the Introduction (AO1). What are the reasons for the mark you have given?

5. Now swap your answer with your partner's and mark each other's responses. What mark (out of 4) would you give the response? Refer to the mark scheme and give reasons for the mark you award.

Sample student answer – the 5 mark question

1. Write an answer to the following question:

   Explain two similarities or differences between what St Augustine and Catherine LaCugna say about the intimacy of God's love. Refer to Christian beliefs in your answer. **[5 marks]**

2. Read the following sample student answer:

   "St Augustine focused on the inner life of the Trinity. He said that God the Father, who is love, and God the Son, who is love, are bound eternally by the Holy Spirit who is also

love, uniting the three person into one God. This love of God flows out as a creative force. Catherine la Cugna focused on the outpouring, creative love, saying that all we could know about God is what God has revealed to us in his active expression of love."

3. With a partner, discuss the sample answer. What are its good points and are there any weaknesses? How do you think the answer could be improved?

4. What mark (out of 5) would you give this answer? Look at the mark scheme in the Introduction (AO1). What are the reasons for the mark you have given?

5. Now swap your answer with your partner's and mark each other's responses. What mark (out of 5) would you give the response? Refer to the mark scheme and give reasons for the mark you award.

Practice questions

1 What is done at the moment of baptism?

   A) The baby is given Holy Communion
   B) The father lights the Paschal candle
   C) The mother kisses the baby's head
   D) The priest pours water over the baby's head [1 mark]

2 Give two ways in which baptism is important for Catholics. [2 marks]

3 Explain two ways in which music influences Catholic worship. [4 marks]

4 Explain two ways in which belief in the Trinity is important for the Catholic understanding of mission. Refer to Christian beliefs in your answer. [5 marks]

5 'The idea of the Trinity is so clearly expressed in the Bible that it does not need to be expressed in any other way, for example by the Nicene Creed or through teachings from the popes.'

Evaluate this statement. In your answer you should:
- give developed arguments to support this statement
- give developed arguments to support a different point of view
- refer to Christian teaching
- reach a justified conclusion. [12 marks]

⭐ Study tip

You should aim to develop contrasting viewpoints to show differences between what is said in the Bible about the Trinity – and how clearly this expresses the idea of three Persons in one God – compared with why Christians developed the Nicene Creed and what the Creed says about God as Trinity. You should aim to refer to Christian teaching in your answer, for example you could refer to passages from the Bible, religious writings or the teaching of Christian Churches or leaders.

4 Redemption

4.1 How church architecture reflects Catholic beliefs

■ Meanings of the word 'church'

For Catholics, **the Church** is the people of God. Christ is present in the people gathered together. As Jesus promised: 'For where two or three are gathered in my name, I am there among them.' (Matthew 18:20). From the earliest days, Christians have met together to share the Eucharist. At first the meetings took place in private houses, and then, as numbers grew, special places were built called 'churches'.

A church is a building that is big enough to allow its members to meet together for worship. For Catholics, the main service is the Eucharist, which is offered on an **altar**, so the altar has to be the central focus of the church. However, Catholics also use the church as a place for quiet, personal devotion, so the church must also be built to enable and inspire personal prayer.

■ Catholic churches built before 1965

The designs of Catholic churches changed dramatically following the Second Vatican Council (1962–1965). Before that Council, churches had been built facing towards Jerusalem, the city where Jesus died and rose again. Because the Mass was in Latin and was said almost in silence by the priest, people were not involved directly in what was taking place. The altar was against the east wall and the priest said Mass with his back to the people. Churches were usually built cruciform (in a cross shape) to remind people of the cross on which Jesus offered himself to God.

As a result of the changes that were made to the liturgy by the Second Vatican Council, many churches were re-ordered. Altars were brought forward, away from the east wall, and there was an attempt to bring the people as close to the altar as possible. However, the shape of the church tended to limit how many changes could be made. The majority of churches used by Catholics in the UK today are pre-1965 churches that have been re-ordered.

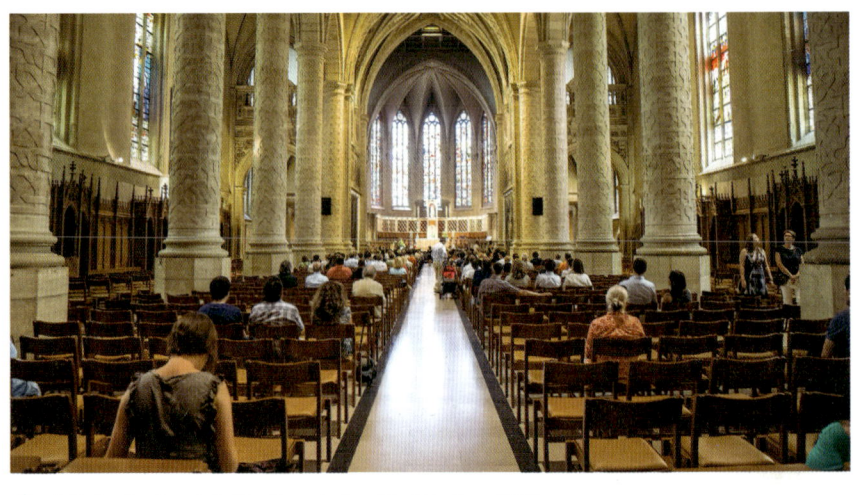

▲ *A Catholic church in Northern Ireland built before 1965*

> **Objectives**
> - Know how Catholic churches are designed and ordered.
> - Understand how Catholic churches help the believer to worship.

> **Key terms**
> - **the Church:** the Holy People of God, also called the Body of Christ, among whom Christ is present and active
> - **a church:** a building in which Christians worship
> - **altar:** the place of sacrifice where the offering of the Mass is made to God
> - **Stations of the Cross:** a series of 14 images that remind Catholics of Jesus' final journey to the cross

Chapter 4 Redemption

■ Catholic churches built after 1965

Churches built since 1965 have been more focused on ensuring that as many people as possible can see and join in with the sacrifice of the Mass. Churches have been built around the altar, with the altar sometimes being physically in the middle of the building, as in Liverpool's Catholic Cathedral. This is to enable everyone to feel fully involved with the sacrifice, and it encourages everybody to join in with all aspects of the Mass.

▲ Liverpool Catholic Cathedral: an example of a Catholic church built after 1965

Catholic churches are decorated to encourage people to reflect on the glory of God. Some people take the view that nothing is too good for God, so some churches are very ornate, using a lot of colour and decoration. In some places, tastes are more muted and people prefer the dignity of simple lines and colours as opposed to rich splendour.

Either approach is meant to help worshippers feel that God is respected. Worshippers are helped to raise their mind to heaven, where God is, and to join in the worship of the angels and saints. Catholic churches often have statues of **saints** – holy people who lived lives pleasing to God and who are now in God's presence. These statues help believers to reflect on God's work in everyday life. They encourage Christians to follow the examples of the saints and to join in their praise of God.

Images like the **Stations of the Cross** also inspire Christians to pray and to reflect on the sufferings of Christ. Most Catholic churches also have side chapels – smaller areas where believers can go into a quiet space to pray and be at one with God.

> ❝ A Christian house of prayer is both a sign of the ecclesial [Church] communion of people at a specific place and also a symbol of the heavenly dwellings that God has prepared for us all. **In God's house we gather together to pray in common or alone** and to celebrate the sacraments, especially the Eucharist. ❞
>
> *Youcat* 190

Research activity
Find two Catholic churches: one that has kept its main features from before 1965 and one that was built after 1965. Make a detailed note of all the differences and similarities between the two buildings.

Activity
'Catholics only need an empty room to pray to God.' Evaluate this statement. Be sure to include more than one point of view, and refer to Catholic beliefs and teachings in your answer.

⭐ Study tip
To help you understand this section better, it is worth visiting a Catholic church to see the physical layout of the building.

Summary
You should now be able to explain how the design and architecture of a Catholic church helps believers to worship.

91

4.2 The main parts of a Catholic church

Catholics believe that Christ is really present in four ways at the Eucharist:

1. in the consecrated Bread (**hosts**) and Wine
2. in the word proclaimed in the readings from the Bible
3. in the priest, working through him – especially at the **consecration**
4. in the worshippers together, as the Body of Christ (the Church).

The main features of a Catholic church help to stress both the presence of Christ and the redemption that Christ brought through his suffering, death and resurrection.

■ The lectern

At every Mass there are at least two readings that are given from the **lectern**. The Old Testament reading is a reminder of how God has guided his people since the beginning and of the promises that God made. Readings from the epistles, Acts and the Book of Revelation in the New Testament guide Christians into leading their lives according to the teachings of Jesus. Readings from the Gospels pass on information about the teachings and actions of Jesus.

Christians believe that as Jesus is the Word of God made flesh, Christ is truly present when the word of God is proclaimed. The lectern should be in a prominent place in the church where people can see and clearly hear the word of God.

■ The altar

The altar is the place of sacrifice. At Mass, people offer God bread and wine in thanksgiving. During the consecration, this offering is joined to Christ's offering of himself to the Father through his death on Calvary (the hill near Jerusalem where Jesus was crucified). Every Mass is absorbed into the great **Paschal sacrifice**: the Last Supper, death and resurrection of Jesus.

As the words of Jesus at the Last Supper are repeated ('This is my Body … This is my Blood'), the bread and wine become the Body and Blood of Christ. Christ is really present on the altar, offering himself to the Father on behalf of humanity. In return, God the Father, through the Holy Spirit, offers the Body and Blood of Christ in Communion to strengthen the lives and faith of believers.

> **Objectives**
> - Know the main features of a Catholic church.
> - Understand how the main features express the mystery of redemption and help worship.

> **Key terms**
> - **hosts:** the small Communion breads that are given out at Communion
> - **consecration:** the point in the Mass when the bread and wine are blessed (consecrated) and become the Body and Blood of Christ
> - **lectern:** the reading stand from which the Bible readings are given and the word of God is proclaimed
> - **Paschal sacrifice:** a term that refers to the Last Supper, suffering, death and resurrection of Jesus
> - **crucifix:** a representation of Jesus on the cross on which he died
> - **tabernacle:** the place in the church where the consecrated hosts are kept

▲ *The altar is the place of sacrifice, where the Eucharist is offered*

Chapter 4 Redemption

■ The crucifix

The **crucifix** is a cross that bears an image of Jesus, usually of him dying in pain. It is a reminder of all that Jesus suffered for the sake of humanity, and of the love that Jesus showed for humans and for his Father in accepting this form of death. It inspires a spirit of gratitude and love for all that Christ has done for humanity. This gratitude best expresses itself in the thanksgiving that is the Eucharist.

■ The tabernacle

Catholics believe that at the words of consecration in the Eucharist, the bread and wine become the Body and Blood of Christ. Some of this consecrated Bread is set aside (reserved) for later use, and placed in the tabernacle. The **tabernacle** houses the Real Presence of Christ in the church, so many Catholics like to pray quietly in front of it. This prayer can give a deep sense of peace to believers, knowing that Christ is still there caring for them.

The consecrated hosts are reserved in the tabernacle in order to take Communion to those who cannot get to church to join in with the Mass, such as people who are too ill to leave their homes. Reservation of the Eucharist is also important in churches where there are not enough priests to say Mass and consecrate the bread every day. Instead, Catholics hold a Communion Service (called a Eucharistic Service) led by a deacon or a lay minister, at which people may receive the Body of Christ that was consecrated at a previous Mass. In this way, people can stay empowered by Christ even when a Mass is not possible.

▲ The tabernacle houses the Real Presence of Christ and is where the consecrated hosts are reserved

Activities

1. Explain the importance of the lectern and the altar for Catholics
2. 'The tabernacle is the most important feature in the church.' Evaluate this statement. Be sure to include more than one point of view, and refer to Catholic beliefs and teachings in your answer.

Discussion activity

Discuss whether the structure of a church in your local area really helps Catholics to appreciate the mystery of Christ's redemption.

★ Study tip

For Catholics, a mystery is a truth that is revealed to humans by God, but its full meaning lies beyond human understanding.

Summary

You should now be able to describe the most important parts of a Catholic church and explain their significance.

93

4.3 Contrasting features and artefacts used by Catholics

The features described on the previous pages appear in most Catholic churches. However, there are variations that appear in some Catholic churches and in other Christian **denominations**. These variations reflect a different but acceptable focus on what is being done in the liturgy. By comparing the differences it is possible to build up a much deeper understanding of what is happening in the Mass.

■ Altar or table

An altar is a place of sacrifice and thanksgiving. In the Old Testament, an altar was where animals were killed as an offering to God. For Catholics, the true altar (the only one that matters) is the cross on which Jesus gave his life. At Mass, Catholics join in with Christ's sacrifice as they offer the bread and wine to God. Most churches have an altar as a reminder that both the offerings of bread and wine, and of Jesus' sacrifice on the cross, are being made.

However, the Mass is also the re-enactment of the **Last Supper**, when Jesus ate with his disciples around a table. Some churches prefer to have a table instead of an altar, as a reminder that Christians are joining in with this meal.

During the Last Supper, Jesus told his disciples to eat his Body and drink his Blood, 'which will be given up for you'. Jesus was referring to the sacrifice he would make through his death on Calvary. By giving himself to his disciples in the form of bread and wine at the Last Supper, Jesus was giving his disciples a share in the effects of his sacrifice. During Mass, both the Last Supper and the events on Calvary are remembered. For this reason the central feature of the church is both a table and an altar.

■ Crucifix, cross or Risen Christ

All Christians accept that the death and resurrection are one event (though spread over a few days). Without the death on the cross, Jesus could not have offered himself to the Father, and the resurrection would not have happened. Equally, the fact that Jesus was raised from the dead gives meaning to his death.

Since it is difficult to represent both the death and the resurrection in one image, some Christians tend to focus more on one aspect of this event than on the other.

Crucifix

A crucifix shows the figure of Christ on the cross, usually as he is dying in pain. Most Catholic churches use crucifixes as a reminder of all that Jesus suffered out of love for humanity, and this helps believers to be grateful for the great love of God.

> **Objectives**
> - Know different ideas about the use of an altar or table, and the crucifix, cross or Risen Christ.
> - Understand how these differences reflect the Catholic understanding of Jesus' death and resurrection (the redemption).

> **Key terms**
> - **denominations:** distinct groups within the Christian faith, with their own organisation and traditions
> - **Last Supper:** the final meal that Jesus ate with his disciples before he died; it is the basis of Holy Communion

▲ A crucifix

Chapter 4 Redemption

Since the Mass re-enacts the sacrifice of Jesus' death on Calvary, many people like to have the crucifix present at this time. For many people, the crucifix is a permanent reminder of the price Jesus paid to free people from their sins.

Cross

Many Christians prefer to use a cross rather than a crucifix. A cross does not include a figure representing Jesus, so there is no suggestion that believers are worshipping an idol. For many believers, the cross is a symbol of the victory over death: Jesus is not on the cross because he has risen. Some believe that the focus on the sufferings of Jesus misses the crucial fact that the resurrection has transformed everything. They believe that Christians must not be people of death but people of new life. The cross is the symbol of triumph over sin and death through the sacrifice of Jesus.

Risen Christ

▲ A cross

▲ A Risen Christ

Some Christians believe that the best image to use is the Risen Christ. The resurrection gives meaning to the whole process of the incarnation, work, suffering and death of Jesus. This is why the image of Jesus should be as the risen, glorified saviour. This also stresses the fact that what Catholics receive in Communion is the Body, Blood, Soul and Divinity of the Risen Christ. It is the resurrection that brings all things to their completion and leads to the fullness of the reign of God.

Activities

1. Explain the different meanings of an altar and a Communion table.
2. 'Only a crucifix truly conveys the importance of what happened to Jesus.' Evaluate this statement. Be sure to include more than one point of view, and refer to Catholic beliefs and teachings in your answer.

Extension activity

Examine the architecture and designs of churches or chapels from three different Christian denominations. Explain what the different features show about the denominations' understanding of the Eucharist.

⭐ Study tip

To help understand this topic, search online to see different pictures of altars and tables in churches, and different versions of crosses and crucifixes.

Summary

You should now be able to explain why some churches use altars and others use tables. You should also be able to explain why some churches or Catholics prefer the crucifix, cross or Risen Christ to represent the death and resurrection of Christ.

95

4.4 The role of Jesus in restoration through sacrifice

■ Free will and sin

Christians believe that God made all creation to be perfect. However, he also gave free will to humans as he did not want them to act like robots, obeying his commands because they could not do anything else. Instead, God wants a real relationship with individuals who can accept or reject him. In the Genesis creation story this is the meaning behind God's command to Adam not to eat from the tree of the knowledge of good and evil (Genesis 2:16–17).

One interpretation of the story of Adam and Eve as a myth is that it shows an important fact about the relationship between God and humans. God wants what is good for humanity, but humans prefer to do what they want rather than what God wants. God accepts this decision, despite the fact that it destroys the harmony between him and creation. It is more important that humans are free and choose to accept God's will than that the world is in a perfect state without any freedom.

Sin is the rejection of the will of God. Christians believe that all humans are born with the tendency to reject God, to commit sin. This is called original sin. However, because of human weakness, humans alone cannot restore the relationship with God that has been broken by sin. Only God can help humans to do this. But if God forced humans to accept this relationship, he would be destroying the important gift of free will. This is the reason God the Son took on the full human condition, to enable the perfect relationship with God to be re-established.

> **Objectives**
> - Know why creation needed to be redeemed.
> - Understand the importance of the death, resurrection and ascension of Jesus in the restoration of creation.

> **Key terms**
> - **atonement:** restoring the relationship between people and God through the life, death and resurrection of Jesus
> - **ascension:** the event, 40 days after the resurrection, when Jesus returned to God the Father in heaven
> - **restoration:** when things are brought back to the way that God intended them to be

■ The death of Jesus

Christians believe that Jesus lived his life in total obedience to the will of God the Father. He perfected the law, the rules that God had given to his people to help them become closer to him. He showed love at all times. His actions towards others, even when they were in the wrong, always tried to win them back to the right path. He never condemned. However, the standards he lived by made other people very uncomfortable. This led to Jesus being rejected by the people he had come to help. They accused Jesus of blasphemy to justify being able to kill him.

Christians believe that Jesus died because he did the right things at all times. He lived by God's law and love. This total obedience of Jesus to the Father restored the relationship that humanity's sin had destroyed. It was the sacrifice of obedience, rather than the sacrifice of pain and blood, that restored the relationship between God and humans. (This is one of the theories of **atonement**, which is supported by Romans 5:12–18.)

▲ *Jesus suffered and died as he obeyed God; his death restored the relationship between humans and God*

■ The resurrection

Because Jesus showed his obedience to God the Father by accepting his own death, fulfilling the Father's will, death could not hold Jesus. ('Death'

96

in this context refers to both the eternal separation from God and to the end of bodily life on earth.) Jesus had not sinned, so hell could not hold him. This means that, as Jesus had never rejected God, the power of sin and death (often referred to as the devil) that tried to permanently separate Jesus from God had no effect on Jesus. God raised Jesus from the dead and this destroyed the ultimate power of sin and death. (The support for this atonement theory is found in Hebrews 2:14.)

Christians believe that through the resurrection, the harmony of creation was restored. Humans still have free will to reject God and people still sin, but the death and resurrection of Jesus have destroyed the ultimate power of sin. However, people still need to accept God and his forgiveness.

The resurrection took place on the first day of the week, Sunday. This shows that Jesus brought in the new creation to balance the original creation, which started on the first day but was damaged by human sin.

> ❝ [Jesus] humbled himself and became obedient to the point of death – even death on a cross. Therefore God also highly exalted him. ❞
>
> *Philippians* 2:8–9 (NRSV)

■ The ascension

Christians believe that as Jesus Christ goes to be with God at the **ascension**, and takes his place at the right hand of the Father, God 'has put all things under his feet and has made him the head over all things' (Ephesians 1:22). 'All things' here refers to the whole of creation. Christ has restored everything to the condition that God wishes.

As Christ is the head of the Church, all people are called to join in with the effects of Jesus' resurrection. The resurrection and the defeat of sin make all things holy: they make things as perfect as God intended them to be from the beginning. This is the meaning of the phrase 'the perfection of the cosmic order', when God will be 'all in all'. In other words, the whole of creation will accept God and God will bring all things together as one. This will be the **restoration** of creation.

▲ *At the ascension, Jesus took his place at the right hand of the Father*

> ❝ Christ, our Redeemer, chose the Cross so as to bear the guilt of the world and to suffer the pain of the world. So he brought the world home to God by his perfect love. ❞
>
> *Youcat* 101

Activities

1 Explain how free will and sin damaged God's creation.
2 Explain how Jesus' death restored creation.
3 'The ascension of Jesus is only important for what it teaches about Jesus.' Evaluate this statement. Be sure to include more than one point of view, and refer to Catholic beliefs and teachings in your answer.

Extension activity

Examine three New Testament passages that refer to Jesus and the new creation brought about by his death (for example, 2 Corinthians 5:11–21, Colossians 1:15–23, Revelation 19–21). What messages are these passages trying to convey?

⭐ Study tip

Think about what you feel you need to do when you have badly hurt a friend. Why is it important that it is you, and not your friend, who takes action?

Summary: You should now understand how Jesus' death, resurrection and ascension brought about the restoration of creation.

4.5 The significance of Jesus' death, burial, resurrection and ascension

Christians believe that through Jesus, God reached down to humans and redeemed them: he freed them from sin and death. God's justice demanded that only a human being could restore the relationship between God and humanity, which had been broken by human sin.

Jesus redeemed humans through his total obedience to God the Father, even though it cost him his life. The death, burial, resurrection and ascension of Jesus are just four steps in one dramatic action that redeemed humanity and restored the relationship between God and humans.

■ The death of Jesus

By accepting death on the cross, Jesus was fulfilling Old Testament prophecies. Even when suffering he forgave his executioners (Luke 23:34), and he promised the thief who admitted he had done wrong that he would also join Jesus in heaven (Luke 23:43). Even in his darkest hour, Jesus continued to love. According to John's Gospel, as Jesus died, he said '"It is finished." Then he bowed his head and gave up his spirit.' (John 19:30). The work Jesus had been sent to do was completed, and his Spirit was given to the world.

The Gospels tell of signs that show the importance of Jesus' death:

- The sky turned dark in the middle of the day and there was an earthquake. This shows that Jesus' death had cosmic significance, which means it affected the whole of creation.
- In the Holy Temple in Jerusalem, the veil that separated the holiest part of the Temple from the rest of it tore in two. This showed that the barrier between God and humanity had been broken down, and humans now had direct access to God.
- Water and blood flowed from the side of Christ where he was pierced (John 19:34–37). This shows the importance of the waters of baptism and the blood of the Eucharist.

Christians believe that through Jesus' death they gain **eternal life**.

■ The burial (or the descent to the dead)

One of Jesus' followers placed his body in a tomb. The early Church fathers reflected on Jesus' death and burial and came to the understanding that when Jesus died, he joined everyone else who had died before him and been separated from the Father by sin. In the Apostles' Creed the phrase is 'he descended into hell'. When Jesus overcame sin and death in the resurrection, all those who had died also rose up to heaven with Jesus.

> **Objectives**
> - Know how Jesus' death, resurrection and ascension are all stages in **redemption**.
> - Understand the meaning of each of these events.

> **Key terms**
> - **redemption:** making up for the wrongs done by other people, to bring humans back into a relationship with God
> - **eternal life:** life after death, that exists forever
> - **resurrection:** Jesus' rising from the dead after dying on the cross

> ❝ Because death is now no longer the end of everything, joy and hope came into the world. ❞
>
> *Youcat* 108

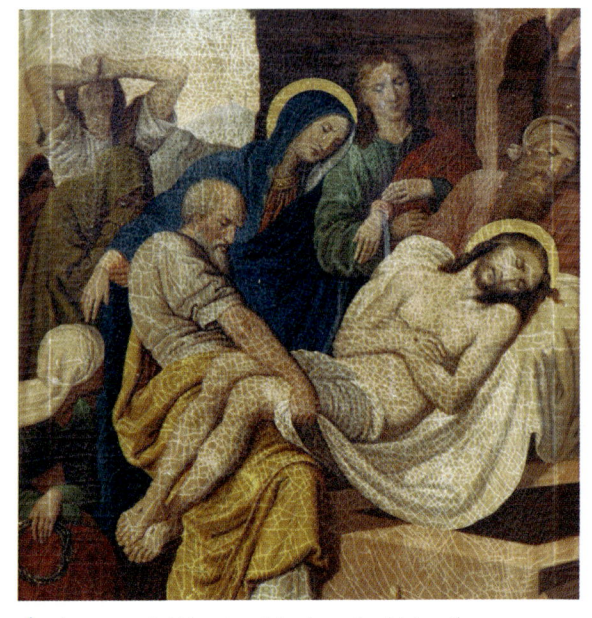

▲ *Jesus was laid in a tomb by Joseph of Arimathea*

Chapter 4 Redemption

For Christians, this act of Jesus also shows that God is with them even in death. Nothing can separate them from the love of God (see Romans 8:38–39).

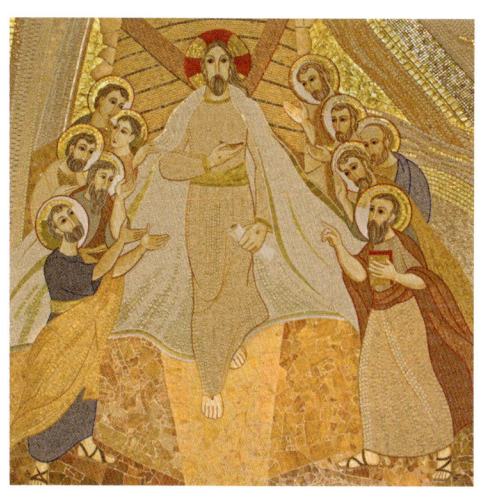

The resurrection

All the Gospels and the epistles point to the reality of the **resurrection**: the fact that it actually happened (rather than being a myth like the creation stories). Accounts of the resurrection appearances can be found in Mark 16:1–8, 9–20, Matthew 28:1–20, Luke 24:1–53, and John 20:1–29 and 21:1–25.

Jesus' apostles were first afraid when they heard that Jesus' tomb was empty. They rejected the early messages from the women who had gone to the tomb and been told that Jesus had risen. It was only when the apostles experienced the presence of Jesus themselves, when he appeared to them in a locked room, that they accepted the fact that Jesus had risen. There are some strange aspects of the appearances:

- Initially Jesus' followers did not recognise him. This suggests that something had changed in Jesus, even though he was still the same person.
- When he appeared Jesus was present in bodily form, for example he could be touched and could eat food.
- Jesus was no longer limited by things that would limit other humans. For example, he could just appear in a locked room.
- Jesus knew what was happening even when he was not visible. This suggests that he is present even when not visible.

St Paul showed the importance of the resurrection for Christians when he wrote: 'if Christ has not been raised, then our proclamation has been in vain and your faith has been in vain. We are even found to be misrepresenting God, because we testified of God that he raised Christ … If Christ has not been raised, your faith is futile and you are still in your sins' (1 Corinthians 15:14–15,17 (NRSV)). Faith is needed to accept the resurrection, but faith in the resurrection transforms the meaning of all lives: life does not end in death.

▲ *When Jesus rose from the dead, all those who had previously died joined in the resurrection*

The ascension

The ascension shows that Jesus is with the Father, sharing his glory for all eternity. Jesus was seen after the resurrection by his followers but then he ascended to heaven. Before he left he promised to send his Spirit, which is the continued presence of Jesus at work in his followers. Christians believe that Jesus no longer works among humans as an individual human being, but he works in and through all of his believers. Where Jesus has gone, he has promised that all his people will follow. For Christians, Jesus is the crown of creation, the perfection of what God wants, and the promise of what awaits believers in heaven.

Research activity

Go through the Gospel accounts of the resurrection and the appearances of Jesus (Mark 16:1–8, 9–20, Matthew 28:1–20, Luke 24:1–53, and John 20:1–18 and 21:1–25). Make a list of all the evidence presented to show that the resurrection was a reality.

Activities

1. Explain the importance of the death of Jesus and Jesus' descent into hell.
2. 'Without the resurrection, there is no Christianity.' Evaluate this statement. Be sure to include more than one point of view, and refer to Catholic beliefs and teachings in your answer.

Summary

You should now be able to explain the meaning of Jesus' death, burial, resurrection and ascension. You should understand why Christians believe that these events redeemed humanity.

⭐ Study tip

You need to be aware of the different Gospel accounts of the resurrection.

99

4.6 Salvation (past, present and future)

■ Different views on salvation

Catholics believe that salvation came through the death and resurrection of Jesus (in the past), grows in the Church and in the life of the believer by doing what God wants (in the present), and will come in full power at the end of time (in the future). Different Christian traditions tend to stress one of these views over another.

Salvation in the past

For many Christians, **salvation** has come through the death and resurrection of Jesus. This event means that sinners have been freed from the power of sin and death, and the gates of heaven have been opened by the sacrifice of Christ. Salvation is an act of God, a free gift to believers, the gift of **grace**. Some Christians maintain that after the death and resurrection of Jesus, nothing else is needed: salvation is complete.

Salvation in the present

Others believe that salvation is an ongoing process. While Christ won the victory over sin, which brings salvation and healing, believers need to allow themselves to be guided by the Holy Spirit every day. This means that they should resist the temptation of sin, but they can also accept forgiveness when they give into sin.

Salvation in the future

Christians believe that the final victory of God's grace will come at the end of time, when **God's Kingdom** is established in full power. When this happens, the power of sin and death will be completely destroyed, and all believers will share in the glory of Christ.

Christians believe that this victory will definitely happen, but they still need to experience the struggle against sin and death themselves. If God simply made everybody join in the glory of heaven without having experienced free will and the negative side of life, heaven would have no meaning. The joy of heaven can only be valued by those who have learned to appreciate the love of God shown in Jesus through the power of the Holy Spirit.

■ How this is reflected in the liturgy

Catholics believe that the offering made by Christ on the cross is re-enacted in Mass, and that redemption is ongoing. The Mass is re-presenting the offering of Christ to the Father.

During Mass, Christians offer themselves up with Christ. At Communion, Catholics receive the Body and Blood of Christ. Christ enters their life to give grace and strength to resist sin and to live for God.

Objectives

- Know how salvation has past, present and future dimensions.
- Understand how salvation is reflected in the liturgy.
- Understand contrasting views on salvation.

Key terms

- **salvation:** freedom from sin, and from the eternal separation from God that is brought about by sin
- **grace:** God's free gift of his unconditional love to the believer
- **God's Kingdom:** the reign of God, when everyone will accept God and live forever in peace and harmony
- **heavenly banquet:** a symbol of the unity and joy of the Kingdom of God, pictured as everyone joining together in one great meal

Link

To learn more about grace read pages 56–57.

Activities

1. Explain how salvation is in three stages: past, present and future.
2. 'For Catholics, joining in the Mass is the only way to celebrate salvation.' Evaluate this statement. Be sure to include more than one point of view, and refer to Catholic beliefs and teachings in your answer.

Chapter 4   Redemption

At the start of Mass, Catholics ask God to forgive their sins so they are more worthy to offer themselves up to God and join in with Christ's sacrifice.

▲ *A priest holding up the consecrated host during Mass*

The Mass is also a chance to experience what the **heavenly banquet** will be like: the victory celebration that shows that God's reign is complete, and sin and death are defeated. This is why Catholics can join in the hymn of praise of the angels in the Sanctus. They can also pray: 'In your mercy keep us free from sin and protect us from all anxiety as we wait in joyful hope for the coming of our Saviour, Jesus Christ.'

The significance of the Mass

Father David says: 'When I offer the Mass, I feel caught up in the sacrifice of Christ on Calvary. It is as if I am in a time warp. I am at the foot of the cross, offering Jesus' death up to the Father. Through my words and actions at the consecration, Christ transforms our poor offering of bread and wine into his own glorious offering. When I receive Christ in Communion, I am gaining the strength I need to carry on, knowing that Christ is with me, and the Holy Spirit is working in me. I feel assured that one day I will be celebrating the great feast of heaven where my joy in Christ will be total.'

Discussion activity

Discuss how important it is for Christians not to sin.

★ Study tip

The idea of salvation having past, present and future dimensions is not as difficult as it may first appear. Compare it with your own life: you are who you are now because of what has happened to you in the past, and you will grow and develop more in the future.

Summary

You should now understand the concept of salvation, and know how this is expressed in the Mass.

4.7 Redemption in the Bible (1)

The idea of redemption is a fundamental belief of Christianity. There is a huge amount of material in the scriptures that talks about this idea. The following passages are typical of Christian teachings about redemption.

■ The crucifixion

> They compelled a passer-by, who was coming in from the country, to carry his cross; it was Simon of Cyrene, the father of Alexander and Rufus. Then they brought Jesus to the place called Golgotha (which means the place of a skull). And they offered him wine mixed with myrrh; but he did not take it. And they crucified him, and divided his clothes among them, casting lots to decide what each should take.
>
> It was nine o'clock in the morning when they crucified him. The inscription of the charge against him read, 'The King of the Jews.' And with him they crucified two bandits, one on his right and one on his left. Those who passed by derided him, shaking their heads and saying, 'Aha! You who would destroy the temple and build it in three days, save yourself, and come down from the cross!' In the same way the chief priests, along with the scribes, were also mocking him among themselves and saying, 'He saved others; he cannot save himself. Let the Messiah, the King of Israel, come down from the cross now, so that we may see and believe.' Those who were crucified with him also taunted him.
>
> When it was noon, darkness came over the whole land until three in the afternoon. **At three o'clock Jesus cried out with a loud voice,** 'Eloi, Eloi, lema sabachthani?' which means, **'My God, my God, why have you forsaken me?'** When some of the bystanders heard it, they said, 'Listen, he is calling for Elijah.' And someone ran, filled a sponge with sour wine, put it on a stick, and gave it to him to drink, saying, 'Wait, let us see whether Elijah will come to take him down.' **Then Jesus gave a loud cry and breathed his last.** And the curtain of the temple was torn in two, from top to bottom. Now when the centurion, who stood facing him, saw that in this way he breathed his last, he said, 'Truly this man was God's Son!'
>
> *Mark* 15:21–39 (NRSV)

This account of the suffering and death of Jesus helps Christians to understand different ways in which the ideas of redemption and atonement can be expressed.

Jesus, the example

In the garden of Gethsemane (see Mark 14:32–42), Jesus was aware of all the pain, both physical and emotional, that he would have to suffer through crucifixion. However, by his courageous decision to be obedient to the will of God, Jesus set an example for all people to follow. The events of the crucifixion show what this loving decision cost him. His total love for God the Father, and for humanity, gave humanity a new way of living which is not self-centred. Through following his example, humanity is saved (see John 15:12–27).

Objectives

- Know how the Bible shows that redemption took place.
- Understand the importance of the death, resurrection and ascension of Jesus for redemption.

Key term

- **crucified:** executed by being fixed to a cross

⭐ Study tip

Each of the Bible passages on pages 102–104 contain useful details so it is advisable to know all of them.

▲ *By dying on the cross, Jesus showed he accepted the will of God*

Chapter 4 Redemption

Jesus, the restorer

Christ is the new Adam, a word that means 'man' (implying 'humanity'). Through sin, represented by the fall of Adam and Eve in Genesis 3, humanity lost its closeness to God. By his total obedience to the will of God, Jesus restored this close relationship between all humanity and God (see 1 Corinthians 15:21–22).

Jesus, the victor

Jesus was fully human. He went through all that the human condition entails, experiencing suffering and death. By bringing the presence of God into these experiences, he defeats them and makes it possible for all human beings to share in their defeat. Because Jesus shared in the human condition, humans are now able to share in the divine condition (see Ephesians 2:10).

> ### Activities
> 1. Explain how Mark's account of the suffering and death of Jesus shows that Jesus accepted his suffering.
> 2. 'John's account of the empty tomb and the appearance of Jesus proves that Jesus rose from the dead.' Evaluate this statement. Be sure to include more than one point of view, and refer to Catholic beliefs and teachings in your answer.

■ The resurrection

> " Early on the first day of the week, while it was still dark, Mary Magdalene came to the tomb and saw that the stone had been removed from the tomb. So she ran and went to Simon Peter and the other disciple, the one whom Jesus loved, and said to them, 'They have taken the Lord out of the tomb, and we do not know where they have laid him.' Then Peter and the other disciple set out and went toward the tomb. The two were running together, but the other disciple outran Peter and reached the tomb first. He bent down to look in and saw the linen wrappings lying there, but he did not go in. Then Simon Peter came, following him, and went into the tomb. He saw the linen wrappings lying there, and the cloth that had been on Jesus' head, not lying with the linen wrappings but rolled up in a place by itself. Then the other disciple, who reached the tomb first, also went in, and he saw and believed; for as yet they did not understand the scripture, that he must rise from the dead. Then the disciples returned to their homes.
>
> But Mary stood weeping outside the tomb. As she wept, she bent over to look into the tomb; and she saw two angels in white, sitting where the body of Jesus had been lying, one at the head and the other at the feet. They said to her, 'Woman, why are you weeping?' She said to them, 'They have taken away my Lord, and I do not know where they have laid him.' When she had said this, she turned around and saw Jesus standing there, but she did not know that it was Jesus. Jesus said to her, 'Woman, why are you weeping? Whom are you looking for?' Supposing him to be the gardener, she said to him, 'Sir, if you have carried him away, tell me where you have laid him, and I will take him away.' Jesus said to her, 'Mary!' She turned and said to him in Hebrew, 'Rabbouni!' (which means Teacher). Jesus said to her, 'Do not hold on to me, because I have not yet ascended to the Father. **But go to my brothers and say to them, "I am ascending to my Father and your Father, to my God and your God."** Mary Magdalene went and announced to the disciples, 'I have seen the Lord'; and she told them that he had said these things to her. "
>
> *John 20:1–18 (NRSV)*

The accounts of Jesus' resurrection in the four Gospels are statements about the transforming effect that this event had on the disciples' lives. The following points are mentioned in John's account:

- The disciples did not understand Jesus' teachings about resurrection, even when the event happened. Their first reaction was to assume that Jesus' body had been stolen. This shows that the idea of the resurrection was not invented by the apostles, as they needed to be persuaded that it actually happened.
- According to the text, Jesus was definitely physically present when he spoke to Mary, but there was something different about him. Even Mary, a person who was close to Jesus, did not recognise him at first, until he said her name. This shows that Jesus has entered a new creation where things were now different, and links to the idea that redemption makes all things new and perfect.

4.8 Redemption in the Bible (2)

■ The ascension

> So when they had come together, they asked him, 'Lord, is this the time when you will restore the kingdom to Israel?' He replied, 'It is not for you to know the times or periods that the Father has set by his own authority. But you will receive power when the Holy Spirit has come upon you; and you will be my witnesses in Jerusalem, in all Judea and Samaria, and to the ends of the earth.' When he had said this, as they were watching, he was lifted up, and a cloud took him out of their sight. While he was going and they were gazing up toward heaven, suddenly two men in white robes stood by them. They said, 'Men of Galilee, why do you stand looking up toward heaven? **This Jesus, who has been taken up from you into heaven, will come in the same way** as you saw him go into heaven.'
>
> *Acts* 1:6–11 (NRSV)

- Before he left his disciples, Jesus promised them that he would send the Spirit to complete his work through them. The disciples were to be witnesses to the redeeming work of Jesus, telling everybody about it so that they could accept it and become part of it.
- Jesus was no longer visible after he ascended to heaven, but the disciples were told that Jesus would return in glory 'on the clouds of heaven' to complete the redemption of the world at the end of time.

▲ The day of Pentecost

■ The Coming of the Holy Spirit

- The power of the Holy Spirit filled the disciples. This is the same Spirit that came to Jesus at his baptism. This Spirit of Jesus leads his followers into the new, redeemed, creation.
- Fire and wind are not controllable but can be used, just like the power and gift of the Spirit. Fire and wind are used in the Old Testament to symbolise the presence of God (see Exodus 3:1–6 and 1 Kings 19:9–18).
- The Spirit transforms the disciples and gives them both the courage and the ability to go out to all people and proclaim the news about Jesus the saviour. In this way, Jesus' followers help other people to join those that Jesus has already redeemed.

Activity

Explain how Jesus promised the Holy Spirit would come, and what happened when this promise was fulfilled.

Extension activity

Examine how St Paul explains the importance of the death and resurrection of Jesus in 1 Corinthians 15.

> When the day of Pentecost had come, they were all together in one place. **And suddenly from heaven there came a sound like the rush of a violent wind,** and it filled the entire house where they were sitting. **Divided tongues, as of fire, appeared among them, and a tongue rested on each of them.** All of them were filled with the Holy Spirit and began to speak in other languages, as the Spirit gave them ability.
>
> *Acts* 2:1–4 (NRSV)

Summary

You should now understand how the four Bible passages on pages 102–104 show how redemption happened through the work of Jesus.

St Irenaeus' and St Anselm's thoughts on salvation

■ St Irenaeus (about 130–202 CE)

For St Irenaeus, **salvation** is part of God's plan for human beings. All humans were affected by the rejection of the will of God, shown when Adam and Eve ate the fruit of the tree. It was Jesus' total acceptance of the will of God, most perfectly shown in the tree of the cross, that saved humanity from the effects of sin.

This salvation **metaphor** makes good use of the parallels between Adam and Jesus, particularly in the symbols of the two trees. Just as humans were lost by eating the fruit of a tree, they were saved by another tree: the cross on which Jesus died. Jesus was totally obedient to the will of God, in contrast to Adam who disobeyed God. Through his obedience, Jesus saved all people who accepted the will of God. It helps believers to value how their own sinfulness is a rejection of God, but the supreme acceptance of the will of God shown by Jesus outweighs all human sinfulness.

The weakness of this metaphor is that it is based on a particular interpretation of Genesis 3 that not all people would agree with.

■ St Anselm (1033–1109 CE)

According to St Anselm, through sin humans reject God and refuse to give him the honour that he deserves. The only way to **atone** or make up for this rejection is for a person to be totally obedient to God. Through his obedience to the point of death, Jesus showed how much he loved God.

St Anselm said that Jesus' obedience 'paid a ransom' for the sins of all humans. He was using a metaphor here from the slave trade. Just as slaves could be freed if enough money was paid, so humans are freed from the effects of their sins by the obedience and death of Jesus.

God's justice required that Jesus suffered. Jesus offered up his life in love of God and in love for all humans. This love far outweighs the rejection of God caused by human sin.

Some Christians are unhappy with the parallel of a ransom being paid in St Anselm's metaphor. They question to whom the ransom is paid, which would imply that there is someone greater than God. However, this is not what St Anselm was trying to say. It was God's honour that had been denied, and this has to be respected by total obedience.

The physical imagery of the two trees used by St Irenaeus appeals to some Christians as the parallels make sense to them. Other Christians prefer St Anselm's image of humanity being slaves to sin, as this reflects what they feel about their own condition.

Activity

Explain how St Irenaeus and St Anselm add to an understanding of salvation.

Objective
- Know what metaphors St Irenaeus and St Anselm used to describe salvation.

Key terms
- **salvation:** freedom from sin, and from the eternal separation from God that is brought about by sin
- **metaphor:** a word or phrase that is applied to something else to suggest the two things are similar
- **atone:** make amends for something that has gone wrong

Discussion activity
Discuss whether it is ever possible or desirable to expect one person to pay the price of another person's failings. What might this show about Jesus and salvation?

★ Study tip
Think how much easier it is for you to understand things when people use images or stories to explain them rather than trying to use complex words. This is why metaphors can be useful to help explain difficult topics.

Summary
You should now understand how St Irenaeus and St Anselm use metaphors to explain salvation.

4.9 The importance of conscience for Christians

The meaning of conscience

Christians believe that **conscience** is the voice of God in their heart and soul. This means that God, though the Holy Spirit, guides each person to make the right choices. Conscience tells a person what is right in each context. The more a person ignores what their conscience is telling them, the more they go against what they feel is right. The more a person sins, the more they block out their conscience.

Christians believe that they need to be in tune with what God is saying to them. With God's help, their conscience guides them to become completely the person they are meant to be.

Conscience does not work on its own: it needs to be educated. For Christians this means that it should take into consideration the many ways that God, through the Holy Spirit, has instructed humanity. For example:

- Human nature is a gift from God that helps to guide people. This is the natural law, which tells humans 'to love good and avoid evil' (*Gaudium et Spes* 16).
- The law of God, which is summarised in the Ten Commandments and the two Great Commandments of Jesus, helps to guide people (Mark 12:29–31).
- The teachings of the Catholic Church are infallibly guided by the presence of the Holy Spirit. This means that the Church's teachings cannot be ignored by Catholics.

Having absorbed all of these factors, in the end it is conscience that is the deciding factor (although a decision should not go against the Church's teachings).

▲ *If you accidentally discovered the answers to a test before you took it, what would your conscience tell you to do? Would how important the test is make a difference?*

Objectives
- Know what is meant by conscience.
- Understand how conscience guides a believer.

Key terms
- **conscience:** for Christians, the voice of God in the heart and soul of a person
- **morality:** a system of ethics about what is right and wrong

Link
Read more about natural law on page 26.

> **Conscience is the inner voice in a man** that moves him to do good under any circumstance and to avoid evil by all means. At the same time it is the ability to distinguish the one from the other.
>
> *Youcat* 295

Chapter 4 Redemption

■ Christian teachings on conscience

> There he is alone with God, Whose voice echoes in his depths. In a wonderful manner conscience reveals that law which is fulfilled by love of God and neighbour.
>
> *Gaudium et Spes* 16

'Conscience' comes from the words meaning 'with knowledge'. Christians believe that people must realise deep in themselves what is the right thing to do before the action is taken. One of the causes of feeling guilty is that people have not listened to their consciences. This must mean that the inner person knew what they should do, but they chose to ignore the promptings of their conscience.

> Christians are joined with the rest of men in the search for truth, and for the genuine solution to the numerous problems which arise in the life of individuals from social relationships. Hence **the more right conscience holds sway, the more persons** and groups turn aside from blind choice and **strive to be guided by the objective norms of morality.**
>
> *Gaudium et Spes* 16

For Christians, conscience helps people to search for and live by the truth. They are called to live by the high standard of doing good and avoiding evil. One person's conscience can inspire other people. A person who is faithful to God in all aspects of life creates an example for others to follow.

Christians believe that each member of the Church must listen to other people to ensure that their conscience is guiding them properly, so they are not ignoring the promptings of the Holy Spirit. All believers can be affected by the conscience of others and each person must consider how their actions might alter another person's actions, particularly by setting either a good or bad example.

Equally, each person must respect the fact that the Church's laws are based on the guidance of the Holy Spirit over hundreds of years. Christians should not easily go against Church teachings.

Some Christians believe that conscience is the guidance offered by an individual's humanity. Some take the view that humans have natural instincts that drive them along specific paths. Some Christians follow St Thomas Aquinas, who said that conscience is applying the knowledge of what is good and bad to help shape an individual's actions. This knowledge is based on the natural law.

Summary

You should now know what conscience means, and understand what the Catholic Church teaches about it.

▲ What does your conscience tell you to do when you see a homeless person on the street?

> Personal conscience and reason should not be set in opposition to the moral law or the Magisterium of the Church.
>
> *Catechism of the Catholic Church* 2039

Activities

1. Explain why conscience is important for a Catholic.
2. 'A Catholic should follow their conscience no matter what the Church teaches.' Evaluate this statement. Be sure to include more than one point of view, and refer to Catholic beliefs and teachings in your answer.

Research activity

Research examples of Christians who have lived and died by following their consciences, such as Oscar Romero or Maximilian Kolbe. Do you think they made the right choices in life? Explain your answer.

★ Study tip

Conscience is often shown in cartoons as an angel on one shoulder and the devil on the other, giving contradictory advice. Catholics believe they should listen to and follow good advice from God.

107

4.10 Redemption and the Mass

The whole structure and intention of the Mass centres round the fact that humans are redeemed in Christ. This means that the Mass is a re-enactment and celebration of Jesus' death, through which humans are freed from their sins and their relationship with God is restored. The two central points of the Mass are the proclamation of the Gospel and the Eucharistic Prayer.

■ The introduction to the Mass

During Mass, Catholics come together to offer worship. Together they form the Body of Christ on earth. As Jesus once said, 'For where two or three are gathered in my name, I am there among them' (Matthew 18:20).

At the start of Mass, Catholics apologise to God and each other for the sins that separate them. This strengthens unity, making people 'at one' with God and with one another as they accept that God has forgiven and redeemed them.

■ The readings

In the readings, Catholics are reminded that God has guided his people through the years. In the Gospel reading, Jesus demonstrates through his words and actions how God loves, heals, restores and forgives all people.

■ The Eucharist

There are three main sections of the Eucharist: the offertory, the Eucharistic prayer (which includes the consecration), and the Our Father and Communion.

Offertory

In the offertory, people present bread (the hosts) and wine to God as a sign of thanksgiving.

Eucharistic Prayer

During the Eucharistic Prayer, at the consecration, the words of Jesus at the Last Supper are repeated over the bread and wine: 'Take this all of you and eat it. This is my body … This is the blood of the new and everlasting covenant which will be poured out for you and all people so that sins may be forgiven. Do this in memory of me'.

In these words:
- Jesus was anticipating his death.
- Jesus was showing that his whole being was present, by saying the bread was his Body and the wine his Blood.

Objectives
- Know how the structure of the Mass reflects Christian beliefs.
- Understand how redemption is celebrated in the Mass.

Key term
- **Communion:** sharing in a meal that unites people with each other and with Christ

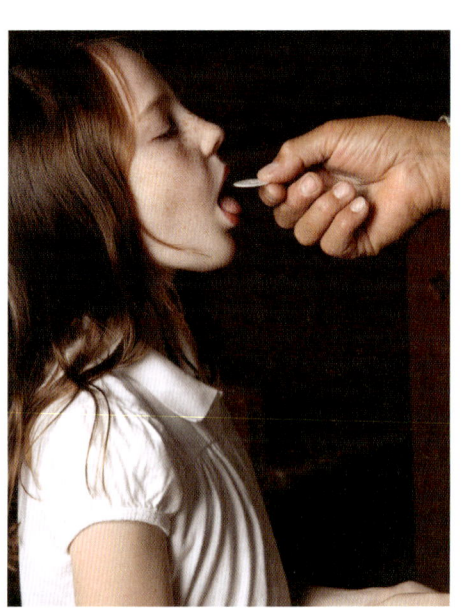

▲ A girl receives Communion

> **Christ is mysteriously but really present in the sacrament of the Eucharist.** As often as the Church fulfils Jesus' command, 'Do this in memory of me' … the same thing takes place today that happened then: Christ truly gives himself for us, and we truly gain a share in him.
>
> *Youcat* 216

- The actions of breaking the bread and pouring the wine symbolise the death of Jesus, which he accepted for the sake of humanity. Both actions reflect the idea of the body and life force being destroyed.
- Jesus' command to eat and drink makes his followers sharers in the offering that he made to the Father on the cross.
- The blood is the blood of the new covenant: the new promise between God and humans. It is different to the Old Testament covenants, which depended on keeping the law and on the regular sacrifice of animals. People often broke these covenants. In contrast, the new covenant that Jesus seals with his blood on the cross will never end; it is a once-and-for-all sacrifice that Catholics join in at Mass.
- The command to 'do this in memory of me' was an order to his disciples not simply to remember the Last Supper, death and resurrection of Jesus as a past event, but to make this event a reality every time his followers meet to celebrate the Eucharist.
- The command to eat emphasises the fact that Catholics join in a celebratory meal that binds them to each other and to God in Christ.
- Just as the Last Supper was a Passover meal that celebrated the time when the Jews were freed from slavery in Egypt, so the Mass is a meal that celebrates the freedom of all believers from their slavery to sin. Humans are redeemed through the blood of Jesus, just like the Jews were saved from death in Egypt by the blood of the Passover lamb (see Exodus 12).

At the end of the Eucharistic Prayer the doxology is said, in which praise is offered to the Father in, with and through Christ in the unity of the Holy Spirit.

The Our Father and Communion

Through Christ's redemption, believers are allowed to call God 'Father'. At this point in the Mass they say the prayer that Christ taught, the 'Our Father'.

In **Communion**, believers receive the Body, Blood, Soul and Divinity of Christ – everything that he is – in the form of bread and wine. Through this action:

- believers are brought even closer to Christ
- they are given power and grace to resist the temptation to sin
- Jesus' words are remembered: 'Those who eat my flesh and drink my blood have eternal life, and I will raise them up on the last day; for my flesh is true food and my blood is true drink. Those who eat my flesh and drink my blood abide in me, and I in them.' (John 6:54–56 (NRSV)).

The end of the Mass

After a period of silent prayer reflecting on the gift received in the Eucharist, Catholics go out into the world and, through their daily actions, share the presence of Christ that they received in the Eucharist with everyone that they meet.

▲ *The hosts and wine used at Mass*

Extension activity

Interview an older Catholic or a priest, ideally someone who knew the old Latin Mass. Ask how the Mass has both changed and remained constant down the centuries. What do these facts suggest about Catholic understanding of the Mass?

Activities

1. Explain the importance of the structure of the Mass as a celebration of redemption.
2. 'Receiving Communion is the most important part of the Mass.' Evaluate this statement. Be sure to include more than one point of view, and refer to Catholic beliefs and teachings in your answer.

★ Study tip

Being able to experience a Mass will help you to appreciate this section more, and help you to understand what happens in a Mass.

Summary: You should now be able to explain how the different parts of the Mass celebrate and reflect the idea of redemption.

4.11 Different Christian understandings of the Eucharist

■ For Catholics

For Catholics, the Mass is the 'source and summit' of Christian life. This means:

- The offering of Christ on the cross is the highest form of prayer to God. All other acts of prayer and praise are simply joining in with Christ's prayer.
- The Mass re-enacts the sacrifice of Christ on the cross, so it is the highest form of prayer that a believer can make.
- All prayers offered by Christians are inspired by the Spirit that flowed from the crucified Christ.
- All acts of love are reflections of the total love for the Father that was shown in the death of Christ, which is repeated in every Mass.
- Without receiving the Eucharist, Christians cannot live the full life that Christ wants. Christ's Body and Blood give life to the soul just as normal food gives life to the human body.
- Offering the Mass on Sunday is the perfect way to 'keep holy the Sabbath day', fulfilling this commandment from God in a Christian way by celebrating the day of resurrection every Sunday.

■ For Orthodox Christians

Orthodox Christians have an understanding of the Eucharist that is very similar to what Catholics believe, although there are a few differences in the practice:

- The Orthodox Eucharist is called the Liturgy and is full of intense symbolism and ritual, more so than in the Catholic Mass.
- In Orthodox churches the consecration takes place behind the Holy Doors of the **iconostasis**, as what happens is considered to be too holy to be seen directly by the congregation. The Holy Doors represent the gateway between heaven and earth, and the Eucharist is on the side of heaven but is given to humans in Communion.
- The Orthodox and Catholic Churches both believe that Christ is fully present in the Eucharist.

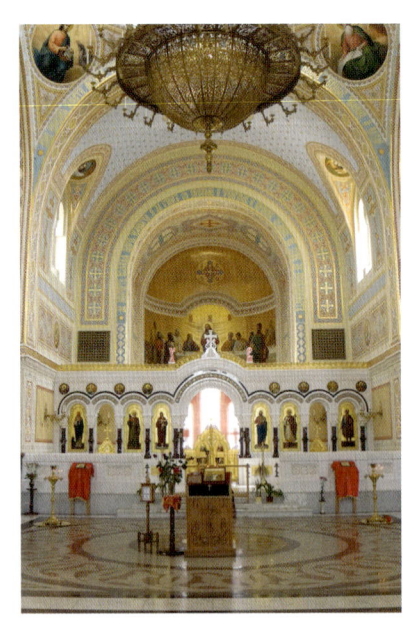

▲ *An Orthodox cathedral in Russia, including an iconostasis*

Objectives

- Know how the Eucharist is the 'source and summit' of Christian life for Catholics.
- Understand how different Christian denominations interpret the Eucharist.

Key terms

- **Orthodox:** A branch of Christianity mainly, but not entirely, practised in Eastern Europe
- **iconostasis:** the screen that divides the holy part of an Orthodox church, including the altar, from the congregation; it represents the meeting place and division between heaven and earth
- **Quakers:** a religious group founded in the seventeenth century; instead of celebrating the Eucharist they gather together for prayer and wait to be inspired by the Holy Spirit
- **Salvation Army:** a Christian group founded in the nineteenth century who see the main purpose of religion as going out to serve and help those in need
- **Nonconformist:** Christians who do not follow the rules laid down by a central authority but are organised at a local level; the Bible forms a central part of their worship

- The Liturgy is a communal activity that the whole group of believers are called to share in, whereas a Catholic priest is allowed to say the Mass in private.

■ For Anglican Christians

There is a range of acceptable beliefs within the Anglican Church about the Eucharist:

- Some share the Catholic understanding that in the Eucharist the bread and wine become the Body and Blood of Christ.
- A larger group believe that the spirit of Christ is received when Communion is given. Christ is spiritually present, but the bread and wine do not literally become the Body and Blood of Christ.
- Christ is present in the community that shares the Eucharist.

■ For Quakers and the Salvation Army

These groups do not celebrate any form of Eucharist. In general, they believe that Christ is present through the Spirit, who inspires their prayers and actions in the service of God and other people. They do not practise sacramental rites as they believe the whole of life is a sacrament.

■ For Nonconformist Christians

There are different **Nonconformist** beliefs about the Eucharist, but many believe that:

- The Eucharist is a memorial of the Last Supper of Jesus. (This means that the purpose of the Eucharist is to remember the Last Supper, rather than to re-enact it in the way that Catholics do.)
- Christ is present in the word of God, the readings from the Bible. Catholics also believe that Christ is present in the words of the Bible, but for Nonconformists, this is where they meet Christ in particular.

Some ask that the Holy Spirit descends so 'that these gifts of bread and wine may be for us the body and blood of Christ'. This means that Christ enters their lives when they receive Communion, whereas Catholics believe that the work of the Holy Spirit actually changes the bread and wine into the Body and Blood of Christ.

▲ A Quaker meeting where people gather together to pray

Research activity

Choose two Christian denominations and research their celebration of the Eucharist. What are the differences and what does this say about their beliefs?

★ Study tip

There are many different Christian understandings about the Eucharist. You are only expected to be aware of the basic differences, not all the details and implications of them.

Summary

You should now understand how and why different Christian groups interpret the Eucharist in different ways.

Activities

1. Explain why some Christians do not celebrate the Eucharist.
2. 'A difference in beliefs about the Eucharist between Christians is not important.' Evaluate this statement. Be sure to include more than one point of view, and refer to Catholic beliefs and teachings in your answer.

4.12 Prayers in the Mass and adoration

Catholics believe that Christ is truly present in the Eucharist. This is called the **Real Presence**. The Bread and Wine are not just symbols of the presence of Christ: Christ is fully present, Body, Blood, Soul and Divinity. The sacrifice of the Mass is the most important form of worship for Catholics.

■ The words of institution

The central part of the Mass is the consecration. Here the priest says the words of Jesus from the Last Supper. These are known as the words of institution.

> At the time he was betrayed and entered willingly into his Passion, he took bread and, giving thanks, broke it, and gave it to his disciples, saying:
>
> TAKE THIS, ALL OF YOU, AND EAT OF IT,/ FOR THIS IS MY BODY,/ WHICH WILL BE GIVEN UP FOR YOU.
>
> In a similar way, when supper was ended, he took the chalice and, once more giving thanks, he gave it to his disciples, saying:
>
> TAKE THIS, ALL OF YOU, AND DRINK FROM IT,/ FOR THIS IS THE CHALICE OF MY BLOOD,/ THE BLOOD OF THE NEW AND ETERNAL COVENANT,/ WHICH WILL BE POURED OUT FOR YOU AND FOR MANY/ FOR THE FORGIVENESS OF SINS./ DO THIS IN MEMORY OF ME.
>
> The words of consecration from Eucharistic Prayer II

Objectives
- Understand the importance of the Words of Institution and the Agnus Dei.
- Know why Catholics respect the Eucharist.

Key terms
- **Real Presence:** Christ is truly present in the consecrated Bread and Wine
- **Blessed Sacrament:** a term that refers to the consecrated Bread and Wine
- **Benediction:** meaning 'blessing'; a service at which the Blessed Sacrament is exposed and Catholics worship Christ in the sacrament

The words in capitals are the actual words of consecration. It is when these words are said that the bread and wine become the Body and Blood of Christ:

- The external features remain bread and wine but the reality changes.
- Christ gave himself in the form of bread and wine so that his followers can become sharers in his suffering, death and resurrection and their effects. This means they can share in the defeat of sin and death, and the promise of eternal life.
- Jesus did not say 'This *symbolises* my body' but 'This *is* my body'.
- Jesus gave his disciples the commission to do what he had done. This means that he made them the first priests with the power to re-enact what he had done. This has been passed on to bishops and priests.
- The word 'memory' does not simply mean 'do not forget'. It means: 'make this a reality to yourself'. This means that whenever Catholics celebrate the Eucharist, they become caught up in what happened to Jesus at his Last Supper, death and resurrection.

▲ *Pope Benedict XVI holds up the Blessed Sacrament in a monstrance*

Chapter 4   Redemption

■ The Agnus Dei

'Agnus Dei' is the Latin translation of the first words of the prayer that is said shortly before Communion:

> Lamb of God, you take away the sins of the world, have mercy on us.
> Lamb of God, you take away the sins of the world, have mercy on us.
> Lamb of God, you take away the sins of the world, grant us peace.

> Not to go to Communion is like someone dying of thirst beside a spring.
>
> St John Vianney

The Last Supper was a Passover meal that celebrated the Jews' escape from Egypt. Passover meals remember the events in Exodus 12, when God ordered each Jewish household to eat a lamb. The blood of this lamb was put on the door of each house to show that they had obeyed God's command. This meant that nobody in that house would be killed by the Angel of Death. The lamb was a sacrifice that saved the Jews.

For Christians, Jesus is the new Lamb of God. His death and blood destroyed the power of sin and death. All people have been saved by the blood of Jesus, the Lamb of God.

■ Eucharistic adoration

Because Catholics believe that Jesus is truly present in the consecrated Bread and Wine, called the **Blessed Sacrament**, they treat the Eucharist with great reverence and respect. Many Catholics receive Communion on the tongue rather than in the hand. This is to remind themselves that they are not dealing with normal bread.

At Mass more hosts are usually consecrated than are required for the people present. The extra hosts are placed into the tabernacle. People pray in front of the tabernacle as they believe the Real Presence of Christ is there.

Link
To read more about the tabernacle see page 93.

Discussion activity
Discuss how important it is for Catholics to respect the Eucharist.

■ Benediction

Since Christ is present in the Eucharist, Catholics can worship Christ fully on earth. Many Catholic churches have **Benediction**. This is when a consecrated host is exposed (put on display) in a monstrance. A monstrance is a large holder in which a large host is placed upright so that people might see it and worship before the Blessed Sacrament. Benediction is a service where the presence of Christ in the Eucharist is praised. At the end of the service, people are blessed with the Real Presence.

★ Study tip
It is important to remember that Catholic actions in relation to the consecrated Bread and Wine are an expression of their beliefs about the Real Presence.

Activities
1. Explain what the words of consecration show about the Eucharist.
2. 'All Catholics should pray in front of the Blessed Sacrament.' Evaluate this statement. Be sure to include more than one point of view, and refer to Catholic beliefs and teachings in your answer.

Summary
You should now understand why the words of Institution and the Agnus Dei are important in the Mass. You should also understand why Catholics treat the Eucharist with great respect.

4 Assessment guidance

Redemption – summary

You should now be able to:

✔ explain how the various features in a Catholic church show what Catholics believe, and explain how they help Catholics to worship

✔ explain the importance of the lectern, altar, crucifix and tabernacle in a Catholic church

✔ explain how different types of architecture and objects within a Catholic church reflect different attitudes and beliefs

✔ explain the importance of the death, resurrection and ascension of Jesus, especially in relation to redemption

✔ explain how Christians see salvation as a past, present and future event, and explain what the gift of grace means to Christians

✔ explain how the liturgy has been influenced by the events of the Last Supper, and the death and resurrection of Jesus

✔ explain how the events described in Mark 15:21–39, John 20:1–18, Acts 1:6–11 and Acts 2:1–4 show the redeeming work of Jesus

✔ explain how St Irenaeus and St Anselm use metaphors to write about salvation

✔ explain the importance of conscience for Christians as the voice of God, and how this affects the way that Christians live

✔ explain the importance of the Mass for Catholics, and explain different Christian understandings of what the Eucharist means

✔ explain the importance of the words of institution, the Agnus Dei, the Real Presence, and the Eucharistic adoration for Catholics.

Sample student answer – the 12 mark question

1. Write an answer to the following question:

   'The Mass is the best way to remind Christians that they are redeemed.'

   Evaluate this statement. In your answer you should:
   - give developed arguments to support this statement
   - give developed arguments to support a different point of view
   - refer to Christian teaching
   - reach a justified conclusion.

   [12 marks]

2. Read the following sample student answers:

Student A

"For Catholics the Mass is the re-enactment of the Last Supper, death and resurrection of Jesus. Other Christians see the Eucharist in different ways. Methodists think that they are just remembering what Jesus did at the last supper and that what they receive at Communion is only ordinary bread. This is different to Catholics who think that they are receiving the body and blood of Jesus. The Mass cannot be a reminder that people are redeemed as it is just a boring event that people feel forced to attend each Sunday. If they felt it was special, then they would take part in it with more energy."

Student B

"At the Last Supper Jesus gave his disciples the bread and wine with the command to take it and eat and drink it, for this was his body and blood that was given up for them. They were also given the command to 'do this in memory of me'. Jesus clearly wanted his followers to remember his sacrifice on the cross, which saved people from the separation from God that is hell.

When Catholics offer the Mass, they are caught up in Jesus' own prayer and offering to God the Father. Jesus saved all people from sin by his death, so when we join in the Mass we are not only celebrating the fact that we are redeemed, but in a way we are caught up in that redemption. Some people might say that they cannot understand how going to Mass and receiving what they think is just a bit of bread and wine can remind them that they are redeemed. This is because they do not have faith.

Some Christians do not have the same beliefs about Jesus being truly present in the Eucharist that Catholics have. For them, the Eucharist is only a reminder of a past event, so they do not focus on redemption in the Eucharist. However, these Christians do not deny that they are redeemed. They only deny that the Mass is the best way to remember the fact. But even for them, since the Eucharist is linked to the Last Supper, which is linked to the death and resurrection of Jesus, they indirectly remember that they are redeemed at the Eucharist."

3. With a partner, discuss the sample answers. For each one, consider the following questions:
   - Does the response answer the question?
   - Does the answer refer to Christian teachings and if so what are they?
   - Is there an argument to support the statement and how well developed is it?
   - Is a different point of view offered and how developed is that argument?
   - Has the student written a clear conclusion after weighing up both sides of the argument?
   - What is good about this answer?
   - How do you think it could be improved?

4. What mark (out of 12) would you give these answers? Look at the mark scheme in the Introduction (AO2). What are the reasons for the mark you have given?

Practice questions

1. Which of these statements best explains for Christians what the conscience is?

   A) It is the voice of God in people's hearts
   B) It is pressure from society for people to conform
   C) It is the temptation to do wrong things
   D) It is following the teachings of the Bible [1 mark]

2. Give two salvation metaphors. [2 marks]

3. Explain two ways that an altar helps Catholics to worship. [4 marks]

4. Explain two Christian beliefs about the importance of the resurrection of Jesus in redemption.

   Refer to Christian teaching in your answer. [5 marks]

> ⭐ **Study tip**
>
> 'Refer to Christian teaching' means that you should refer to the Bible or Church documents, or the words of Christian leaders as part of your answer.

5. 'The architecture, design and decoration of a Catholic church has no importance for Catholic worship.'

   Evaluate this statement. In your answer you should:
   - give developed arguments to support this statement
   - give developed arguments to support a different point of view
   - refer to Christian teaching
   - reach a justified conclusion. [12 marks]

5 Church and the Kingdom of God

5.1 Pilgrimage and the Stations of the Cross

■ The pilgrim people of God

Catholics think of the Church as the **pilgrim** people of God:

> **❝** Christians, on pilgrimage toward the heavenly city, should seek and think of these things which are above. **❞**
>
> *Gaudium et Spes* 57

Pilgrimage is a movement forward to a final destination. Christians believe they are on their way to meet God at death. Therefore during life, a Christian's daily prayer and actions should reflect the idea of making progress. In this way, Christians are on a sacred journey of service throughout their lives. A Christian who sees life as a pilgrimage will do their best to ensure that all the people they meet are touched by their sense of purpose and by the presence of God, which is reflected in their attitude and actions.

■ The Stations of the Cross

Jesus was a great pilgrim. His mission took him throughout Judea, preaching and caring for those in need. The final stage of his journey was from Pilate's house to the hill of Calvary, the place of crucifixion, carrying his cross. In every Catholic church there are 14 images that remind Catholics about events that happened during this painful journey. These images are collectively called the **Stations of the Cross**.

During **Lent** many Catholics like to make the Stations of the Cross. This means that they walk between the Stations and say a prayer at each one as they think about Jesus' last journey. This can be done in a group or as individuals.

This is a form of **dramatised prayer**. Drama is a form of expression that uses action and performance to convey a meaning and to get people involved in what is happening. Prayer is a raising of the heart and mind to God. Many people believe that for prayer to make an impact, it needs to include a physical dimension as well as mental and verbal expression.

When Catholics reach each of the 14 Stations, they usually reflect on a short reading about the event depicted, such as the way Simon helped Jesus to carry his cross, or the way in which Jesus fell under the weight of the cross. A prayer is said and then they move on to the next Station.

Objectives

- Understand why Catholics call the Church the pilgrim people of God.
- Understand how the Stations of the Cross help a Catholic to join in with the final journey of Jesus to his crucifixion.
- Understand why Catholics go on pilgrimage to Jerusalem.

Key terms

- **pilgrim:** a person on a religious journey, which reflects the journey through life to heaven
- **Stations of the Cross:** a series of 14 images that remind Catholics of Jesus' final journey to the cross
- **Lent:** the 40 days before Easter, during which Christians reflect on the sufferings of Jesus
- **dramatised prayer:** a form of prayer that includes actions, like moving from one place to another or acting out the intention of the prayer

Chapter 5 Church and the Kingdom of God

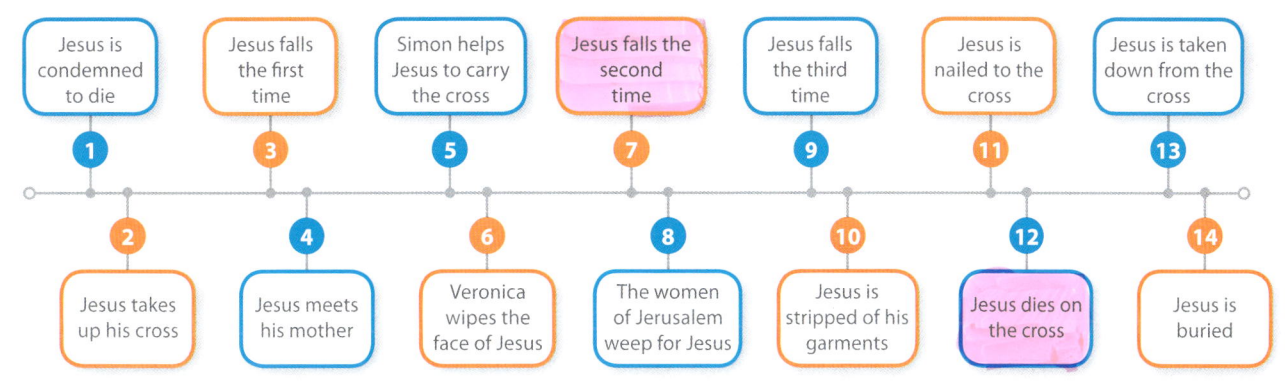

The 14 Stations of the Cross

1. Jesus is condemned to die
2. Jesus takes up his cross
3. Jesus falls the first time
4. Jesus meets his mother
5. Simon helps Jesus to carry the cross
6. Veronica wipes the face of Jesus
7. Jesus falls the second time
8. The women of Jerusalem weep for Jesus
9. Jesus falls the third time
10. Jesus is stripped of his garments
11. Jesus is nailed to the cross
12. Jesus dies on the cross
13. Jesus is taken down from the cross
14. Jesus is buried

The movement is a way to accompany Jesus on his journey, to act out a form of sharing in Jesus' sufferings as a sign of gratitude. The physical movement also allows the person praying to maintain focus, as sometimes sitting or kneeling in the same place for a time can make the person's mind drift on to other topics.

Pilgrimage to Jerusalem

Most Catholics cannot afford the time or the money to go to Jerusalem on pilgrimage (the city in Israel where Jesus died). For them, making the Stations of the Cross in their local church allows them to follow the footsteps of Jesus in spirit if not in body. Those Catholics who can make a pilgrimage to Jerusalem usually do the Stations of the Cross on the Via Dolorosa, the street through which Jesus carried his cross. By walking in the footsteps of Jesus, Catholics hope to follow him to heaven.

In Jerusalem, most Catholics also visit the tomb in which it is thought Jesus was buried and from which he rose again. Once people have made the journey to Jerusalem, they usually go to the other towns and places in the area where Jesus lived and taught. These holy sites enable pilgrims to make direct contact with the founding events of their religion. This allows them to renew their faith and commitment to Jesus. Most pilgrims return home with a new determination to live out their faith, both in prayer and in action, in a more committed way.

▲ *Jesus is nailed to the cross*

Link

To read about pilgrimage to Rome, Lourdes and Walsingham see the next page.

★ Study tip

It would be useful to visit a Catholic church to see where the Stations of the Cross are.

Activities

1. Explain why some Catholics like to make the Stations of the Cross.
2. 'The only way to make the Stations of the Cross in a meaningful way is in Jerusalem.' Evaluate this statement. Be sure to include more than one point of view, and refer to Catholic beliefs and teachings in your answer.

Research activity

Find one of the published sets of prayers that may be used when making the Stations of the Cross. Read the prayers and make notes on the significance of each of the 14 Stations.

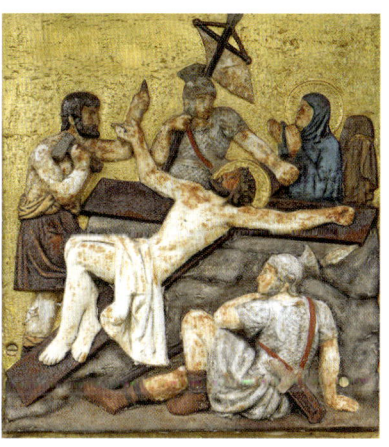

Summary

You should now know why pilgrimage is important to Catholics. You should also understand how making the Stations of the Cross – as a type of dramatised prayer – helps Catholics to become closer to Jesus, and understand why Catholics visit Jerusalem on pilgrimage.

117

5.2 Pilgrimage to Rome, Lourdes and Walsingham

A **pilgrimage** is a dramatised journey. It is a journey of spiritual and religious significance. Pilgrims go to a place that they believe has been touched in a special way by the presence of God. Pilgrimage sites might be connected to events in the life of Jesus or one of the saints, or they might be where visions have been received.

There are many reasons people go on pilgrimage, for example:

- to express thanks to God
- to ask forgiveness for sins
- to seek spiritual and physical healing
- to renew commitment to their faith
- to experience the support of other believers
- to physically express the inner journey of faith.

■ Rome

Many Catholics go on pilgrimage to Rome (the capital city of Italy) as it is the centre of the Catholic faith. St Peter, the leader of the apostles (see Matthew 16:18–19), went to Rome to preach the Christian faith. He was crucified and buried on a hill in Rome where the Vatican now stands. The Bishops of Rome (the popes) are the successors to St Peter, and the authority that Jesus gave to Peter has been passed on in an unbroken line to the present pope.

Pilgrims from around the world come to Rome to show their commitment to the Catholic Church and their unity with the Pope and all Catholics. In Rome, Catholics visit the tomb of St Peter in St Peter's Basilica. They also visit the cathedral of St John Lateran, the Pope's cathedral, which is the mother church (the most important of all Catholic churches).

■ Lourdes

Lourdes, a town in France, is a very popular place of pilgrimage. Many Catholics believe that in 1858, St Bernadette, a teenage peasant, saw 18 visions of a woman who identified herself as the **Immaculate Conception**. In the visions, Mary gave Bernadette three instructions:

- to pray the rosary (to say one 'Our Father', ten 'Hail Marys' and one 'Glory be to the Father', repeating this five times)
- to come in procession (to meet up with other Catholics and walk together as a sign of faith, while saying prayers)
- to build a church.

Mary also told Bernadette to dig. When she dug, a spring came from the ground. Since that time, many people have bathed in the waters of this spring. A number of unexpected cures have taken place, some of which have been declared miracles by the International and Medical

Objectives

- Know how pilgrimage is seen as a reflection of the journey of life.
- Understand why Catholics go on pilgrimage to Rome, Lourdes and Walsingham.

Key terms

- **pilgrimage:** a journey by a believer to a holy site for religious reasons; an act of worship and devotion
- **basilica:** a large church that is not a cathedral
- **Immaculate Conception:** a title given to Mary that refers to the belief that Mary was conceived without original sin
- **the Body of Christ:** (1) the consecrated host (Bread) in the Eucharist (2) a community of believers, the Church

Links

To read about pilgrimage to Jerusalem see the previous page.

▲ *The grotto at Lourdes where Bernadette saw visions of Mary*

Chapter 5 Church and the Kingdom of God

Committee of Lourdes, after scientific and medical study could find no natural explanations for the sudden healings.

Pilgrims often go to Lourdes in large groups, taking with them people who are ill and need the support of others to make the journey. This care shows the idea of **the Body of Christ** in practice. St Paul used the image of all Christians united together like a body, doing the work of Christ on earth (see 1 Corinthians 12:12–30). Often on pilgrimages the stronger parts of the body look after the weaker parts.

Even when there is no physical change in a person, they often feel stronger and more at peace after a pilgrimage, ready to accept the challenges of life with an increased trust in the love and power of God. This effect of the pilgrimage applies as much to healthy people as it does to sick people.

■ Walsingham

For many people, going abroad on pilgrimage is not an option. However, it is quite possible to do a day pilgrimage to a local shrine. The Catholic national shrine in England is at Walsingham, a village in Norfolk.

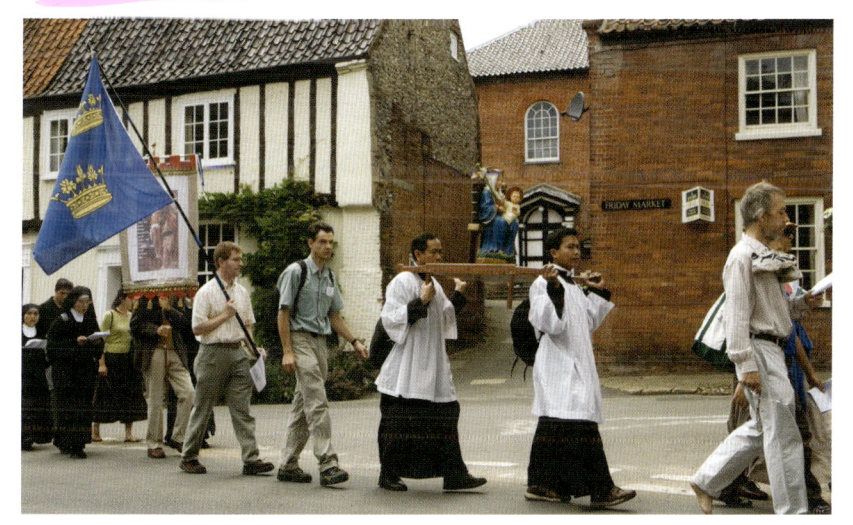

▲ Catholics process through the streets of Walsingham

Many Catholics believe that in 1061, Richeldis de Faverches, a Saxon noblewoman, had a vision in which she saw the house in Nazareth where Mary had lived. Richeldis had a copy of this house made. It became a major place of pilgrimage throughout the Middle Ages until it was destroyed on the command of Henry VIII in 1538.

In the nineteenth century, people started to return to Walsingham as pilgrims. The centre for Catholic pilgrimage today is the Slipper Chapel, a small fourteenth-century building where pilgrims would leave their shoes before walking the final mile to the Holy House barefoot.

Now thousands of people every year come to Walsingham. They sometimes process through the streets of Walsingham, starting at the Slipper Chapel and ending at the ruins of the destroyed abbey. The holy mile reflects the journey of life to God's presence. People sing hymns, go to confession and attend Mass. This pilgrimage makes people more aware of their faith and their place in the community of believers, the Church.

> *Someone who goes on a pilgrimage 'prays with their feet' and experiences with all his senses that his entire life is one long journey to God.*
>
> Youcat 276

Extension activity

Compare two places of Christian pilgrimage. Examine their history, what they reflect about Christian beliefs, and the activities that take place there.

Activities

1 Explain why Catholics go on pilgrimage.

2 'A pilgrimage is nothing more than an excuse for a holiday.' Evaluate this statement. Be sure to include more than one point of view, and refer to Catholic beliefs and teachings in your answer.

⭐ Study tip

It might help you to compare a pilgrimage with a journey that shows dedication, like going a long distance to support a football team or to see your favourite band.

Summary

You should now be able to explain why Catholics go on pilgrimage to Rome, Lourdes and Walsingham.

5.3 Mission and evangelism in drama

■ Showing mission and evangelism in drama

Catholics believe they are part of the Church's **mission** to take the message about Jesus, his life and his teaching to the people they meet, particularly through their actions. **Evangelism** is the preaching of the Gospel, particularly in words.

There are many kinds of drama that show the message of Christianity. These include films, plays, musicals and comedies. The action in a dramatic work can help people to relate to how the message of Christianity is both received and ignored.

Often the Christian message is presented subtly; it is only once you have seen the whole work that you can see the unfolding of the story in a religious light. *Les Miserables* is an example of this type of drama.

Other dramatic productions are explicitly built around a religious story or theme, and people can more easily assess the value of the religious message through the action. The film *The Mission* is an example of this type of drama.

■ Les Miserables

Les Miserables is a novel by the French writer Victor Hugo, which has been used as the basis for a number of dramatic works, including a musical and a film. It centres round the power of love and forgiveness, and shows how the kind act of one person can have major effects on other people's lives. It reflects the Christian duty to love all people, and shows how this is best done in actions rather than words. Here are a few examples from the 2012 film that show this:

- The ex-convict Valjean steals a lot of silver from the Bishop of Digne. When the police catch Valjean with the silver, he tells them that it was a gift from the bishop. The bishop tells the police that this was the case and when the police have left, the bishop urges Valjean to use this new opportunity to do some good. This touches Valjean and he decides to change his ways. He sets up a factory to try to help other people benefit from the wealth that the bishop has given him.
- Since Valjean broke his parole from prison, he is a wanted man. Javert, his former jailer, constantly chases him, not being willing to forgive him. Javert believes that no man can change. But Javert is then captured by revolutionaries, who ask Valjean to kill him. Valjean chooses to let Javert go free.
- When Javert finally corners Valjean, he cannot kill him, but neither can he forgive himself for not killing him. Javert shows how easy it is to let hardheartedness destroy a life, while Valjean shows how difficult yet rewarding it is to try to live by the Christian principle of showing love, even to your enemies.

Objectives

- Know how mission and evangelism are shown through drama.
- Understand the impact that dramatic works can have on people's understanding of Christianity.

Key terms

- **mission:** 'sending out' people with a job or function to perform
- **evangelism:** preaching the good news about Jesus to other people

Link

To read more about the differences between mission and evangelism see pages 74–75.

Activities

1. Explain how one other play or film, such as *Amazing Grace* or *Lord of the Rings*, expresses beliefs that are important to Christians. Do you think this play or film could be used to help convert people to Christianity?

2. 'Using drama is one of the best methods for converting people to Christianity.' Evaluate this statement. Be sure to include more than one point of view, and refer to Catholic beliefs and teachings in your answer.

- The message of the whole musical is summed up in the line from one of the final songs: 'To love another person is to see the face of God', which reflects the central message of Christianity.

The Mission

This film from 1986 reflects the situation in South America in the eighteenth century, when some Europeans were trying to enslave the native population, and some Christian missionaries were trying to convert them to the Christian faith. There are many examples in this film that show the power of faith and forgiveness. Here are a few:

- A former slave trader kills his stepbrother. He feels so bad about this that he goes to work among the people he used to enslave. He has to drag a heavy load around, representing his past, and it is only when one of the ex-slaves releases him from the load that he accepts that he is forgiven. This shows the power of Christian forgiveness in action.
- The European priests convert the native people by working with them, and they become committed to Christianity because of the example set by the priests. When the native people are attacked by the slave traders, some of the priests fight to defend them. This is an example of Jesus' teaching: 'No one has greater love than this, to lay down one's life for one's friends' (John 15:13). This also shows how both mission and evangelism demand total commitment.
- The priests were ordered by their bishops to abandon the native people to the slavers for political reasons. However, the priests rejected these orders in favour of following their consciences.

> **The production and showing of films that have value** as decent entertainment, humane culture or art, especially when they are designed for young people, **ought to be encouraged** and assured by every effective means. This can be done particularly by supporting and joining in projects and enterprises for the production and distribution of decent films, by encouraging worthwhile films through critical approval and awards, by patronizing or jointly sponsoring theaters operated by Catholic and responsible managers.
>
> *Inter Mirifica* 14

▲ In The Mission the Jesuit priest Father Gabriel supports and works with the native population

In both *Les Miserables* and *The Mission* there is a central conflict between law and grace. In both films what the law demands does not match up with what goodness demands; the 'heroes' in the films either ignore the demands of civil law (in the case of *Les Miserables*) or Church law (in the case of *The Mission*).

Discussion activity

Discuss whether plays or films should ever deal with religion.

⭐ Study tip

It is often easier to see mission and evangelism in drama once you have watched the whole play or film. Often the messages are hidden in the storyline.

Summary

You should now understand how drama can be used for mission and evangelism, and how it can show examples of mission and evangelism.

5.4 The Kingdom of God and the Lord's Prayer

■ The Kingdom of God

According to Mark's Gospel, Jesus' first teaching was: 'The time is fulfilled, and the **Kingdom of God** has come near; repent, and believe in the good news' (Mark 1:15). This is a summary of Jesus' whole teaching. Jesus constantly referred to the Kingdom of God, sometimes called the Kingdom of Heaven.

'Kingdom of God' is perhaps better translated as 'Reign of God'. This is because Jesus was not referring to a place, but to the idea of God's sovereignty and authority.

It is helpful to think about the Kingdom of God as a gradual process:

- God's power came to earth in the person and teaching of Jesus. Jesus said to his disciples, 'the Kingdom of God is among you' (Luke 17:21).
- The Kingdom established itself through the resurrection of Jesus and the sending of the Holy Spirit at Pentecost. God's reign is seen among those who follow Jesus. The Church, the Body of Christ on earth, is the sign of the Kingdom of God present on earth.
- The Kingdom will be completed at the end of time when God comes in power and all people enjoy the eternal happiness of heaven.

> **Objectives**
> - Know what is meant by the Kingdom or Reign of God.
> - Understand how the Lord's Prayer shows the meaning of the Kingdom of God.

> **Key terms**
> - **Kingdom of God:** also called the Reign of God, where all people live as God intends
> - **The Lord's Prayer:** the prayer taught to the disciples by Jesus; also known as the 'Our Father'

■ The Lord's Prayer

'**The Lord's Prayer**' is so called because Jesus taught it to his disciples. Most Catholics refer to the prayer as the 'Our Father' after the first words of the prayer. The usual version of the prayer used by Catholics is this translation of a passage from Matthew 6:9–13:

> " Our Father, who art in heaven,
> hallowed be thy name;
> thy kingdom come,
> thy will be done
> on earth as it is in heaven.
> Give us this day our daily bread,
> and forgive us our trespasses,
> as we forgive those who trespass against us;
> and lead us not into temptation,
> but deliver us from evil. "
>
> *The Lord's Prayer*

▲ *Jesus taught his disciples how to pray*

'Our Father, who art in heaven'

This prayer starts by using the Aramaic word *Abba*, translated as 'Father', which shows Jesus' intimate relationship with God the Father. Jesus wants all his followers to have the same type of trusting relationship with God that he has.

'Hallowed be thy name'

When believers pray that God's name is accepted as holy, they are not just referring to the name of God but all that God is. When people respect the otherness, majesty and holiness of God, they recognise the importance of God in their own lives. In doing this, they are accepting the call to become members of God's Kingdom.

'Thy kingdom come'

When people pray for God's Kingdom to come, they are not just looking forward to the end of time, the final establishment of God's rule; it is a prayer for people to accept the rule of God in their own hearts. In this way, the Kingdom will spread on earth through each person recognising their place as a child of God.

'Thy will be done, on earth as it is in heaven'

The will of God is done by all members of the heavenly Kingdom. Those who are happy in the presence of God delight to do his will, as it brings them a sense of fulfilment as well as showing great respect to God. The prayer asks that all people on earth might share in this attitude to God's will. When everybody does the will of God, the world will be perfect and God's Kingdom will be fully established.

'Give us this day our daily bread'

Daily bread is the requirement for survival, not for luxuries. When people ask for their daily bread, they are asking that God remove need from their lives so they can focus more on God.

'And forgive us our trespasses'

Sins separate a person from God and from other people. When sins are forgiven, barriers are removed and God's power and love can be experienced more fully. Forgiveness has to be shared fully to be effective. This is the only part of the prayer that is conditional: forgive my sins to the extent that I forgive those who sin against me.

'Deliver us from evil'

The evil one is trying to prevent the growth of the Kingdom of God, by tempting people to sin and reject God. The prayer accepts that humans need help to resist temptation, but with the grace of God this will happen.

> **"** When we pray, 'Thy Kingdom come,' we call for Christ to come again, as he promised, and for God's reign, which has already begun here on earth, to prevail definitively. **"**
>
> *Youcat* 520

Extension activity

Research different interpretations given to the words 'the Kingdom of God'. Explain which interpretation is most meaningful for you.

⭐ Study tip

In the days of Jesus and for many centuries afterwards, the king was a leader who could demand almost anything and the people would obey him. This is the starting point of talking about God as king.

Summary

You should now be able to explain what 'the Kingdom of God' means. You should also understand what the Lord's Prayer teaches about the Kingdom of God.

Activities

1. Explain why the Kingdom of God is important in Christianity.
2. 'The Lord's Prayer is dealing only with the Kingdom of God.' Evaluate this statement. Be sure to include more than one point of view, and refer to Catholic beliefs and teachings in your answer.

5.5 Signs of the Kingdom: justice, peace and reconciliation

Christians believe that the Kingdom of God is the perfect kingdom, where all things that go against what God wants have been removed.

> [Y]ou anointed your Only Begotten Son,/ our Lord Jesus Christ, with the oil of gladness/ as eternal Priest and King of all creation,/ so that … he might present to the immensity of your majesty/ an eternal and universal kingdom,/ a kingdom of truth and life,/ a kingdom of holiness and grace,/ a kingdom of justice, love and peace.
>
> *Preface: Christ, King of the Universe*

The aim of Christians should be to help the Kingdom of God grow on earth. All things that work against the good of other people and the harmony of society are limiting the spread of the Kingdom.

Justice

Justice ensures all people have what they are entitled to as human beings. Injustice creates divisions and resentment. Catholics believe that all people are created equal and are loved equally by God. They are called upon to help ensure that the dignity of every person, regardless of sex, race, colour or religion, is recognised and supported. This should not be simply on a personal level but also applies to institutions within society. Catholics have a duty to reject any movement by a political or pressure group that undermines the dignity of any human being.

> Man is himself the author, centre, and goal of all economic and social life. The decisive point of the social question is that **goods created by God for everyone should in fact reach everyone** in accordance with justice and with the help of charity.
>
> *Catechism of the Catholic Church* 2459

It is not enough for Catholics to try to live in a way that respects the rights of other people: they should also work to change the systems that allow injustice to flourish. Christians believe that justice comes from God, and any attempt to ensure that justice exists on earth is spreading the Kingdom of God. 'Give the king your justice, O God … May he judge your people with righteousness, and your poor with justice' (Psalms 72(71):1–2 (NRSV)).

Peace

The Hebrew word for **peace** is *shalom*, which does not just refer to a lack of conflict. Peace is better thought of as a state of total trust and unity between all people. Peace flows from justice. While there is any form of injustice, there can be no peace.

Objectives

- Know what justice, peace and reconciliation mean.
- Understand how justice, peace and reconciliation are signs of the Kingdom of God.

Key terms

- **justice:** bringing about what is right and fair, according to the law, or making up for a wrong that has been committed
- **peace:** a state of total trust and unity between all people
- **reconciliation:** (1) the restoring of harmony after relationships have broken down (2) a sacrament in the Catholic Church

> Peace is but an empty word, if it does not rest upon that order which … is founded on truth, built up on justice, nurtured and animated by charity, and brought into effect under the auspices of freedom.
>
> *Pacem in Terris* 167

Peace is the removal of tensions that are caused by suspicion, resentment and mistreatment. To create peace, all people must learn to accept the rights of every individual. Catholics believe that peace is not an external quality but something that comes from a person's heart. When people learn to trust and accept each other, to support the weak and the defenceless, then there is a chance that peace will begin to flourish.

Catholics should support all agencies that are working to establish peace and harmony in the world. This is not just referring to anti-war movements but to organisations that work for justice and unity. In this way, Catholics believe that the peace of God's Kingdom may be experienced here on earth.

■ Reconciliation

Reconciliation is the bringing back together of people who have broken apart. This division may be caused by many factors, but it tends to increase bitterness. People who have been reconciled can learn to appreciate each other more because they learn to accept and live with their differences, without there being any tension. Reconciliation is based on an attitude that is willing to accept that the past has happened but that it should not have happened. It requires people to learn from the past and work together to ensure that the same type of situation does not happen again.

Through reconciliation, the barriers that caused separation are removed. For Christians, this allows God's peace and justice to spread, which helps the Kingdom of God to flourish on earth.

The Warrington bombing

In 1993 two young boys, Tim Parry (12 years old) and Jonathan Ball (3) were killed when two IRA bombs exploded in the main shopping street in Warrington (England). Tim Parry's parents were deeply affected by the death of their son but they decided that they would try to get communities to work together to get rid of the violence. They built a safe place called The Peace Centre, where young people of all religions, races and backgrounds could come together, to share and appreciate what they have in common. In this way, violence was overcome by reconciliation.

▲ *The River of Life – a memorial to remember the victims of the IRA bombings in Warrington. The dome is imprinted with the handprints of local school children.*

> **❝ It is my duty to build bridges and to help all men and women, in any way possible, to do the same** … The contemporary world, with its open wounds which affect so many of our brothers and sisters, demands that we confront every form of polarisation which would divide it into … two camps. **❞**
>
> Pope Francis
> 24 September 2015

Activities

1. Explain fully what is involved in the idea of peace.
2. 'Without justice there can never be peace and reconciliation in the world.' Evaluate this statement. Be sure to include more than one point of view, and refer to Catholic beliefs and teachings in your answer.

Research activity

Research one of the following reconciliation projects: Corrymeela in Northern Ireland or the Truth and Reconciliation Commission in South Africa. How successful has the project been in achieving its aims? How much of its work was based on Christian teachings?

⭐ Study tip

To help understand these ideas think about a time when you had a major argument with a friend or relative. What was needed to resolve the situation?

Summary
You should now understand the concepts of peace, justice and reconciliation, and know how they are linked to the Kingdom of God.

5.6 The hierarchy of the Catholic Church and the Second Vatican Council

The hierarchy of the Catholic Church

The Catholic Church has a **hierarchy**: a ranking system that brings about unity and recognises people's authority and responsibility. At the top of the Catholic hierarchy is the **Pope** (the Bishop of Rome). He is the successor of St Peter, who was chosen by Jesus to be the leader of the apostles. The promise to Peter (whose name means 'rock') was:

> ❝ **'You are Peter, and on this rock I will build my church,** and the gates of Hades will not prevail against it. I will give you the keys of the kingdom of heaven, and whatever you bind on earth will be bound in heaven, and whatever you loose on earth will be loosed in heaven.' ❞
>
> *Matthew* 16:18–19 (NRSV)

The powers that Jesus gave to Peter have been passed down in an unbroken line to the present pope.

Below the Pope, in order of importance, are:

- Cardinals, who are appointed by the Pope. It is the task of the cardinals to elect the new pope when the previous pope dies or retires.
- **Bishops**, who are the successors to the apostles. Bishops are the heads of the local churches; they are responsible for an area called a diocese. Senior bishops, who have more responsibility, are called archbishops.
- Priests, who are **ordained** to administer the sacraments and to preach the word of God. Most priests look after a small area of the Church called a parish.
- Deacons, who are ordained to preach the word of God and to assist the priest. They can administer baptism, lead the celebration of marriage and perform funerals.
- Lay people, who are non-ordained members of the Church. They share in the priestly office of Christ through their baptism.

Objectives

- Know the hierarchy of the Catholic Church.
- Understand how the **Second Vatican Council** made changes to the Church.

Key terms

- **Second Vatican Council:** a series of important gatherings of all the Catholic bishops between 1962 and 1965, which updated many Catholic teachings
- **hierarchy:** a ranking system that gives structure to the Church
- **Pope:** the Head of the Catholic Church, the successor to St Peter
- **bishops:** high-ranking clergymen who have the power to confirm and ordain
- **ordained:** made a priest

▲ *Pope Francis and Cardinals attending a Mass*

> ❝ Christ the Lord instituted in His Church a variety of ministries, which work for the good of the whole body. For those ministers, who are endowed with sacred power, serve their brethren, so that all who are of the People of God … may arrive at salvation.

> **The college or body of bishops has no authority unless it is understood together with the Roman Pontiff [the Pope]**, the successor of Peter, as its head. ❞
>
> *Lumen Gentium* 18, 22

126

Chapter 5   Church and the Kingdom of God

■ The Second Vatican Council

All authority in the Church lies with the Pope. However, the Pope sometimes wants to consult other members of the hierarchy and can do this both formally and informally. When the Pope wants to consult formally with all the bishops over issues that affect the whole Church, he might call a Council.

The last Council was the Second Vatican Council, summoned by Pope John XXIII, which met between 1962 and 1965. Pope John called the bishops together to 'open the windows of the Church'. He felt that the Church had become cut off from the world and was too closed in on itself. The bishops made major changes to the everyday administration of the Church, including the forms of worship. They also reasserted the eternal truths held by the Church, but sometimes in a form of language that was easier for people to understand and appreciate.

The Council documents

Many of the documents that the more conservative bishops had drawn up for the approval of the Council were rejected immediately. Pope John ordered that the documents be removed and that new ones be produced that reflected a more modern approach to the Church and the world.

Pope John died in June 1963, but his successor Paul VI continued with the Council.

The Council produced four major documents:

- **Dei Verbum (The Word of God).** This dealt with the importance and the interpretation of scripture. The Council accepted that the books of the Bible were written at a particular time in different ways, and with different messages. It is people's duty to take the messages from scripture seriously as they come from God, but Catholics should not read the Bible in a literal way.
- **Lumen Gentium (On the Church).** This dealt with the nature of the Church, the role of each of its members and the idea that the Church is the Kingdom of God on earth. The words *Lumen Gentium* mean 'The Light of the Peoples'. The First Vatican Council had focused on the role of the Pope as infallible. *Lumen Gentium* stressed how all other members of the Church also have important roles to play. It emphasised the idea of the pilgrim Church moving forward, rather than being an immovable fortress that has to withstand the attacks of modern society.
- **Sacrosanctum Concilium (On the Sacred Liturgy).** This dealt with the way the liturgy and services needed to be changed to allow people to take a full part in the worship of God. This document called for a major revision of all forms of worship. This included allowing all Catholics to hear Mass in their own language, and to include aspects of their own culture in worship.
- **Gaudium et Spes (The Church in the Modern World).** This dealt with issues relating to family life, the development of culture, political and economic life, and peace and harmony between nations. The words '*Gaudium et Spes*' mean 'joy and hope'. The Church now sees itself as the guide to all people living in the modern world, responsible for and responsive to the challenges that modern technology, politics and economics offer. The Church is not separated from the world, but works in and through people's lives.

▲ *Gaudium et Spes* attacks economic policies that lead to social inequality. Should the Church express views on matters like this?

Activities

1. Explain the Church's hierarchy.
2. 'All Catholics are equal.' Evaluate this statement. Be sure to include more than one point of view, and refer to Catholic beliefs and teachings in your answer.

Discussion activity

Discuss whether you think the Church needs a pope.

★ Study tip

To understand the idea of a hierarchy, think about the structure within your own school or the local football team. Some people are needed at the top to make decisions on behalf of everybody else.

Summary

You should now be able to describe the hierarchy of the Catholic Church. You should also be able to explain why the Second Vatican Council was important, and how the documents it produced reflected new ways of thinking.

127

5.7 The importance of Mary and the Magnificat

■ The importance of Mary

Mary, the mother of Jesus, has always had a special position within Christianity. Her willing acceptance of the will of God (Luke 1:26–38) was the moment that allowed the incarnation to take place. Just before he died, Jesus entrusted his mother to the beloved **disciple**, who is the symbol for all the followers of Jesus.

Christians believe that Mary was the perfect disciple. She listened to and accepted the word of God. She stood by Jesus, even at the darkest moment of his life, in trust and in faith. She was a woman of prayer.

■ The Magnificat

During the annunciation, Mary was told that her older cousin Elizabeth was also pregnant, so Mary went to visit her. When Elizabeth saw Mary, she praised her as the mother of the Lord. In answer, Mary sang the praises of God in the **Magnificat**.

Mary's awareness of what God had done in her and for her is perfectly expressed in the Magnificat. The title of this prayer is the first word of the prayer in Latin.

> Mary said, **'My soul magnifies the Lord,**
> **and my spirit rejoices in God my Saviour,**
> for he has looked with favour on the lowliness of his servant.
> Surely, from now on all generations will call me blessed;
> for the Mighty One has done great things for me,
> and holy is his name.
> His mercy is for those who fear him
> from generation to generation.
> He has shown strength with his arm;
> he has scattered the proud in the thoughts of their hearts.
> **He has brought down the powerful from their thrones,**
> **and lifted up the lowly;**
> he has filled the hungry with good things,
> and sent the rich away empty.
> He has helped his servant Israel,
> in remembrance of his mercy,
> according to the promise he made to our ancestors,
> to Abraham and to his descendants for ever.'
>
> *Luke* 1:46–55 (NRSV)

Objectives

- Know how Mary is a model of discipleship.
- Understand how the Magnificat can be seen as both a hymn of praise to God and a revolutionary prayer.

Key terms

- **disciple:** a follower of Jesus; one who learns
- **Magnificat:** the name of the prayer that Mary said when Elizabeth greeted her during her visit

> Meanwhile, standing near the cross of Jesus were his mother, and his mother's sister, Mary the wife of Clopas, and Mary Magdalene. When Jesus saw his mother and the disciple whom he loved standing beside her, **he said to his mother, 'Woman, here is your son.' Then he said to the disciple, 'Here is your mother.'** And from that hour the disciple took her into his own home.
>
> *John* 19:25–27 (NRSV)

Links

To learn more about the annunciation and Mary's willing acceptance of the incarnation see pages 36–37.

Chapter 5 Church and the Kingdom of God

- In this prayer, Mary praises God for his greatness. All that God has done in and for Mary reflects God's care for all people.
- God has fulfilled the promises he made to the people of Israel though the prophets.
- When Mary accepted God's will for herself, she allowed his Kingdom to grow in her heart, but more importantly in her body. She became the mother of Jesus, who himself brought God's Kingdom to earth.
- Mary is always humble in this hymn of praise. All that has happened is because God has shown his mercy, forgiveness and love for his people. When Mary talks about people calling her blessed, it is not because she is big-headed. It is because people will be accepting all that God has done, in and for Mary and, through her, for the whole human race.
- However, this prayer also contains a great deal of trust in the power of God working on behalf of the poor and the oppressed. Mary herself as a pregnant unmarried teenager was running the risk of being killed for adultery – yet she believed that God would protect her as she was doing his will.
- Throughout the prayer, there is a great sense of revolution. The prayer has been banned by governments on occasions as it makes people believe that God is on the side of the weak and helpless (which Christians believe he is). The prayer says that God will cast those in power down and raise up the humble. Some people think that this supports those who are rebelling against governments (rather than those who are vulnerable in society). However, others think that the prayer means that people who trust in God will be saved, but those who trust in themselves – believing that they are gods – will end up losing everything.

▲ *A protest in Greece against austerity measures. Can the Magnificat be used to justify protests like this?*

Why is Mary special?

Paul says: 'I like praying in front of the statue of Mary. I don't understand people who say that Mary is not special. God chose Mary and she was the mother of Jesus. God must think of her as special. After all, it was Mary who taught Jesus how to pray as a young boy. I remember a priest once saying to me: if Jesus does not answer your prayer, go and tell his mother and she will sort it out for you.'

Activities

1. Explain why Mary is important to many Catholics.
2. 'The Magnificat supports political revolutions.' Evaluate this statement. Be sure to include more than one point of view, and refer to Catholic beliefs and teachings in your answer.

Discussion activity

Discuss whether Catholics focus too much on Mary.

Summary
You should now know why Mary is important to Catholics, who see her as an example of a perfect disciple. You should also understand different interpretations of the Magnificat.

⭐ **Study tip**

Think about how important mothers are. This will help you to understand why Catholics value Mary as the mother of Jesus.

129

5.8 The four marks of the Church and apostolic succession

The four marks of the Church

The Church is 'the Body of Christ'. This means that all Christians are united together like a body, doing the work of Christ on earth. At baptism, each Christian becomes a child of God and is filled with the Holy Spirit. In the Eucharist, Catholics receive the Body and Blood of Christ to draw them closer to Christ: 'The union is so strong that it joins [Christ] and us like the head and members of a human body and makes us one' (*Youcat* 126).

There are four qualities or marks of the Church without all of which the Church would not exist. These marks also distinguish the Church from any other institution. These qualities are: one, holy, **catholic** and **apostolic**.

One

Just as God is one and Christ is one, so the Church is one. Since the Church is the Body of Christ, it has to be one body. All believers unite together in this one body (see 1 Corinthians 12:12–30). While there are many individual local churches or dioceses, they are all part of the one Church, just as limbs form parts of one human body. At the Last Supper, Jesus prayed to God about his followers that 'they may all be one' (John 17:21).

Holy

The Church is a community of sinners. Jesus said: 'I have come to call not the righteous but sinners to repentance' (Luke 5:32). However, every Christian is made holy (they are sanctified) in the waters of baptism. Each person and the whole community is guided by the presence and power of the Holy Spirit. God is at work in the whole Body of Christ, in both individuals and in the community. The presence of God makes the Church holy.

Catholic

The word 'catholic' literally means 'related to the whole' or 'worldwide'. The teachings of the Church are the beliefs held by Catholics everywhere.

Apostolic

Jesus chose 12 apostles to be his witnesses, and to be the foundation of the people of God. After the resurrection Jesus told his apostles to go and preach his message to all people. The message that the apostles preached is the foundation of Catholic belief today.

> **Objectives**
> - Know the four marks of the Church and their significance.
> - Understand how the idea of **apostolic succession** gives authority to the Magisterium.

> **Key terms**
> - **apostolic succession:** the power of the apostles passed on to the next generations of bishops
> - **Catholic:** (1) a term used to describe something that is worldwide and all-inclusive (2) referring to the Roman Catholic Church
> - **apostolic:** based on what the apostles taught
> - **Magisterium:** the teaching authority of the Catholic Church, exercised by the Pope and the bishops

▲ *Many individual churches join together to form the one Church, the Body of Christ*

Chapter 5   Church and the Kingdom of God

■ Apostolic succession

The leader of the 12 apostles was Peter, who was chosen by Jesus during his time on earth. Peter's position was reaffirmed by Jesus after the resurrection (John 21:15–17), even though Peter had denied knowing Jesus when Jesus was on trial (Mark 14:66–72). The other apostles accepted the leadership of Peter. Peter left Jerusalem and moved to Rome, which at the time was the centre of the known world.

When Peter was executed in Rome, Linus took over as Bishop of Rome. Since then there has been an unbroken succession (though not always immediate or uncontested) of bishops of Rome. They have taken on the leadership of the whole Church that Peter once had.

The apostles preached in different areas and they appointed leaders of the local churches to take their place after them. These local leaders were called bishops. The bishops are the successors to the apostles, in an unbroken line, and they protect and hand on the message of the apostles.

▲ *Catholics believe that at the Last Supper, Jesus made the apostles the first priests*

The Magisterium

The combined authority of the bishops and the Bishop of Rome (who is now known as the Pope) is called the **Magisterium**. This is the teaching authority of the Church. Catholics believe that as the whole Church is guided by the Holy Spirit, the Church is infallible. This means that it cannot go wrong in its definitive teachings. When the Pope makes a formal declaration of an official doctrine of the Church, he is speaking as Head of the Church, the Vicar of Christ on earth. On those (rare) occasions, the Pope speaks infallibly, which means he cannot be wrong.

> ❝ The Church is holy, not because all her members are supposedly holy, but rather because God is holy and is at work in her. All members of the Church are sanctified by baptism. ❞
>
> *Youcat* 132

Extension activity

Examine why people say that the survival of the Church can only be explained by the working of the Holy Spirit.

Being part of the Catholic Church

Jan, a mother of two from Aintree, says: 'I am proud to belong to the Catholic Church. People ask me how I can justify all the abuses. My only answer is that I can't justify them. The Church is made up of weak human beings, and we are all sinners. Jesus called us as sinners and called us to try to live better lives. This is what the Church is doing. I feel supported in my weak efforts to try harder, knowing that I am surrounded by other people who are trying.'

⭐ Study tip

Remember that the Bishop of Rome (the Pope) is the successor to St Peter, who was the leader of the apostles. All the other bishops can be thought of as successors to the other apostles.

Activities

1. Explain what the four marks of the Church show about Catholic beliefs.
2. 'The apostolic succession guarantees that the Church is always right in its teachings.' Evaluate this statement. Be sure to include more than one point of view, and refer to Catholic beliefs and teachings in your answer.

Summary

You should now know the meanings of the four marks of the Church. You should also understand how the authority of Magisterium is connected with the apostles.

131

5.9 The conciliar and pontifical nature of the Church

The meanings of conciliar and pontifical

The Church as conciliar

The Magisterium is the teaching authority of the Church that is held by the Pope and the bishops. At times, there may be meetings of all the bishops and heads of the religious orders of priests and monks. These meetings are called **Councils**. Some Catholics claim that a Church Council expresses the voice of the whole Church, and therefore the Church Council should be the highest authority in the Church. However, the official teaching of the Church is that:

- The Pope is the Supreme Head of the Church.
- The Pope may summon Councils whenever he chooses to discuss and advise on topics chosen or permitted by the Pope.
- If the Pope dies during the Council, the Council stops and will only resume if the new pope agrees to it continuing. This happened when John XXIII died in 1963.
- The decisions of a Council have no authority until they are approved by the Pope.

However, Councils are important as they allow the Pope to understand the feelings of the whole Catholic community. They help the Pope to make important decisions that affect the rest of the Church. This is how the Catholic Church can be thought of as **conciliar**.

> **Objectives**
> - Know how the Magisterium is both conciliar and pontifical.
> - Understand the role of the Magisterium in providing Catholic social teaching.

> **Key terms**
> - **Council:** a gathering of bishops to make decisions about important issues for the Church
> - **conciliar:** when the authority of the Magisterium is expressed through the Pope in a council
> - **pontifical:** when the teachings of the Church are presented by a pope

> **"** The Church sincerely professes that all men, believers and unbelievers alike, **ought to work for the rightful betterment of this world** in which all alike live; such an ideal cannot be realized, however, apart from sincere and prudent dialogue. **"**
>
> *Gaudium et Spes* 21

▲ *A meeting of the Second Vatican Council (1962–1965)*

The Church as pontifical

The word **pontifical** comes from one of the Latin titles for the Pope: *Pontifex Maximus* (the Great Bridge-builder, which refers to building a bridge between earth and heaven). A pontifical Church is one where the highest authority can be exercised by a pope. Catholics believe that the

Bishop of Rome, the Pope, is the successor to St Peter (the leader of the apostles), and that all the authority given to St Peter to lead the Church has been passed down to him. This is how the Catholic Church can be thought of as pontifical.

The Pope is guided by the Holy Spirit in a unique way. He is the Vicar (representative) of Christ on earth. The Pope's teachings should be taken with great seriousness, and when solemnly declared as such, as infallible. The Pope appoints all the bishops to assist him in running the local churches. All bishops have to give an account of their leadership to the Pope on a regular basis.

▲ *Pope Francis in 2014*

■ The Magisterium and Catholic social teaching

In the last 120 years, particularly since Pope Leo XIII's encyclical *Rerum Novarum* in 1891, the Church has strongly expressed its thoughts about the condition of society. This springs from an awareness that the Church is made up of human beings, and that God loves all people. This love needs to be shown in the way the Church – both as an institution and on an individual level – supports the weakest or poorest members of society.

> ❝ The joys and the hopes, the griefs and the anxieties of the men of this age, especially those who are poor or in any way afflicted, these are the joys and hopes, the griefs and anxieties of the followers of Christ. Indeed, **nothing genuinely human fails to raise an echo in their hearts.** ❞
>
> *Gaudium et Spes* 1

The Church believes that Catholics should not let their fellow human beings suffer, especially when their suffering is due to the effects of economic exploitation and greed on the part of other people:

> ❝ **Today we ... have to say 'thou shalt not' to an economy of exclusion and inequality.** Such an economy kills. How can it be that it is not a news item when an elderly homeless person dies of exposure, but it is news when the stock market loses two points? This is a case of exclusion ... Today everything comes under the laws of competition and the survival of the fittest, where the powerful feed upon the powerless. As a consequence, masses of people find themselves excluded and marginalized: without work, without possibilities, without any means of escape ...
>
> The culture of prosperity deadens us; we are thrilled if the market offers us something new to purchase. In the meantime all those lives stunted for lack of opportunity seem a mere spectacle; they fail to move us. ❞
>
> *Evangelii Gaudium* 53–54

The teaching authority of the Church is trying to lead by example. This is why Pope Francis has tried to simplify the lifestyle and structures of the Church leadership, and the recent popes have sold off Church valuables to give aid to those who need it.

Activities

1. Explain the similarities and differences between a conciliar and a pontifical Church.
2. 'The Church should not give any teachings concerning social issues.' Evaluate this statement. Be sure to include more than one point of view, and refer to Catholic beliefs and teachings in your answer.

Research activity

Choose one papal encyclical to do with social issues (for example *Laudato Si* of Francis, *Sollicitudo Rei Socialis* of John Paul II or *Populorum Progressio* of Paul VI) and explain five of the main points made in it by the Pope.

⭐ Study tip

Remember that for Catholics the Pope is the head of the Church on earth. The Pope will call a Council when he feels a topic needs an in-depth discussion.

Summary

You should now understand how the Catholic Church can be considered to be both conciliar and pontifical. You should also understand why it provides social teachings for Catholics.

5.10 The Church as the Body of Christ: the importance of charity for Catholics

How charities work locally, nationally and globally

Christians have always been aware of the importance of God's command to love. This is best expressed in two quotes from the New Testament:

> The second [commandment] is this, 'You shall love your neighbour as yourself.' There is no other commandment greater than these.
>
> *Mark* 12:31 (NRSV)
>
> Those who do not love a brother or sister whom they have seen, cannot love God whom they have not seen.
>
> *1 John* 4:20 (NRSV)

Anyone in need is a brother or sister to a Christian (see the Parable of the Good Samaritan in Luke 10:29–37). Christians believe they should show love to those in need. In this case love cannot just be words; it has to become action. This action is sometimes divided into three categories:

- **Local** – this is help given to people living in the immediate area. Christians might see these people on a daily basis and can personally go to their aid. Christians can also join locally with others to ensure that the help they give is effective and long-lasting. Examples of Christian groups that help locally are the SVP (St Vincent de Paul Society) and Life. Their work addresses practical issues on an individual basis.
- **National** – this is help offered on a countrywide basis. One of the major tasks for Christians is to get changes made to the policies and laws that cause the problems – to prevent them from happening in the first place – rather than just helping to solve the problems after they have occurred. Examples of groups doing this type of work are CSAN (Caritas Social Action Network) and SPUC (Society for the Protection of Unborn Children).
- **Global** – this is help offered to people in other countries. Christians can support agencies that tackle problems in other countries (such as natural disasters like earthquakes or drought) through raising awareness and funds. They can also put pressure on international companies to improve their ways, by shaming them publicly and boycotting their products. Examples of Catholic organisations that work globally are Missio and CAFOD.

SVP (St Vincent de Paul Society)

The SVP is an international Catholic **charity**. It has nearly 600,000 members around the world, who work in small groups at a local level. This makes the SVP an example of a charity that works locally.

Objectives

- Know the work of two Catholic charities.
- Understand how the work of these charities fulfils Christ's command to love.

Key term

- **charity:** (1) providing help and love to those in need (2) an organisation that does not make a profit, whose main purpose is to help those in need (3) another term for 'love'

> Our Vision, which is inspired by Christ's message to love our neighbour as ourselves, is for individuals and families who are in any form of need to have hope, together with a sense of dignity, worth, well-being and peace of mind.
>
> St Vincent de Paul Society

Chapter 5 Church and the Kingdom of God

SVP was started by students in 1833 in Paris, and its members are dedicated to going out into the local community to help people in need. Its work is divided into two types:

- Membership activity: This is where members visit people in need in their homes, in hospitals, in care homes and in prisons. They go to offer support by visiting the sick and elderly, showing friendship and concern. They address practical needs like helping with shopping, providing food for those who are without money, or helping to improve a home so that people can have a better quality of life.
- Special works: these include slightly bigger projects that help the local community, such as soup runs for the homeless, summer camps for children, furniture stores to provide free furniture, and advice for asylum seekers.

The main aim of SVP is to give practical help to individual people in need. SVP's members attend local meetings that start with prayer and Bible readings, where they can share their work with each other.

■ CAFOD (Catholic Agency for Overseas Development)

CAFOD was started in 1962 and is the official charity organisation of the Catholic Church in England and Wales. It is part of Caritas International, the charity organisation of the whole Catholic Church. CAFOD's activities include:

- providing emergency aid in places where natural disasters or war and conflict have ruined lives
- supporting people through long-term aid, such as irrigation schemes, education, healthcare and so on
- challenging national policies and laws that damage the lives of the poor, for example in relation to inequality or climate change.
- supporting people who are trying to keep control of their lives in the face of threats from large companies; for example, providing legal assistance when poor farmers are in danger of losing their land.

The central aim of CAFOD is to make everybody self-reliant. A saying that its members frequently use is: 'Give a man a fish and he has a meal. Teach him to fish and he can feed himself for life.'

▲ CAFOD aims to help people to become self-reliant through providing long-term aid, such as education on sustainable farming

Activities

1. Explain why Catholics feel the need to show charity.
2. 'Christians should only help people in need in their local area.' Evaluate this statement. Be sure to include more than one point of view, and refer to Catholic beliefs and teachings in your answer.

Extension activity

Research the work of one Catholic charity that works locally, and one Catholic charity that works nationally and globally. Investigate the sort of activities that they do and how these activities help people.

Links

To read more about the work of CAFOD see pages 33 and 332.

★ Study tip

Make sure you know about the work of two Catholic charities: one that works locally, and one that works nationally and globally. You could study the two examples given here or pick your own.

Summary

You should now know why Catholics think it is important to show charity. You should also be able to describe the work of two Catholic charities.

5.11 Kingdom values in different vocations

■ What are Kingdom values?

Kingdom values refer to the values, or standards of living, that God wants people to have as members of his Kingdom. The best example of **Kingdom values** in practice was given by Jesus. He lived by the standards he taught. Serving other people, by showing love through action, was key to his work and mission. Jesus taught: 'whoever wishes to be great among you must be your servant' (Matthew 20:26); he even washed his disciples' feet, a job usually reserved for the lowest servant (John 13:1–15). Kingdom values are stated in the Beatitudes (Matthew 5:1–12): humbleness, gentleness, a wish to do what is right, mercy, a desire for peace, and so on.

■ Christian vocations

Christians follow Jesus' example in different ways, depending on their vocation. A **vocation** is a calling by God for a person to go along a particular path in life. Each person has their own vocation. Christians believe that God has given everybody a unique combination of gifts, talents, inclinations and personalities. Following the call from God will enable people to be totally happy within themselves and with the world.

Examples are given below of a few different vocations that Catholics are called to.

Priesthood

A **priest** gives his life to God as one of service to the people. A priest is a man of prayer, who builds all that he does on his commitment to and relationship with God. Because a priest takes a promise of celibacy (a promise not to marry or have sex), he commits himself, body and soul, to God. Since he has no family, he is free to be always available for the needs of others. This availability shows that the priest is a servant of others, following Jesus' example. The priest takes a promise of obedience to the bishop, knowing that he is obeying the voice of God. These promises are never easy, yet by his life he shows the Kingdom of God to be present in the community.

Family life

A couple get married to make the commitment to each other for life. This is a sign to each other and to the community that love is strong in them. St John wrote: 'God is love' (1 John 4:16) and Christians believe that any expression of love is the work of God active in the lives of people. This is especially the case in marriage. The husband and wife give their whole mind, body and soul to each other 'and they become one flesh' (Genesis 2:24). In the physical expression of their love, God creates new life through the union of the husband and wife.

Objectives

- Understand the terms 'Kingdom values' and 'vocation'.
- Understand how a vocation shows Kingdom values.

Key terms

- **Kingdom values:** the standards of living that God wants his people to follow
- **vocation:** a call from God to fulfil a particular role in life
- **priest:** an ordained minister of the Catholic Church; one who is chosen to celebrate Mass, preach and forgive sins
- **monk:** a male member of a religious community who lives under solemn vows
- **nun:** a female member of a religious community who lives under solemn vows

Links

To learn more about God's Kingdom see page 122.

Links

The Beatitudes are discussed in more detail on pages 50–51.

Chapter 5 Church and the Kingdom of God

Married life can be very demanding, but a couple that is prepared to work at the relationship can make it a genuine sign of the Kingdom of God on earth. Catholic parents try to show love and obedience to each other, and to set a good standard that their children can appreciate and follow. In this way, they help the Kingdom of God to spread on earth.

Religious life

Some Catholics prefer to embrace a religious life more fully. This could be:

- Living as a **monk** or **nun**, in a community that usually follows the Rule of St Benedict, often shut off from the world. Monks and nuns live a life centred round prayer. They take vows of poverty, chastity and obedience to show that they have committed themselves to God's values. They want to live in the service of God, in as simple a way as possible. Monasteries are a centre of prayer for the whole community. Other people can come to share in the life and the sense of peace that comes from doing the will of God, and can take these qualities back to the world in their everyday lives.

- Living as a religious brother or sister. They also take the vows of poverty, chastity and obedience, but they work in the world at the service of other people. Religious brothers and sisters centre their lives round both prayer and active service. They might take on roles such as teachers, nurses or care workers, using their talents to help those in need. Their day starts and ends with prayer. Their work translates those prayers into action. By their care and commitment, they show other people the love of God and express the Kingdom values.

> ❝ Through Baptism Christ has made us into a kingdom of 'priests to his God and Father' (Rev 1:6). Through the universal priesthood, **every Christian is called to work in the world in God's name** and bring blessings and grace to it. ❞
>
> *Youcat* 259

▲ Mother Teresa was an influential religious sister and missionary, who helped many people around the world

Discussion activity

Discuss whether there is any need for monks and nuns, and religious brothers and sisters today.

⭐ Study tip

See if you can talk to a priest, monk, nun or a married person about their vocation. This will help you to understand why their vocation is important.

Activities

1. Explain how Kingdom values are lived out by one type of vocation.
2. 'It is easy for a family to live by Kingdom values.' Evaluate this statement. Be sure to include more than one point of view, and refer to Catholic beliefs and teachings in your answer.

Summary

You should now know what Kingdom values are, and understand how these can be shown in different vocations.

137

5.12 Kingdom values in the life of a Catholic

■ Kingdom values in practice

There are many individual Catholics whose lives bear witness to Kingdom values. Everything that they do demonstrates their belief in concepts such as justice, peace and reconciliation. Even if the individual never mentions these words in particular, their underlying approach to life testifies that these values are important to them. Sometimes it is blatantly obvious that these qualities shape their lives. Recent examples of well-known Catholics who have lived by Kingdom values are Mother Teresa and Pope Francis.

■ Pope Francis

- Jorge Mario Bergoglio was born on 17 December 1936 in Buenos Aires (Brazil).
- He entered the Society of Jesus (an organisation for priests) on 11 March 1958.
- He was ordained a priest on 13 December 1969.
- He was named Auxiliary Bishop of Buenos Aires in 1992.
- He became Metropolitan Archbishop of Buenos Aires on 28 February 1998.
- He was elected Pope on 13 March 2013 and chose the name Francis.

Justice

Here are some of the ways that Pope Francis has contributed to and asked for justice:

- When he became Archbishop of Buenos Aires he increased the number of priests working in the shanty towns and among the poor.
- He leads by example, and does not allow money to be wasted on himself. As Pope, he uses the same iron pectoral cross that he used when he was archbishop, instead of a gold one. He lives in a small flat in a guesthouse rather than in the official papal apartments in the Vatican.
- Both as archbishop and as Pope, he has criticised economic policies that lead to inequality. He speaks out against all forms of abuse and exploitation. He tries to make all people realise that abuse in any form damages all people's lives and leads to injustice.

Peace

These are some of the ways that Pope Francis has helped to create peace:

- During 2014–15, he played a major role in restoring relations between Cuba and the USA. There had been tension between these two countries since 1958.
- He has welcomed leaders of countries that have been at war or in disagreement, including the Palestinian and Israeli presidents. In 2014, he met and prayed with both these leaders together.

Objectives

- Know how Kingdom values have shaped the life of a leading Catholic figure.
- Understand the importance of these values in a Christian's life.

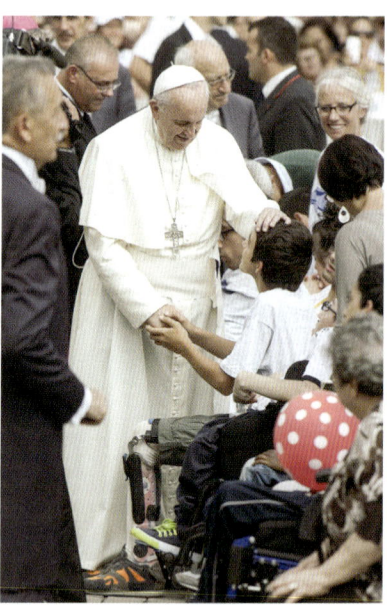

▲ Pope Francis greeting pilgrims in St Peter's Square during his weekly general audience

Links

To read more about justice, peace and reconciliation as signs of the Kingdom of God see pages 124–125.

❝ Many things have to change course, but it is we human beings above all who need to change. ❞

Pope Francis, *Laudato Si* 202

138

Chapter 5   Church and the Kingdom of God

- During the 1970s he sheltered people who were being hunted by the Argentine dictator Jorge Rafael Videla. After Videla was replaced, Pope Francis worked quietly but ceaselessly to try to stop the Argentine government's continuing abuse of power.
- He uses his public addresses to pray for peace, in particular praying for areas of great conflict and tension.

▲ Pope Francis washing the feet of local prisoners on Maundy Thursday

Reconciliation

Here are some of the ways that Pope Francis has worked to achieve reconciliation:

- As archbishop, he was responsible for Greek Orthodox Christians in South America, because he was open to their way of life and prayer.
- Both as archbishop and as Pope, every Maundy Thursday he goes to a local prison and washes the feet of 12 prisoners, including Muslims. In this way, he shows the prisoners that they are accepted and not rejected from the community.
- In both Argentina and Rome, he has welcomed non-Catholic Christians, including some groups that in the past have been very critical of Catholics. He has often asked these people to pray for him, even kneeling down in their presence and having them place their hands on him as they prayed.
- He has visited areas of tension in the world, trying to restore harmony. People have accepted his good intentions because they can see that he is not moved by anything other than truth and justice.
- He has helped to break down some of the barriers of tension and suspicion that exist between many Muslim groups and Catholics, and between some Jewish groups and Catholics. As archbishop, he arranged services in his cathedral at which Orthodox and Presbyterian Christians, and Muslim and Jewish religious leaders, all prayed together with him.

Activities

1. Explain how peace, justice and reconciliation have been important in the life of Pope Francis.
2. 'If enough Christians live by Kingdom values the whole world will begin to follow their example.' Evaluate this statement. Be sure to include more than one point of view, and refer to Catholic beliefs and teachings in your answer.

Research activity

Research the life of another leading Catholic figure (such as Mother Teresa or Pope John Paul II) and explain how Kingdom values shaped their life.

⭐ Study tip

Make sure you know how Kingdom values have been expressed in the life of one important Catholic figure. The choice of which figure is up to you: here we talk about Pope Francis but you could pick someone else, and make similar notes on their life based on the notes given here.

Summary

You should now understand how the values of justice, peace and reconciliation are shown in the life of Pope Francis.

139

5. Assessment guidance

Church and the Kingdom of God – summary

You should now be able to:

- ✔ explain how dramatised prayer, including the Stations of the Cross, reflects the idea of the pilgrim Church
- ✔ explain the importance of pilgrimage for Catholics, including the importance of going on pilgrimage to Jerusalem, Rome, Walsingham and Lourdes
- ✔ explain how mission and evangelism are expressed in drama
- ✔ explain the meaning of the Kingdom of God, especially in the Lord's Prayer
- ✔ explain Catholic teachings about justice, peace and reconciliation, as a reflection of beliefs in the Kingdom of God
- ✔ explain how the Catholic Church operates, including how it consults in councils
- ✔ explain the importance of the Second Vatican Council and the documents it produced
- ✔ explain the importance of Mary as a disciple, and explain how the Magnificat is a controversial prayer
- ✔ explain the importance of the four marks of the Catholic Church (one, holy, catholic and apostolic), and explain why apostolic succession is important to Catholics
- ✔ explain what the Magisterium is, and its role in Catholic teaching
- ✔ explain how two Catholic agencies follow the command to 'love your neighbour' in their work
- ✔ explain how Kingdom values are lived out in the priesthood, family and religious life
- ✔ explain how one important Catholic figure works for justice, peace and reconciliation.

Sample student answer – the 4 mark question

1. Write an answer to the following question:

   Explain two ways in which dramatised prayer, like the Stations of the Cross, help Catholics to understand the Church as being a people of God on a pilgrimage. [4 marks]

2. Read the following sample student answer:

   "Dramatised prayer can help people to get involved physically as well as mentally in the prayer life of the Church. It helps people appreciate the fact that they are part of the Church, which is a pilgrim people, on its journey through life to reach God's Kingdom. The Stations of the Cross are a powerful dramatised prayer as people join in the journey of Jesus to his death which brought salvation for everyone."

3. With a partner, discuss the sample answer. Is the focus of the answer correct? Is anything missing from the answer? How do you think it could be improved?

4. What mark (out of 4) would you give this answer? Look at the mark scheme in the Introduction (AO1). What are the reasons for the mark you have given?

5. Now swap your answer with your partner's and mark each other's responses. What mark (out of 4) would you give the response? Refer to the mark scheme and give reasons for the mark you award.

Sample student answer – the 5 mark question

1. Write an answer to the following question:

   Explain two teachings about the reign of God that are expressed in
   the Lord's Prayer. Refer to Christian beliefs in your answer. **[5 marks]**

2. Read the following sample student answer:

   "Jesus taught the Lord's Prayer to his disciples when they asked him to teach them to pray. In it he said 'May your kingdom come'. This means that Christians are hoping that what God wants will be done by people on earth. When people obey God, they are increasing the reign of God on earth and showing other people how great God's power is. Earth will become like heaven: 'Your will be done on earth as it is in heaven'."

3. With a partner, discuss the sample answer. What are its good points and are there any weaknesses? How do you think the answer could be improved?

4. What mark (out of 5) would you give this answer? Look at the mark scheme in the Introduction (AO1). What are the reasons for the mark you have given?

5. Now swap your answer with your partner's and mark each other's responses. What mark (out of 5) would you give the response? Refer to the mark scheme and give reasons for the mark you award.

Practice questions

1 Which of the following best shows the idea of the Body of Christ on earth?

   A) Members of CAFOD going to help people in a disaster area
   B) Football supporters booing the opposition
   C) People in a cinema joining in a sing-along
   D) Workers going on a strike **[1 mark]**

2 Give two ways in which Kingdom values are seen in the life of a Catholic monk or nun.

[2 marks]

> ⭐ **Study tip**
>
> Remember that there is only one mark available here for each way that you state. This means that you do not need to give any detailed explanation.

3 Explain two ways in which the belief that the Catholic Church is apostolic influences believers' reactions to the Magisterium. **[4 marks]**

4 Explain two ways in which justice and peace are expressions of the Kingdom of God. Refer to Christian beliefs in your answer. **[5 marks]**

5 'The four marks of the Catholic Church guarantee that what the Church teaches is true.'

   Evaluate this statement. In your answer you should:
   - give developed arguments to support this statement
   - give developed arguments to support a different point of view
   - refer to Catholic teaching
   - reach a justified conclusion. **[12 marks]**

6 Eschatology

6.1 The Paschal candle

■ The Paschal candle in the Easter Vigil

One of the most meaningful and noticeable symbols used in Catholic churches is the **Paschal** candle.

The Paschal candle is one of the first and most important features of the **Easter Vigil** ceremony. The Easter Vigil ideally takes place during the hours of darkness. When the congregation is assembled, preferably outside the church, the priest lights a fire, the light of which breaks the darkness. This reflects the light of Christ rising from the grave, destroying the power of sin and death. Then the priest blesses and lights the Paschal candle. This is a large beeswax candle that represents the Risen Christ.

▲ *The blessing of the Easter fire, with the server holding the Paschal candle*

The design on the Paschal candle is very symbolic, and the prayers said by the priest, as he traces this design with his hand, show the meaning of the symbols. As the priest traces the Alpha and Omega symbols and the numbers of the current year, he says:

'Christ yesterday and today;/ the Beginning and the End;/ the Alpha;/ and the Omega;/ All time belongs to him;/ and all the ages;/ To him be glory and power;/ through every age and for ever. Amen.'

Then the priest inserts five little holders, each containing a grain of incense, into the candle. These represent the five wounds that Christ

Objectives

- Know the symbolism of the Paschal candle.
- Understand how the Paschal candle reminds Christians that the light of the Risen Christ should be evident in their lives.

Key terms

- **Paschal:** relating to Easter, so the Paschal candle is the Easter candle
- **Easter Vigil:** the service that takes place in the hours of darkness between Holy Saturday and Easter Sunday, during which the resurrection of Jesus is proclaimed and celebrated, and the first Mass of Easter is held
- **Eastertide:** the 50-day period between Easter Sunday and Pentecost

Links

To read more about the Risen Christ see pages 94–95.

Links

To learn more about the Alpha and Omega symbols see pages 44–45.

received in his hands, feet and side during his crucifixion. As the priest does this, he says:

'By his holy/ and glorious wounds,/ may Christ our Lord/ guard us/ and protect us. Amen.'

Then, taking a light from the bonfire, the priest lights the Paschal candle and says:

'May the light of Christ rising in glory/ dispel the darkness of our hearts and minds.'

The priest then carries the candle into church and places it on a tall stand on the altar. During the procession he chants three times:

'The light of Christ' ('*Lumen Christi*' in Latin).

To which the congregation replies:

'Thanks be to God' ('*Deo gratias*' in Latin).

During the procession, a light is taken from the Paschal candle and given to every member of the congregation, so that at the end of the procession everyone is holding a lighted candle. This shows that all believers share in the risen glory of Christ.

■ Other uses of the Paschal candle

One Paschal candle lasts for the whole year, until the next Easter Vigil. It is lit during every Mass in **Eastertide**, at every baptism, and at every funeral. The lit candle shows the presence of the Risen Christ.

Christians believe that in a baptism, the person is filled with the light of Christ and becomes another bearer of Christ. When a person is baptised, they are given a candle lit from the Paschal candle. The priest says:

'Parents and godparents, this light is entrusted to you to be kept burning brightly. This child of yours has been enlightened by Christ. He (she) is to walk always as a child of the light. May he (she) keep the flame of faith alive in his (her) heart. When the Lord comes, may he (she) go out to meet him with all the saints in the heavenly kingdom.'

At a funeral, the Paschal candle is lit to show that the deceased has joined Christ in the resurrected life. The promise made by God to all believers through the resurrection of Jesus has now been fulfilled for the dead person.

The significance of the Paschal candle

Jane, a 42-year-old Catholic from Ormskirk, says: 'I think the Easter Vigil is the most moving of all the church ceremonies. To see the lighted bonfire outside break the darkness makes a big impact on me. When we go into the dark church, gradually people receive the light from the Paschal candle so that everyone is standing in the glow of one light. This reminds me that we are all bearers of the Risen Christ, we all have to carry Christ in our lives to other people. When my sister died, at the funeral it was comforting to see her coffin beside the lighted Paschal candle as I knew that Christ is with her in death.

▲ *A Paschal candle with the Alpha and Omega symbols*

Activities

1. Explain the symbolism of the Paschal candle.
2. 'The most important use of the Paschal candle is at a Catholic funeral.' Evaluate this statement. Be sure to include more than one point of view, and refer to Catholic beliefs and teachings in your answer.

Research activity

Study the whole Easter Vigil ceremony and examine how the symbolism that is used reinforces the ideas presented by the Paschal candle.

⭐ Study tip

Go into a Catholic church and study the shape and design of the Paschal candle. Also notice where it is positioned in the church, and what time of year your visit takes place.

Summary

You should now understand why the Paschal candle is important to Christians and how it represents Christ's resurrection.

6.2 Michelangelo's *The Last Judgement*

Pope Clement VII commissioned Michelangelo to paint *The Last Judgement* in the Sistine Chapel in Rome. It took Michelangelo four years to complete, between 1537 and 1541. In his painting Michelangelo used mostly Christian teachings but also included some figures from Roman mythology. The painting depicts the time when Christ judges all people and decides whether to reward or condemn them.

Objectives

- Understand the imagery and symbolism that is used in Michelangelo's *The Last Judgement*.
- Understand how this reflects Catholic teachings about judgement and the afterlife.

Jesus and Mary

The central (and dominant) figure of the painting is Jesus Christ. He is shown as a powerful being, but he still carries the wounds of his crucifixion. This shows that Jesus came to his glory and his role as judge through obedience and suffering.

All of the characters in Michelangelo's original painting, except Jesus and Mary, are totally naked (although another artist was ordered by a later pope to cover up some of the nudity). This shows that in **the Last Judgement** all people are equal before God, regardless of their status in life. Mary is sitting beside her son, Jesus, with an expression of calm trust.

▲ Michelangelo's The Last Judgement *covers the wall behind the altar in the Sistine Chapel, Rome*

Key terms

- **the Last Judgement:** the time when all people will have to account for their actions and will be rewarded or condemned by God
- **the last day:** the end of time, when the earth will be destroyed and all people will face judgement
- **archangel:** a powerful spiritual being who carries out the will of God
- **hell:** the state of total separation from God

The seven angels

Towards the bottom of the painting there are seven angels blowing trumpets. These refer to the angels in the Book of Revelation, chapters 8–10. When these angels blow their trumpets, devastation comes to the earth and the end of the world is announced, followed by God's judgement.

The saints

Near to Jesus are some saints who are holding the instruments that were used for their own torture and death. St Bartholomew is carrying the knife with which he was tortured. St Lawrence is holding the gridiron

> **The Last Judgement will take place at the end of the world, at the second coming of Christ.** 'All who are in the tombs will hear his voice and come forth, those who have done good, to the resurrection of life, and those who have done evil, to the resurrection of judgement' (Jn 5:29).
>
> *Youcat* 163

on which he was roasted. St Catherine is carrying part of the wheel on which she was broken. There are also other saints depicted, including St John the Baptist and St Peter.

All of these saints are shown as having perfect bodies – without any signs of their torture – reflecting the belief that in the resurrection all will be renewed. This also reflects the promise made by Jesus that those who stand firm to the end will be saved (Mark 13:13). This means that the people who do not betray Jesus and who stick to their faith, no matter what happens to them, will share in Christ's resurrection.

The faithful

The rest of the painting reflects the Parable of the Sheep and the Goats (Matthew 25:31–46), in which Jesus promises that the good will be on his right and the wicked on his left. (Remember that the directions are swapped when you look at the painting, so Jesus' left side is your right side.)

At the bottom of the painting, on the left, Michelangelo shows the dead who are being raised up for judgement in the presence of Christ. The depiction of people leaving their graves shows that all people will be raised on **the last day**. Jesus' right hand is raised, showing both his power to raise people from the dead and his power to raise those on his right to the glory of heaven.

The **archangel** Michael is shown with the group of seven angels, holding the book of those who have been faithful and who will be rewarded by heaven. This book is not big in comparison to the book held by the angel next to him, which contains the names of those who are destined for **hell**. The message here is the same that Jesus gave (for instance in Matthew 7:13–14): do your best to ensure that you are in the book of those rewarded rather than those punished. There is no room for complacency.

The condemned

On the right of the painting, Michelangelo shows some people who are destined for hell. These people express their despair for the future in the looks on their faces and the way they hold their bodies.

The general movement on the right of the painting is downwards. Towards the bottom are shown the River Styx and Charon the boatman. These are taken from Roman mythology. The river is the one crossed by those who are to be sent to hell and Charon is the ferryman who takes people to hell. Michelangelo does not show hell itself, but he shows a gaping blackness that is the gateway to hell, beyond which people will not return. Michelangelo's hell has no light in it, which is a sign that the light of Christ cannot reach people who have rejected God.

Summary

You should now be able to explain how Michelangelo's *The Last Judgement* reflects Catholic beliefs about God's judgement and the afterlife.

▲ *Jesus is the central figure of the painting, with Mary by his side*

Links

To read more about the Parable of the Sheep and the Goats see page 51.

Discussion activity

Discuss whether you think Michelangelo has been successful in depicting the Last Judgement. What are the painting's strengths and weaknesses?

Activities

1 Explain three types of symbolism used in Michelangelo's *The Last Judgement*.

2 'No one knows what will happen at the end of time so there is no need for anyone to worry about it.' Evaluate this statement. Be sure to include more than one point of view, and refer to Catholic beliefs and teachings in your answer.

⭐ Study tip

Michelangelo was commissioned to paint pictures that got across a message, as most people during his time couldn't read. Remember that you need to look for the meaning in the picture, not just the artistic quality.

6.3 Memorials for the dead

Catholic beliefs about burial

Catholics believe in the resurrection of the body. (This means that at judgement the whole person, both body and soul, will come into God's presence.) During a person's life, their body is a temple of the Holy Spirit (see 1 Corinthians 6:19). Therefore the body must always be treated with respect, even after death. Catholic teachings forbid anything that seems to undervalue the body. In the past, the Church also believed that Genesis 3:19 ('you are dust, and to dust you shall return') taught that the body should be allowed to corrupt naturally. This meant that cremation was banned until the 1960s, when it became accepted partly for practical reasons.

Tombstones

A **tombstone** indicates the location of the earthly remains of the person who has died, so that the place can be treated with respect. It also includes information about the deceased, such as their name and which years they lived. Many Christian tombstones contain religious messages, particularly the letters R.I.P. This is an abbreviation of the phrase '*Requiescat in pace*' or 'May (s)he rest in peace'. This phrase is a prayer for the deceased to be in the presence of God in heaven, enjoying the happiness and peace of eternal life.

Many Catholic tombstones are shaped in the form of a cross. This is to indicate that the deceased believed in Jesus. The message is that as the person joined Christ in his death, so they might rise with him to eternal life. Through the suffering that led to death, unending life has come.

Some Catholic graves, particularly those for children, have an angel carved on them. This is an indication of the belief that all people have their own guardian angel who takes care of them in this life and who presents the dead person to God for judgement, asking for a merciful judgement.

Monuments

Many civilisations have erected **monuments** over the burial place of an important person. Some of these monuments are very prominent, for example the pyramids in Egypt and the Taj Mahal in India.

The Catholic Church allows some important people to be buried inside churches, though the more usual practice has been to bury everybody in the grounds around a church. Occasionally, monuments have been built to indicate how special a person was. Some monuments have been erected over the tombs of saints, and people come in pilgrimage to pray there. Two examples are the shrines of St Edward the Confessor in Westminster Abbey (London), and St Thomas Becket in Canterbury Cathedral.

Objectives

- Know the different types of burial that are accepted by the Catholic Church.
- Understand how these practices reflect Catholic beliefs about the afterlife.

Key terms

- **tombstone:** a large carved stone that is placed (either lying or standing) over a burial site
- **monument:** something that is built to remember an important person or event
- **cremation:** the burning of the bodily remains of a person
- **remembrance garden:** an area designed for the remains of the deceased, where mourners can come and reflect in quiet

> ❝ Eternal rest give unto them, O Lord, and let perpetual light shine upon them. May they rest into peace. Amen. ❞
>
> *Eternal Rest*, a Catholic prayer for the dead

Monuments often have an effigy (sculpture) of the deceased on them, usually lying down with their hands joined in prayer. Different artistic styles have been used on monuments through the ages. In the Early Roman Christian burials, some wealthy people were buried in sarcophagi (highly decorated coffins), often with religious symbols like the Chi-Rho on them to indicate the deceased person's belief in Christ. In the Middle Ages, it was common practice to decorate monuments with skeletons and other reminders of decay. The message of these monuments was that no matter how important the deceased had been, they face the same bodily corruption and the same call to account for their actions as all other people.

▲ *A Christian sarcophagus showing the Chi-Rho symbol on the side*

Remembrance gardens

Many Catholics now choose **cremation** instead of burial, often because of the practical issue of there not being enough land for burial. The Catholic Church insists that the remains of the dead person must be treated with dignity, even as ashes. When a Catholic is cremated, the ashes are kept in a single container or urn and are not scattered. Urns must be placed in a formal site for burial, like a cemetery or **remembrance garden**.

▲ *Remembrance gardens provide a peaceful space for people to mourn*

Remembrance gardens are places of quiet dignity where the bereaved can mourn their loved ones. The beauty and peace of the surrounding garden are meant to help the mourners reflect on the beauty and peace of heaven, where they hope the deceased is now at peace. They are also places where mourners can still feel close to the deceased, as their bodily remains rest in that place.

Extension activity

Examine the use of different Christian methods of remembering the dead down the ages. What message does each method convey?

Activities

1. Explain the importance of Christian tombstones for believers.
2. 'Remembrance gardens are of little value to Catholics.' Evaluate this statement. Be sure to include more than one point of view, and refer to Catholic beliefs and teachings in your answer.

⭐ Study tip

A visit to a cemetery or a remembrance garden might help you to appreciate the importance of memorials for all people.

Summary

You should now understand how Christian beliefs about the afterlife are expressed in different memorials.

6.4 Eschatology and life after death

■ What is eschatology?

Eschatology is the study of what happens at the end of time. It includes topics like death, judgement, heaven and hell. Christians believe it is difficult to say for sure what will happen at the end of time, as Jesus is the only person who has been able to provide any real insight into the afterlife.

However, the Bible gives some ideas of what might be involved. Jesus talked about the end of time in passages such as Mark 13, Matthew 24–25 and Luke 21. Some of the teachings in these passages were a warning to Jesus' followers about the devastation that would take place during the siege of Jerusalem in 68–70 CE. Other passages deal with the coming of the Son of Man on the clouds of heaven to judge the whole of creation. The coming of the Son of Man will be preceded by **cosmic disasters**:

> ❝ The sun will be darkened, and the moon will not give its light, and the stars will be falling from heaven, and the powers in the heavens will be shaken. ❞
>
> *Mark* 13:24–25 (NRSV)

These events reflect the end of this world order and the establishment of the Reign of God in glory.

▲ *Jean Cousin's painting of the Last Judgement shows Christ in glory, with a sickle in his hand, separating the good from the bad*

Objectives

- Know what is meant by 'eschatology'.
- Understand how the resurrection of Jesus has influenced Christian eschatology.

Key terms

- **eschatology:** the study of what will take place at the end of time
- **cosmic disasters:** frightening events in the universe that will indicate the end of time

Links

To learn more about the Son of Man read page 42.

> ❝ In death body and soul are separated. **The body decays, while the soul goes to meet God** and waits to be reunited with its risen body on the Last Day. ❞
>
> *Youcat* 154

Chapter 6 Eschatology

■ Eschatology and the resurrection

The resurrection of Jesus was the power of God at work in a new way on earth. It was the beginning of the end of the reign of sin and death. In the resurrection, Jesus showed that life continued beyond the grave, in the presence of God.

For the early Christians, the resurrection of Jesus totally transformed their understanding of life and death. They believed that the end of the world was imminent and that Jesus' resurrection would be quickly followed by all people being taken into the presence of God.

As time passed and nothing seemed to change, the Christian view of the end of time took on a different meaning. The resurrection still showed the defeat of sin and the eternal separation from God that is symbolised by death. However, Christians realised they had to live in the life of the resurrection here on earth, which meant resisting the power of evil and allowing the Holy Spirit to guide them into living by the values and standards that Jesus followed. This would prepare them to meet the Son of Man, both when they died and in the final judgement.

St Paul's letters on resurrection

For Christians, the resurrection of Jesus proves that in death 'life is changed not ended' (Preface I for the Dead). Christians often question what the afterlife will be like. In his earlier letters, St Paul deals with the subject of the resurrected life, particularly in 1 Thessalonians 4:13–18 and 1 Corinthians 15:

> ❝ So it is with the resurrection of the dead. What is sown is perishable, what is raised is imperishable. It is sown in dishonour, it is raised in glory. It is sown in weakness, it is raised in power. It is sown a physical body, it is raised a spiritual body. If there is a physical body, there is also a spiritual body. ❞
>
> *1 Corinthians* 15:42–44 (NRSV)

Paul here compares the relationship of the earthly body and the heavenly body to the relationship of a seed and the plant that grows from it. Nobody can deny that the seed brings forth the new plant and therefore they must be the same thing. However, the resemblance between the two stages of the plant is such that it is difficult for the human mind to comprehend; all it can do is accept.

When the risen Jesus appeared to his disciples, he was not limited by any physical barrier, yet he was fully present and touchable (John 20:19–29). Jesus promised that he would take those who were faithful with him to heaven:

> ❝ In my Father's house there are many dwelling-places. If it were not so, would I have told you that I go to prepare a place for you? And if **I go and prepare a place for you,** I will come again and will take you to myself, so that **where I am, there you may be also.** ❞
>
> *John* 14:2–3 (NRSV)

Links

To read more about the resurrection of Jesus see pages 96–99.

Research activity

Look up all the passages in the Bible referred to in this chapter. What information do they give about the end of time and the afterlife?

Activities

1. Explain the importance of the end of time for Christians.
2. 'It is impossible for Catholics who are still alive to make sense of what will happen after death.' Evaluate this statement. Be sure to include more than one point of view, and refer to Catholic beliefs and teachings in your answer.

★ Study tip

Remember that in this section, we are dealing with future events. Some of the ideas might seem strange but sometimes it is only the expressions used that are unusual, not the underlying ideas.

Summary

You should understand what eschatology is, and know how the resurrection affects Christian beliefs about the afterlife.

6.5 The four last things

'The four last things' is the term for what Christians believe all people will have to encounter at the end of their earthly existence: death, judgement, heaven and hell.

■ Death

Christians believe that even though the earthly body will come to an end, this is not the end of the individual. Catholic teachings emphasise that a person consists of body and soul. While the body may corrupt, the soul passes beyond the veil of death and goes to meet God to wait for the end of time, when the body and soul will be reunited in a perfect form.

For Christians, death is a transition to a new phase of life: eternal life without the limitations of the earthly body. Death is not something to fear. As St Therese of Lisieux said when facing a very early death: 'I am not dying, I am entering life' (quoted in *Youcat*).

■ Judgement

Christians believe that after death, a person is taken to be judged by God and will have to give an account of all their deeds and failings in life. This is the moment of truth when people can no longer hide or deceive themselves. In the presence of the total love of God, people have to accept responsibility for all their actions. They become fully aware of how little they have fulfilled God's plan for themselves.

Traditional Catholic teaching is that people stand before God who judges them. Some would say that people also judge themselves in the light of God's love. However, Christ died so that all people might be saved. If people hold on to this belief, **judgement** will be merciful.

■ Heaven

For Christians, **heaven** is the place of total, eternal happiness in the presence of God, when all believers are aware of the love of God for each individual as well as for the whole community. In heaven, the absorbing love of God removes all cares and worries. All people rejoice that they are in the love of God.

The traditional image of angels playing harps on the clouds of heaven is trying to capture this idea of the beauty, freedom and total absorption in the love and praise of God. Heaven is the reward for those who have lived by God's love and guidance.

Christians believe that God is loving and so wants all people to join in the happiness of heaven. However, this can only happen when people choose to accept

> **Objectives**
> - Know the importance of the four last things.
> - Understand how the love of God is shown in the four last things.

> **Key terms**
> - **judgement:** the belief that God judges a person based on their actions, and either rewards or punishes them as a result
> - **heaven:** the state of eternal happiness in the presence of God
> - **hell:** the state of total separation from God

> ❝ **Heaven is the endless moment of love** … Together with all the angels and saints we will be able to rejoice forever in and with God. ❞
> *Youcat* 158

▲ *A fresco depicting heaven*

God. God cannot and will not force people to be happy in heaven. God's love respects the free choices of each individual.

Hell

For Christians, **hell** is the state of separation from God. Those people who choose to reject God, who harden their hearts to his love and forgiveness, choose to live for all eternity without God in their life. They remain in a state of spiritual darkness, aware of what they have willingly thrown away, and unwilling to accept anything from God.

> **Hell is the condition of everlasting separation from God,** the absolute absence of love. Someone who consciously and with full consent dies in serious sin, without repenting, and refuses God's merciful, forgiving love forever, excludes himself from communion with God and the saints … our freedom makes that decision possible.
>
> *Youcat* 161

▲ A fresco showing the separation of those going to heaven and those going to hell

Christians believe that God does not damn people to hell. Those in hell have damned themselves in their failure to recognise and accept God. God does not want people to be in hell, but respects the choices individuals make. God has given every person free will and that means that some people will choose to reject God. God accepts that this is the price to pay for creating people who are free.

Those in hell remain for all eternity with a sense of frustration and an awareness of what they have thrown away. The traditional picture is to show hell as a place of endless burning. It is possible to see this as an image for the self-inflicted frustration and anger that people in hell experience.

Discussion activity

Discuss to what extent people should be afraid of death.

Links

To read more about free will see page 16.

⭐ Study tip

Remember that because Christians believe people have been given free will, they are responsible for their own actions and will have to face the consequences of those actions, both good and bad. This idea is important for Christian beliefs about the afterlife.

Summary

You should now be able to explain Christian beliefs about the four last things.

Activities

1. Explain the differences between heaven and hell.
2. 'People should not have to accept responsibility for all their actions; God should just forgive them.' Evaluate this statement. Be sure to include more than one point of view, and refer to Catholic beliefs and teachings in your answer.

6.6 Purgatory and judgement

■ Purgatory

Christians believe that when people are judged before the total love of God, many want to accept the offer of God's presence for all eternity. However, the overwhelming love of God will make the person ashamed of how they have not responded well to the love of God throughout their life. They will be very conscious of the sins they have committed.

Catholics know that God is forgiving. However, even in an everyday relationship, people feel uncomfortable in the presence of someone they have wronged until they do something to make up for the offence. It is not the other person who demands this; the individual simply wants to make things better. The same applies to a relationship with God. The person cannot feel at ease in the presence of God while they are still conscious of their own sins, even though these have been forgiven.

> ❝ When Peter had betrayed Jesus, the Lord turned around and looked at Peter: 'And Peter went out and wept bitterly' – a feeling like being in purgatory. Just such a purgatory probably awaits most of us at the moment of our death: **the Lord looks at us full of love – and we experience burning shame and painful remorse** over our wicked or 'merely' unloving behaviour. ❞
>
> *Youcat* 159

Purgatory is a cleansing process, rather than a place, in which the effects of sins are removed so that the person can feel happy in the full presence of God. Purgatory is not a half-way point between heaven and hell, as all those who are in purgatory are on their way to heaven. Purgatory is often thought of as a state of pain, but it is also a state of hope. The sense of pain comes from the removal of the effects of sins. Hope comes from the fact that the person knows that heaven awaits them once this purifying is finished. Those in purgatory need the support and the prayers of other people so that the cleansing process might be completed quickly.

■ Individual and final judgement

The Catholic Church believes that when a person dies, they are taken into the presence of God and judged on a personal basis. The person's response to God at this point will be the deciding factor in whether they go to heaven, to purgatory or to hell. This is **particular judgement**.

Jesus also talked about **final judgement**. This is when Christ will come in glory at the end of time and the whole of creation will be judged. Then the Reign of God will be established and all those who have

Objectives
- Know Catholic teachings about purgatory.
- Understand different Christian beliefs about the afterlife.

Key terms
- **purgatory:** a state of cleansing to remove the effects of sin, to help a person accept the full presence of God
- **particular judgement:** the time when a person is judged by God after they die, and has to accept the responsibility for their actions when alive
- **final judgement:** sometimes called the Last Judgement; when Christ comes at the end of time and the whole of creation is judged

▲ *Imagine you broke your parents' favourite vase. How would this make you feel? Is it better to try to deny what you have done or to admit it?*

Chapter 6 Eschatology

▲ At the final judgement, all people will stand before the judgement seat of Christ

accepted God's invitation will join him forever in glory. This will be the completion of the new creation, when God will make everything perfect.

■ Other Christian beliefs about the afterlife

All Christian denominations believe in the resurrection and in heaven. However, there are different interpretations of some scriptural passages that lead to different teachings about the afterlife. Many groups refer to the Book of Revelation. This book contains a great amount of imagery and some people believe that it presents a good picture of what will happen after death.

- Some Christians believe that the moment of judgement after death is decisive. It is when an individual will either totally accept God and go to heaven or totally reject God and go to hell. Many Christians do not believe in purgatory; they believe instead that people either accept God, so are in a state of grace in heaven, or reject God and are in hell.
- Some believe that all people will wait for the second coming of Christ in their graves and then they will be called to a once-for-all judgement, ending up in either heaven or hell.

Purgatory and prayer

Peggy, a 62 year old Catholic from Formby, says: 'I like to pray for the holy souls in purgatory. They cannot help themselves so I like to help them through prayer. They can also pray for my needs. I am sure that their support to my prayers also helps them to show God that they are no longer selfish so they are ready for heaven.'

Summary

You should now understand the concept of purgatory, and be able to compare different Christian beliefs about the afterlife.

Research activity

Research beliefs about the afterlife that are held by two Christian denominations other than Catholics. What are the differences?

Activity

'Purgatory is a sign of God's love.' Evaluate this statement. Be sure to include more than one point of view, and refer to Catholic beliefs and teachings in your answer.

Extension activity

Examine how the different Christian beliefs about the afterlife are linked to various passages from the Bible, such as 1 Corinthians 15:1–58, 1 Thessalonians 4:13–18 and John 11:20–44.

⭐ **Study tip**

To begin to understand the idea of purgatory, think about how you would feel if someone wanted to let you off for something really bad that you had done to them, without you having to do anything to make up for it.

153

6.7 The Parable of the Rich Man and Lazarus

■ What are heaven and hell like?

Christians have very little evidence of what the afterlife is like. However, there is some information in the Bible to indicate its nature. Jesus' teachings about the afterlife talk about a place of torment and a place of happiness.

The place of torment is pictured in different ways. In Matthew it is described as 'the outer darkness, where there will be weeping and gnashing of teeth' (Matthew 25:30), where the unrighteous will go to 'eternal punishment' (Matthew 25:46).

Similarly, the place of happiness is referred to in various ways, such as 'eternal life' (Matthew 25:46) and a 'banquet' (Matthew 22:2–10).

■ The Parable of the Rich Man and Lazarus

One passage that unites images of both heaven and hell is the **Parable** of the Rich Man and Lazarus:

> There was a rich man who was dressed in purple and fine linen and who feasted sumptuously every day. And at his gate lay a poor man named Lazarus, covered with sores, who longed to satisfy his hunger with what fell from the rich man's table; even the dogs would come and lick his sores. The poor man died and was carried away by the angels to be with Abraham. The rich man also died and was buried. In Hades, where he was being tormented, he looked up and saw Abraham far away with Lazarus by his side. He called out, 'Father Abraham, have mercy on me, and send Lazarus to dip the tip of his finger in water and cool my tongue; for I am in agony in these flames.' But Abraham said, 'Child, remember that during your lifetime you received your good things, and Lazarus in like manner evil things; but now he is comforted here, and you are in agony. Besides all this, between you and us a great chasm has been fixed, so that those who might want to pass from here to you cannot do so, and no one can cross from there to us.' He said, 'Then, father, I beg you to send him to my father's house – for I have five brothers – that he may warn them, so that they will not also come into this place of torment.' Abraham replied, 'They have Moses and the prophets; they should listen to them.' He said, 'No, father Abraham; but if someone goes to them from the dead, they will repent.' He said to him, **'If they do not listen to Moses and the prophets, neither will they be convinced even if someone rises from the dead.'**
>
> Luke 16:19–31 (NRSV)

Objectives

- Know the Parable of the Rich Man and Lazarus.
- Understand what this parable tells Christians about the afterlife.

Key terms

- **parable:** a story with a religious message; particularly used for the stories told by Jesus
- **Hades:** the word used for 'hell' in Greek mythology; a place of torment

▲ Matthew 22:2–10 compares heaven to a wedding banquet to which everyone is invited

The rich man (who is not named, unlike Lazarus) had everything that he wanted in life, but he completely ignored the poor man sitting by the gates of his house. This is a warning about the hard-heartedness

Chapter 6   Eschatology

that can come from wealth and fame, which can destroy people's empathy for others if they are not careful. It is this lack of warmth for the needs of others, rather than his wealth, that condemns the rich man to **Hades**.

Hades (or hell) is the place where people are cut off from any relationship with God. The suffering and despair of hell are depicted through the rich man's plea for a drop of water to ease his torment.

> ❝ God does not damn men. Man himself is the one who refuses God's merciful love and voluntarily deprives himself of (eternal) life by excluding himself from communion with God. ❞
>
> *Youcat* 162

▲ *A fresco depicting heaven and hell*

Those condemned to hell are aware of the happiness of those in heaven, who are by the side of Abraham (the father of the Jews). Abraham was rewarded for his faith and trust in God, and those who have been faithful will share in the reward given to Abraham. The awareness of the happiness in heaven increases the suffering of those in hell, as they know that they have brought this suffering on themselves through their attitudes and actions in life.

When the rich man makes his plea, Abraham points out that no movement between heaven and hell can take place: people's actions and earlier choices have created the future for them. The rich man pleads that his brothers be made aware of the effect of their choices before it is too late for them. Abraham points out that the brothers have all the information they need in the scriptures.

The rich man says that this is not enough, but if his brothers were to see someone rise from the dead, their attitudes would change. Abraham points out that people's hard-heartedness would not change no matter how much evidence was presented to them.

This parable teaches that an awareness of the value and the needs of others results in a closeness to God in the afterlife. In contrast, a lack of this awareness leads to eternal separation from God.

Activities

1. Explain the imagery and descriptions used in this Parable to show heaven and hell.
2. 'The only point Jesus is making in the Parable of the Rich Man and Lazarus is that Catholics should care for the poor.' Evaluate this statement. Be sure to include more than one point of view, and refer to Catholic beliefs and teachings in your answer.

Extension activity

Examine other parables of Jesus that include reference to the afterlife, and explain the imagery used in them (for example Matthew 25:1–13, 25:14–30 and 25:31–46).

⭐ Study tip

Remember that parables are important for the messages they give, but are not to be taken literally.

Summary

You should now understand what the Parable of the Rich Man and Lazarus shows about Christian beliefs about the afterlife.

155

6.8 Cosmic reconciliation

Jesus' role in restoring harmony

While Catholics consider the story of the fall of Adam and Eve in Genesis 3 to be a myth, it contains some great insights into human nature. It shows that humans have a tendency to sin: to reject what God wants. God made all things to live in harmony, which includes humans having a freely chosen and meaningful relationship with God. Sin, which breaks this relationship, has an impact on the rest of creation. God's hopes have been undermined by human rejection and the whole of creation has lost its balance. Things are not how God wants them to be.

Paul shows how the death of Jesus restores the relationship between humanity and God. But it does more than that: Jesus' death also restores the harmony of all creation.

▲ Adam and Eve's disobedience reflects human rejection of God

> He is the image of the invisible God, the firstborn of all creation; for in him all things in heaven and on earth were created … He himself is before all things, and in him all things hold together. **He is the head of the body, the church; he is the beginning, the firstborn from the dead,** so that he might come to have first place in everything. For in him all the fullness of God was pleased to dwell, and through him God was pleased to reconcile to himself all things, whether on earth or in heaven, by making peace through the blood of his cross.
>
> *Colossians* 1:15–20 (NRSV)

Objectives

- Know what is meant by the cosmic reconciliation of all things.
- Understand how this relates to God's creation.

Links

To read more about the defeat of sin and restoration see pages 96–97.

Paul reminds his readers that God made the whole of the created order through his Word, God the Son. All things are united in Christ. Through his death and resurrection, Jesus has destroyed the power of sin and death that disrupted God's perfect creation. Through Jesus' obedience, the disharmony caused by disobedience has been overturned.

> **Since death came through a human being, the resurrection of the dead has also come through a human being;** for as all die in Adam, so all will be made alive in Christ. But each in his own order: Christ the first fruits, then at his coming those who belong to Christ. Then comes the end, when he hands over the kingdom to God the Father, after he has destroyed every ruler and every authority and power. For he must reign until he has put all his enemies under his feet. The last enemy to be destroyed is death. For 'God has put all

▲ Julian is named after St Julian's Church in Norwich, where she lived in a small cell to devote herself to God

> things in subjection under his feet.' … When all things are subjected to him, then the Son himself will also be subjected to the one who put all things in subjection under him, so that God may be all in all. **"**
>
> *1 Corinthians* 15:21–28 (NRSV)

■ Julian of Norwich

Julian of Norwich (c1342–1416) was a medieval writer. When she was in her late 20s, she had a severe illness and was given the last rites. Over a five-hour period she had a series of revelations from Jesus, which she called 'showings', followed by a further showing the next day. She recovered her health and then dedicated her life to being an anchoress: someone who withdraws from the world to live a solitary life of prayer. She therefore shut herself up in a small room to devote her life to God. Twenty years later, she dictated her showings to a scribe.

One of the questions she asked Jesus was why there was sin and hell.

> **"** In my folly, before this time I often wondered why, by the great foreseeing wisdom of God, the onset of sin was not prevented … This impulse [of thought] was much to be avoided, but nevertheless I mourned and sorrowed because of it, without reason and discretion.
>
> But Jesus, who in this vision informed me of all that is needed by me, answered with these words and said: **'It was necessary that there should be sin; but all shall be well, and all shall be well, and all manner of thing shall be well.'**
>
> These words were said most tenderly, showing no manner of blame to me nor to any who shall be saved. **"**
>
> Julian of Norwich, *Revelations of Divine Love* 32

The answer Jesus gave to Mother Julian reflects Paul's teachings about Christ reconciling the world. The main idea is that sin is needed for people to be able to make free choices for or against God. Hell is needed for those who choose to totally reject God, even though God does not want anyone to be lost.

However, in the love of Jesus, all things will be brought back together. **Cosmic reconciliation** does not just affect human beings but it includes the whole of the created order. The disharmony that is reflected in the story of the Fall, as a result of Adam and Eve's disobedience, has been destroyed. All things will be made perfect at the end of time.

Summary

You should now understand what cosmic reconciliation means, and how Jesus' death and resurrection are important for restoring it.

Links

For an explanation of the last rites see pages 160–161.

Activities

1. Explain how creation lacks harmony. Refer to Christian ideas about human sin in your answer.
2. 'It is pointless to hope that all things will be perfect in the end.' Evaluate this statement. Be sure to include more than one point of view, and refer to Catholic beliefs and teachings in your answer.

Discussion activity

Discuss whether you think the thoughts of a medieval writer have any value for the twenty-first century.

Key term

- **cosmic reconciliation:** the time when all things in creation will be brought together in harmony

★ Study tip

Don't be too worried about the use of different tenses here. Remember that the defeat of sin is a gradual process: although it happened in the resurrection, sin is still present because people live sinful lives. Sin will totally be defeated when all things are made perfect at the end of time.

6.9 The Church's teachings on the end of time

■ The three parts of the Church

The Church has always considered itself to consist of three distinct yet related parts:
- the Church Militant – the people on earth who are struggling against the temptations of sin and evil
- the Church Suffering – the souls of the faithful who are in purgatory
- the Church Glorious – the faithful who are enjoying the happiness of heaven.

These three sections of the Church are dependent on each other:
- People on earth pray to God with the assistance of the faithful in heaven.
- Those on earth pray for the souls who are being purified in purgatory.
- Those in purgatory are dependent on those who are alive for help, and they also pray for the needs of the living.

> **Objectives**
> - Know what the Second Vatican Council taught about the role of the Church in preparing for the end of time.
> - Understand how a Catholic's life and relationship to the Church prepares them for the end of time.

▲ The Vatican is the centre of the Church, where many Catholics gather each week

■ Teachings of the Second Vatican Council

Preparing for the end of time

The Second Vatican Council showed that one of the roles of the Church is to prepare for the end of time.

Christians believe that Christ has promised he will come in glory at the end of time as judge and as saviour, and they must live on earth in this hope. They are empowered by the Holy Spirit to live by the same standards and values as Christ did, and to perform good deeds on earth.

Jesus told his followers to be constantly prepared for the end. This applies to the death of the individual as well as to the end of the world. The Council echoed Jesus' teachings:

> ❝ The Church's task is to make the kingdom of God, which has already begun with Jesus, germinate and grow in all nations … **the Church, for all her weakness, is a formidable bit of heaven on earth.** ❞
>
> *Youcat* 123

> ❝ **The promised restoration which we are awaiting has already begun in Christ, is carried forward in the mission of the Holy Spirit and through Him continues in the Church** in which we learn the meaning of our terrestrial life through our faith, while we perform with hope in the future the work committed to us in this world by the Father, and thus work out our salvation. ❞
>
> *Lumen Gentium* 48

Chapter 6 Eschatology

> **Since however we know not the day nor the hour, on Our Lord's advice we must be constantly vigilant** so that, having finished the course of our earthly life, (Heb 9:27) we may merit to enter into the marriage feast with Him and to be numbered among the blessed (Mt 25:31–46) and that we may not be ordered to go into eternal fire (Mt 25:41) like the wicked and slothful servant, (Mt 25:26) into the exterior darkness where 'there will be the weeping and the gnashing of teeth'.
>
> *Lumen Gentium 48*

The Council stressed the idea that the Church on earth is not yet in its perfect form: it is a community of sinners, trying to reach perfection but limited by human weakness. All people are called to belong to the Church. The hope is that all people will be saved and, through Christ, reach heaven and be in the presence of God.

> The Church, to which we are all called in Christ Jesus, and in which we acquire sanctity through the grace of God, **will attain its full perfection only in the glory of heaven,** when there will come the time of the restoration of all things. At that time the human race as well as the entire world, which is intimately related to man and attains to its end through him, will be perfectly re-established in Christ.
>
> *Lumen Gentium 48*

Free will and hell

Christians believe that God's love brings people into existence, and God's love does not end. This means that people must continue to live once their life on earth is over; if they didn't then God's unending love would have to end, which is a contradiction. God wants all people to be happy, and to experience eternal happiness in heaven. However, God loves each individual so intensely that he gives each person free will. God cannot force people to accept him and God must respect the wishes of those who reject him.

The *Catechism of the Catholic Church* – a book that summarises all the teachings of the Church – teaches that there are people in hell, but this is because people have made that choice, not because God wants them there. People who do actions that are a total rejection of God commit **mortal** (deadly) **sins**. All sins can be forgiven, but the person must confess and be sorry for their sin. A total refusal to admit the sin means that the person has rejected God's love.

Summary

You should now understand what the Second Vatican Council taught about the role of the Church in preparing for the end of time. You should also understand Catholic beliefs about what happens at the end of time.

Research activity

Research the Bible passages referred to in these pages. What do they indicate about life after death for Christians?

Activities

1. Explain why the Catholic Church teaches that some people are in hell.
2. 'There is no way in which the Catholic Church can help people prepare for the end of time.' Evaluate this statement. Be sure to include more than one point of view, and refer to Catholic beliefs and teachings in your answer.

> **God predestines no one to go to hell;** for this, a willful turning away from God (a mortal sin) is necessary, and persistence in it until the end.
>
> *Catechism of the Catholic Church* 1037

Key term

- **mortal sins:** offences against God, yourself or other people that totally destroy the relationship with God

⭐ Study tip

Remember that the Church's teachings on the end of time and the afterlife are based on the logical extension of Jesus' teachings.

159

6.10 The last rites

The last rites are the prayers and blessings that take place when a person is approaching death. They include the anointing of the sick, the last confession, the last Communion (Viaticum) and the commendation of the dying.

The anointing of the sick

One of the seven sacraments is **the anointing of the sick** (often called the sacrament of the sick). When a person is seriously ill, facing a major operation or showing signs of the weakness of old age, the sacrament of the sick is often received.

The letter of St James describes the origin of the sacrament, its format and its effects:

> Are any among you sick? They should call for the elders of the church and have them pray over them, anointing them with oil in the name of the Lord. **The prayer of faith will save the sick,** and the Lord will raise them up; and anyone who has committed sins will be forgiven.
>
> James 5:14–15 (NRSV)

The rite of the anointing of the sick involves the following stages:
- The priest sprinkles the room and the patient with holy water as a reminder of baptism.
- The sick person may confess their sins to the priest.
- There is a reading from the Bible.
- A short litany (a list of saints' names with 'Pray for us' after each name) and prayers for the sick are said.
- The priest lays his hands on the head of the sick person, calling down the power and strength of the Holy Spirit.
- A small amount of oil (the oil of the sick) is blessed.
- The priest anoints the forehead and hands of the sick person with this oil, saying: 'Through this holy anointing may the Lord in his love and mercy help you with the grace of the Holy Spirit. May the Lord who frees you from sin, save you and raise you up.'
- The 'Our Father' is said.
- Holy Communion is given.

This rite is full of meaning:
- The power of the Holy Spirit fills the sick person to give them the strength to resist both the temptation of sin, and the sense of doubt and despair that some people feel when facing death.

Objectives
- Know what the last rites are.
- Understand the importance of the last rites for Catholics.

Key terms
- **the anointing of the sick:** one of the seven sacraments that gives healing, strength and forgiveness
- **commendation of the dying:** the prayers that are said when a person is at the point of death
- **Viaticum:** meaning 'with you on the way'; the last Communion before death to show that Christ is with the person in death

Links
To read more about the seven sacraments see pages 58–59.

▲ A priest performing the anointing of the sick

160

- The sacrament includes the forgiveness of sins so that the sick person can face the future with a clear conscience. Sometimes, an awareness of sins can be a contributing factor in a negative attitude towards sickness. With forgiveness, people often feel better about themselves, and more able to face whatever is to come.
- The anointing may bring physical as well as mental and spiritual healing.
- The reception of Holy Communion shows that Christ is present with the person in their sickness, supporting them.
- The anointing gives hope of a new life, whether it be a restoration to full health in this life or the promise of eternal happiness with God.

■ Commendation of the dying

The **commendation of the dying** is a short service that is centred round the reception of the dying person's last Communion, called Viaticum.

- The dying person may hold a crucifix as a reminder that they are sharing in Christ's death.
- The baptismal promises may be renewed (the vows the person said when they were baptised). In these, the dying person is reminded of their faith in God and is made more confident about the love of God that is waiting to greet them in heaven.
- A short passage from the Bible may be read, for example: 'Even though I walk through the darkest valley, I fear no evil; for you are with me' (Psalms 23:4).
- There is a Litany of the Saints, asking for their prayers as the dying person faces judgement.
- All present will receive Communion. For the dying person this is **Viaticum**, the last Communion. Viaticum shows that Jesus is with them on the journey through death to new life. Since Christ has been through death, they can be assured that Christ is with the person in death.
- At the moment of death the following prayer might be said: 'Go forth, Christian soul, from this world/ in the name of God the almighty Father,/ who created you,/ in the name of Jesus Christ, Son of the living God,/ who suffered for you,/ in the name of the Holy Spirit,/ who was poured out upon you,/ go forth, faithful Christian./ May you live in peace this day,/ may your home be with God in Zion,/ with Mary, the virgin Mother of God,/ with Joseph, and all the angels and saints.'

Summary
You should now be able to explain what happens in the last rites, and understand why these are important for Catholics.

▲ A stained-glass window representing the anointing of the sick, showing the oil that is used as part of the sacrament

Activities

1. Explain the importance of both the anointing of the sick and Viaticum.
2. 'It is not important whether a Catholic receives the last rites or not.' Evaluate this statement. Be sure to include more than one point of view, and refer to Catholic beliefs and teachings in your answer.

Discussion activity

Discuss whether the last rites and Viaticum should be given in private or in the presence of family and friends.

★ Study tip

Don't confuse the last rites with a funeral, which takes place after a person has died.

6.11 The funeral rite

The Catholic **funeral** rite reflects Catholic beliefs about the afterlife. It usually involves the following stages:

■ Reception of the body

- The body is taken to church. This represents the deceased being presented back to God.
- At the church doors, the coffin is sprinkled with **holy water**, as a reminder of baptism. The deceased was baptised into Christ's death, so now joins in Christ's resurrection.
- The coffin is placed beside the lit Paschal candle. This represents the light of the Risen Christ shining on the person.

▲ The priest sprinkles the coffin with holy water as it is carried into the church

■ The funeral Mass

- The priest will usually wear either purple or white vestments.
- The funeral Mass is often called a **requiem**. The word 'requiem' is Latin and means 'rest'. It comes from a prayer that starts with the line 'Eternal rest give unto them, O Lord'. The whole Mass is centred around praying that the deceased may be in the presence of God in heaven, with all their sins forgiven.
- The readings of the Mass focus on the effects of Christ's resurrection. One reading often used is Jesus' discussion with Martha (John 11:1–44), in which Jesus proclaims: 'I am the resurrection and the life. Those who believe in me, even though they die, will live, and everyone who lives and believes in me will never die.' (John 11:25–26 (NRSV)).
- During the Eucharistic Prayer, a special prayer for the deceased may be said: 'Remember your servant (Name),/ whom you have called/ from this world to yourself./ Grant that he/she who was

Objectives
- Know what happens during a Catholic funeral.
- Understand how a Catholic funeral shows beliefs about life after death.

Key terms
- **funeral:** a ceremony to mourn the dead person
- **holy water:** blessed water that is used in baptism
- **requiem:** the Mass for the dead
- **crematorium:** a building where the dead are cremated

Links
Read more about the Paschal candle on pages 142–143.

> ❝ A Christian funeral is a service performed by the Christian community for the benefit of its dead. It expresses the sorrow of the survivors, yet it always has a Paschal character. **Ultimately, we die in Christ so as to celebrate with him the feast of the Resurrection.** ❞
>
> *Youcat* 278

united with your Son in a death like his,/ may be one with him in his Resurrection,/ when from the earth/ he will raise up in the flesh those who have died,/ and transform our lowly body/ after the pattern of his own glorious body.'

The committal

- At the end of Mass, the priest will say a prayer asking that any sins committed by the deceased during their life may be forgiven.
- The coffin is again sprinkled with holy water as a reminder of baptism.
- The priest waves the smoke from burning incense over the coffin. During life, the dead person's body was a temple of the Holy Spirit. They were filled with the gifts of the Holy Spirit and the work of the Sprit was evident in their life. God had given the deceased to the living community for a time. Now their family is returning the deceased back to God, in thanksgiving for all that the dead person meant to them.
- The rising smoke of the incense represents the prayers of the faithful being offered up to God on behalf of the deceased.
- As the coffin is blessed, the congregation pray or sing: 'May the angels lead you to paradise and with poor man Lazarus of old may you enjoy eternal life.'
- A prayer is said for the mourners, that they may live in the hope that they will meet with the deceased again in the new life of heaven.

▲ *During the committal the priest waves the smoke from burning incense over the coffin*

At the grave or in the crematorium

- The 'Our Father' is said, reflecting the belief that the dead person was a child of God who has now been received back into his loving care.
- The grave or the coffin is sprinkled with holy water.
- The prayers reflect the hope that the deceased will quickly gain the eternal happiness of heaven.

Trusting in God

Sue, a 73-year-old Catholic widow from Melling, says: 'When Bill died it was a great blow. We had been married for 44 years, so his death totally changed my life. The funeral service was a very sad time for me, but it also gave me comfort. To see his coffin taken into church made me feel that he was going home to God. The symbols of water and the incense made me more aware of just how much Bill had been a child of God. I know that we will meet again, forever in God's love, so our separation is only a temporary thing. I just need to keep trusting that God knows what is best.'

Activities

1. Explain the symbolism used during a Catholic funeral.
2. 'Catholic funerals should be happy occasions.' Evaluate this statement. Be sure to include more than one point of view, and refer to Catholic beliefs and teachings in your answer.

Extension activity

Compare a Catholic funeral with burial customs from other Christian traditions. Explain your thoughts about each of the customs you have examined.

⭐ Study tip

Remember that a Catholic funeral is often in two stages: the first part in the church and the second part at the graveside or in the crematorium.

Summary

You should now be able to explain what happens in a Catholic funeral, and understand how this reflects Catholic beliefs about the afterlife.

6.12 The care of the dying and euthanasia

■ The sanctity of life

The Catholic Church maintains that all life comes from God. Every individual is special and precious to God. This means that every life and all life is holy.

This belief in the **sanctity of life** is a fundamental principle that shapes Catholic teachings about the care given to every human life in all its stages.

> ❝ Everyone has the duty to lead his or her life in accordance with God's plan. That life is entrusted to the individual as a good that must bear fruit already here on earth, but that finds its full perfection only in eternal life. ❞
>
> *Declaration on Euthanasia* I

Catholics believe that all life belongs to God, and if anyone damages or destroys a human life intentionally then they are rejecting a gift from God.

■ The care of the dying

The Catholic Church accepts the fact that life on earth is finite, but it believes that it is also the gateway to eternal life. The Church teaches that people should value both aspects of this idea. Life has to be respected while it is being lived. When the body starts to break down, it needs help and support and this should be provided.

Objectives

- Know what 'sanctity of life' and 'euthanasia' mean.
- Understand how beliefs about the sanctity of life guide Catholic teachings on the care of the dying and euthanasia.

Key terms

- **sanctity of life:** all life is holy as it is created and loved by God; human life should not be misused or abused
- **euthanasia:** killing someone painlessly and with compassion, to end their suffering

▲ The Catholic Church teaches that all people should be treated with respect and care, including the elderly

> ❝ Life is a gift of God, and on the other hand death is unavoidable; it is necessary, therefore, that **we, without in any way hastening the hour of death, should be able to accept it with full responsibility and dignity.** It is true that death marks the end of our earthly existence, but at the same time it opens the door to immortal life. ❞
>
> *Declaration on Euthanasia*
> Conclusion

Those who are nearing death often need special care. Illness, fragility and old age should be treated with all due care for the rights and dignity of the individual. People in need must not be made to feel that they are an unnecessary burden. When people know they are valued, their own sense of self-worth increases.

Euthanasia

Many sick Christians are willing to accept their suffering as a way of sharing in the suffering of Jesus. Suffering is an integral part of being human. It is not pleasant and when there are reasonable treatments that can ease suffering, Catholics are free both to use them for themselves and to assist other people.

> According to Christian teaching, however, suffering, especially suffering during the last moments of life, has a special place in God's saving plan; **it is in fact a sharing in Christ's passion** and a union with the redeeming sacrifice which He offered in obedience to the Father's will.
>
> *Declaration on Euthanasia* Conclusion

The Catholic Church does not agree with **euthanasia**, a term that means 'good death'. Euthanasia describes a situation in which someone helps another person to die to end their suffering. For example, if a doctor deliberately gives a patient a large dose of medication and knows that they will die as a result, this is euthanasia.

Great care has to be given to the dying, which might include the administration of pain-relief drugs in order to make the patient more comfortable. Even though these drugs might quicken the process of death, that is not their intention. For the Catholic Church, the intention of showing care for the person who is loved by God is central to any decisions about the type of treatment they receive. Anything that is done to deliberately bring about the death of another person is considered to be murder and against the moral law, and thus is totally rejected by the Church.

The Catholic Church believes that euthanasia, suicide and assisted suicide are wrong. It believes that all these processes lower the value and dignity of life. However, the Catholic Church does not believe that a person's life should be deliberately prolonged by treatments that will have no real benefit for the dying person. It is against Catholic teaching to give any treatment that will deliberately prolong the suffering of a dying person. Nature should be allowed to take its course.

> When inevitable death is imminent in spite of the means used, it is permitted in conscience to take the decision to refuse forms of treatment that would only secure a precarious and burdensome prolongation of life, so long as the normal care due to the sick person in similar cases is not interrupted.
>
> *Declaration on Euthanasia* IV

> Today people often try to get around the Fifth Commandment with seemingly humane arguments. But neither euthanasia nor abortion is a humane solution.
>
> *Youcat* 379

Activities

1. Explain what the terms sanctity of life and euthanasia mean.
2. 'The Catholic Church should allow euthanasia in extreme cases of persistent suffering.' Evaluate this statement. Be sure to include more than one point of view, and refer to Catholic beliefs and teachings in your answer.

Research activity

Research a local hospice, examining the help given to the dying and their families. Comment on the strengths and weaknesses of what happens in a hospice.

⭐ Study tip

Remember that euthanasia can take different forms. The Catholic Church will not accept any action that deliberately ends a person's life, though it accepts that sometimes actions are taken that will almost inevitably bring about the end of life.

Summary

You should now understand what the Catholic Church teaches about the sanctity of life and euthanasia.

6 Assessment guidance

Eschatology – summary

You should now be able to:

- ✔ explain the features and meaning of the Paschal candle
- ✔ explain the meaning and religious ideas in Michelangelo's *The Last Judgement*
- ✔ explain how memorials show Christian beliefs about life after death
- ✔ explain Catholic beliefs about eschatology and life after death, including the importance of the resurrection of Jesus
- ✔ explain the importance of the four last things (death, judgement, heaven and hell), and Catholic beliefs about purgatory and judgement
- ✔ explain what the Parable of the Rich Man and Lazarus teaches about life after death
- ✔ explain what Julian of Norwich's *Revelations of Divine Love* 32 teaches about the idea of cosmic reconciliation
- ✔ explain how the Second Vatican Council influenced Catholic teachings about eschatology
- ✔ explain how the last rites are seen as signs of reconciliation, healing and hope
- ✔ explain how the prayers and actions of the funeral rite reflect Catholic beliefs about life after death
- ✔ explain how the idea of the sanctity of life affects Catholic views about the care of the dying and euthanasia.

Sample student answer – the 12 mark question

1. Write an answer to the following question:

   'Catholics should be afraid of the four last things: death, judgement, heaven and hell.'

   Evaluate this statement. In your answer you should:
   - give developed arguments to support this statement
   - give developed arguments to support a different point of view
   - refer to Catholic teaching
   - reach a justified conclusion.

   [12 marks]

2. Read the following sample student answer:

   "The four last things happen at the end of a person's life. Nobody alive has personally experienced any of the four last things. Though some people might claim that they have died and come back to life, they have not died for good and there is no guarantee that what they experienced was real death. It is the lack of knowledge of what is going to happen after death that makes most people, including many Catholics, afraid of death.

   What is even more frightening is the fact of having to stand before God and be judged on how you have lived your life. Everybody is ashamed of something that they have done. In the presence of God, there is no hiding the truth. Most people do not want to accept the truth about themselves, but at the Last Judgement it cannot be avoided. However, Jesus said, 'the truth will set you free'. If a person can accept the truth about themselves at judgement and be sorry for what they have done wrong, they can be sure of God's love and forgiveness. Jesus promised, 'there are many rooms in my Father's house', so this must mean that many sinners are in heaven, so there is hope for anyone facing judgement.

   The existence of hell makes many Catholics afraid as they do not want to be damned to eternal suffering away from the presence of God. The Catechism tells us that God does not predestine anybody to hell but that those people who choose knowingly and deliberately to reject God have chosen hell for themselves. Maybe these are the people who should be afraid of death, but then again, God is respecting their choices by allowing them to cut themselves off, so maybe they will get what they want. Very few people will be scared of the prospect of heaven, the state of perfection and eternal happiness in the presence of God. What most people are afraid of is not getting to heaven.

The Catholic belief in purgatory, a state of cleaning that people can go through to prepare them for the happiness of heaven, is a great source of hope, not fear. While people might have to endure some suffering and cleansing, they know that they are on the way to heaven, so that should remove any fear. For a true believer, Jesus has gone ahead to prepare a way to heaven, so there is nothing to be afraid of because God loves everybody."

3. With a partner, discuss the sample answer. Consider the following questions:
   - Does the response answer the question?
   - Does the answer refer to Catholic teachings and if so what are they?
   - Is there an argument to support the statement and how well developed is it?
   - Is a different point of view offered and how developed is that argument?
   - Has the student written a clear conclusion after weighing up both sides of the argument?
   - What is good about this answer?
   - How do you think it could be improved?

4. What mark (out of 12) would you give this answer? Look at the mark scheme in the Introduction (AO2). What are the reasons for the mark you have given?

Practice questions

1. Which of the following shows the religious meaning of the Parable of the Rich Man and Lazarus?

   A) If people are rich they will be happy in the afterlife
   B) Everybody is destined to go to heaven
   C) How well people care for each other will affect how they spend their afterlife
   D) Only poor people will get to heaven [1 mark]

2. Give two points from Mother Julian's teachings about cosmic reconciliation. [2 marks]

3. Explain two ways in which Catholic beliefs about life after death influence the types of memorials that are chosen to remember people. [4 marks]

> ⭐ **Study tip**
> Remember that you have to give two different ways, including some development or explanation in your answer.

4. Explain two ways in which the prayers and actions in a Catholic funeral express beliefs about an afterlife. Refer to Christian beliefs in your answer. [5 marks]

5. 'Catholic funerals should be happy occasions.'

   Evaluate this statement. In your answer you should:
   - give developed arguments to support this statement
   - give developed arguments to support a different point of view
   - refer to Christian teaching
   - reach a justified conclusion. [12 marks]

Part 2: World religions

7 Islam: beliefs and teachings

7.1 The Oneness of God and the supremacy of God's will

■ Introduction to Islam

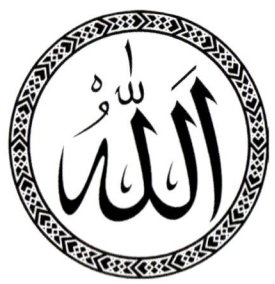

▲ The word 'Allah' in Arabic

Muslims believe **Islam** was gradually revealed to humanity through various prophets over many centuries. It was first revealed to Adam, the first man. The final and most complete revelation was made to Muhammad in the seventh century.

The word 'Islam' in Arabic means 'surrender', 'obedience' or 'submission'. Muslims believe that they should surrender to the will of **Allah**. Islam also means 'peace', as it is through obeying God's will that a person will achieve peace in themselves.

■ The Oneness of God

One of the most important beliefs in both Sunni and Shi'a Islam is **Tawhid**: the belief that there is only one God. Like Christianity, this makes Islam a **monotheistic** religion. The Arabic word for God, 'Allah', means 'the God', that is 'the one and only God'. This belief is expressed in Surah 112:

> Say, 'He is God the One, God the eternal. He begot no one nor was He begotten. No one is comparable to Him.'
>
> *Qur'an* 112:1–4

This belief is repeated daily in the Shahadah: 'There is no God but Allah and Muhammad is his prophet.'

A Muslim's most important duty is to declare faith in the one God. Muslims believe that God is an undivided entity. This means that God is not made up of different persons nor has a son. No one else and no other object has God's attributes or qualities. Muslims believe the only sin that God will not forgive is attributing God-like qualities to any other being or thing.

God is unique. There is nothing like God. No one can picture or describe God because there is nothing to compare God to. This is one reason why there are no images or pictures of God in mosques (the

Objective

- Understand Muslim beliefs in the Oneness of God and the Supremacy of God's will.

Key terms

- **Muslim:** one who has submitted to the will of God and has accepted Islam
- **Islam:** the name of the religion followed by Muslims; to surrender to the will of God; peace
- **Allah:** the Arabic name for God
- **Tawhid:** the Oneness and unity of God
- **monotheistic:** a religion that believes there is only one God
- **supremacy:** supreme power or authority; a quality of God

Links

To learn about the differences between Sunni and Shi'a Islam see pages 170–171.

Links

To learn more about the Shahadah see page 191.

Muslim place of worship) or in Muslim books or homes. Mosques are often beautifully decorated with verses from the Qur'an instead.

The supremacy of God's will

For Muslims, God is the one and only creator and controller of everything; therefore nothing takes place unless God allows it to happen. No matter whether something is good or bad, Muslims believe it is God's will, and that God must have had a good reason for letting it happen. For Sunni Muslims, the **supremacy** of God's will is an important article of faith.

Muslims believe they should accept whatever happens as the will of God, trusting in God's good intentions for people. God's will is supreme (above all things). What God wants and expects of people is the most important thing.

Muslims often add the words 'God willing' (inshallah) after a promise to do something. This shows their belief that they are not in control of what happens: only God is in control. This idea leads some Muslims to believe that God controls everything human beings do and that humans do not have free will. Others think that God does not force people to act in certain ways, but that God has allowed people freedom to choose how to behave.

> You who believe, obey God and the Messenger.
>
> *Qur'an* 4:59

The impact of these beliefs on Muslims

For Muslims, it is not enough just to believe in one God: they must show that belief in the way they live their lives. This means that only God should be worshipped. Muhammad is respected as a prophet but he is not worshipped. That would be idolatry (worshipping an idol), which is forbidden in Islam. Muslims must never make anything in their lives more important than God, including their family, money or jobs.

Believing in the supremacy of God's will means that Muslims have to try to accept that even the bad things that happen in life are 'meant to be'. God's plans are mysterious and cannot be fully known by humans. The word Muslim means 'one who has submitted to God', and so a Muslim tries both to accept God's will and to live according to God's will in everyday life.

> Misfortunes can only happen with God's permission.
>
> *Qur'an* 64:11

Summary

You should have now learnt about Muslim beliefs in the Oneness of God and the supremacy of God's will.

Mosques are often highly decorated inside, but with patterns or text from the Qur'an rather than images of God

Activities

1. Explain the belief in Tawhid in your own words.
2. Explain four qualities of God described in Surah 112.
3. Why might a Muslim add the words 'God willing' when talking about their future plans?
4. Explain how belief in the supremacy of God's will might affect a Muslim's attitude to life.

Research activity

Recall Christian beliefs about the Trinity or look up Hindu beliefs about the deities. Explain why many Muslims disapprove of these ideas about God.

Discussion activity

With a partner or in a small group, discuss the following statement: 'If God controls everything, then people are not responsible for their actions.' Try to consider different points of view and include a Muslim perspective.

⭐ Study tip

It is easy to find differences between religions, but try considering the beliefs about God that Muslims and Christians share.

7.2 Key beliefs of Sunni Islam and Shi'a Islam

■ Sunni and Shi'a Islam

Sunni Islam

When Muhammad died, the majority of Muslims thought that only the **Qur'an** (the Muslim holy book) and the **Sunnah** (Muhammad's teaching and actions) had the authority to guide the beliefs and behaviour of Muslims. They elected Abu Bakr to be their leader (Caliph), to act on behalf of God and Muhammad to make sure people followed God's laws.

The Caliphs did not make the laws; they enforced them once the community had considered the views of scholars who studied the Qur'an and the Sunnah. This group of Muslims came to be called '**Sunni**', meaning followers of the Sunnah.

Shi'a Islam

Another group of Muslims believed that Muhammad had named his cousin Ali as his successor. Ali was one of the earliest converts to Islam and was married to Muhammad's daughter, Fatima. Ali and his supporters thought that the true leader (called the Imam) had to be a descendent of Muhammad and chosen by God. Each Imam would identify the next one before he died.

Ali's claims to be leader were ignored by many Muslims. Over time a split developed between the followers of Ali's party, known as the **Shi'a**, and the Sunni Muslims. Today, the Shi'a have their own interpretation of Islamic laws and only accept sayings of Muhammad that have been passed down through Ali or his followers.

Shi'a and Sunni Islam hold many elements in common such as belief in God, the prophethood of Muhammad, the guidance of the Qur'an, and following the Sunnah. They only differ in interpretations of certain aspects of belief and law, and in the emphasis they put on expressing key beliefs, as you will see below.

■ The key beliefs of Sunni and Shi'a Islam

The six articles of faith in Sunni Islam

Sunni Muslims hold these six main beliefs:

1. There is only one God. 'Allah' combines the two Arabic words 'al' (the) and 'ilāh' (God).
2. Angels communicate the message of God to humans.
3. The Qur'an (meaning 'recitation') is the most important writing and the highest authority in Islam.
4. Muhammad, whose name means 'highly praised', is the most important prophet of God.
5. The Day of Judgement is when all humanity will be judged by God and sent to paradise or hell.

Objectives

- Know the origins of Sunni Islam and Shi'a Islam.
- Know the key beliefs of Sunni Islam and Shi'a Islam.

Key terms

- **Qur'an:** the holy book revealed to Muhammad by the angel Jibril; God's final revelation to humankind
- **Sunnah:** the teachings and deeds of Muhammad
- **Sunni:** Muslims who believe in the successorship to Muhammad of Abu Bakr, Umar, Uthman and Ali
- **Shi'a (Shi'i):** Muslims who believe in the Imamate, the successorship of Ali

Links

To read more about Muhammad see pages 184–185.

▲ Sunni Muslims follow the Qur'an and the Sunnah

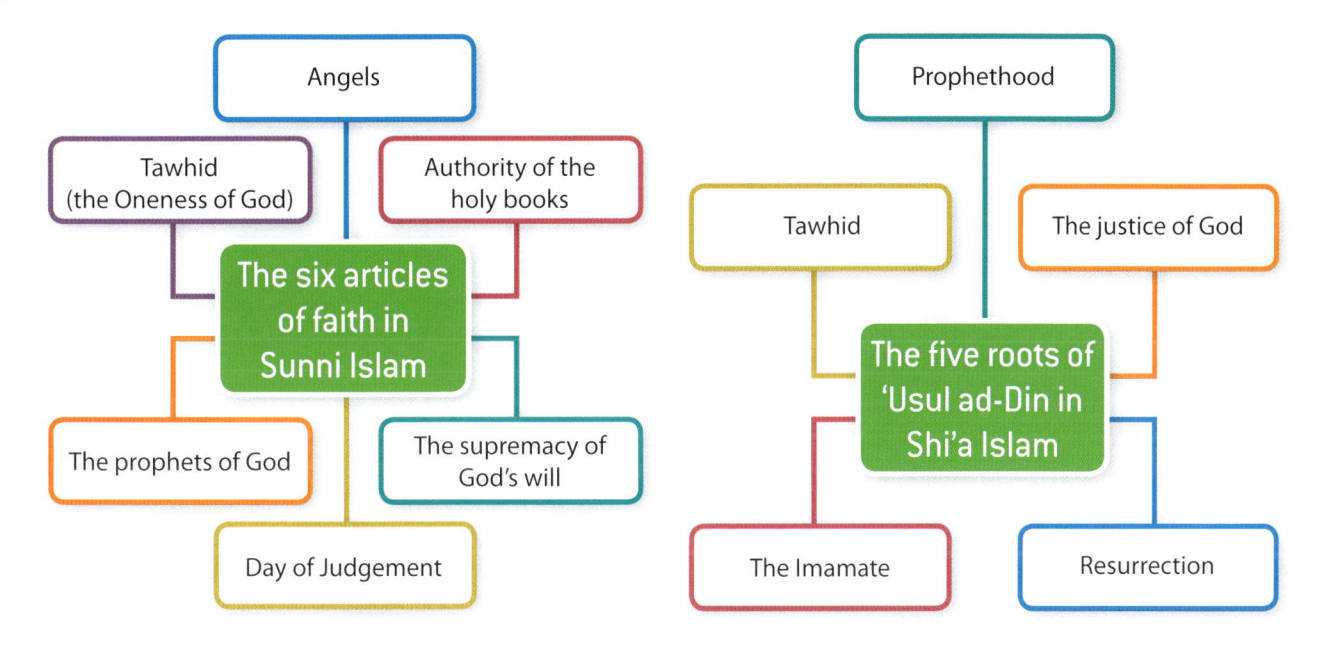

Chapter 7 Islam: beliefs and teachings

The six articles of faith in Sunni Islam
- Tawhid (the Oneness of God)
- Angels
- Authority of the holy books
- The prophets of God
- The supremacy of God's will
- Day of Judgement

The five roots of 'Usul ad-Din in Shi'a Islam
- Tawhid
- Prophethood
- The justice of God
- The Imamate
- Resurrection

6. The supremacy of God's will means that God already knows but also makes happen everything that occurs in the world and in human lives.

The five roots of 'Usul ad-Din in Shi'a Islam

'Usul ad-Din means the 'principles (or roots) of religion'. The roots of a tree keep it alive and firmly attached to the source of its life. For Shi'a Muslims, these five principles keep them firmly rooted in God, the source of life.

1. Tawhid means that God is One; God is not made up of different persons.
2. Prophethood means accepting that Muhammad is God's last prophet, and that God's revelations through him are true.
3. God is just and wise, cannot do wrong, and holds humans accountable for their actions.
4. The Imamate means accepting that the twelve Imams are the leaders of Islam and guard the truth of the religion without error.
5. Shi'a Muslims believe that after death they will be resurrected to be judged by God.

▲ Millions of Shi'a Muslims visit the burial place of Imam Ali, whom they believe was Muhammad's true successor

★ Study tip
It is important to understand the beliefs that Shi'a and Sunni Muslims hold in common as well as why they have differences.

Activities
1. Explain the meaning of the word 'Islam'.
2. Give two beliefs that Sunni and Shi'a Muslims share.
3. Explain two differences between the beliefs of Sunni Muslims and Shi'a Muslims.

Summary
You should now be able to identify the six articles of faith in Sunni Islam and the five roots of 'Usul ad-Din in Shi'a Islam. You should also be able to explain the origins of Sunni Islam and Shi'a Islam.

7.3 The nature of God

■ 'God is the greatest'

Every day Muslims hear and say the words 'Allahu Akbar', meaning 'God is the greatest'. Muslims believe that God is so great he is beyond human understanding, and greater than anything humans can imagine. Yet Muslims have firm beliefs about what God is like. Where do these ideas come from?

■ The names of God

Muslims believe God has revealed himself to people through Muhammad and the holy books. There are 99 names of God in the Qur'an and Hadith (Muhammad's sayings), which can help Muslims to understand something of God's nature. Each name describes a quality that God has revealed about himself.

▲ Muslims use prayer beads to help them recite the names of God

Many Muslims memorise the names of God and recite them when they are praying privately. Each name helps them to feel God's presence. Some names show God's power, might and authority; others show God's love and care for human beings.

> ❝ The Most Excellent Names belong to God: use them to call on Him. ❞
>
> *Qur'an* 7:180

■ Qualities of God

A young child might ask 'Where is God?'. It is not an easy question to answer! Muslims believe that God is **immanent**, within all things and close to his people. But God is also **transcendent**, beyond all things.

Objective
- Understand Muslim beliefs about the nature of God.

Key terms
- **immanent:** the idea that God is present in and involved with life on earth and in the universe; a quality of God
- **transcendent:** the idea that God is beyond and outside life on earth and the universe; a quality of God
- **omnipotent:** almighty, having unlimited power; a quality of God
- **beneficent:** benevolent, all-loving, all-good; a quality of God
- **merciful:** the quality of God that shows compassion or forgiveness to humans, even though he has the power to punish them
- **fairness:** the idea that God treats people fairly and impartially without favour or discrimination
- **justice:** the idea that God is just and fair and judges human actions, rewarding the good and punishing the bad
- **Adalat:** the concept of justice in Shi'a Islam

Our limited human thinking makes us wonder, 'How can God be both?' For Muslims, God can be both because God is creator of the universe, therefore outside and not limited by the physical world, yet he is also within all things and compassionate towards people.

Muslims also believe God is **omnipotent** (all-powerful), as God is the creator, sustainer and owner of all things. He is also all-knowing, aware of everything including human actions and thoughts.

> ❝ This is God, your Lord, **there is no God but Him, the Creator of all things,** so worship Him; **He is in charge of everything.** No vision can take Him in, but He takes in all vision. He is the All Subtle, the **All Aware.** ❞
>
> Qur'an 6:102–103

> ❝ He is with you wherever you are. ❞
>
> Qur'an 57:4

Research activity

Muslims and Christians share a belief that God is the creator of all things. Find out more about how Muslims and Christians view God as the creator, and summarise the similarities and differences between their beliefs.

God is **beneficent**, the source of all goodness. His generosity is seen in his gift to humans of life on earth.

God's beneficence is linked to his mercy and compassion. In their daily prayers, Muslims begin by saying 'In the name of God, the Lord of Mercy, the Giver of Mercy'. This phrase is called the 'Bismillah' and Muslims say it to dedicate everything they do to God. They believe that God is **merciful**: he understands their suffering, cares for them and forgives them if they are truly sorry for any wrong they have done.

God acts with **fairness** and **justice**. He treats people equally and justly, and requires that they do the same to their fellow human beings. God will judge people in fairness on the Day of Judgement.

▲ God's beneficence is seen in his gift to humans of life on earth

One of the five roots of 'Usul ad-Din in Shi'a Islam is the justice of God (**Adalat**). Since God is perfect, he is just and therefore never acts unjustly to his creations. Also, God is not happy when people do wrong and will hold them to account. Humans have full responsibility for their own actions and God will judge them accordingly.

Activities

1. Make a list of the seven qualities of God and explain them in your own words. Try to learn the seven qualities off by heart.
2. How might the belief of Shi'a Islam in the justice of God (Adalat) affect people's attitudes towards suffering in life?
3. 'God cannot be both immanent and transcendent.' Evaluate this statement. Be sure to include more than one point of view, and refer to Muslim beliefs and teachings in your answer.

Extension activity

Look up the 99 names of Allah online. What do the names show Muslims believe about the nature of God?

⭐ Study tip

It is important to remember that although Muslims believe God is beyond human understanding, he does make himself known in ways people can partly understand.

Summary: You should now be able to explain Muslim beliefs about the nature of God.

7.4 Angels

■ What are angels?

Muslims believe that **angels** bring the word of God to the prophets or messengers of God. For Sunni Muslims the belief in angels is one of the six articles of faith.

Angels are part of the unseen world. They are supernatural beings, created by God from light.

> ❝ Praise be to God, Creator of the heavens and earth, who made angels messengers with two, three, four [pairs of] wings. ❞
>
> *Qur'an* 35:1

■ What do angels do?

Muslims believe that angels are able to receive God's words directly from him and pass them on to the prophets of God. They can do this because they are pure and sinless. Angels have no free will so they cannot do anything to displease God. They ceaselessly praise and worship God.

For Muslims, angels are involved in the lives of human beings from soon after conception until the moment of death. Some are guardian angels who take care of each person throughout their lives (Qur'an 13:11). Others are responsible for recording in a 'book of deeds' everything each person thinks, says or does (Qur'an 18:49). The book will be presented as evidence before God on the **Day of Judgement**.

According to tradition, the angel Israfil will blow a trumpet to announce the Day of Judgement. The angel of death and his helpers take people's souls to God (Qur'an 32:11). Angels also escort people into paradise and guard the gates of hell.

Muslims believe that God has given the angels the power to take on human form when appearing to people to whom he wishes to give a message. For example, angels appeared to Ibrahim (Abraham) and to Maryam (Mary) as men.

■ Jibril

Jibril (Gabriel) is the angel most familiar to Christians and Jews as well as to Muslims. He is an archangel (a special angel with higher status than others) who is a trusted messenger of God. Jibril was the angel who relayed the Qur'an to Muhammad from God.

Muslims believe that Jibril first appeared to Muhammad when the prophet was a child. In one story, Jibril, together with Mika'il, came to Muhammad during the night and purified his heart so that later in life Muhammad would be able to receive God's revelation. When Muhammad was 40 years old, Jibril returned to him in a blaze of light when he was meditating at Mount Hira. Jibril told Muhammad what

Objective
- Understand Muslim beliefs about angels.

Key terms
- **angels:** spiritual beings believed to act as messengers of God
- **Day of Judgement:** a time when the world will end and every soul will be judged by God, and either rewarded or punished
- **Jibril:** the Arabic name for Gabriel, the archangel who brought God's message to the prophets, particularly to Muhammad
- **Mika'il:** the Arabic name for Michael, the archangel of mercy who rewards good deeds and provides nourishment to people

Links
More about the role of angels after death can be found on pages 178–179.

> ❝ Each person has angels before him and behind, watching over him by God's command. ❞
>
> *Qur'an* 13:11

Chapter 7   Islam: beliefs and teachings

▲ An early handwritten copy of the Qur'an, which is a record of the message that Jibril brought to Muhammad from God

> The record of their deeds will be laid open and you will see the guilty, dismayed at what they contain, saying, 'Woe to us! What a record this is! It does not leave any deed, small or large, unaccounted for!' **They will find everything they ever did laid in front of them:** your Lord will not be unjust to anyone.
>
> Qur'an 18:49

God wanted him to do and inspired him with the revelations of the Qur'an. God continued to guide Muhammad throughout his entire life, often communicating through Jibril.

■ Mika'il

Mika'il (Michael) is another high-ranking archangel who is also known to Christians and Jews. Muslims believe that Mika'il is an angel of mercy. God has assigned Mika'il to reward righteous people for the good they do during their lives on earth. God has also given Mika'il responsibility for sending rain, thunder and lightning to earth.

The Qur'an mentions Mika'il when it warns that anyone who is an enemy of God's angels, Jibril and Mika'il, is also an enemy of God (Qur'an 2:98).

Muslims believe that Jibril and Mika'il have brought nourishment to human beings: Jibril brought the spiritual nourishment of God's words in the Qur'an, and Mika'il brings nourishment for the earth and human life through the rain.

▲ Mika'il is believed to bring life to earth through rain

Activities

1. Write down three Muslim beliefs about angels.
2. Explain the importance of Jibril for Muslims.

Research activities

1. Find out either Jewish or Christian beliefs about Mika'il (Michael) the archangel. How are they similar or different to Muslim beliefs?
2. Look up the visit of the angels to Ibrahim in Qur'an 51: 26–28. What made Ibrahim suspicious of his visitors?

Discussion activity

With a partner or in a small group, discuss how you would feel knowing that angels were recording every one of your thoughts, words and actions throughout your life. List the advantages and disadvantages.

⭐ Study tip

Try to list the different roles angels play in the lives of Muslims.

Summary

You should now understand Muslim beliefs about angels, including the roles they play in the lives of Muslims. You should know about the importance of Jibril and Mika'il in particular.

175

7.5 Predestination

Predestination in Islam

There are different ideas about **predestination** in Islam. Some Sunni Muslims believe that God has already determined everything that will happen in the universe. He has written down everything that will happen in a 'book of decrees'. God creates all things, including the actions of his creatures, so they must act according to his will.

> **Only what God has decreed will happen to us.** He is our Master: let the believers put their trust in God.
>
> *Qur'an 9:51*

This is linked to the Sunni belief in the supremacy of God's will. Some Sunni Muslims believe that because God's will is so powerful, he can determine everything that is going to happen. This view places greater emphasis on God's omniscience and less emphasis on human freedom, but it does not mean that people have no choice about how they behave.

Human freedom

Many Shi'a Muslims believe that God *knows* everything that is going to happen, but this does not mean that he *decides* what is going to happen. This means that people still have free will, so they can make their own choices.

Here is one way to think about it: a mother of a little boy knows her child very well, and knows in advance what he is going to do. If he is given a choice between a bowl of peas and an ice cream, she is very sure he will choose the ice cream. That's not to say the boy was forced to eat the ice cream – it was his choice. Another time he might be offered peas or spinach, and he might choose the peas then if he likes them better. Just because a mother might be able to predict what will happen does not mean the boy is not being given a real choice.

Or imagine you have travelled in time 100 years into the future. You spend some time observing what people are doing and writing down their actions. You take this written record back with you to the present year. Does this mean that the people you observed 100 years in the future suddenly have no free choice? No; those people are still deciding for themselves what they want to do – you just happen to have been able to see in advance what they are going to decide.

Another way to think about it is this: God is the creator of time so is not bound by it. For God there is no past, present and future – for him it is as if everything has already happened. Human events happen in time due to cause and effect or human free will, but God is outside time. Therefore many Muslims do not see any conflict between the supremacy of God's will, and human freedom to act freely and make choices.

Objectives

- Understand Muslim beliefs about predestination and human freedom.
- Know how these beliefs relate to the Day of Judgement.

Key term

- **predestination:** the idea that God knows or determines everything that will happen in the universe

▲ A mother knows what her child will choose

> **“** God does not change the condition of a people [for the worse] unless they change what is in themselves. **”**
>
> *Qur'an 13:11*

Links
To read more about the supremacy of God's will see page 169.

■ The Day of Judgement

We will learn more about the Day of Judgement in the next two pages. Muslims believe that on the Day of Judgement, God will judge humans according to everything they have done throughout their lives. Many Muslims believe that as God has given humans free will, they themselves are responsible for whether God rewards or punishes them for the choices they have made. This emphasises the point that even though God knows everything that is going to happen, people are still responsible for their actions and will be rewarded or punished because of them.

> **“** Those who believe, do good deeds, keep up the prayer, and pay the prescribed alms will have their reward with their Lord. **”**
>
> *Qur'an 2:277*

▲ Muslims believe that God will judge them on the choices they make in their lives, including how well they follow their faith

Activities

1. Explain the Muslim idea of predestination.
2. 'Predestination means that humans have no freedom.' Evaluate this statement. Be sure to include more than one point of view, and refer to Muslim beliefs and teachings in your answer.

Summary
You should now understand what Muslims believe about predestination and human freedom, and how this affects what happens on the Day of Judgement.

⭐ Study tip
Take care not to confuse the Muslim belief in predestination with the idea that people have already been chosen to go to heaven or hell regardless of their behaviour.

177

7.6 Life after death

Life after death

All religions believe that there will be a time of perfect peace and happiness that can be reached by living a good life on earth. For Muslims, death is not the end but the beginning of a new stage of life called **Akhirah**.

Many Muslims believe that after death the person still has a conscious existence in the grave. Here they will enter a state of waiting called 'barzakh', which means 'a barrier': no one can cross the barrier to amend things they have done wrong or warn the living. They are waiting for the Day of Judgement.

Muslims believe that as they lie in the grave, God sends two angels to question them about their faith. If people answer correctly, they will see the rewards to come, but if they deny God, they will see the punishments they will have to endure. Some believe the punishments start right away. Others think that people sleep in their graves until the end of the world when the Day of Judgement will come.

▲ Muslims believe they are questioned by angels while lying in the grave

The Day of Judgement and resurrection

Muslims believe that a day will come when God's purpose for the universe has been fulfilled. Only God knows when that will be. On this day the angel Israfil will blow a trumpet to announce that the world will be destroyed. The present world will be totally transformed into a new world (Akhirah) and then the angel Israfil will blow the trumpet again. Everyone who has ever lived will be raised from the dead (**resurrection**) and judged by God.

People will be given new bodies and the book of their life will be handed to them to read out. Just as human DNA is a sort of 'book' that dictates how the body develops, the book of deeds dictates how one lives in the

Objectives

- Consider Muslim beliefs about life after death.
- Understand the importance of human responsibility and accountability for Muslims.

Key terms

- **Akhirah:** everlasting life after death
- **resurrection:** rising from the dead or returning to life
- **heaven:** the state of eternal happiness in the presence of God; also called paradise
- **hell:** the state of total separation from God

Discussion activity

In small groups discuss what you think happens after death. Share your ideas with the class.

Activities

1. Explain what is meant by Akhirah.
2. Describe what happens after a person's death, according to Muslims.
3. Can God be both merciful and a judge who punishes? Explain your opinion.
4. 'If there is no life after death, there is no point in living a good life.' Evaluate this statement. Be sure to include more than one point of view, and refer to Muslim beliefs and teachings in your answer.

afterlife. If people are given it in their right hand they will go to **heaven**; if they receive it in their left hand they will go to **hell**.

On this day everyone will be faced with their good and bad deeds and realise what they have done. If they are believers who have shown sorrow for their failings, God will forgive them. God sorts the souls by making them cross the narrow 'Sirat Bridge' that spans the fires of hell. Good people are transported across the bridge quickly and enter heaven.

Heaven and hell

▲ *Paradise is often imagined as a beautiful garden*

Heaven is described in the Qur'an as gardens of happiness (Qur'an 22:23). It is the reward for faith and good deeds.

> On couches of well-woven cloth they will sit facing each other; everlasting youths will go round among them with glasses, flagons, and cups of a pure drink that causes no headache or intoxication; [there will be] any fruit they choose; the meat of any bird they like; and beautiful-eyed maidens like hidden pearls: **a reward for what they used to do.**
>
> *Qur'an 56:15–24*

The Qur'an describes hell as a place of fire and great torment. It is the punishment for those who reject God and do evil.

> They will dwell amid scorching wind and scalding water in the shadow of black smoke, neither cool nor refreshing.
>
> *Qur'an 56:42–44*

> Garments of fire will be tailored for those who disbelieve; scalding water will be poured over their heads, melting their insides as well as their skins; there will be iron crooks to restrain them; whenever, in their anguish, they try to escape, they will be pushed back in and told, 'Taste the suffering of the fire'.
>
> *Qur'an 22:19–22*

Muslims accept God's word in the Qur'an but have different interpretations of these verses. Some think they are exactly what heaven and hell are like. Others think they are just hints or suggestions because heaven and hell are beyond human understanding. Others think they are symbolic of the spiritual life a person will live after their death, either in the presence or absence of God.

The importance of belief in life after death

Belief in life after death is one of the six articles of faith for Sunni Muslims and one of the five roots of 'Usul ad-Din in Shi'a Islam. It is an important belief because it encourages human responsibility and accountability: the idea that people must be responsible for their own actions as they will be held accountable for them by God.

Belief in life after death urges people to avoid sin and do the right thing. It also satisfies a deep human need for justice. Sometimes it seems that some people get away with almost anything in life; the belief in God's judgement means that one day they will be held accountable and punished for their wrongdoing. For those good people who have suffered in life, there is something better to look forward to.

⭐ Study tip

You should know Muslim beliefs about life after death but also be able to explain (with reasons) your own viewpoint.

Summary

You should now understand Muslim beliefs about life after death (Akhirah) and their impact on the lives of believers.

7.7 Prophethood and Adam

■ What is prophethood?

Muslims believe that God has chosen many prophets to bring the message of Islam to people. This belief in the **prophets** and their importance is known as **Risalah**. **Prophethood** – when someone is made a prophet – is a gift given by God to help humankind understand his message.

The prophets are important for Muslims because they provided a method of communication between God and human beings. In order for Muslims to know how to live in the way God desires, it was necessary for instructions to be conveyed to people through the prophets. When humans forgot, misunderstood or changed God's message, he sent prophets to call people back to the right path.

Many Muslims believe there have been around 124,000 prophets, of which 25 are named in the Qur'an. The most important prophets are called messengers or apostles. These have been sent by God to every nation on earth.

Muslims believe that the prophets and messengers are important role models to follow, as they were good people who lived according to God's will. Some of the most important prophets in Islam include Adam, Ibrahim (Abraham), Musa (Moses), Isa (Jesus) and Muhammad.

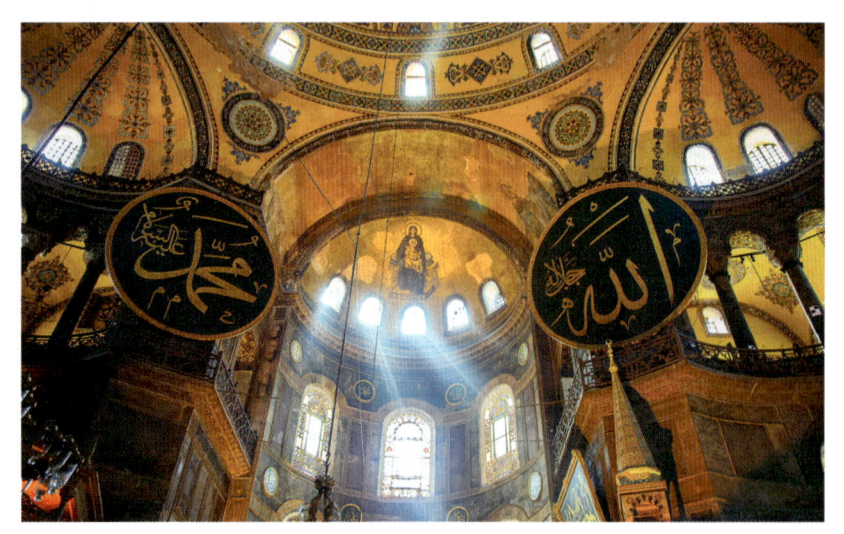

▲ Images of God or the prophets are not allowed in Islam, so mosques are often decorated instead with Arabic calligraphy. The Hagia Sophia museum in Istanbul, Turkey, was originally a church that was later converted to a mosque, so displays both Christian images and Arabic calligraphy.

■ Adam

Muslims believe that Adam was the first man on Earth and the first prophet of Islam. Created by God from the dust of the ground, he is regarded as the father of the human race and so is treated with reverence and great respect.

Objectives

- Understand the concept of prophethood (Risalah).
- Understand the role and importance of Adam as a prophet.

Key terms

- **prophet:** a person who proclaims the message of God
- **Risalah:** the belief that prophets are an important channel of communication between God and humans
- **prophethood:** when God makes someone a prophet to communicate his message to people
- **Iblis (Satan):** a spiritual being, created from fire, who was thrown out of paradise for refusing to bow to Adam

> **Every community is sent a messenger,** and when their messenger comes, they will be judged justly; they will not be wronged.
>
> Qur'an 10:47

Discussion activity

In small groups or in pairs, discuss the reasons why Muslims believe that prophets make good role models.

Chapter 7   Islam: beliefs and teachings

> One of His signs is that He created you from dust and – lo and behold! – you became human and scattered far and wide.
>
> *Qur'an 30:20*

> He first created man from clay … Then He moulded him; He breathed from His Spirit into him; He gave you hearing, sight, and minds.
>
> *Qur'an 32:7 & 9*

God gave Adam understanding and the names of all things:

> **He taught Adam all the names [of things],** then He showed them to the angels and said, 'Tell me the names of these if you truly [think you can].' They said, 'May You be glorified! We have knowledge only of what You have taught us. You are the All Knowing and All Wise.'
>
> *Qur'an 2:31–32*

God then asked Adam to tell the angels the names of some objects that they did not know but he did. God told the angels to bow down to Adam out of respect and admiration for his knowledge, but **Iblis** refused. His defiance resulted in him being thrown out of paradise and he vowed to tempt humans to sin against God.

In order to prevent Adam from being lonely, God created Hawwa (Eve) and they lived in the Garden of Bliss. There was one rule they had to obey: 'O Adam! Dwell thou and thy wife in the Garden, and enjoy (its good things) as ye wish: but approach not this tree, or ye run into harm and transgression' (Qur'an 7:19). Iblis deceived them into eating the fruit from the tree and they were thrown out of the garden. Their actions brought sin into the world. All humans would now be judged on the Day of Judgement.

Adam is important to Muslims as a prophet because God gave him understanding and Adam in turn passed on his knowledge to the rest of the human race through his descendants. He was the first person to learn to plant seeds, harvest crops and cook food. God revealed to him the food that Muslims are allowed to eat, how to repent for wrongdoing and how to bury the dead. Adam and Hawwa (Eve) had many children including Cain and Abel.

▲ Adam was the first person to learn how to plant seeds and harvest crops

Research activity

Isa (Jesus) is an important prophet in Islam who Muslims believe was sent by God to help guide them in their faith. There are a number of shared beliefs in Christianity and Islam about Jesus; for example, that Jesus was born of a virgin mother, performed miracles, and was a messenger of God. However, there are also a number of differences, including the Muslim belief that Jesus was fully human, so is not divine in nature and is not the Son of God.

Find out more about the differences and similarities between how Christians and Muslims view Jesus.

★ Study tip

Remember that it is important to learn the key definitions and be able to use them appropriately when answering questions.

Activities

1. Explain what is meant by prophethood (Risalah).
2. What was the main purpose of the prophets?
3. Name five of the most important prophets in Islam.
4. Why did Iblis get thrown out of heaven?
5. Explain the importance of the prophet Adam for Muslims.

Summary

You should now understand Muslim beliefs about prophethood (Risalah), and know the importance of the first prophet, Adam.

7.8 Ibrahim

■ Why is Ibrahim important?

> ❝ Who could be better in religion than those who direct themselves wholly to God, do good, and follow the religion of Abraham, who was true in faith? God took Abraham as a friend. ❞
>
> *Qur'an* 4:125

Ibrahim is the Arabic name of the prophet Abraham. Muslims believe that he fulfilled all the tests and commands given to him by God, and so was promised to be the father of all nations. They believe that the prophet Muhammad was descended from Ibrahim through his first son, Ishmael.

The Qur'an presents Ibrahim as a role model because of his obedience to God, his kindness and compassion, and his refusal to worship idols. (His close relative Aazar was a sculptor who carved statues and idols, which at the time were worshipped widely by the people of Arabia.)

Ibrahim (or Abraham) is an important religious figure in Islam, Christianity and Judaism; for this reason these three faiths are called 'Abrahamic religions'.

■ Ibrahim and idol worship

As a young man, Ibrahim was determined to discover who created the universe. He wanted his people to know who had made the stars, moon and sun, which many people worshipped in those days. He declared that he wished to submit to the creator of the universe. He declared his belief in one God (Allah) and was determined to stop idol worship.

One day when there was a big feast by the riverbank he saw his opportunity. As everyone left the town, he took an axe and destroyed all the idols in the temple except for the largest one. He left the axe tied around the neck of this statue. When the people returned they were angry and demanded to know what had happened. Ibrahim replied that the biggest statue had destroyed all the rest and that they could ask the statue if this was so. When the people objected that their idols could not speak, Ibrahim rebuked them, asking why they worshipped statues that cannot speak, hear, see or defend themselves.

The people were furious and demanded that Ibrahim be burned alive. An enormous fire was prepared on the orders of the king and Ibrahim was thrown into it. A miracle occurred and the fire only burned his chains and he walked out completely unscathed, much to the amazement of the people. As a result many began to follow Allah.

Objectives

- Understand the importance of the prophet Ibrahim.
- Know how Muslims remember Ibrahim through their actions today.

Key terms

- **Ka'aba:** the black, cube-shaped building in the centre of the Grand Mosque in Makkah (Mecca); the holiest place in Islam
- **Id-ul-Adha:** a Muslim festival that celebrates the prophet Ibrahim's willingness to sacrifice his son for God
- **Hajj:** the annual pilgrimage to Makkah (Mecca) that every Muslim should try to make at least once in their life

▲ *Pilgrims walking to Mina to throw stones at the Jamarat, representing the stones that Ibrahim threw at the devil*

Chapter 7 Islam: beliefs and teachings

■ The Ka'aba, Ishmael and Hajj pilgrimage

The **Ka'aba** is a small building in the centre of the Masjid al-Haram mosque in Makkah (Mecca). It is considered to be the house of God and the holiest place in Islam. Muslims believe that the original Ka'aba was built by Adam but it was destroyed by the flood at the time of Noah. With his son Ishmael, Ibrahim rebuilt it on the same site.

▲ *Pilgrims surround the Ka'aba in the Masjid al-Haram mosque in Makkah*

Many Muslims believe that Ibrahim had a dream in which God asked him to sacrifice his son to him. God did not take the boy although Ibrahim was willing to sacrifice him, showing his willingness to be obedient and that he was a man of faith. During the festival of **Id-ul-Adha** each year, Muslims slaughter an animal to remember Ibrahim's willingness to sacrifice his son.

Ibrahim is also remembered when Muslims go on the **Hajj** pilgrimage. For some Muslims this pilgrimage is a way to return to the perfection of Ibrahim's faith. At Mina, Muslims often throw stones at the Jamarat in the same way that Ibrahim threw stones at the devil that tempted him to disobey God. When pilgrims run between the two hills and drink the water of Zamzam, they remember the story of Ibrahim's wife Hagar. She searched desperately for water for her young son Ishmael and God rewarded her search with the gift of the well. Makkah is sometimes referred to as 'the city of Ibrahim.'

Ibrahim is important in Islam because he was a man of faith who denounced the worship of idols, rebuilt the Ka'aba and gave the message that there is only one God. In Arabia at that time people worshipped many gods and statues.

Activities

1. How is Ibrahim presented in the Qur'an?
2. Describe what Ibrahim did to stop idol worship.
3. How was Ibrahim to be punished for destroying statues and how did he escape?
4. What event does Id-ul-Adha remember?
5. Explain the importance of Ibrahim to Muslims.

Research activity

Use a library or the internet to find out about the story of Ibrahim and the four birds (Qur'an 2:260). What does the story show Muslims?

Links

To read more about the Id-ul-Adha festival see pages 206–207.

★ Study tip

It is important to be able to explain why Ibrahim is revered by Muslims as a prophet today.

Summary

You should now know why Ibrahim is important in the teachings of Islam.

183

7.9 Muhammad and the Imamate

■ Muhammad

Muslims believe that Muhammad received the final revelation of Islam from God. He is known as the last and greatest of the prophets.

> ❝ Muhammad is not the father of any one of you men; **he is God's Messenger and the seal of the prophets:** God knows everything. ❞
>
> Qur'an 33:40

Born around 570 CE in Makkah (Mecca), a city in present-day Saudi Arabia, Muhammad became an orphan at an early age and was brought up by his uncle Abu Talib. He became a merchant and gained a good reputation for honest dealing. When he was 25 he married his employer, a wealthy widow named Khadijah.

From an early age he was religious and on occasions he went to a cave in the mountains for meditation and prayer. There on Mount Hira in 610 CE he had an experience that changed his life. The angel Jibril (Gabriel) appeared to him with a message from God. This was his first revelation from God. For more than 20 years, Muhammad received further revelations and these were combined together to form the Qur'an, the Muslims' most important holy book.

Objectives
- Know the important events in Muhammad's life.
- Understand the importance of Muhammad for Muslims.
- Understand the role and significance of the Imamate in Shi'a Islam.

Key terms
- **Caliph:** a person considered to be a political and religious successor to the prophet Muhammad, and the leader of the Sunni Muslim community
- **Imam:** (1) a person who leads communal prayer (2) in Shi'a Islam, the title given to Ali and his successors
- **Imamate:** the divine appointment of the Imams

▲ Pilgrims at the cave on Mount Hira where the angel Jibril revealed the Qur'an to Muhammad

Muhammad's preaching

Three years after the first revelation, Muhammad began preaching the words he had received and he spent the remainder of his life proclaiming that God is One, and that complete surrender to God is the only acceptable way to live. He challenged the people of Makkah to give up cheating, drinking alcohol, gambling and idol worship. This was not a message the leaders of Makkah wanted to hear and he fled persecution with his followers to Madinah in 622 CE. This event is known as the Hijrah (departure), and marks the beginning of the Ummah (the worldwide family of Islam). The Islamic calendar starts from this date and the years are numbered AH (after Hijrah).

Muslims believe that before the Hijrah, Muhammad had an amazing experience which is recorded in the Qur'an. The angel Jibril took Muhammad on a miraculous journey to Jerusalem. In this event, known as the Night Journey, Muhammad was carried on a horse-like creature with wings, called al-Buraq. From Jerusalem he ascended into heaven, saw magnificent signs of God and spoke to prophets such as Isa (Jesus). He was told that people should pray five times every day.

In Madinah, Muhammad united the tribes and gathered an army of 10,000 Muslim converts. He marched on Makkah and conquered the city in the name of Allah. The 360 idols at the Kaaba were destroyed and Muhammad set about introducing Muslim law. Muhammad's teachings and practices (Sunnah), which are found in the Hadith and Sira texts, are still used as sources of Islamic law (Shariah). Muhammad won many battles but in 632 CE he returned to Madinah, became ill and died. He was buried in a simple grave.

■ The Imamate

When Muhammad died it wasn't clear who should succeed him. Muslims split into two groups, Sunni and Shi'a. Sunnis elected Abu Bakr as their first **Caliph**. Shi'as believe that Muhammad named his cousin and son-in-law, Ali ibn Abi Talib, as his successor – so Ali became the Shi'as' first **Imam**. For Shi'as, it was important that Ali took control because they believed the prophet had appointed him by divine instruction, and that leadership should follow the family line. When Ali died, his son became the Imam. Each Imam that followed was the son of the previous Imam (with the exception of Husayn ibn Ali, who was the brother of Hasan ibn Ali).

The Twelver branch of Shi'a Islam believes that there have been twelve Imams in total. The last of the Imams is Muhammad al-Mahdi, who they believe has been kept alive by God and hidden somewhere on earth, and who will return with Jesus Christ to bring justice and equality.

The Twelvers believe that the Imams not only rule justly but are able to maintain and interpret the Qur'an and Shariah law without fault. They believe that the receiving of God's law was completed through Muhammad, but that guiding people, and preserving and explaining the divine law, continued through the Imams. The **Imamate** is important because people need divine guidance to know how to live correctly. The Twelvers believe that, in each generation, there has always been an Imam who is the divinely appointed authority on all matters of faith and law, and is part of the Ahl al-Bayt (family of Muhammad).

▲ One of the largest mosques in the world now sits above Muhammad's grave

Activities

1. Describe what happened in 610 CE that changed the life of Muhammad.
2. What was the main message that Muhammad started preaching?
3. Describe what happened to Muhammad in 622 CE and explain its importance to Muslims.
4. Explain the importance of Muhammad for Muslims.
5. Explain the importance and significance of the Imamate for Shi'a Muslims.

Discussion activity

In small groups or in pairs discuss why Muhammad is often referred to as 'the seal of the prophets.' What do you think it means?

★ Study tip

Focus on learning an overview of the life of Muhammad, and his importance to Muslims as the last and greatest prophet.

Summary

You should now understand the importance of Muhammad for Muslims, and know why the Imamate is important in Shi'a Islam.

7.10 The holy books in Islam

■ The Qur'an

The importance of the Qur'an

Muslims believe that the Qur'an is the word of God, which was revealed to Muhammad via the angel Jibril over a period of around 22 years. It contains the foundation of every believer's faith, and is the most sacred text of Islam. It is believed to be an infallible source of authority for all matters of doctrine, practice and law. Islamic scholars regard the Qur'an as a literary work that is beautifully written in perfect Arabic. The original Qur'an is believed to be in heaven, so when Muslims read the Qur'an they believe that God's words are speaking directly to them.

> " This is the Scripture in which there is no doubt, containing guidance for those who are mindful of God. "
>
> *Qur'an 2:2*
>
> " This is truly a glorious Qur'an [written] on a preserved Tablet. "
>
> *Qur'an 85:21–22*

The name 'Qur'an' means 'the Recital', as Muhammad recited by heart each revelation that he received, and passed it on to his followers.

His followers memorised them and scribes wrote them down. After Muhammad died, his successor Abu Bakr commissioned an official copy to be compiled by Zayd ibn Thabit, one of Muhammad's companions. Soon converts of different nationalities started to read and write the Qur'an and some parts were in danger of being misread or miswritten. So Uthman, the third Caliph, commissioned a team of Muslim scholars to oversee the compilation of one official written version to be followed everywhere. They completed their work around 650 CE.

Objectives

- Understand how the Qur'an was revealed, and why it has authority in Islam.
- Know about the Torah, the Psalms, the Gospel and the Scrolls of Abraham.

Key terms

- **Torah:** the five books revealed by God to Moses
- **Psalms:** a holy book revealed by God to David
- **Gospel:** a holy book revealed by God to Jesus
- **Scrolls of Abraham:** a holy book revealed by God to Abraham

The contents of the Qur'an

Similar to the Christian Bible, the Qur'an contains a mixture of historical accounts and advice on how to follow God. There are 114 surahs (chapters) in total. It begins with a short surah called 'al Fatihah', which means 'The Opener'. This is a prayer to God for guidance, and is used in daily prayers. The remaining surahs are arranged approximately in order of length with the longest

▲ *Muslims often study the Qur'an in a mosque*

first (286 verses) and the shorter chapters last. The content is not arranged in the order it was revealed. Apart from the ninth surah, each chapter begins with the words 'In the name of God, the Lord of Mercy, the Giver of Mercy.'

Muslim children are encouraged to learn Arabic so they can read the Qur'an in its original language. Qur'anic recitation is highly valued as Muslims believe that it brings blessings. Those who are able to recite the whole Qur'an from memory are given the title 'hafiz'.

■ Other holy books

Muslims believe there are other holy books that have been revealed by God. These include the **Torah** (revealed to Moses), the **Psalms** (revealed to David), and the **Gospel** (revealed to Jesus). Some Muslims think that these books have been lost, while others believe they can be found in the Christian Bible (although the original text has been corrupted or distorted, so does not have the same authority as the Qur'an).

The Torah (Tawrat)

Muslims believe that the Torah was given to Moses (Musa). It is mentioned 18 times in the Qur'an. Some Muslims think the Torah is essentially the first five books in the Bible, but over time additions and subtractions have been made to the original text.

The Psalms (Zabur)

The Psalms were revealed to David, and are mentioned on three occasions in the Qur'an. Many Muslims believe these are similar to the Psalms in the Bible.

The Gospel (Injil)

The Gospel is mentioned in the Qur'an and it is believed that this refers to a book divinely revealed to Jesus (Isa). It is thought that this Gospel has been lost but that some of its message is still found in the Bible. The word Injil occurs 12 times in the Qur'an.

> ❝ We sent Jesus, son of Mary, in their footsteps, to confirm the Torah that had been sent before him: **We gave him the Gospel** with guidance, light, and confirmation of the Torah already revealed – a guide and lesson for those who take heed of God. ❞
>
> *Qur'an 5:46*

The **Scrolls of Abraham** (Ibrahim) are also referred to in the Qur'an, but these have been lost and no longer exist. They are thought to have been one of the earliest scriptures of Islam, which were revealed to Ibrahim.

Muslim children are encouraged to learn Arabic so they can read the Qur'an in its original language

Activities

1. Who revealed the Qur'an to Muhammad and how long did it take?
2. Why do you think it was necessary to have an official version of the Qur'an?
3. How many surahs (chapters) does the Qur'an contain? What order are they in?
4. Why does the Qur'an have more authority than any other holy books in Islam?

Extension activity

Use the internet or a library to find out more about the first encounter Muhammad had with the angel Jibril. Describe how you think Muhammad would have felt when the Qur'an was being revealed.

★ Study tip

Remember that for Muslims, the Gospel refers to something different to the four gospels in the Christian Bible (although some Muslims believe that parts of the Injil can still be found in the four gospels in the Bible).

Summary

You should now know why the Qur'an is important to Muslims. You should also know about the other holy books in Islam.

7 Assessment guidance

Key beliefs – summary

You should now be able to:

- ✓ explain Muslim beliefs in the Oneness of God (Tawhid) and the supremacy of God's will
- ✓ identify the six articles of faith in Sunni Islam, and the five roots of 'Usul ad-Din in Shi'a Islam
- ✓ explain the names and qualities that Muslims use to describe God, including immanent, transcendent, omnipotent, beneficent, and merciful
- ✓ explain the meaning of God's fairness and justice (Adalat in Shi'a Islam)
- ✓ explain Muslim beliefs about angels, including Jibril and Mika'il
- ✓ explain Muslim beliefs about predestination and human freedom, and their relationship to the Day of Judgement
- ✓ explain Muslim beliefs about life after death (Akhirah), resurrection, heaven and hell
- ✓ explain the importance of human responsibility and accountability in relation to life after death.

Authority – summary

You should now be able to:

- ✓ explain Muslim beliefs about prophethood (Risalah), and the roles and importance of Adam, Ibrahim and Muhammad
- ✓ explain the role and significance of the Imamate in Shi'a Islam
- ✓ identify the holy books in Islam and explain Muslim beliefs about their authority
- ✓ explain the significance of the Qur'an as revelation and as authority.

Sample student answer – the 4 mark question

1. Write an answer to the following question:

   Explain two ways in which a belief in the supremacy of God's will influences Muslims today. [4 marks]

2. Read the following sample student answer:

   "Often you hear Muslims say 'inshallah' which means 'God willing' after they promise to do something. For example, if they were going to a football match they might say to a friend that they would meet them there 'God willing'. That is because some Muslims believe that God is completely in charge of everything they do. If it is God's will that they go to the match, they will be there, otherwise they won't. They believe that even the bad things that happen in life are part of God's will. This influences them because it means they have to accept what God has planned for them even if it is painful or unpleasant."

3. With a partner, discuss the sample answer. Is the focus of the answer correct? Is anything missing from the answer? How do you think it could be improved?

4. What mark (out of 4) would you give this answer? Look at the mark scheme in the Introduction (AO1). What are the reasons for the mark you have given?

5. Now swap your answer with your partner's and mark each other's responses. What mark (out of 4) would you give the response? Refer to the mark scheme and give reasons for the mark you award.

Sample student answer – the 5 mark question

1. Write an answer to the following question:

   Explain two Muslim teachings about life after death.
   Refer to scripture or sacred writings in your answer. **[5 marks]**

2. Read the following sample student answer:

   "Muslims believe that when you die you are judged by God. If you are good you go to heaven and if you are bad you go to hell. You have to wait for the Day of Judgement. The state of waiting is called 'barzakh'. Some angels question you about your faith. If you get the answers right they will let you into heaven. If you get the answers wrong you will be condemned to punishment in hell."

3. With a partner, discuss the sample answer. It makes some good points but it fails to do something which is important. How do you think the answer could be improved?

4. What mark (out of 5) would you give this answer? Look at the mark scheme in the Introduction (AO1). What are the reasons for the mark you have given?

5. Now swap your answer with your partner's and mark each other's responses. What mark (out of 5) would you give the response? Refer to the mark scheme and give reasons for the mark you award.

Practice questions

1. Which one of the following best describes the meaning of Risalah?

   A) Tawhid   B) Justice   C) Prophethood   D) Predestination **[1 mark]**

2. Name two Muslim holy books. **[2 marks]**

3. Explain two ways in which a belief in prophethood influences Muslims today. **[4 marks]**

4. Explain two Muslim teachings about predestination.

   Refer to scripture or sacred text in your answer. **[5 marks]**

5. 'The best way of understanding God is to describe God as transcendent.'

   Evaluate this statement. In your answer you should:
   - give reasoned arguments in support of this statement
   - give reasoned arguments to support a different point of view
   - refer to the teaching of Islam
   - reach a justified conclusion. **[12 marks]**

> ⭐ **Study tip**
> Read the statement carefully and make sure that your answer is fully focused on what it is saying. Check that you have followed the guidance in the bullet points under the statement.

8 Islam: practices

8.1 The Five Pillars, the Ten Obligatory Acts and the Shahadah

■ The Five Pillars

The Five Pillars are central to Muslim practices, and they have a great impact on daily life. Muslims believe that they support the main principles and beliefs of Islam, just as pillars are used to support a building. They can be seen as the key to living a perfect Muslim life. They help to give Muslims an identity as one community who share a faith, and enable them to show their obedience and dedication to God.

The Five Pillars are:

1. Shahadah – the declaration of faith.
2. Salah – prayer.
3. Zakah – charitable giving.
4. Sawm – fasting.
5. Hajj – pilgrimage.

▲ *Pillars being used to support a mosque in Iran*

■ The Ten Obligatory Acts in Shi'a Islam

For Muslims who follow Twelver Shi'a Islam, there are ten duties called **the Ten Obligatory Acts** (also known as the Ancillaries of the Faith). These include all the Five Pillars except Shahadah (which is covered by some of the additional acts). They are:

1. Salah – prayer.
2. Sawm – fasting.
3. Zakah – charitable giving.
4. Khums – a 20 per cent tax on income once all expenses are deducted. Half goes to charity and half goes to Shi'a religious leaders.
5. Hajj – pilgrimage.
6. Jihad – the struggle to maintain the faith and defend Islam. For many Muslims this means the struggle to live by their faith as well as possible, for example by obeying the Five Pillars, contributing to the community or doing voluntary work.

Objectives
- Know the Five Pillars and the Ten Obligatory Acts.
- Understand the importance of the Shahadah.

Key terms
- **the Five Pillars:** the five most important duties for all Muslims: to believe, to pray, to give to charity, to fast and to go on pilgrimage
- **the Ten Obligatory Acts:** ten important duties for Shi'a Muslims, which include the Five Pillars
- **Shahadah:** the Muslim declaration of faith

Discussion activity
If you wanted to develop actions or duties for a group of people to give them a distinct identity, and help them to show obedience and dedication to a higher power, what would you do? Discuss this with a small group and give explanations to support your suggestions.

Links
Twelver Shi'a Islam is explained in more detail on page 185.

7. Amr-bil-Maruf – encouraging people to do what is good.
8. Nahi Anil Munkar – discouraging people from doing what is wrong.
9. Tawallah – to be loving towards the friends of God, including Muhammad and the Imams.
10. Tabarra – disassociating from the enemies of God.

Shahadah

The basic belief of Islam is expressed in the Shahadah. In Arabic it is 'La ilaha illa Allah wa – Muhammad rasul Allah', which in English translates to 'There is no God but Allah and Muhammad is the Prophet of Allah'. Sincerely reciting this statement in front of Muslim witnesses is the only requirement for joining the Muslim community. It is recited many times during a lifetime. It is said when a baby is born, so the first thing they hear is this basic belief of the faith they are born into. It is also included in the daily prayers. If possible, it becomes the last words of a Muslim before they die.

▲ The national flag of Saudi Arabia includes the Shahadah

As well as being the first of the Five Pillars, the Shahadah also provides the foundation for the other four. These four pillars are actions that put a Muslim's faith, expressed in the Shahadah, into practice. (This also applies to the additional five Obligatory Acts found in Shi'a Islam.)

The Shahadah in Shi'a Islam

Many Shi'a Muslims add an extra phrase to the Shahadah: 'and Ali is the friend of God'. This demonstrates their belief that Ali, Muhammad's cousin and son-in-law, was the true successor of Muhammad, and that only he and his descendants know the true meaning of the revelation given to Muhammad.

Activities

1. Draw a diagram to show that the Five Pillars of Islam support the Muslim faith. Include the names of the pillars within your diagram.
2. Explain how the Ten Obligatory Acts differ from the Five Pillars. What extra duties do they involve?
3. Explain what Shi'a Muslims add to the Shahadah.

Research activity

When do Muslims use the Shahadah? Try to find as many times and ways as possible.

Links

The Five Pillars are discussed in more detail on the following pages.

⭐ Study tip

It is important to learn both the Arabic and English terms for the Five Pillars.

Summary

You should now know what the Five Pillars and the Ten Obligatory Acts are. You should also know what the Shahadah means and be able to explain when it is used in a Muslim's life.

8.2 Salah: the daily prayers (1)

■ The times of prayer

To observe the second pillar of Islam (**salah**), Sunni Muslims are required to pray at five set times during the day. The times are worked out from the times of sunrise and sunset, so they change slightly each day. Muslims refer to prayer timetables based on where they are in the world so they know that the times are right.

The times of the five prayers are:

Fajr	Just before sunrise
Zuhr	Just after midday
Asr	Afternoon
Maghrib	Just after sunset
Isha	Night

The first prayer is earlier in the summer than the winter because sunrise is earlier. This places demands upon Muslims but is all part of the self-discipline required in submitting themselves to God.

Shi'a Muslims combine the midday and afternoon prayers, and the sunset and night prayers, so they pray three times a day.

▲ A digital prayer timetable in a mosque

■ How Muslims prepare for prayer

It is important that Muslims are spiritually clean before they pray. This is achieved by ritual washing (or ablution) called **wudu**. Muslims follow detailed instructions in order to make sure that they do this properly. These are outlined in the Qur'an:

Objectives
- Know when Muslims pray and how they prepare for prayer.
- Understand the importance of facing Makkah when praying.
- Know how prayer happens inside a mosque.

Key terms
- **salah:** prayer with and in worship of God, performed under conditions set by the prophet Muhammad
- **wudu:** ritual washing before prayer
- **mihrab:** a niche in a wall that indicates the direction of Makkah
- **qiblah wall:** the wall in a mosque that contains the mihrab

Discussion activity
With a partner, discuss any benefits you think Muslims would get from regular prayer. Write down any conclusions you come to.

Research activity
Without downloading it, search for a mobile phone app that tells the times for prayer. Read the supporting information about the app and any reviews that users have posted.

> "You who believe, when you are about to pray, wash your faces and your hands up to the elbows, wipe your heads, wash your feet up to the ankles and, if required, wash your whole body."
>
> *Qur'an* 5:6

Mosques have two special rooms set aside for washing, one for men and one for women. Washing is done under running water rather than using a basin. If water is not available, for example in a desert, a dry form of washing is allowed using sand or dust. This illustrates that it is not physical cleanliness that is required but spiritual cleanliness, and wudu is a form of spiritual preparation or purification to allow Muslims to focus fully on God in their prayers.

The direction of prayer

It is very important that while praying, Muslims face the holy city of Makkah. This means that all Muslims are physically and mentally focusing on one place associated with God, in the same way that all Muslims should focus every part of their lives on God. If the prayers are taking place in a mosque, this is easy to achieve. All mosques have a **mihrab**. This is a semi-circular niche built into the **qiblah wall**, which shows the exact direction of Makkah from the mosque. Muslims face this in order to pray.

If prayer is taking place anywhere outside a mosque, a special compass is used to show the direction of Makkah. This is sometimes a part of the mat that Muslims kneel on when they pray.

Prayer inside a mosque

Many mosques have special carpets that look like separate rows of prayer mats, facing the mihrab. This gives each person a suitable space to carry out their prayers properly.

The prayers are led by an imam who is positioned in front of the congregation but also facing the mihrab. Men and women pray at the same time but in separate spaces; they are either separated by a partition or curtain or they pray in separate rooms. It is normal for the voice of the imam in the men's prayer room to be broadcast in the women's prayer room at the same time, so he can lead their prayers along with the men's.

▲ *A washroom in a mosque in Istanbul, Turkey*

▲ *A mihrab in a mosque in Cairo, Egypt*

⭐ Study tip

Do not confuse the imam with the twelve Imams in Shi'a Islam. The 'imam' is a title given to the person who leads the prayers in a mosque, while the twelve Imams are specific religious leaders and descendants of Muhammad.

Activities

1. Explain when Muslims are expected to pray and how they know when these times are.
2. Why do you think Muslims organise their prayers in such a way?
3. What is wudu? Explain why Muslims believe it is important.
4. Why do Muslims have to face Makkah in order to pray?
5. Explain how the layout of a mosque makes it easier for Muslims to pray correctly.

Summary

You should now know how Muslims pray, and begin to understand why prayer forms a significant part of Muslim life.

8.3 Salah: the daily prayers (2)

The rak'ah

> So woe to those who pray but are heedless of their prayer.
>
> *Qur'an* 107:4–5

The daily prayers are made up of a number of **rak'ah**. This is a set sequence of actions and **recitations**. For example, the morning prayer is made up of two rak'ah and the night prayer is made up of four rak'ah. The rak'ah changes slightly depending on which prayer it is used in, and whereabouts it occurs in the overall sequence, but it includes the following basic actions (all the recitations are said in Arabic):

- While standing, Muslims recite the first chapter from the Qur'an.
- While bowing, Muslims say in Arabic 'Glory be to my Lord who is the very greatest' three times. The bowing position shows they believe God to be great.
- Returning to an upright position, they make a recitation praising God.
- They then kneel with their forehead, nose, hands, knees and toes touching the floor. This is called **prostration** and shows complete obedience to God. (Shi'a Muslims rest their heads against a clay tablet or piece of wood when they prostrate, while Sunni Muslims touch their heads directly against the floor.) They recite 'How perfect is my Lord the most high'.
- Muslims then sit while reciting 'God is the greatest', and after pausing for a few seconds prostrate themselves once more while repeating 'God is the greatest'.

Once the required number of rak'ah is completed, in a kneeling position Muslims turn their face to the right and then to the left, reciting in Arabic 'Peace be upon you, and the mercy and blessings of God'.

▲ *Muslims praying at a mosque in Istanbul, Turkey*

Objectives

- Have an overview of the movements and recitations used in prayer.
- Know what makes the Jummah prayer different.
- Understand the importance of prayer for Muslims.

Key terms

- **rak'ah:** a sequence of movements in ritual prayer
- **recitation:** repeating a passage of text from memory
- **prostration:** kneeling with the forehead, nose, hands, knees and toes touching the floor, in submission to God
- **Jummah prayer:** a weekly communal prayer performed after midday on Friday, which includes a sermon

Research activity

Use the internet to watch a video of a Muslim performing a rak'ah.

Personal prayers (Du'a prayers) may be added on to the end of the final rak'ah. These do not have to be in Arabic and do not follow any set form. Muslims believe that God answers their prayers in the way that God knows is best for them.

■ Jummah prayer

The midday prayer every Friday is considered to be special, and is called the **Jummah prayer**. All male Muslims are expected to attend a mosque for this prayer, and women may do so if they wish. Once the prayer is complete, the imam will deliver a sermon that reminds Muslims of their obligations and duties to God. Although Friday is not a day of rest, Muslims must leave their work or close their businesses in order to attend the Jummah prayer, and then return to work afterwards.

■ Prayer at home

Muslims are allowed to pray at home. They must perform wudu before prayer, but they do not need a special room in their home to pray. Provided the room is clean, it is suitable. Many Muslims will use a prayer mat, which they position so it is facing Makkah, in the same way as it would in a mosque. Muslim women in particular can find it useful to pray at home, especially if they have children to look after.

■ The significance of prayer

Prayer has its own importance as one of the Five Pillars. However, for Muslims it is more than that – it is what God has commanded them to do. Prayer creates a greater awareness of God, which in turn motivates them to do God's will.

Prayer also unites Muslims worldwide because they all pray in the same way. A Muslim can go into any mosque anywhere in the world and be able to participate with fellow Muslims. In addition, reciting from the Qur'an during the prayers reminds Muslims of its importance. The actions of bowing and prostrating remind them that God is greater and more important than they are.

As the most significant instruction in the Qur'an, prayer is the most important aspect of worship for all Muslims. However, some Muslims may emphasise its ritualistic aspects while others point out the spiritual quality with which it should be performed. Many Muslims believe that a prayer performed without reflection, understanding and humility of the heart gives little benefit to the worshipper.

> ❝ Your Lord says, 'Call on Me and I will answer you'. ❞
>
> Qur'an 40:60

> ❝ Believers! When the call to prayer is made on the day of congregation, hurry towards the reminder of God and leave off your trading. ❞
>
> Qur'an 62:9

▲ A Muslim woman praying at home

⭐ Study tip

Remember you should only put quotation marks around a quote if you are writing it out exactly. If you are putting the quote into your own words or summarising it, you do not need to use quotation marks.

Summary

You should now know what a rak'ah is, and what type of actions and words it contains. You should also know what the Jummah prayer is, and understand why prayer is important to Muslims.

Activities

1. Explain what Muslims do when they pray.
2. Do you think having a set sequence for prayer is a good idea? Explain your opinion.
3. Why do you think Muslims pray in Arabic rather than English?
4. If Muslims are allowed to pray at home, why do you think many go to a mosque to pray?
5. Explain how a Muslim might answer the question: 'Why do you pray?'

8.4 Sawm: fasting during Ramadan

■ Ramadan

Ramadan is the ninth month of the Islamic calendar and for Muslims, the most important. They believe it was during Ramadan that the Qur'an started to be revealed to Muhammad. Many Muslims will recite the whole of the Qur'an, in daily sections, over the 30 days of Ramadan. The daily readings from the Qur'an help Muslims to remember its teachings and its importance in their lives.

During the month of Ramadan, Muslims focus on **fasting** (sawm), charity and pleasing God.

■ Fasting

Ramadan is known as the month of fasting because Muslims fast during daylight hours for the whole month, going without food or drink. They get up every day before sunrise in order to eat and drink enough to keep them going until sunset. Then the fast is broken and Muslims are allowed to eat until sunrise the next day. The evening meal is often shared with family and friends, then followed with extra prayers and readings from the Qur'an.

The command to fast can be found in the Qur'an, and it has been obligatory for Muslims to fast during Ramadan since the seventh century.

For Muslims, fasting is not just to do with food and drink; smoking and sex are also forbidden during daylight hours. Muslims who live in non-Muslim countries may find this month particularly difficult, since there can be more temptation to break the fast. For example, in the UK it can be very difficult for those in school to resist temptation or participate in PE lessons without being able to drink to rehydrate themselves. Many schools at break and lunchtimes provide special rooms during Ramadan, where Muslims students can go so that they may avoid the temptation to eat or drink.

▲ Many Muslims break their fast at the end of each day during Ramadan by drinking water and eating dates

The whole focus during the month of Ramadan is on God, for which purity of thought is required in order to cleanse the soul and free it from harm. Fasting requires considerable self-discipline, but it allows Muslims to show they can sacrifice their physical needs as evidence of their submission to God.

Exceptions to fasting

Not all Muslims have to fast during Ramadan, although those excused from fasting are supposed to make up for it later if they can. People

Objectives

- Know the origins, duties, benefits and exceptions to fasting during Ramadan.
- Understand why the Night of Power is important.

Key terms

- **Ramadan:** the ninth month of the Muslim calendar, during which Muslims have to fast from dusk to sunset
- **fasting:** not eating or drinking for a certain length of time, usually for a religious reason
- **the Night of Power:** (1) the night when the first revelation of the Qur'an was made to Muhammad (2) the festival that marks the start of God's revelation to Muhammad

Links

At the end of Ramadan, Muslims celebrate the festival of Id-ul-Fitr. To learn about this see page 206.

> ❝ It was in the month of Ramadan that the Qur'an was revealed as guidance for mankind … So any one of you who is present that month should fast, and anyone who is ill or on a journey should make up for the lost days by fasting on other days later. ❞
>
> *Qur'an* 2:18

196

can be excused for health reasons – for example pregnant women, mothers nursing babies, children, and those who are ill do not have to fast. Some children, fast for a shorter length of time to help train themselves.

Charity

One of the positive elements to feeling hungry during the day is that it serves as a reminder that the poor feel that way all the time if they cannot afford to eat properly. This greater awareness inspires many Muslims to find ways to help the poor. This may include inviting the poor to share their meal that breaks the fast at sunset. Many Muslims choose to pay Zakah during Ramadan.

■ The Night of Power

The Night of Power is an important festival that marks the beginning of God's revelation to Muhammad. The exact date this happened is not agreed on, but it is believed to be one of the odd-numbered dates in the second half of Ramadan. The first verses of the Qur'an that were revealed to Muhammad on this night (96:1–5) describe how the angel Jibril instructed him to start reading:

> Read! In the name of your Lord who created: He created man from a clinging form [a blood clot]. Read! Your Lord is the Most Bountiful One who taught by [means of] the pen, who taught man what he did not know.
>
> *Qur'an 96:1–5*

The night's importance is explained in the Qur'an:

> What will explain to you what that Night of Glory is? The Night of Glory is better than a thousand months.
>
> *Qur'an 97:2–3*

This means that observing the Night of Power gives Muslims the benefits of worshipping for a thousand months. Because of this, Muslims try to keep awake throughout the night on each of the possible dates, devoting themselves to prayers and studying the Qur'an.

Activities

1. Explain why the Qur'an is a major focus in the observance of Ramadan.
2. Explain the rules that Muslims must obey to ensure they fast properly.
3. How does fasting help Muslims to focus on the poor?
4. Explain why some Muslims are excused from fasting.
5. 'It is easier to observe Ramadan in a Muslim country than it is in the UK.' Evaluate this statement. Be sure to include more than one point of view, and refer to Muslim beliefs and teachings in your answer.
6. Explain how the Night of Power changes the routine of many Muslims during Ramadan.

★ Study tip

Although Ramadan is best known as a time of fasting, don't forget it involves other important elements too.

Links

For more about Zakah see pages 198–199.

Discussion activity

With a partner, share your ideas about the advantages and disadvantages of fasting in the daylight hours for a month.

▲ Studying the Qur'an is an important part of Ramadan

Summary

You should now understand how and why Muslims change their actions and behaviour during Ramadan.

8.5 Zakah: almsgiving

What is Zakah?

The third pillar of Islam is **Zakah**. This means giving alms (giving money to the poor). For Muslims who have enough savings, it is compulsory to give 2.5 per cent of those savings every year to help the poor. Many Muslims will work out how much they owe and give the money at the end of Ramadan.

By giving Zakah, Muslims are acknowledging that everything they own comes from God and belongs to him, and that they should use their wealth to remember God and give to those in need. It frees people from desire, and teaches self-discipline and honesty.

Zakah literally means to purify or to cleanse. Muslims believe that giving Zakah helps to purify the soul, removing selfishness and greed.

The origins of Zakah

The giving of Zakah began as a response to an instruction in the Qur'an:

> They ask you [Prophet] what they should give. Say, 'Whatever you give should be for parents, close relatives, orphans, the needy, and travellers. **God is well aware of whatever good you do.'**
>
> *Qur'an 2:215*

Objectives

- Know the origins of Zakah.
- Understand how and why Zakah is given, and who benefits from it.
- Understand the Shi'a practice of Khums.

Key terms

- **Zakah:** purification of wealth by giving 2.5 per cent of savings each year to the poor
- **Sadaqah:** good actions or voluntary payments that are undertaken for charitable reasons
- **Khums:** a 20 per cent tax paid by Shi'a Muslims on their excess income

The Qur'an does not specify how much should be given in Zakah; the figure of 2.5 per cent of savings was worked out at a later date by Muslim scholars.

How Zakah is given and who receives it

Only Muslims with savings greater than a certain figure (known as the nisab) are required to give Zakah. The nisab is either worked out as the value of 87 grams of gold, which in 2015 was around £2200, or 612 grams of silver, which in 2015 was around £200. Muslims can choose which figure they use and therefore how much they pay, although using the gold nisab is more common.

As an example, this means that a Muslim with savings of £1000 would not be required to give Zakah if they were using the gold nisab, whereas a Muslim with savings of £4000 would pay £100 (2.5 per cent of £4000).

▲ *Zakah is calculated as 2.5 per cent of savings*

Zakah can be donated directly to a charity such as Islamic Relief or Muslim Aid. Alternatively, it can be put into a collection box in the mosque to be distributed among the poor. The Qur'an makes it clear who should receive Zakah:

Chapter 8 Islam: practices

> **Alms are meant only for the poor, the needy,** those who administer them, those whose hearts need winning over, to free slaves and help those in debt, for God's cause, and for travellers in need.
>
> *Qur'an 9:60*

In addition to giving Zakah, Muslims are encouraged to voluntarily give their money and time to charity at any point of the year. This is called **Sadaqah**.

▲ *Zakah can be given to Islamic Relief to support projects such as this one in Ethiopia*

■ The significance of Zakah

- In giving Zakah, Muslims are fulfilling a duty imposed by God. The Qur'an makes it clear that giving Zakah is a sign of a true Muslim.
- Paying Zakah gives Muslims a good attitude towards money. They learn to share it and not be greedy with it.
- Zakah strengthens communities by making the rich support the poor.
- Zakah links well with salah (prayer). Prayers should make Muslims feel concern for others, and Zakah puts this concern into action.

■ Khums

Khums is an important part of Muslim practice in Shi'a Islam in addition to giving Zakah. It literally means 'fifth'. Originally it referred to a requirement for Muslims to donate 20 per cent of the spoils of war to the leader representing the state of Islam. Today, it refers to the excess income or earnings that a Shi'a Muslim makes, and is still set at 20 per cent. Half of the money collected as Khums goes to Shi'a religious leaders, to be spent on behalf of God on things considered necessary for religious matters, while the rest is given to charity or the poor.

Research activity

Find out about some projects that Islamic Relief and/or Muslim Aid are involved in.

Discussion activities

1. Should Shi'a Muslims in the UK be expected to give Khums as well as paying UK taxes? Discuss this with a partner and write down your conclusions, with reasons.
2. Four bullet points are given above on the significance of Zakah. Which of these do you think is the most important reason to give Zakah? Discuss with a partner.

Activities

1. Explain what Zakah is, and how it is calculated.
2. What do you think the obligation to give Zakah teaches Muslims?
3. How does Sadaqah differ to Zakah?

⭐ Study tip

Try to learn and remember the differences between Zakah, Sadaqah and Khums.

Summary

You should now understand the practice of Zakah, including how and why it is given. You should also know about Khums.

8.6 Hajj: pilgrimage (1)

What is Hajj?

A **pilgrimage** is a journey made for religious reasons. **Hajj**, the fifth pillar of Islam, is a pilgrimage that should be made at least once during a Muslim's lifetime, provided they are healthy and wealthy enough to do so. Some communities will provide financial support for a poor Muslim to make the pilgrimage because it is a religious obligation and not a holiday.

Hajj starts and ends in the holy city of Makkah (Mecca) in Saudi Arabia. It always takes place from the 8th to the 12th of Dhul-Hijjah, which is the last month of the Islamic calendar. During this time, around 3 million Muslims take part in the pilgrimage.

There are several references to Hajj in the Qur'an, for example:

> " Pilgrimage to the House is a duty owed to God by people who are able to undertake it. "
>
> *Qur'an* 3:97

The origins of Hajj

Muslims believe that around 4000 years ago, the prophet Ibrahim was told by God to take his wife Hajira and son Ishmael to Arabia. He was then told to leave Hajira and Ishmael on their own with some supplies of food and water. Within a few days, the supplies ran out and Hajira and Ishmael were suffering from hunger and dehydration.

Looking for help, Hajira ran up and down two hills called Safa and Marwah before collapsing beside her son. She prayed to God for help. Ishmael struck his foot on the ground, which caused water to gush up from the earth. They traded some of this water for food and other supplies. When Ibrahim returned he was told by God to build a shrine dedicated to him. This became the **Ka'aba**. Ibrahim was told to make the Ka'aba a pure place of worship and to call people to perform Hajj there.

Many centuries later, the city of Makkah was established nearby using the water from Ishmael's well (the well of Zamzam). Over the years, the people of Makkah became used to worshipping idols, many of which were stored in the Ka'aba. In 628 CE, Muhammad journeyed from Madinah to Makkah with a large group of Muslims in what is now seen as the first pilgrimage in Islam. In 630 CE, the Ka'aba was returned to the worship of God alone.

It is this story that is reflected in Hajj.

Objectives

- Understand the importance of Hajj.
- Understand the origins of Hajj and know how the pilgrimage begins.

Key terms

- **pilgrimage:** a journey by a believer to a holy site for religious reasons; an act of worship and devotion
- **Hajj:** the annual pilgrimage to Makkah (Mecca) that every Muslim should try to make at least once in their life
- **Ka'aba:** the black, cube-shaped building in the centre of the Grand Mosque in Makkah (Mecca); the holiest place in Islam

▲ *Hajj begins with pilgrims circling the Ka'aba in the Masjid al-Haram (Grand Mosque) in Makkah*

Activities

1. What is a pilgrimage?
2. In your own words, tell the story that explains how Hajj originated.
3. Explain why Makkah has become such an important city for Muslims.

How Hajj is performed

Entering a state of Ihram

Before Hajj begins, pilgrims must enter a sacred state called Ihram. This involves performing ritual washing, praying and putting on Ihram clothing. For men this is two sheets of white cloth that they wrap around their body. The white cloth is a sign of equality and purity. Women wear clothes of a single colour that cover the whole of their body apart from their face.

They are now ready for the pilgrimage to begin.

Circling the Ka'aba

Hajj begins in Makkah at the Ka'aba. Pilgrims circle the Ka'aba in an anti-clockwise direction seven times. If possible, they touch the black stone built into the Ka'aba or raise their hand to acknowledge it. This stone is revered by Muslims as an ancient Islamic relic; it is considered by some to be the only surviving stone from the original Ka'aba built by Ibrahim. However, the origins of the stone are unclear. Some believe it is a meteorite; others believe it was given by God to Adam to erase his sin and allow him a path into heaven; others believe it was brought from a nearby mountain by the archangel Jibril, or that it came from paradise.

As Muslims circle the Ka'aba they recite the pilgrims' prayer: 'Here I am. Oh Lord, at your service. Praise and blessings to you.'

Travelling to Arafat

The crowd then walks along a covered walkway linking the hills of Safa and Marwah, which feature in the story of Ibrahim, Hajira and Ishmael. After completing seven circuits of this walk they return to the Ka'aba to collect bottles of water from the well of Zamzam.

Muslims then face the prospect of a 13 mile walk or ride to Arafat, possibly in high temperatures that many are not used to. Halfway there they stop for the night at Mina, where they pray and read the Qur'an.

▲ Thousands of tents are provided at Mina for pilgrims to sleep in

Discussion activity

1. With a partner discuss how Ihram is a sign of purity and equality.
2. While on Hajj, pilgrims must not shave, cut their nails, wear scent, argue or have sex. Why do you think this is the case?

> Safa and Marwa are among the rites of God, so for those who make major or minor pilgrimage to the House it is no offence to circulate between the two.
>
> Qur'an 2:158

★ Study tip

Try to find a map or diagram online that shows the different places pilgrims visit on Hajj, as this will help you to understand what happens on the pilgrimage.

Summary

You should now understand the significance of Hajj and know how it originated. You should also be able to explain how the pilgrimage begins.

8.7 Hajj: pilgrimage (2)

How Hajj is performed (continued)

Standing at Arafat

At dawn of the 9th day of Dhul-Hijjah, pilgrims walk from Mina to Arafat, where Muhammad preached his last sermon. Here they spend the whole afternoon praying under the hot summer sun. The heat of the sun is a reminder of what the Day of Judgement will be like. Some Muslims spend the whole afternoon standing to show the depth of their faith, and the afternoon is sometimes called 'the standing at Arafat'. The authorities provide water supplies and toilets, just for this one day in the year.

Islam teaches that God will forgive the sins of all who complete the standing at Arafat, but only if they know they have done wrong, are determined not to do wrong again, and are prepared to try to make up for their sins.

Throwing pebbles at Mina

At the end of the day, Muslims walk to Muzdalifah, where they spend the night. On the way, they collect 49 small pebbles to be used next day at Mina. At Mina, there are three stone walls called the Jamarat. These walls represent the devil and temptation. On the 10th of Dhul-Hijjah, pilgrims throw the pebbles they have collected at the walls to show that they reject evil.

Many pilgrims then sacrifice an animal (a sheep, cow, camel or goat). This is repeated throughout the world as part of the celebration of Id-ul-Adha. The leftover meat that cannot be eaten is frozen or canned and given to the poor. To follow teachings in the Qur'an and the example of Muhammad, pilgrims then cut their hair. Women normally just cut off a small lock of their hair while men shave their heads.

▲ *Pilgrims throwing pebbles at the Jamarat in Mina*

Returning to Makkah

The next day, pilgrims return to Makkah to circle the Ka'aba seven more times. They then return to Mina to spend two more nights there, remembering God and reflecting on his blessings, before Hajj ends.

Once Hajj is completed, many pilgrims take the opportunity to travel to Madinah to visit Al-Masjid an-Nabawi (the Prophet's Mosque). This is a huge mosque, placed on the site of a much smaller mosque that

Objectives

- Know how the pilgrimage continues and ends.
- Understand the significance of Hajj for Muslims.

Key term

- **Hajji:** someone who has completed Hajj

Links

To read more about the celebration of Id-ul-Adha see pages 206–207.

Activity

Create a Hajj flowchart. Include all of the main places that pilgrims visit on Hajj, in the correct order. Include brief captions to describe what happens at each place.

Muhammad built in 622 CE. It contains the tomb of Muhammad and of some early Muslim leaders.

The Prophet's Mosque in Madinah – the tomb of Muhammad is located beneath the green dome

The significance of Hajj

Hajj has great significance for Muslims. Even though it is a requirement to go on Hajj once in a lifetime, many Muslims go a number of times, especially if they live close to Makkah. Once someone has completed Hajj, they can be referred to as a **Hajji**.

Hajj is so important to Muslims for a number of different reasons:
- It can bring about a deep spiritual transformation that makes the Hajji a better person. Their consciousness of God grows and they become more aware that God is with them and watching them.
- It teaches sincerity and humility in a person's relationship with God.
- It produces inner peace, which is shown in the values of justice, honesty, respect, kindness, mercy and forgiveness.
- It shows self-discipline. The physical and mental demands it imposes are great. Not all are able to complete it.
- It emphasises unity and equality. The Ihram clothing ensures there is no distinction between rich and poor, and the thousands of tents that pilgrims stay in at Mina strengthen the feeling of brotherhood and sisterhood.
- It reminds Muslims of the faith and examples set by Ibrahim, Hajira and Ishmael.
- It can lead to forgiveness for sins.

Summary

You should now know what happens during Hajj, and understand why it is important for Muslims.

Research activity

Search online to read people's diaries or accounts of Hajj. How has the experience been significant for them?

Activity

Produce a spider diagram with Hajj in the middle, surrounded by the benefits it has for a Muslim. Try to think of simple illustrations to represent each of the benefits and add them to your diagram.

★ Study tip

When writing about what happens during Hajj, remember there is no need to include the visit to the Prophet's Mosque at Madinah, as this is not part of Hajj.

203

8.8 Jihad

■ What is jihad?

Jihad is an important concept for Muslims. It refers to struggling against evil, either as an individual or as the collective fellowship of Islam. Jihad requires Muslims to strive to improve themselves and the societies in which they live in a way that God would approve of. The origins of jihad go back as far as Muhammad, as the concept appears many times in the Qur'an and the Hadith (the sayings of Muhammad):

> **This is My path, leading straight, so follow it,** and do not follow other ways: they will lead you away from it – 'This is what He commands you to do, so that you may refrain from wrongdoing.'
> *Qur'an* 6:153

> But those who have believed, migrated, and striven for God's cause, it is they who can look forward to God's mercy: God is most forgiving and merciful.
> *Qur'an* 2:218

There are two elements to jihad: greater jihad and lesser jihad. Although they are strongly linked, there are distinct differences between them.

■ Greater jihad

Greater jihad is a personal inward struggle of all Muslims to live in line with the teachings of their faith. This means they must observe the Five Pillars of Islam, which bring them closer to God:

- The Shahadah and salah lay the foundations for their faith, by putting God above everything else.
- Zakah requires them to care for others as a duty.
- Sawm requires them to show discipline by putting God above their bodily needs for a whole month.
- Hajj means that for ten days they leave behind worldly concerns and dedicate themselves to God's will.

All of this is required as part of greater jihad, which for Muslims is a constant struggle to purify one's heart from all evil traits, and to establish instead all types of virtues.

Muslims must also devote their lives to God by avoiding such temptations and distractions as drugs, alcohol, greed and jealousy. Anything that takes them away from their submission to God must be avoided. Some Muslims take their development as devout followers of their faith even further. For example, some learn the Qur'an by heart, which requires great discipline and patience.

Others make great efforts to improve life for people in the community. Not only do they give Zakah, they also choose to give extra sums of money to charity. This is called

Objectives

- Understand the origins, influence and significance of jihad.
- Understand both lesser and greater jihad, and the differences between them.

Key terms

- **jihad:** a struggle against evil; this may be an inward, personal struggle or an outward, collective struggle
- **greater jihad:** the personal inward struggle of all Muslims to live in line with the teachings of their faith
- **lesser jihad:** the outward struggle to defend one's faith, family and country from threat
- **holy war:** fighting for a religious cause or God, probably controlled by a religious leader

▲ *Muslims volunteering to pack food for families in need*

Sadaqah. Others also give their time by working with the poor and vulnerable, both locally and globally.

In all these ways, Muslims improve themselves spiritually and deepen their relationship with God.

■ Lesser jihad

As the term **lesser jihad** suggests, it is considered less important than greater jihad, which Muslims believe is required every single moment of their lives. Lesser jihad is seen as the outward struggle to defend Islam from threat. In the early days of the faith, this was important when Muslims were being persecuted and they needed to protect their freedom to practise their faith.

▲ *These Syrian refugees left their homes in 2015 as a result of what some believe to be a lesser jihad in their country*

There are several instances in the Qur'an that appear to allow extreme violence in the name of lesser jihad, but it must be remembered that they were written in the seventh century CE when the new faith of Islam was under severe threat. Some might argue that in the context of war, behaving in such a violent way is justified, but this does not mean that lesser jihad can be used to justify terrorism that targets innocent civilians.

Fighting for a religious cause is sometimes referred to as a **holy war**. Some of the criteria for a holy war are:

- It must only be declared by a fair religious leader.
- It cannot be used to make people convert to Islam.
- It must be in response to a threat to the faith.
- It must not be used to gain territory or wealth.
- It must be the last resort – all peaceful methods must have been tried first.

As the above criteria suggest, neither lesser jihad nor holy war should be used to justify terrorist acts, whether or not there is a perceived threat to the faith. However, this is how lesser jihad is sometimes misinterpreted in modern times. Muslim extremists are often called jihadists, but no Muslim for whom greater jihad is an important element in their faith would justify such violent actions by referring to terrorism as struggling to live in the way that God intends. For Muslims, jihad is essentially an important spiritual practice that brings them closer to God.

Discussion activity

With a partner, discuss and decide which (if any) of the holy war criteria are acceptable.

Activities

1. Explain the meaning of jihad, including the differences between greater and lesser jihad.
2. Describe different ways in which Muslims practise greater jihad.
3. Explain why many Muslims believe it is impossible to justify terrorism as an example of lesser jihad or holy war.

Links

To read more about holy war see page 303.

★ Study tip

When you are writing about jihad, it is best to include both greater and lesser jihad unless you are asked to write about just one of them.

Summary

You should now understand what jihad means to Muslims. You should also be able to explain the differences between lesser and greater jihad.

205

8.9 The festivals of Id-ul-Fitr and Id-ul-Adha

■ The origins of Id-ul-Fitr and Id-ul-Adha

It is said that when Muhammad arrived in Madinah, he noticed that some people were celebrating two specific days with entertainment and festivities. When he asked about this he was told that before Islam came to their city, they had celebrated two grand carnivals each year. Muhammad replied that God had appointed two other days that are better to celebrate, the days of **Id-ul-Fitr** and **Id-ul-Adha**.

■ Id-ul-Fitr

Why is Id-ul-Fitr important?

Id-ul-Fitr (also written as Eid-ul-Fitr) means the 'festival of breaking of the fast'. It has several other names including the Sugar Feast, the Sweet Festival or Lesser Eid. The festival marks the end of the month of Ramadan. Muslims are not only celebrating the end of a whole month of fasting, but are thanking God for the strength and help he has given them to fast for a month. Muslims also give thanks to God for providing his guidance and wisdom in the Qur'an, the first revelation of which was made during the month of Ramadan.

How is Id-ul-Fitr celebrated?

Id-ul-Fitr may be celebrated for one, two or three days. Muslims gather together in mosques or large outdoor areas to say special prayers. The imam's sermon usually reminds Muslims that they should forgive and forget any differences or disputes that have occurred during the year, and focus instead on helping the poor.

Everyone wears their best clothes or new clothes for the occasion, and homes are decorated. Special foods are eaten and processions take place through the streets. There is a festive atmosphere, and cards and presents are exchanged.

Although Id-ul-Fitr is not a recognised national public holiday in Britain, in areas where many Muslims live they may be granted the day off to attend morning prayers and enjoy the festival. Many also go to their local cemetery to remember family members who have died and to pray for them.

■ Id-ul-Adha

Why is Id-ul-Adha important?

Id-ul-Adha (also written as Eid-ul-Adha) is the festival of sacrifice or Greater Eid. It is celebrated on the 10th day of the month of Dhul-Hijjah, and lasts for four days.

Objectives

- Understand the origins and meanings of Id-ul-Fitr and Id-ul-Adha.
- Know how the Id-ul-Fitr and Id-ul-Adha are celebrated.

Key terms

- **Id-ul-Fitr:** a Muslim festival that celebrates the end of Ramadan
- **Id-ul-Adha:** a Muslim festival that celebrates the prophet Ibrahim's willingness to sacrifice his son for God

Links

To read more about Ramadan and fasting see pages 196–197.

▲ *Women decorate their hands with henna for Id-ul-Fitr*

Chapter 8 Islam: practices

Celebrating Id-ul-Fitr

Sumaiya, from Luton in England, recounts her experience of Id-ul-Fitr: 'Preparations for Id-ul-Fitr begin the night before with the women decorating their hands and feet with henna. Baklava and special biscuits, called finger biscuits, are also made.

In the morning the men go the mosque to attend a special Id prayer and the women will usually stay at home to put on new outfits. Throughout the day different family members visit each other and guests will be given drinks, biscuits and baklava, and the children are usually given toys as gifts.'

▲ Special sweet foods are made for Id-ul-Fitr

This festival remembers and honours the prophet Ibrahim, who was willing to sacrifice his son Ishmael on God's command. The Qur'an 37:100–112 records how Ibrahim had a recurring dream in which God told him to sacrifice his son. Ibrahim loved his son dearly, but decided he must obey God's command, provided his son agreed with him. Ibrahim informed his son and his son replied that he must do what God had told him.

However, as Ibrahim was about to carry out the sacrifice, God prevented it and gave Ibrahim a ram to sacrifice instead. He had passed the test of being willing to carry out God's commands.

How is Id-ul-Adha celebrated?

This festival forms part of Hajj, but is celebrated by Muslims all over the world. In Britain, it is a time of celebration when people visit family and friends, and enjoy festive meals. It begins with prayers in the mosque, where the imam preaches a sermon about sacrifice and reminds those who attend why the festival is celebrated.

During Id-ul-Adha animals are slaughtered to remember Ibrahim's sacrifice. On Hajj many pilgrims sacrifice an animal, but this is not allowed in Britain. Instead some British Muslims buy an animal from their local slaughterhouse. This animal will have been killed in a certain way, following Islamic law. The family usually keeps a third of the meat, gives another third to relatives, friends and neighbours, and the remaining third is given to the poor. However, many in Britain prefer to give money instead of meat to support those in need.

Cards and presents are given and community celebrations are often organised. Those living on their own receive invitations to share meals with their neighbours. Those in hospital receive lots of visitors as every effort is made to ensure that no one is left out.

Activities

1. Give two other names for the festival of Id-ul-Fitr.
2. What are Muslims celebrating during Id-ul-Fitr?
3. Explain how Id-ul-Adha is celebrated in Britain today.
4. Why do you think that many Muslims in the UK prefer to make the sacrifice of giving money rather than meat to the poor?

Extension activity

Use the internet to find out more about the celebration of Id-ul-Adha by pilgrims on Hajj. Record any similarities or differences that you find between the celebrations that take place during Hajj and those that take place elsewhere.

Links

Hajj is described in detail on pages 200–203.

⭐ Study tip

Remember that Muslims are not only celebrating but also making a sacrifice, as Ibrahim did, by giving meat or money to their neighbours, friends and the poor.

Summary

You should now be able to explain the origins and meanings of Id-ul-Fitr and Id-ul-Adha, and describe how these festivals are celebrated.

207

8.10 The festival of Ashura

■ The origins and meaning of Ashura

The **Day of Ashura** (Day of Remembrance) is a major Shi'a festival that takes place on the 10th day of the month of Muharram. Ashura means 'tenth.'

Sunni Muslims also observe Ashura, but they refer to it as the Day of Atonement, and remember it as the day when the Israelites were freed from slavery in Egypt. Others believe that traditionally Ashura remembers the day Noah (Nuh) left the ark after the flood. After going to Madinah, Muhammad nominated Ashura as a day of fasting from sunset to sunset, and it is still a voluntary fast day for Sunni Muslims. To Shi'a Muslims, however, Ashura is a day of great sorrow because of the tragic events of Karbala.

Shi'a Muslims remember the death of Husayn (Hussein), son of Imam Ali and grandson of Muhammad, on 10 October, 680 CE, in Karbala, Iraq. It is a day of mourning for the martyrdom of Husayn. The battle at Karbala was fought between Husayn and his supporters against the army of Caliph Yazid I. It lasted all day as Husayn, with around 70 men plus women and children, fought against the much larger army. Eventually Husayn's supporters were overwhelmed near the river Euphrates, and it is said that their camp was set on fire and their bodies were trampled upon by the horses of their enemy. Husayn and his male followers were killed and their property looted. The women were allowed to live but were taken as captives.

This event had a profound effect on the surviving relatives and supporters of Husayn, as they mourned for him and all his companions who were killed. Poems were written to retell the story and it is remembered by Shi'a Muslims with much sorrow. Husayn's martyrdom is widely seen by Shi'a Muslims as a symbol of the struggle against injustice, tyranny and oppression.

■ How is Ashura commemorated?

In many Muslim countries like Afghanistan, Iraq and Pakistan, a public holiday takes place to remember the events at Karbala. During the day Shi'a Muslims take part in a public expression of grief and mourning. Some even go so far as to beat themselves on the back with chains, pound their head or cut themselves. They do this in an attempt to connect with Husayn's sufferings and death.

> **Objectives**
> - Understand the origins and meaning of Ashura.
> - Know how Ashura is commemorated by both Sunni and Shi'a Muslims.

> **Key term**
> - **Day of Ashura:** a festival that is important for Shi'a Muslims in particular, who remember the battle of Karbala and death of Husayn on this day

▲ *The shrine of Husayn, which many Shi'a Muslims visit during Ashura*

Shi'a Muslims beating themselves during Ashura in London

Recently some of these practices have been condemned by some Shi'a religious authorities, who have stated that they are the wrong actions for Muslims to take. Re-enactments and plays are performed to retell the story of Husayn's death so that people will remember the events at Karbala.

In London, several thousand Shi'a Muslims go to Marble Arch for a procession of mourning and to listen to speeches. In cities such as London and Manchester, Shi'a Muslims gather in the street and some men beat themselves (slap themselves on their bare chests in unison) as part of the mourning ritual. Some British Shi'a Muslims believe that they should shed blood to remember Husayn. Rather than beating and cutting themselves, some UK religious leaders encourage them to donate blood to the blood transfusion service instead.

In Iraq, many Shi'a pilgrims go to the Mashhad al-Husayn, the shrine in Karbala which is believed to house the tomb of Husayn. During the reign of Saddam Hussein in Iraq, Ashura commemorations were banned as Saddam saw the gathering of thousands of people as a potential threat to his regime. After Saddam Hussein was removed from power, the pilgrimage began again despite the dangers from bomb attacks. For example, in 2004, bombs killed and wounded hundreds of pilgrims in Karbala at the time of Ashura. In Iran, the festival became a major political symbol during the Islamic Revolution. The Day of Ashura has become a point of difference between some Sunni and Shi'a Muslims, and security in many countries is heightened for the occasion.

For Sunni Muslims, Ashura is a day when many fast voluntarily. Many give to charity, show kindness to their family and to the poor, recite prayers and learn from Islamic scholars. It is not such an important festival or as solemn an occasion as it is for Shi'a Muslims.

Activities

1. When does Ashura take place?
2. Explain why Sunni Muslims take part in Ashura.
3. Describe the historical event that Shi'a Muslims remember on the day of Ashura.
4. Give three things that Shi'a Muslims see Ashura as a symbol of the struggle against.
5. Describe how Ashura is commemorated by a) Sunni Muslims and b) Shi'a Muslims.

Discussion activity

In small groups or in pairs, discuss whether or not you think it is important to have a special day every year to remember significant events that happened years ago in a religion. Should the past influence what people do today?

★ Study tip

You need to be able to write about what Shi'a Muslims do at Ashura, but you should also be aware of the historical event they are commemorating. It is also useful to know the differences between Sunni and Shi'a Muslims concerning Ashura.

Summary

You should now understand the origins of Ashura, and know what Sunni and Shi'a Muslims do and remember at this festival.

8 Assessment guidance

Worship – summary

You should now be able to:

✔ explain the Five Pillars of Sunni Islam and the Ten Obligatory Acts of Shi'a Islam

✔ explain the Shahadah, including its importance for Muslims and how it is used in worship

✔ explain how and why Muslims pray, including the significance of prayer, the differences between how Sunni and Shi'a Muslims pray, the importance of the Jummah prayer, and how prayer is carried out in the mosque and home.

Duties and festivals – summary

You should now be able to:

✔ explain how Muslims celebrate Ramadan and explain its significance

✔ explain Zakah and Khums, including the origins of Zakah and how and why it is given

✔ explain Hajj, including the different actions the pilgrimage involves and their significance

✔ explain the concept of jihad, including the differences between greater and lesser jihad

✔ describe and explain the festivals of Id-ul-Fitr, Id-ul-Adha and Ashura, and their importance for Muslims in Great Britain today.

Sample student answer – the 12 mark question

1. Write an answer to the following question:

   'It is important that Muslims celebrate their festivals in Great Britain today.'

   Evaluate this statement. In your answer you should:
   - give reasoned arguments in support of this statement
   - give reasoned arguments to support a different point of view
   - refer to the teaching of Islam
   - reach a justified conclusion. [12 marks]

2. Read the following sample student answer:

   "Of course it is important that Muslims celebrate their festivals in Great Britain today. If Muslims did not celebrate their festivals, it would be the same as Christians not celebrating Christmas and Easter and nobody would think that was right. It is quite difficult for them to celebrate their festivals because Great Britain is not a Muslim country but they definitely need to make the effort.

   I think Id-ul-Fitr is the most important because it starts when Ramadan finishes. Successfully completing a month-long fast should be celebrated and this is what Id-ul-Fitr does. Although there is a happy side to the festival, they also remember that there are poor people in the world and they should be looked after. If this is all the festival teaches them then it is very important. This is also when Zakah is usually given, which is one of the Five Pillars. Many schools in Great Britain allow Muslim children to have a day off school to celebrate Id-ul-Fitr and this is the right thing to do.

   Another festival is Id-ul-Adha, which is celebrated at the same time that many Muslims are on their pilgrimage. It celebrates the obedience and faith that Ibrahim showed when he was asked to sacrifice his son Ishmael. It is a very joyful festival with presents, parties and feasting. The poor are invited to join in. Muslims also go to a mosque and they sacrifice a goat to provide food as well. Sacrifice isn't allowed in Great Britain so a local halal slaughterhouse may be asked to do this. Some of the meat is eaten during Id-ul-Adha, some given to the poor and some given to family members and friends.

So of course it is important that Muslims celebrate festivals in Great Britain today because it helps them remember the poor and Allah wants them to do this."

3. With a partner, discuss the sample answer. Consider the following questions:
   - Does the answer refer to Muslim teachings and if so what are they?
   - Is there an argument to support the statement and how well developed is it?
   - Is a different point of view offered and how developed is that argument?
   - Has the student written a clear conclusion after weighing up both sides of the argument?
   - Are there logical steps in the argument?
   - What is good about this answer?
   - How do you think it could be improved?

4. What mark (out of 12) would you give this answer? Look at the mark scheme in the Introduction (AO2). What are the reasons for the mark you have given?

5. Now swap your answer with your partner's and mark each other's responses. What mark (out of 12) would you give the response? Refer to the mark scheme and give reasons for the mark you award.

Practice questions

1 How many Obligatory Acts are there in Shi'a Islam?

   A) 5   B) 7   C) 10   D) 12   **[1 mark]**

2 Give two places pilgrims visit while on Hajj. **[2 marks]**

3 Explain two ways in which a belief in the importance of prayer influences Muslims today.

   [4 marks]

> ⭐ **Study tip**
>
> This question asks about how a belief influences Muslims today. You must make sure you apply the belief to the present day, rather than just describing it.

4 Explain two Muslim beliefs about the importance of festivals.
   Refer to scripture or sacred text in your answer. **[5 marks]**

5 'The Shahadah is the most important pillar of Islam.'

   Evaluate this statement. In your answer you should:
   - give reasoned arguments in support of this statement
   - give reasoned arguments to support a different point of view
   - refer to the teaching of Islam
   - reach a justified conclusion. **[12 marks]**

> ⭐ **Study tip**
>
> A good way of answering a question that asks you to decide the importance of something is to give arguments to support it, then give arguments to support something else being more important.

9 Judaism: beliefs and teachings

9.1 The nature of God: God as One

■ The concept and nature of God

The belief in one God is the most basic principle in Judaism. Like Christianity, this makes Judaism a **monotheistic** religion. Jews believe that it is God who has had the major effect and influence on the world and their place within the world. Although there are important people in the history of the faith, there has never been any suggestion that any of them have been a part of God or a god themselves. It is God who is the source of all Jewish morality, beliefs and values, which affect Jews' decisions about how to live correctly.

Jews believe that this overwhelming importance and significance of God is seen in his role as the creator. In addition to being the creator, God also sustains his creation by caring for people and requiring loyalty in exchange. Jews believe that God has given laws to his people, and is the true judge of how people follow these laws.

Jews believe that they can see the work of God in history, and that by carefully studying history they can learn more about God. The historical content in the Tenakh (also commonly spelled Tanakh – the Jewish scriptures) is considered important for what it reveals about God. The idea of seeing God at work, and learning more about him, is also extended into the present and the future because Jews believe God is constantly at work.

While Judaism is a monotheistic religion, there is considerable diversity in how the faith is practiced and how the Jewish scriptures are interpreted. You will learn more about some of these differences in the following pages.

> **Objectives**
> - Understand the concept and nature of God for Jews.
> - Understand the Jewish belief that God is One.

> **Key terms**
> - **monotheistic:** a religion that believes there is only one God
> - **Shema:** a Jewish prayer affirming belief in the one God, found in the Torah

> **Research activity**
> While Jews and Christians both believe in only one God, Christians believe that God consists of three distinct Persons. Read pages 70–71 to find out more about this.

■ God or G-d?

Some Jews prefer not to write the word God. They use G-d instead as a sign of respect. When written in Hebrew, God's name can never be erased or destroyed. The Hebrew letters of the name for God are YHWH, and this is never said out loud by Jews. When it appears in scripture or liturgy, instead of saying it, Jews substitute the Hebrew word 'Adonai', which means 'my Lord'. Any book containing the Hebrew name of God is treated with respect and is never destroyed or thrown away. When it is too old to be used it is kept in a special place in the synagogue before being properly buried in a Jewish cemetery.

▲ *Old Jewish books containing the Hebrew name of God, stored in a synagogue in Israel*

212

Chapter 9   Judaism: beliefs and teachings

Some Jews think it is acceptable to write the word God, as they view it as a title, not a name. It is important to note that God and G-d refer to exactly the same one God and not different gods or parts of God.

■ God as one

For Jews, monotheism is not just the belief there is only one God; it is a way of viewing the world and all the contents of the world that they believe God created. It is God who is ever present in people's lives; every sight they see, sound they hear, and experience they are aware of is regarded as a meeting with God. This is the true meaning of the idea that God is One and is best expressed in the first two verses of the Shema, an important Jewish prayer that derives from passages in the books of Deuteronomy and Numbers. It begins with an expression of the unity of God, and the way humankind should respond to this belief:

> ❝ Hear, O Israel! The Lord is our God, the Lord alone. You shall love the Lord your God with all your heart and with all your soul and with all your might. ❞
>
> *Deuteronomy 6:4–5*

The reference to loving God with all your heart implies that God requires total loyalty, just like loyalty is needed in a full loving relationship. The mention of the soul shows that Jews need to have spiritual dedication to the one God.

▲ The Shema prayer being recited in a synagogue. Many Jews put their hand over their eyes while saying the first line, to avoid distractions.

For Jews, God is a single, whole, indivisible entity who cannot be divided. He is infinite and eternal, beyond the full understanding of humankind. This makes him the only being who should be praised.

Activities

1. What does the term monotheism mean?
2. Explain fully the Jewish belief that God is One.
3. Write out the first two verses of the Shema.
4. Explain what you think the Shema means to Jews.

Discussion activity

'It is God who is the source of all Jewish morality, beliefs and values, which affect Jews' decisions about how to live correctly.'

With a partner, discuss what you think this means to individual Jews who are keen to follow their faith properly. After five minutes, compare your conclusions with two other people.

Extension activity

Read the next part of the Shema from Deuteronomy 6:7–9. What instructions does this give about ways in which the Shema should be used?

⭐ Study tip

You are allowed to write G-d rather than God in your exam and will not be penalised for doing so. Whichever version you choose, it is respectful to use an upper case G.

Summary

You should now understand key Jewish beliefs about the concept and nature of God, including the belief that God is one.

9.2 The nature of God: God as creator

Jewish beliefs about creation

The **Torah** begins with these words:

> " When God began to create heaven and earth … "
>
> *Genesis* 1:1

So right from the very start of the Torah, the belief that God is the **creator** is established. Jews believe that God created the universe out of nothing, exactly how he wanted it to be.

The book of Genesis tells how God took six days to create the universe and everything in it. Many **Orthodox** and **ultra-Orthodox Jews** believe that this is a literal truth and that it happened around 6000 years ago. They reject scientific theories of evolution. Other Jews accept that an evolutionary theory may be correct and that the universe is much older, but that God made everything happen. They still believe that God is the creator, but do not take the creation story in Genesis literally.

According to the creation story, it took four days for God to get the universe fit to support life and a further two days to create all living creatures. On the seventh day, God rested and made it a holy day. Jews remember this every week between sunset on Friday to sunset on Saturday during the observance of **Shabbat**. In doing so, Jews are regularly reminded of God's importance and role in the creation of everything.

▲ *The earth seen from the moon*

Evil and free will

Jews believe that in order for God to have the ability and power to create the universe, it is essential he has characteristics that no other living being has. Jews believe that God is:

Objectives

- Understand the Jewish belief that God is the creator and the sustainer.
- Understand how this relates to the concepts of evil and free will.

Key terms

- **Torah:** (1) the five books of Moses, which form the first section of the Tenakh (the Jewish Bible) (2) the Jewish written law
- **creator:** the one who makes things and brings things about
- **Orthodox Jews:** Jews who emphasise the importance of following the laws and guidance in the Torah; they believe the Torah was given directly by God to Moses, so should be followed as closely as possible
- **Ultra-Orthodox Jews:** Jews who are even more committed than Orthodox Jews to strictly following the laws and guidance in the Torah
- **Shabbat:** the Jewish holy day of the week; a day of spiritual renewal starting shortly before sunset on Friday and continuing to sunset on Saturday
- **omnipotent:** almighty, having unlimited power; a quality of God
- **omniscient:** knowing everything; a quality of God
- **omnipresent:** being everywhere at all times; a quality of God

Chapter 9   Judaism: beliefs and teachings

- **omnipotent** – all powerful
- **omniscient** – all knowing
- **omnipresent** – being everywhere at all times.

Jews believe that God is the creator of everything; there is no concept in Judaism that evil was created by the devil. They believe that God, as the only creator, must have created evil himself. However, he also gave people the free will to choose what they know is right, and to reject evil as being completely against God.

Jews believe that in order for people to have free will, they have to be able to make their own choices between good and bad, which is why evil needs to exist. Being able to *choose* to do good also makes the act of doing good more significant.

Some find it difficult to accept that God created the potential for evil – particularly when remembering events such as the Holocaust, when Jews faced extreme persecution – but it is considered to be a necessary consequence of giving humans free will.

The belief in one God who creates everything, including the potential for evil, is reinforced in Isaiah 45:6–7.

▲ 'God saw all that He had made, and found it very good' (Genesis 1:31)

■ God the sustainer

Jews believe that God not only created the universe but also sustains it. This means that God provided sufficient resources on the planet to feed and provide for all species. The fact that resources are distributed unequally, so that some have less than they need, is a result of human free will, granted by God. Those who follow Jewish teaching by helping to provide resources for others who have too little are helping to fulfil God's plan for the world he created.

Research activity

Read pages 14–17 and 24–25 to find out how Christians view God as the creator of everything. Summarise the similarities and differences between Jewish and Christian beliefs in God as the creator.

★ Study tip

The three words beginning with omni, meaning 'all' – omnipotent, omniscient and omnipresent – are important words to remember when referring to Jewish beliefs about the nature of God.

Activities

1. Carefully explain the Jewish belief that God is the creator.
2. Why can it be difficult to accept that God created evil as well as good?
3. Explain what it means when Jews call God 'the sustainer'.

> **I am the Lord and there is none else**, I form light and create darkness, I make weal and create woe – I the Lord do all these things.
>
> *Isaiah 45:6–7*

Discussion activity

With a partner, discuss what Isaiah 45:6–7 means in regards to the Jewish belief in one God.

Summary

You should now understand what it means when Jews call God 'the creator' and 'the sustainer'. You should also understand Jewish beliefs about evil and free will.

215

9.3 The nature of God: God as lawgiver and judge; the divine presence

God as lawgiver

In order to help people to exercise their free will in the way he would like them to, God gave the Jews many laws that he expects them to obey. The foundation for these laws are the **Ten Commandments**. God gave these to Moses after he rescued the Jewish slaves from Egypt, probably in the thirteenth century BCE. They were originally inscribed on two tablets of stone and Jews still consider these laws to be of great importance.

Altogether the Torah contains 613 laws that govern how people should behave. These are called **mitzvot** and they form the basis of the Halakhah, which is the accepted code of conduct for Jewish life. By obeying these various laws, Jews believe they are doing what God requires of them and fulfilling his will on earth.

In providing the Ten Commandments and the other mitzvot, Jews believe that God has set the basis of his relationship with his people, and that that is the purpose of God being the lawgiver.

▲ *Studying and obeying the mitzvot in the Torah is very important to Jews*

God as judge

Jews believe that God not only gave them laws to follow, but also judges them for how well they follow those laws. They believe that God judges everyone – whether they are a Jew or not – based on their actions, behaviour and beliefs. Jews believe that God's judgements are fair and always tempered by his loving, **merciful** nature; the qualities of justice and mercy are perfectly balanced.

For Jews there are two main times when God's judgement happens. The first is once a year during the festival of Rosh Hashanah (the Jewish new year), when God judges people for their actions over the past year and decides what the coming year will bring them. This festival offers Jews

Objectives

- Understand the Jewish belief that God is the lawgiver and judge.
- Understand the concept of the divine presence (Shekhinah).

Key terms

- **Ten Commandments:** ten laws given by God to Moses over 3000 years ago
- **mitzvot** (singular **mitzvah**): Jewish rules or commandments
- **merciful:** the quality of God that shows compassion or forgiveness to humans, even though he has the power to punish them
- **Shekhinah:** the divine presence of God
- **Temple:** the centre of Jewish worship at the time of Jesus; the meeting place between God and the priest

Links

For more on Moses and the Ten Commandments see pages 224–225.

Links

For more on mitzvot see pages 230–231.

★ Study tip

Wherever you see a link to another section of the book, try to find the time to look at it, as it will provide useful background information and help you to understand the topic in more depth.

Chapter 9   Judaism: beliefs and teachings

the chance to reflect on their behaviour over the year, repent for their wrongdoings and pray for goodness and happiness for themselves and their families.

Many Jews also believe they will be judged after death, when God determines where they will spend their afterlife.

■ The divine presence (Shekhinah)

The word **Shekhinah** does not appear in the Tenakh, but its meaning is present in many passages. Shekhinah means 'God's manifested glory' or 'God's divine presence'. It refers to the presence of God on earth.

Many Jewish writings refer to the Tabernacle – a portable structure, similar to a tent – as being the early dwelling place for the divine presence of God. The Jews carried the Tabernacle with them on their journey after their exodus from Egypt, through the wilderness, to the conquering of the land of Canaan.

At times, the Tenakh mentions that the Jews were led on this journey by a pillar of fire or a cloud, which were also possible manifestations of the Shekhinah. So the Shekhinah is associated with God's presence among his people and their experience of the Spirit of God. It is seen as a sign of his power and glory.

After Canaan was conquered, the Tabernacle was replaced with Solomon's **Temple** in Jerusalem in the tenth century BCE. Several of the prophets, including Isaiah, Jeremiah and Ezekiel, made reference to the presence of God in the temple.

> In the year that King Uzziah died, **I beheld my Lord seated on a high and lofty throne**; and the skirts of His robe filled the Temple. Seraphs stood in attendance on Him.
>
> *Isaiah 6:1–2*

▲ *An early twentieth-century model of Solomon's Temple*

A small number of Jews believe that the Shekhinah is the feminine presence of God, because in Hebrew Shekhinah is a feminine word.

Research activity

Over the centuries, there were two temples built or rebuilt on Temple Mount: Zerubbabel's Temple and Herod's Temple. Find out when and why they were built, and who built them. Then find out about the Holy of Holies.

Discussion activity

With a partner, discuss what might be meant by the feminine presence of God.

Activities

1. Carefully explain God's role as lawgiver.
2. Explain how laws help people to use their free will responsibly.
3. Explain the Jewish belief in the Shekhinah. Exodus 40:34–35 gives an example that will help you.

Summary

You should now understand how Jews view God as the lawgiver and judge, and understand the meaning of Shekhinah.

9.4 Life after death, judgement and resurrection

■ Jewish customs surrounding death

Jews believe that because it is part of God's plan, death is an inevitable part of life. Judaism teaches that Jews should not die alone, although of course this is not always possible to achieve. The dying person's family should make every effort to visit and look after them, and ensure there is always somebody with them. It is considered to be an act of great kindness to be present at the time of death and to close the dead person's eyes. Upon hearing of a death of a loved one, Jews make a blessing to God:

> " Blessed are You, Lord our God, King of the universe, the True Judge. "

Intense mourning follows a person's death, especially while waiting for their burial, then for seven days after the burial, followed by a further 30 days of lesser mourning.

Jews follow these traditional customs to show respect to the dying person, and to show they accept that God has taken their loved one's life.

■ Jewish beliefs about the afterlife

There is little teaching about life after death in the Jewish holy books, and beliefs about it have developed over the centuries. This has led to differences between Jews in their ideas about what happens after death. Some believe that life after death will be a physical life, while others believe it will be spiritual.

Heaven and Sheol

Teachings about the afterlife imply that the good will enter paradise (Gan Eden) while others will go to a place sometimes referred to as Sheol. This is seen as a place of waiting where souls are cleansed. Even though many Jews believe that those who follow their faith properly will be judged good enough for heaven, there is no clear teaching about what heaven is like. It is believed that heaven will be with God, but it is not known whether it is a state of consciousness, or an actual physical or spiritual place.

Judgement and resurrection

Some Jews believe they will be judged by God as soon as they die; this view is supported for example by Ecclesiastes 12:7, which suggests that **judgement** happens upon or shortly after death.

Objective
- Understand what Jews believe about what happens after death.

Key terms
- **judgement:** the belief that God judges a person based on their actions, and either rewards or punishes them as a result
- **resurrection:** rising from the dead or returning to life
- **rabbi:** a Jewish religious leader and teacher

Links
To learn more about mourning rituals see pages 254–255.

▲ Graves in a Jewish cemetery marked with the Star of David – a symbol commonly used to represent Judaism

Some believe that God will judge everyone on the Day of Judgement, after the coming of the Messiah. This is when God will decide who goes to heaven and who goes to hell. This is the view taken in Daniel 12:2.

Daniel looks forward to a time of **resurrection** at some point in the future. In Judaism, resurrection is the idea that at some point after death, people will rise from their graves to live again. However, many Jews reject the idea of resurrection, whether physical or spiritual. They have no firm view on what happens after death.

One of the reasons for the lack of agreement about the afterlife is that Jews believe the present is more important, and they should focus on living in a way that is pleasing to God. The idea that it is best to focus on the present rather than the afterlife is told in the following story by Rabbi Benjamin Blech (a contemporary American **rabbi**):

> A very wealthy man, not known for his piety, stood in a long line of those waiting to have their lives assessed by the heavenly court. He listened attentively as those who were being judged before him recounted both their spiritual failings and achievements. A number of them seemed to have the scales weighted against them until they suddenly remembered acts of charity they had performed, which dramatically tipped the scales in their favour. The rich man took it all in and smiled to himself.
>
> When it was his turn, he confidently said, 'I may have committed many sins during my lifetime, but I realise now what has the power to override them. I am a very wealthy man and I will be happy to write out a very large cheque to whatever charity you recommend.'
>
> To which the court replied, '**We are truly sorry, but here we do not accept cheques – only receipts**.'
>
> Rabbi Benjamin Blech, 'Life after death', www.aish.com

▲ Jews believe they should focus on living in a way that is pleasing to God, for example by observing the mitzvot or helping the poor; here Jewish volunteers are putting together kosher food packages

> **Many of those that sleep in the dust of the earth will awake**, some to eternal life, others to reproaches, to everlasting abhorrence.
>
> Daniel 12:2

> And the dust returns to the ground/ As it was,/ And the lifebreath returns to God/ Who bestowed it.
>
> Ecclesiastes 12:7

Activities

1. Why do you think Jews prefer to focus on this life rather than the next?
2. Do you agree that this is a good idea? Explain your reasons.
3. Explain different Jewish views about judgement after death.
4. Why do you think there are few references to life after death in the Tenakh?

Discussion activity

With a partner, discuss what, if anything, you think happens after death.

★ Study tip

If you are writing about a topic like resurrection or judgement, try to include different views to show that some Jews believe one thing while others believe differently.

Summary

You should now understand what Jews believe about life after death, including different views on judgement and resurrection.

219

9.5 The nature and role of the Messiah

■ Origins of the Messiah

In the twelfth century Rabbi Moses ben Maimon, also known as Maimonides, compiled the 'Thirteen Fundamental Principles of Jewish Faith', based on the Torah. The twelfth principle is 'The belief in the arrival of the **Messiah** and the Messianic era.' The nature and role of the Messiah is the cause of great debate among many in the Jewish community.

The word Messiah means 'anointed one', and was originally used in the Tenakh to refer to the kings of Israel. The first king of Israel was Saul, who lived around the eleventh century BCE. In anticipation of Saul being made king, the prophet Samuel anointed him to show that he was chosen by God:

> ❝ Samuel took a flask of oil and poured some on Saul's head and kissed him, and said, 'The LORD herewith anoints you ruler over His own people.' ❞
>
> *1 Samuel* 10:1

Samuel also made a prediction about Saul which came true immediately:

> ❝ The spirit of the LORD will grip you, and you will speak in ecstasy along with them; you will become another man. And once these signs have happened to you, act when the occasion arises, for God is with you. ❞
>
> *1 Samuel* 10:6–7

▲ Saul is anointed by Samuel

Objectives
- Understand the nature and role of the Messiah.
- Consider different beliefs about the Messiah.

Key terms
- **Messiah:** 'the anointed one'; a leader of the Jews who is expected to live on earth at some time in the future
- **Messianic age:** a future time of global peace when everyone will want to become closer to God, possibly through the intervention of the Messiah

Activities
1. Explain different Jewish beliefs about the role of the Messiah.
2. What do Jews believe the Messianic age will be like?
3. If the Messiah came this year, what do you think Jews would want him to do? Explain your reasons.
4. Explain why the belief in the Messiah might provide comfort to Jews in bad times.

Chapter 9 Judaism: beliefs and teachings

■ The nature of the Messiah

Today, many Jews use the term 'Messiah' to refer to a future leader of the Jews. There is no suggestion in Judaism that Saul is connected to the coming Messiah, especially as he disobeyed God once he became king. However, the way that God changed Saul is also likely to apply to the future Messiah. The Messiah is expected to be a future king of Israel – a descendent of Saul's successor, King David – who will rule the Jews during what is known as the **Messianic age**.

Jews who believe in the future Messianic age debate about what it will be like and when it will come. Some believe the dead will be resurrected and live in a time of peace in a restored Israel. The prophet Micah describes it as a time when war will end and people will live in universal peace and harmony:

> And they shall beat their swords into plowshares/ And their spears into pruning hooks. **Nation shall not take up/ Sword against nation**; They shall never again know war.
>
> *Micah 4:3*

Orthodox Jews believe that in every generation there is a descendent of King David who has the potential to be the Messiah. If the Jews are worthy of redemption, this person will be directed by God to become the redeemer and will rule over all humanity with kindness and justice. He will also uphold the law of the Torah and will be the ultimate teacher of it. In addition, he will rebuild the temple in Jerusalem and gather all Jews back to the land of Israel. He will usher in world peace and unite humanity as one. Each of these expectations is outlined in the Tenakh.

In contrast, many in Reform Judaism reject the idea of a Messiah. Instead of believing in one specific person who will unite the world in peace, they believe that everyone should work together to achieve that peace. They still believe in a future Messianic age, but one that is achieved through people's collective actions, including observance of religious obligations, rather than as the result of the leadership of one person.

▲ *The star of David appears on the flag of Israel and is named after the king from whom the Messiah will be descended*

Although Christians believe that Jesus was the Messiah, Jews firmly do not. This is because Jesus did not fulfill the expectations that the Jews have for their Messiah, especially in his observance of Torah law and because Jews do not believe he established the Messianic age.

The belief in the coming of the Messiah has provided some hope and comfort for Jews facing persecution and hardship. Many Jews murdered in the death camps during the Second World War went to their deaths proclaiming their belief in God and in the coming of the Messiah.

Discussion activity

'People should work together to establish peace on earth rather than waiting for the Messiah to do it.'

With a partner, discuss whether you agree with this statement and give reasons that support and oppose your opinion.

Research activity

Research the differences between Jewish and Christian beliefs about the Messiah.

⭐ Study tip

When writing about the Messiah, remember that different groups of Jews have different beliefs about the Messiah's role and importance.

Summary

You should now understand the nature and role of the Messiah. You should also have considered different Jewish beliefs about the Messiah.

9.6 The Promised Land and the covenant with Abraham

Abraham and the Promised Land

According to Jewish tradition, Abraham was born in the city of Ur in Mesopotamia, probably in the twentieth or nineteenth century BCE. At that time, it was common for people to worship idols of many different gods. From an early age, Abraham became convinced that there could be only one God who created everything, and that worshipping idols was wrong. He tried to spread this message to the people of Ur but with little success. The belief that there is only one God is called **monotheism**.

▲ *The city of Ur was excavated in 1929*

Abraham, together with his wife Sarah, father Terah and some other family members, left Ur to travel to Canaan. However, they did not reach Canaan, choosing instead to settle on the way at Haran in Northern Mesopotamia where, sometime later, Terah died.

The book of Genesis tells that God told Abraham to continue the journey to Canaan and made a promise to him:

> The LORD said to Abram [Abraham], 'Go forth from your native land and from your father's house to the land that I will show you./ **I will make of you a great nation,/ And I will bless you**;/ I will make your name great,/ And you shall be a blessing./ I will bless those who bless you,/ And curse him that curses you;/ And all the families of the earth/ Shall bless themselves by you.'
>
> *Genesis* 12:1–3

Once Abraham and Sarah reached Canaan, God told Abraham to look all around him and said that, 'for I give all the land that you see to you and your offspring forever' (Genesis 13:15).

God's promises to Abraham mean that Canaan (which includes present-day Israel) has become known as the **Promised Land**.

Objectives

- Know about Abraham and the Promised Land.
- Understand the idea of a covenant.

Key terms

- **monotheism:** belief in one God
- **Promised Land:** the land of Canaan that God promised to the Jews
- **covenant:** an agreement; in Judaism it refers to an agreement between individuals, often on behalf of the Jews, and God
- **circumcision:** the removal of the foreskin from the penis

Activities

1. Using Genesis 12:1–20 and the map for reference, write an account of Abraham's journeys. Describe the route that Abraham took, and add in any other details about the journey that you can find in Genesis 12:1–20.
2. Why do you think Abraham built altars in different places?
3. What does the fact that Abraham was prepared to leave Haran and travel to Canaan tell you about his faith in God?

Extension activity

Read the full story of Abraham. It can be found in Genesis 12:1–17:27 and 21:1–25:11.

Chapter 9 Judaism: beliefs and teachings

■ The covenant with Abraham

The word **covenant** means agreement. A covenant benefits both parties; it includes promises and sometimes responsibilities that should be undertaken. Jews believe that the covenants that God has made in history with people such as Adam, Abraham and Moses were binding for those individuals, the people they represented and God. Jews believe the covenants still apply to them today. Even though in the past some people have broken their side of the covenant (indeed some Jews broke the covenant between God and Moses soon after it had been agreed), Jews believe that God never has and never will break his side.

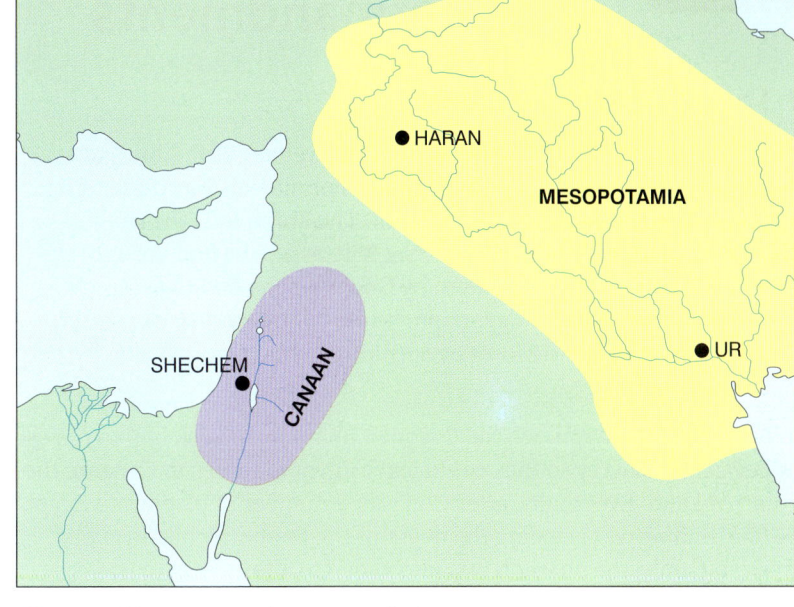

▲ Map of the area around Canaan in Abraham's time

The existence of covenants between the Jews and God has led to a belief that Jews were specially chosen by God to be his people (see Deuteronomy 14:2).

Although some have interpreted statements such as this as meaning that Jews believe they are in some way superior to all others, this is a misunderstanding. Jews themselves focus on the responsibilities of being chosen by God with no thought of superiority.

Covenants are sealed by oaths, often supported by a special action such as a sacrifice. In the case of the covenant with Abraham, it was supported by the action of **circumcision**. Once God had told Abraham the terms of the covenant, which was that he would make Abraham the father of many nations if Abraham would 'walk in My [God's] ways and be blameless' (Genesis 17:1), Abraham proved his acceptance by being circumcised himself and by circumcising all the males in his household.

To make it possible for Abraham to become the father of a great nation, God enabled Abraham's wife Sarah to conceive despite the fact that she was very elderly and had previously been unable to conceive. Coming so soon after the covenant was established, Sarah's pregnancy and the birth of a son, Isaac, may be seen as a gift from God to mark the covenant between God and Abraham.

> ❝ For you are a people consecrated to the LORD your God: of all the peoples on earth the LORD your God chose you to be His treasured people. ❞
>
> *Deuteronomy 7:6*

Links

For more about circumcision in present-day Judaism see pages 248–249.

⭐ Study tip

If you are referring to a particular covenant, try to remember to include the name of the person with whom God made the covenant (most likely Abraham or Moses).

Activities

1. Explain the meaning of the term covenant.
2. Explain the promise God made to Abraham as his side of the covenant.
3. How did Abraham support the oath he made to God?
4. How did God make it possible for Abraham to be the father of a great nation?

Summary

You should now know about Abraham's journey to the Promised Land, and understand the covenant that was made between Abraham and God.

9.7 The covenant at Sinai and the Ten Commandments

■ The escape from Egypt

About 400 years after God established the covenant with Abraham, the Jews found themselves as slaves in Egypt. For many it was difficult to follow the faith established by Abraham. The Torah tells the story of Moses, who was rescued from the river Nile as a baby and brought up in the royal palace. He was chosen by God when he fled to escape being put to death for killing an Egyptian who was ill-treating a Jewish slave. God gave instructions to Moses by speaking to him through a bush that appeared to be on fire.

God told Moses to approach the Egyptian pharaoh and ask him to release the Jews from slavery so they could leave Egypt to return to Canaan, the Promised Land. Eventually, after God sent a number of plagues to Egypt, the final and worst one being the death of the firstborn child in every Egyptian family, the pharaoh was persuaded to allow them to leave. They travelled across the Sea of Reeds (also referred to as the Red Sea), once God had parted the waters to allow them through. Estimates of the number of Jews who escaped from Egypt range from several thousand to around 3 million (the latter number is more consistent with the story in the Torah, which refers to around 600,000 men, most of whom probably had wives and children travelling with them).

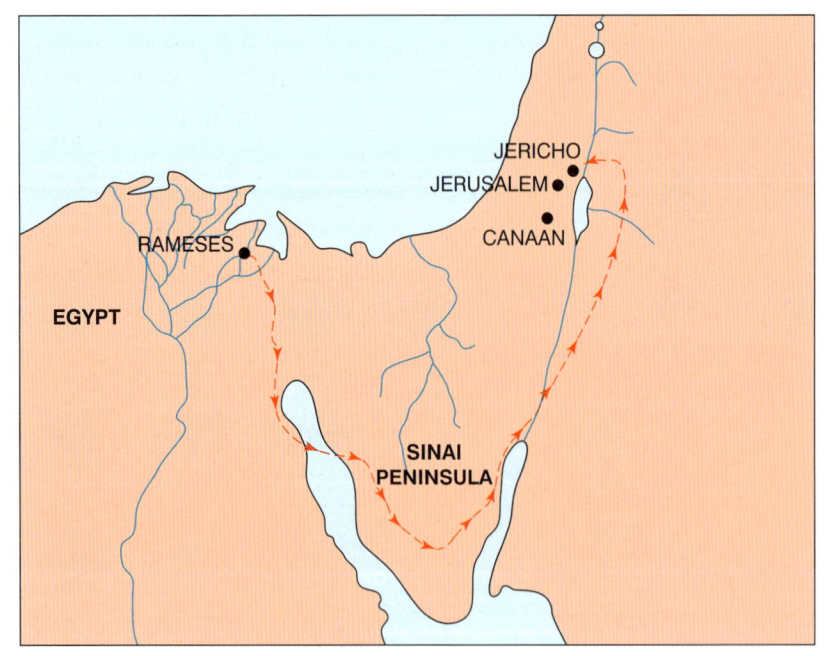

▲ Map of the possible route taken by the Jews as they escaped Egypt

■ The Ten Commandments

Once across the Sea, the Jews wandered for many years in the desert in the Sinai region between Egypt and Canaan. When they arrived

> **Objectives**
> - Know about the covenant at Sinai, including the role and importance of Moses in establishing the covenant.
> - Know the Ten Commandments and understand their importance.

> **Key term**
> - **Ten Commandments:** ten laws given by God to Moses over 3000 years ago

> **Discussion activity**
> The Jews have developed a belief that they are God's chosen people. With a partner, discuss how you think the story of Moses and the covenant has contributed to this belief.

at Mount Sinai, Moses ascended the mountain, leaving the Jews at the base. While on Mount Sinai, God gave Moses ten laws, four of them concerning the relationship between the Jews and God and six concerning their relationships with each other. These were carved on two tablets of stone that Moses carried down the mountain. In this way the **Ten Commandments** were given to the Jews.

The Ten Commandments are recorded in Exodus 20:1–17 and also in Deuteronomy 5:6–21.

> **❝** I the Lord am your God who brought you out of the land of Egypt, the house of bondage: You shall have no other gods besides Me.
>
> **You shall not make for yourself a sculptured image, or any likeness** of what is in the heavens above, or on the earth below, or in the waters under the earth. You shall not bow down to them or serve them …
>
> **You shall not swear falsely by the name of the Lord your God;** for the Lord will not clear one who swears falsely by His name.
>
> **Remember the sabbath day and keep it holy**. Six days you shall labor and do all your work, but the seventh day is a sabbath of the Lord your God … For in six days the Lord made heaven and earth and sea, and all that is in them, and He rested on the seventh day; therefore the Lord blessed the sabbath day and hallowed it.
>
> **Honor your father and your mother**, that you may long endure on the land that the Lord your God is assigning to you.
>
> **You shall not murder. You shall not commit adultery. You shall not steal. You shall not bear false witness against your neighbor.**
>
> **You shall not covet** your neighbor's house: you shall not covet your neighbor's wife, or his male or female slave, or his ox or his ass, or anything that is your neighbor's. **❞**
>
> *Exodus* 20:1–17

Activities

1. Explain why Moses asked the pharaoh to allow the Jews to leave Egypt.
2. What special event happened to Moses on Mount Sinai? (See Exodus 19:16–25.)
3. Explain why God gave the Ten Commandments to Moses.

⭐ Study tip

When referring to the Ten Commandments, it is acceptable to use a simplified version rather than the full version from Exodus 20:1–17.

Summary

You should now understand how the Ten Commandments were given to the Jews, and why they are important. You should also understand the terms of the covenant between God and the Jews.

The Ten Commandments form the basis of the covenant between God and the Jews. The terms of the covenant were that God would be the God of the Jews and would protect them from harm, provided they obeyed his laws in return. This is the basis of the belief that the Jews are the chosen people of God. The Ten Commandments gave the Jews important guidance on how to create a society where people had basic rights and were able to live in peace with each other.

Moses died in Moab, just before the Jews reached the Promised Land of Canaan. He was succeeded by Joshua, who led the Jews across the River Jordan into the Promised Land. After winning several battles, including a famous one at Jericho, the Jews settled into their new home.

▲ *The possible location of Mount Sinai, in the Sinai Peninsula in Egypt*

9.8 Key moral principles in Judaism

As with all religions, most Jews see Judaism as a complete way of life. In addition to providing opportunities and methods to acknowledge and worship God, it also provides guidance to help believers to live in a way that is pleasing to God. The last six of the Ten Commandments outline ways in which this can be achieved, and they are further developed in other Jewish teachings.

Justice

For Jews, pursuing **justice** is a sacred duty that can only be achieved when accompanied by truth and peace. It can be defined as bringing about what is right and fair, according to the law, or making up for a wrong that has been committed. According to the prophet Micah, God requires his people 'to do justice and to love goodness, and to walk modestly with your God' (Micah 6:8).

The prophet Amos expresses the wish that people should:

> **"** But let justice well up like water,/ Righteousness like an unfailing stream. **"**
>
> *Amos* 5:24

Jews believe that the Torah and the prophets were sent by God to help people understand and bring about justice in a way that demonstrates mercy. The laws in the Torah give important guidance on the treatment of the poor and vulnerable, in order that justice can be achieved for them as well as for the rich and powerful. For Jews there is never any reason to ignore justice or the suffering of others. Creating a just society requires all individuals to contribute by living their lives correctly, following the laws of the Torah.

Healing the world

The concept of healing (or repairing) the world is very important in Judaism. While Jewish scholars have debated it widely, many see it simply as an action that draws people closer to God. For many Jews it motivates them to get involved in work designed to increase social justice, for example by volunteering for a **charity** that helps the poor or protects the environment.

Some Jews believe this understanding of healing the world by doing charity work or similar actions is too limited. They believe the term should encompass much more, including obeying the mitzvot and trying to become closer to God spiritually, for example through prayer.

Objective
- Understand the Jewish moral principles of justice, healing the world, and kindness to others.

Key terms
- **justice:** bringing about what is right and fair, according to the law, or making up for a wrong that has been committed
- **healing the world:** being involved in God's work to sustain the world; it can involve work to increase social justice or to preserve the environment
- **charity:** (1) providing help and love to those in need (2) an organisation that does not make a profit, whose main purpose is to help those in need
- **kindness to others:** positive, caring actions that should be shown to all living things

▲ *Jewish and Muslim volunteers prepare Christmas day meals for the homeless*

Chapter 9 Judaism: beliefs and teachings

▲ Young Jews in Israel plant trees to help the environment

World Jewish Relief

World Jewish Relief (WJR) is a UK-based international humanitarian agency. Inspired by the Jewish belief in healing the world, their main aim is to help tackle Jewish poverty and provide support for Jewish communities. However, they also provide assistance to people of all faiths and ethnicities, particularly in response to international disasters. Some of the ways they help include:

- helping unemployed Jews in Eastern Europe to develop the skills needed to find work
- providing practical and emotional support for older Jews living in poverty
- providing emergency aid, such as food and shelter, in response to international disasters like the 2015 earthquake in Nepal.

■ Kindness to others

Kindness to others is an important concept in Judaism. Many of the laws of the Torah spell out how to be kind to others and this is something Jews must aim to achieve. The Torah laws not only forbid murder and other negative actions, but also provide positive laws to encourage acts of kindness. These should be shown to all living things, both Jews and non-Jews alike.

Leviticus 19 twice instructs Jews to love people as they love themselves (verses 18 and 34):

> ❝ You shall not take vengeance or bear a grudge against your countrymen. **Love your fellow as yourself**. ❞
> *Leviticus* 19:18

> ❝ The stranger who resides with you shall be to you as one of your citizens; **you shall love him as yourself**, for you were strangers in the land of Egypt. ❞
> *Leviticus* 19:34

Research activity
Find out about one project in which World Jewish Relief helps healing of the world.

Extension activity
Leviticus 19 contains a large number of laws that are designed to help people show kindness to others. Read Leviticus 19:1–18 and write down five laws that you think show kindness to others most strongly.

Activities
1. Explain what justice is.
2. Explain how Judaism interprets the moral principle of justice.
3. Choose the quote from either Micah or Amos and explain what it says about justice.
4. Explain the meaning of healing the world.
5. Explain how the Torah law shows the importance of showing kindness to others.

★ Study tip
You may find it helpful to consider and refer to the concepts of justice, healing the world and kindness to others in other sections of your course, especially in the ethical themes.

Summary
You should now understand the moral principles of justice, healing the world and kindness to others.

227

9.9 Sanctity of life

What does the 'sanctity of life' mean?

Belief in the **sanctity of life** is important in many faiths, including Judaism. For Jews, the belief stems from the story of creation in Genesis, when humans were created in the image of God. The story tells that God breathed life into Adam and into the whole of creation. Life is therefore seen to be holy and sacred because it is given by God. This is the meaning of the phrase 'sanctity of life'. It particularly applies to humans (rather than animals) because they were made in God's image.

How this affects Jewish beliefs about ending life

Believing in the sanctity of life helps Jews to work out whether an action is moral and acceptable to God. It is a key consideration in such areas as war, murder, abortion, euthanasia and capital punishment. Put simply, belief in the sanctity of life means that life is sacred, special and valuable because it belongs to God. God gives life to humans and that means only he has the right to take it away.

As life belongs to God, preserving life is a duty in Judaism. Death cannot be made to come more quickly than it would from natural causes. For Jews this rules out such practices as active euthanasia and murder.

However, advances in medical technology mean that making life and death decisions is more complex today than it was in the past. While Jewish law states that people have a duty to preserve life, there are different opinions among scholars about what this means in practice.

Some Jews think that patients should be kept alive at all costs, while others believe that you shouldn't prolong a natural death if the patient is in great pain. For example, if a dying patient is being kept alive with a ventilator, some Jews believe it would be acceptable to remove the ventilator as it is preventing a natural death.

An important teaching about preserving life is found in the **Talmud**:

> **"** He who destroys one soul of a human being, the Scripture considers him as if he should destroy a whole world, and him who saves one soul of Israel, the Scripture considers him as if he should save a whole world. **"**
>
> *Sanhedrin* 4:5

The first half of this quote is engraved on the Medal of the Righteous, which the Yad Vashem organisation in Jerusalem awards to those who rescued Jews and saved their lives during the Second World War.

Objectives

- Understand the Jewish belief in the sanctity of life.
- Understand the Jewish concept of saving a life (pikuach nefesh).

Key terms

- **sanctity of life:** all life is holy as it is created and loved by God; human life should not be misused or abused
- **Talmud:** a commentary by the rabbis on the Torah – it consists of the Mishnah and Gemara together in one collection
- **pikuach nefesh:** the obligation to save a life, even if doing so breaks Jewish law

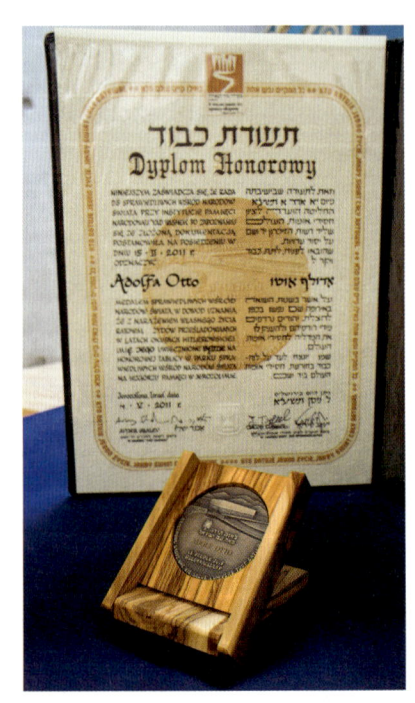

▲ The Medal of the Righteous presented in 2011

Chapter 9 Judaism: beliefs and teachings

■ Saving a life (pikuach nefesh)

> "Do not profit by the blood of your fellow."
>
> *Leviticus* 19:16

Although life is sacred and only God can give or take it, there are circumstances in which Jews believe that humans have a responsibility to take part in preserving life. In Judaism, the obligation to save life – **pikuach nefesh** – emphasises how valuable human life is for Jews, as it takes precedence over other responsibilities and most Jewish laws.

Transplant surgery is a way of preserving life in cases of disease or failure of certain organs. Many Jews agree with transplant surgery and feel it is a great honour to donate organs to save another person's life, although some disagree because they believe that the body should be complete when buried and donated organs make this impossible.

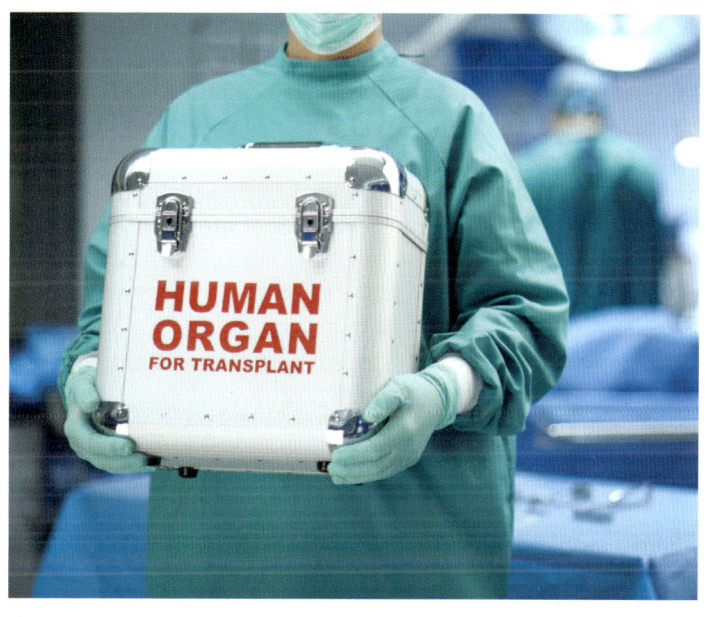

Jews are required to observe Shabbat, which means they are not allowed to do certain types of 'creative' work from sunset on Friday until sunset on Saturday. Logically this would prevent saving life if it involved work. However, the principle of pikuach nefesh allows Shabbat law to be set aside if it is in order to save a life.

The Talmud contains several instances where it is permissible to break Shabbat law in order to save life. These include rescuing a child from the sea, breaking apart a wall that has collapsed on a person and putting out a fire that is endangering life. In more modern times, it might include driving a sick or injured person to hospital or performing a life-saving operation.

▲ Some Jews believe that transplant surgery respects the sanctity of life and pikuach nefesh

Extension activity

Find out what some people did to be awarded the Medal of the Righteous.

★ Study tip

You will not be expected to know many Hebrew terms, but pikuach nefesh is one that may be helpful for you to know and use.

Activities

1. Referring to the belief in the sanctity of life, explain why ending life early is against Jewish beliefs and teachings.
2. How does believing in the sanctity of life help Jews to live in the way God wants them to?
3. Explain why deciding how to respect the sanctity of life may be more difficult today than in the past.
4. Explain how believing in pikuach nefesh helps Jews to respect the sanctity of life.

Summary

You should now understand what belief in the sanctity of life means, and why it is important to Jews. You should also understand the concept of pikuach nefesh.

9.10 Free will and mitzvot

■ Free will

The story of Adam and Eve's disobedience in Genesis 3 teaches Jews that God has allowed them to choose how they can live their lives. This is called **free will**. However, these choices will always have consequences. Choosing to act in a way that pleases God should bring about a life of fulfilment, and a guarantee that God will judge Jews favourably on the Day of Judgement. However, Jews believe that using free will to justify actions that are wrong – such as stealing or worshipping different gods – will not bring them closer to God in life or after death. In the story of Adam and Eve, it is made clear that when Eve disobeyed God and persuaded Adam to do the same, the consequences were severe and continue to affect humankind today.

▲ Young Jewish women studying the Torah

■ Mitzvot

Mitzvot is the plural of mitzvah, which literally means commandment. However in modern times it is also used as a term for a good deed or a charitable act.

There are 613 mitzvot in the Torah and others in the Talmud, which cover such things as the correct way to worship, family issues and conduct in society. It is generally accepted that there are 248 positive mitzvot (traditionally corresponding to the number of bones in the male human body). Obeying these helps Jews to strengthen their bond with God. The 365 'negative' mitzvot (corresponding to the number of days in the year), which tell people what not to do, attempt to prevent the bond between God and humans from being damaged.

Objectives

- Understand the relationship between free will and mitzvot.
- Understand the different types of mitzvot: mitzvot between man and God and mitzvot between man and man.
- Understand the importance of the mitzvot.

Key terms

- **free will:** belief that God gives people the opportunity to make decisions for themselves
- **mitzvot:** Jewish rules or commandments

Links

To read more about Jewish beliefs in life after death see pages 218–219.

⭐ Study tip

Try not to think of the idea of free will as a way to justify people choosing and being allowed to do whatever they want.

As the Torah mitzvot are believed to have been given by God to the Jews while they were in Sinai under the leadership of Moses, following them carefully makes it impossible to disobey God. The mitzvot help Jews to use their free will correctly by providing divine guidance on how to live. They help Jews to make responsible choices, and ensure that the results of their choices are good and pleasing to God. This is why Jews believe they are important.

Mitzvot between man and God

The first four of the Ten Commandments govern a person's relationship with God. They tell Jews that God is the only God and that they should not make images of him or any other god, nor should they misuse his name. On the seventh day of every week they should have a day of rest and worship to honour God. Many of the mitzvot that are based on the first four commandments give further guidance on how an individual can improve their relationship with God, including in the areas of ritual, worship, sacrifice, food laws and the observance of festivals.

Mitzvot between man and man

In the Torah there are instructions that a person must love God and also love their neighbour; for Jews these are very important and cannot be separated. They believe that obeying the mitzvot that involve people's relationships with each other is pleasing to God. Indeed, a person who does not love other people cannot be said to be showing love for God.

The mitzvot between man and man cover areas such as the treatment of workers, how to settle disputes, and the types of food that can and cannot be eaten. They are not just rules telling Jews what not to do; many of them give positive advice and guidance that will help them to live as true members of their faith and their community.

▲ Observing mitzvot regarding the types of food that can be eaten helps Jews to obey God

Discussion activity

'People should only do what they want if the results are good and pleasing to God.' With a partner, discuss what this quote means and whether you agree with it. Give your reasons.

Activities

1. Explain why Jews do not see free will as an excuse to do whatever they want.
2. Explain how free will is linked to consequences.
3. How many mitzvot are there and what do the number of positive and negative ones correspond to?
4. Why is it important that Jews observe the mitzvot?
5. Explain in detail the difference between mitzvot between man and God and mitzvot between man and man.
6. Why do you think Jews consider the mitzvot to be so important? Give as many reasons as you can.

Summary

You should now understand how the mitzvot help Jews to use their free will. You should also understand the different types of mitzvot and why they are important to Jews.

9 Assessment guidance

Key beliefs – summary

You should now be able to:
- ✔ explain Jewish beliefs about the nature of God, especially the beliefs that God is One, the creator, the lawgiver and judge, loving and merciful
- ✔ explain the concept of the divine presence (Shekhinah)
- ✔ explain Jewish beliefs about life after death, including judgement and resurrection
- ✔ explain Jewish beliefs in the nature and role of the Messiah, including different views on the role and importance of the Messiah.

The covenant and the mitzvot – summary

You should now be able to:
- ✔ explain the terms and significance of the covenant with Abraham, and explain Abraham's journey to the Promised Land
- ✔ explain the covenant at Sinai and its importance to Jews, including the role of Moses and the Ten Commandments
- ✔ explain key moral principles in Judaism, including justice, healing the world, charity and kindness to others
- ✔ explain the importance for Jews of the sanctity of human life, including the concept of 'saving a life' (pikuach nefesh)
- ✔ explain the importance of the mitzvot for Jews and how they relate to free will, including the different types of mitzvot: those between man and God, and those between man and man.

Sample student answer – the 4 mark question

1. Write an answer to the following question:

   Explain two ways in which Jewish beliefs about life after death influence Jews today. [4 marks]

2. Read the following sample student answer:

   "Jews are unclear about what happens to them after death. Therefore it is difficult for them to be influenced by them. They do believe in life after death so whatever form it takes, they do try to make sure it is good for them. This means they follow the mitzvot because this means they are doing what God wants them to. This also means they treat people properly. So even though they don't know what may happen, it does influence their lives and makes them better."

3. With a partner, discuss the sample answer. Is the focus of the answer correct? Is anything missing from the answer? How do you think it could be improved?

4. What mark (out of 4) would you give this answer? Look at the mark scheme in the Introduction (AO1). What are the reasons for the mark you have given?

5. Now swap your answer with your partner's and mark each other's responses. What mark (out of 4) would you give the response? Refer to the mark scheme and give reasons for the mark you award.

Sample student answer – the 5 mark question

1. Write an answer to the following question:

   Explain two Jewish teachings about God the creator.
   Refer to scripture or sacred text in your answer. **[5 marks]**

2. Read the following sample student answer:

   "Jews believe that God is the creator and that he created the earth and all living things. This information is in Genesis.

   The creation was God's choice. He created humans with a job to do. Genesis says that this job is to look after the earth for him."

3. With a partner, discuss the sample answer. It makes some good points but it fails to do something which is important. How do you think the answer could be improved?

4. What mark (out of 5) would you give this answer? Look at the mark scheme in the Introduction (AO1). What are the reasons for the mark you have given?

5. Now swap your answer with your partner's and mark each other's responses. What mark (out of 5) would you give the response? Refer to the mark scheme and give reasons for the mark you award.

Practice questions

1. How many mitzvot are there in the Torah?

   A) 513   B) 563   C) 613   D) 663 **[1 mark]**

2. Name two people who had covenants with God in the Tenakh. **[2 marks]**

3. Explain two ways in which a belief in the sanctity of human life influences Jews today. **[4 marks]**

4. Explain two Jewish beliefs about the divine presence (Shekhinah).

   Refer to scripture or sacred text in your answer. **[5 marks]**

5. 'The mitzvot help Jews to use free will properly.'

   Evaluate this statement. In your answer you should:
   - give reasoned arguments in support of this statement
   - give reasoned arguments to support a different point of view
   - refer to the teaching of Judaism
   - reach a justified conclusion. **[12 marks]**

> ⭐ **Study tip**
>
> Your answer to this question will be also assessed for the quality of your spelling, punctuation and grammar. You should try not to make careless errors in the way you write.

10 Judaism: practices

10.1 The importance of the synagogue

What is a synagogue?

A **synagogue** is a house of assembly (the Hebrew term is Beit K'nesset) where Jews meet for prayer, worship and study. Jews can pray anywhere but there are certain prayers that can only be said in the presence of a **minyan** – a group of at least 10 adults. (In Orthodox Judaism, this needs to be 10 men over the age of 13; in Reform Judaism women can be part of the minyan as well.) Jews believe that it is good to pray together in a group, and the synagogue provides the facility to do so. As a result it is sometimes called Beit T'filah (House of Prayer).

> **Objective**
> - Explore the importance of the synagogue in Judaism.

> **Key terms**
> - **synagogue:** a building for Jewish public prayer, study and gathering
> - **minyan:** a group of at least 10 adults; the minimum number of Jews required for a Jewish religious service
> - **menorah:** a many-branched candlestick that holds either seven or nine candles
> - **Star of David (Magen David):** a symbol of Judaism said to represent the shield of King David, who ruled Israel in the tenth century BCE

▲ The Star of David in the wall of a synagogue

Synagogues are usually rectangular in shape but they can be any shape and size. There are no rules about what the building should look like from the outside, but there are usually symbols associated with Judaism that make it recognisable as a synagogue. There is sometimes a representation of a **menorah** or the **Star of David**. There are often stained glass windows showing patterns or pictures in coloured glass. The second of the Ten Commandments forbids making and worshipping idols of humans or animals, so images of humans or animals are not usually found in synagogues.

▲ A young Jew lighting a menorah

234

Various names are used for the synagogue. Many Orthodox Jews often refer to the synagogue as 'shul', which means 'school' or 'place of study'. Some Reform Jews use the word 'temple' because they consider the synagogue to be a replacement for the Temple in Jerusalem, which was an important centre of worship for Jews before it was destroyed by the Romans in 70 CE.

The importance of the synagogue

The synagogue is important because it forms the centre of the Jewish religious community. It is a place of prayer, study and education, social and charitable work, as well as a social centre. It provides a focal point for the celebration of festivals and rites of passage such as a Bar Mitzvah, Bat Mitzvah or a marriage.

An important function of the synagogue is to provide a house of study (Beit Midrash). Some synagogues provide classes for the learning of Hebrew, which is the language used in Jewish prayer. Learning this is important for helping young Jews to prepare for their Bar and Bat Mitzvahs. The importance of education, however, spans the whole life of those who follow the Jewish faith. Most synagogues have a well-stocked library to enable adults to improve their knowledge and understanding of the Jewish faith, its sacred texts and its culture.

▲ *A synagogue is a place of study*

Most synagogues have a social hall that is used for religious and non-religious activities. The synagogue often functions as a sort of town hall where matters of importance to the community, both religious and non-religious, can be discussed. It also provides a venue for collecting money or other items to be distributed to the poor and needy, both at a local and international level. For example, Jews frequently support the work of organisations such as World Jewish Relief, and they often hold charity events to provide aid in the time of a natural disaster. The social hall can be used for a variety of activities for young children, teenagers and adults. Youth clubs, music, drama and sports groups, lunch clubs and other clubs for senior citizens may all meet there.

Activities

1. What is meant by Beit K'nesset?
2. How might a synagogue be recognised from the outside?
3. Explain why pictures of animals or humans are not usually found in synagogues.
4. Why do some Jews use the word 'shul' when referring to a synagogue?
5. Explain the importance of the synagogue to the Jewish community.

Links

To learn about Bar and Bat Mitzvahs see pages 250–251.

Discussion activity

In small groups or in pairs discuss the following statements:

'The synagogue is so important to Jews that without it the religion might not survive.'

'Jewish worship does not need to be in a synagogue.'

★ Study tip

If you are asked to explain the importance of the synagogue to the Jewish community, don't forget to include both worship and all the other activities which take place there.

Summary

You should now be able to explain the importance of the synagogue for Jews, and describe the activities that happen in a synagogue.

10.2 Interior features of a synagogue

■ The prayer hall

The prayer hall of a synagogue is usually rectangular in shape, often with seats on three sides facing inwards towards the **bimah**. The fourth side includes the focal point of the synagogue – the holy Ark (**Aron Hakodesh**). The prayer hall will contain a seat for the **rabbi** and a pulpit from where sermons are delivered. Most halls also have a seat for the chazzan (a trained singer) who leads the prayers.

Patterns, Jewish symbols or extracts from the scriptures may be used as decoration, but pictures of the prophets or other human beings are not, as that would break the second commandment not to have idols.

■ The Ark (Aron Hakodesh)

The Ark (Aron Hakodesh) is regarded as the holiest place in the synagogue. This is because it is where the sacred Torah scrolls are kept and because it represents the original Ark of the Covenant. Jews believe that the original Ark was created to hold the stone tablets which contained the Ten Commandments that God gave Moses at Mount Sinai. This Ark was eventually taken to Jerusalem and placed in the Temple built by King Solomon, and was the focus of Jewish worship. In many synagogues Jews are reminded of this because above the ark there are two stone tablets on which the start of each of the Ten Commandments is written.

▲ *The Ark when opened, showing the Torah scrolls inside*

The Ark is situated at the front of the synagogue, usually set into the wall facing Jerusalem (the eastern wall in British synagogues). This means that when worshippers face the Ark, they are facing towards the city where the Temple once stood. The Aron Hakodesh is usually reached by climbing up steps, as a reminder to worshippers that God is above his people and that the sacred Torah is above humanity.

> **Objective**
> - Understand the design and religious features of a synagogue, including their importance and their use in worship.

> **Key terms**
> - **bimah:** a platform in a synagogue from where the Torah is read
> - **Aron Hakodesh:** the Ark – the holiest part of the synagogue, which contains the Torah scrolls
> - **rabbi:** a Jewish religious leader and teacher
> - **ner tamid:** eternal light; a light that is kept burning in the synagogue above the Ark

> **Activities**
> 1. Name three features that can be found in the prayer hall of a synagogue.
> 2. Explain the importance of the Aron Hakodesh (Ark) in the synagogue.
> 3. Explain why the ner tamid is kept burning at all times.
> 4. Describe the bimah and explain its purpose in worship.
> 5. Explain how features in the synagogue's prayer hall are reminders of the Temple in Jerusalem.

The Ark itself is an ornamental container or cupboard that houses the handwritten Torah parchment scrolls (Sefer Torah). It is only opened during special prayers and when removing the Torah to read during services. The remainder of the time it is covered with a curtain called the Parochet. This symbolises the curtain that was in the Temple in Jerusalem.

> ❝ [He] brought the ark inside the Tabernacle. **Then he put up the curtain for screening, and screened off the Ark of the Pact** – just as the LORD had commanded Moses. ❞
>
> *Exodus* 40:21

Research activity

Look up Exodus 25:10–22 to find details of the original Ark of the Covenant.

Extension activity

Find out about the connection between the ner tamid and the Jewish festival of Hanukkah.

Every action involving the Ark is full of ceremony and it is considered an honour to be the person who climbs the steps, opens the doors and parts the inner curtain so that the Torah scroll may be removed.

■ The ever-burning light (ner tamid)

Each synagogue has a light that is kept burning at all times. It is placed in front of, and slightly above the Ark, and is called the **ner tamid** (eternal flame or ever-burning light). It symbolises God's presence and so is never put out. It is also a reminder of the menorah that was lit every night in the Temple in Jerusalem. Originally synagogues used an oil lamp, but now most use electric lights with an emergency power source in the event of an electricity cut.

■ The reading platform (bimah)

▲ *A synagogue with the bimah in the centre*

The bimah is a raised platform situated in most synagogues in the very centre. It is used when reading from the Torah and often by the person leading services. When the Torah scrolls are being read, the bimah is the focus of worship, and the raised platform makes it easier for the congregation to hear what is being said. To some it is a reminder that the altar was the central feature of the courtyard of the Temple in Jerusalem.

★ Study tip

Make sure you are familiar with the Jewish terms used to describe the features in a synagogue, and are able to use them appropriately when answering questions.

Discussion activity

In pairs or a small group discuss and evaluate the following statement: 'The ner tamid is the most important feature of a synagogue.' Give reasons for and against this statement.

Summary

You should now be able to describe the interior features of a synagogue, and explain their function and importance.

237

10.3 Worship in Orthodox and Reform synagogues

■ Different Jewish groups

Within modern Judaism there are different religious groups who have their own interpretation of the faith and ways of worshipping. The main groups in Britain today are the **Orthodox** and **Reform Jews**.

Orthodox Judaism

Orthodox Judaism is the traditional branch of the Jewish religion and was the only form of Jewish practice until the eighteenth century. Orthodox Jews emphasise the importance of obeying God's instructions as laid down in the Torah and the Talmud. They also believe that there are different roles for men and women, which result in different religious duties and responsibilities.

Reform Judaism

Reform Judaism, which is a type of Progressive Judaism, emphasises the importance of individual choice in deciding how to worship and practise the faith. Reform Jews believe that their religion should change its practices to become more relevant to modern life. They believe that it is the overall spiritual and moral code within the Torah and Talmud that must be obeyed, rather than each individual law. They also believe in equality for men and women.

■ Public worship

Jews are expected to pray three times a day and often this takes place in a synagogue. The services in the synagogue are led by either a rabbi, a **cantor** (chazzan) or a member of the congregation.

Orthodox synagogue services

In an Orthodox synagogue, the person leading the service has his back to the congregation so he is facing the Ark (Aron Hakodesh), and prays facing the same direction as the congregation. The service is conducted in Hebrew and the singing is unaccompanied. Men and women sit separately; traditionally the women sat in an upstairs gallery or at the back of the synagogue. Nowadays this arrangement is often replaced by a symbolic dividing structure between men and women sitting at the same level. Orthodox Jews believe that a greater level of personal connection with God can be achieved through prayer when men and women pray separately.

Within the Orthodox tradition, women have been working towards change in recent times, promoting greater equality, looking at ways of expanding their roles in prayer services, and taking greater community leadership roles. Currently Orthodox rabbis are all male.

In Orthodox services, it is not uncommon for some of the congregation to arrive late and for people to catch up at their own pace. This may mean that for a time the late arrivals are doing things differently to everyone else.

> **Objective**
> - Understand some of the differences between worship in Orthodox and Reform synagogues.

> **Key terms**
> - **Orthodox Jews:** Jews who emphasise the importance of following the laws and guidance in the Torah; they believe the Torah was given directly by God to Moses, so should be followed as closely as possible
> - **Reform Jews:** Jews who believe the laws and guidance in the Torah can be adapted for modern times; they believe the Torah was inspired by God but written by humans, so can be interpreted according to the times
> - **cantor (chazzan):** a person who leads or chants prayers in the synagogue

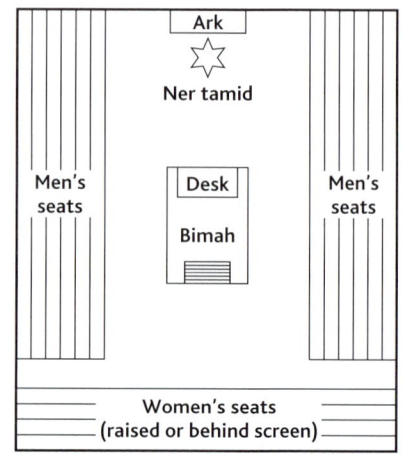

▲ An example of the layout of an Orthodox synagogue

Chapter 10 Judaism: practices

▲ A service in a Reform synagogue, where women and men sit together

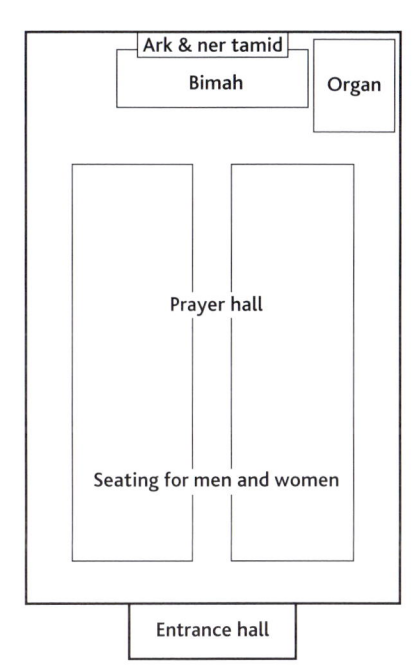

▲ An example of the layout of a Reform synagogue

Orthodox Jewish men always cover their heads when attending the synagogue, and some cover their heads at all times. They wear a skull cap known as a kippah or yamulkah. Some also wear a hat over the kippah. The covering of the head is a sign of respect for and fear of God; it shows that the worshipper recognises that God is above humankind. Married women also cover their heads by wearing a scarf or a hat.

Reform synagogue services

Many Reform synagogues do not hold daily services, but concentrate instead on celebrating Shabbat and festivals. In Reform synagogues the men and women sit together and the person leading the service faces the congregation most of the time. The Reform communities allow women to take a more active part than in the Orthodox tradition. Women can perform all rituals traditionally reserved for men such as becoming a rabbi, publicly reading the Torah, being a cantor and being part of the minyan. Reform services are shorter than Orthodox ones but tend to be more rigidly structured; there is a set time and all worshippers are usually present at the beginning.

Reform services are conducted in both Hebrew and the country's own language (English in the UK), and the singing may be accompanied by musical instruments. In larger synagogues in America, there is often a choir to lead the singing, but this is not common in the UK.

In a Reform service, most men wear a head-covering and some female worshippers wear a kippah or a hat.

Activities

1. Name two different groups or movements within Judaism in Britain today.
2. Explain the reasons why these groups have some different practices in worship.
3. Who leads worship in the synagogue?
4. Explain the major differences in worship between Orthodox and Reform Jews.
5. Give two reasons why Jews cover their heads in worship.

Extension activity

Look up Psalm 150, which is used as part of morning worship. Explain what it says about God and how God should be worshipped.

★ Study tip

Make a chart to show the differences between Orthodox and Reform beliefs and practices. It will help you to learn the differences.

Summary

You should now be able to explain some of the differences between the worship of Orthodox and Reform Jews.

239

10.4 Daily services and prayer

■ Tallit and tefillin

During morning prayers Orthodox Jewish men wear the **tallit** and, on weekdays, the **tefillin**, and in the Reform tradition some men and women wear them as well. The tallit is a prayer shawl made from wool or silk, with a long tassel called a tzitzit attached to each corner. It is usually white with blue or black stripes. The tallit reminds Jews that they are obeying God's word whenever they wear it.

The tefillin are a pair of black leather boxes (phylacteries) containing passages of scripture, including some of the words of the Shema. One is fastened with leather straps to the centre of the forehead. The other is wound around the upper arm in line with the heart. This reminds Jews that during prayers their total concentration should be on God and the prayers should be completely from the heart.

> And this shall serve you as a sign on your hand and as a reminder on your forehead – **in order that the Teaching of the Lord may be in your mouth** – that with a mighty hand the Lord freed you from Egypt.
>
> *Exodus* 13:9

Objectives

- Understand how Jews worship in public.
- Understand the significance of prayer for Jews, including the Amidah.

Key terms

- **tallit:** a prayer shawl
- **tefillin:** small leather boxes containing extracts from the Torah, strapped to the wearer's arm and forehead for morning prayers
- **Amidah:** also known as the 'standing prayer', it is the central prayer of Jewish worship

■ The format of Jewish services

Prayer is extremely important to Jews as they believe that it builds the relationship between God and humankind. Devout Orthodox Jews pray three times a day. Formal prayer services are held in Orthodox synagogues in the morning, afternoon and evening, although such services need not take place in a synagogue. For Sabbath and daily services all that is required is a minimum of ten adult males (in the Orthodox tradition) or ten men and women (in the Reform tradition) to be present. Daily prayers are taken from a book called a siddur, which sets out the order of the prayers.

The opening prayers vary depending on the service, but might consist of a series of prayers and psalms that praise and give thanks to God.

The Shema is the Jewish statement of belief, which begins, 'Hear O Israel, the Lord our God, the Lord is One'. It is accompanied by blessings (prayers), which are said before and after the Shema.

▲ The tzitzit tassels on a tallit represent the 613 Jewish laws

Research activity

Use the internet to find out more about the Jewish daily prayers and how the three services differ.

Chapter 10   Judaism: practices

The **Amidah** is also called the 'standing prayer' or the 'eighteen blessings' (although the blessings now number nineteen). On a weekday it forms the core of all Jewish prayer services, and is prayed in silence while standing and facing Jerusalem. It consists of a series of blessings:

- The first three blessings in the Amidah praise God; they also inspire the worshipper and ask for God's mercy.
- The middle thirteen blessings are prayers of petition and intercession (requests for God's help): they consist of six personal requests, six requests for the community, and a final request that God accept the prayers.
- The final three blessings thank God for the opportunity to serve him and pray for peace, goodness, kindness and compassion.

▲ *Tefillin are fastened to the forehead and the upper arm*

The Amidah is sometimes followed by a reading from the Torah.

The final prayers include the closing Aleinu prayer. This prayer is recited at the end of each of the three daily services and gives praise and thanks to God.

■ The importance of prayer

Jews believe that prayer is vital for communicating with God. They believe that prayer brings them closer to God as it enables them to focus their hearts, minds and souls on him. It reinforces their faith by helping them find new insights into their relationship with God. Formal prayer in the synagogue also helps them to remember what their faith is all about and strengthens the sense of Jewish community.

Activities

1. Why do Jews wear the tallit and tefillin at morning prayers?
2. How many times a day is an observant Jew expected to pray?
3. Describe what happens during a typical morning prayer service in the synagogue.
4. What is the Amidah?
5. Explain why prayer is seen as very important in Judaism.

Summary

You should now be able to describe the main features of daily prayer in Judaism, and explain why prayer is important to Jews.

Extension activity

Look up Deuteronomy 6:4–9 and write down what this passage is telling Jews to do. Explain why these instructions are important to Jews.

Discussion activity

In small groups or in pairs evaluate the following statements:

'Jews can pray whenever they wish so they don't need set times.'

'Jews should wear the tallit and tefillin for all their prayers.'

⭐ Study tip

When learning about Jewish prayer, it is important not only to know how Jews pray but also to understand why it is a central part of their religion.

10.5 Shabbat in the synagogue

What is Shabbat?

Every week Jews celebrate a special holy day called **Shabbat** (the Sabbath day). It is seen as a gift from God of a day of rest and renewal. Described in Jewish literature, music and poetry as a bride or queen, Shabbat provides the opportunity to relax and temporarily forget the concerns of everyday life. It is also a time to worship God and enjoy family life.

Shabbat begins just before sunset each Friday and lasts until an hour after sunset on Saturday, approximately 25 hours in total. All the shopping, cooking and cleaning is done in advance – such work isn't allowed during Shabbat itself, which is a day of rest – and Jews look forward to a very special time. It is considered the most important holy day as it was explicitly commanded by God in the Ten Commandments:

> **Remember the sabbath day and keep it holy.** Six days you shall labor and do all your work, but the seventh day is a sabbath of the Lord your God: you shall not do any work.
>
> *Exodus* 20:8–10

Celebrating Shabbat is a reminder of the agreement (covenant) made between God and the Jewish people, and is an occasion to rejoice that God has kept his promises. The idea of rest comes from the Genesis story in which God created everything in six days and rested on the seventh day. So Shabbat is seen as a time when the demands of a busy life can be replaced by an oasis of calm, when no work should be done. It is a time to forget distractions such as the television and internet, and instead relax and worship together as a family. Shabbat is observed and celebrated in different ways in Judaism; the following pages describe customs that are common to many Jews.

Shabbat services

On the Friday evening there is a brief service (which lasts around 45 minutes) in the synagogue. Shabbat is welcomed like a bride coming to meet her husband, the Jewish people. Some synagogues hold services specially designed for families with children on either Friday evening or Saturday morning. These include storytelling, discussion, games and music. At the end of the Friday service, the prayer leader takes a cup of wine and recites a blessing (Kiddush) thanking God for having given Shabbat to the Jewish people.

The Saturday morning service is longer than the weekday services and includes not only the prayers and blessings, but also a reading from the Torah and often a sermon. The Torah is divided into sections so that each week a different part is read, meaning that the entire five books of Moses are completed in a year.

Objectives

- Understand the significance of Shabbat for Jews.
- Understand how Shabbat is celebrated in the synagogue.

Key term

- **Shabbat:** the Jewish holy day of the week; a day of spiritual renewal starting shortly before sunset on Friday and continuing to sunset on Saturday

▲ *A yad is used as a pointer when reading the Torah scroll*

Chapter 10 Judaism: practices

The Torah

During the Saturday morning service, when the doors or curtains of the Ark (Aron Hakodesh) are opened to reveal the Torah scrolls, it is customary for the congregation to stand. This is a reminder of how the Israelites stood at the bottom of Mount Sinai when Moses returned with the Ten Commandments. The congregation chants Numbers 10:35, and the Torah is taken from the Ark and dressed with a cover and various ornaments, such as a breastplate, crown or belt. This reminds Jews of the vestments worn by the priests in early Judaism.

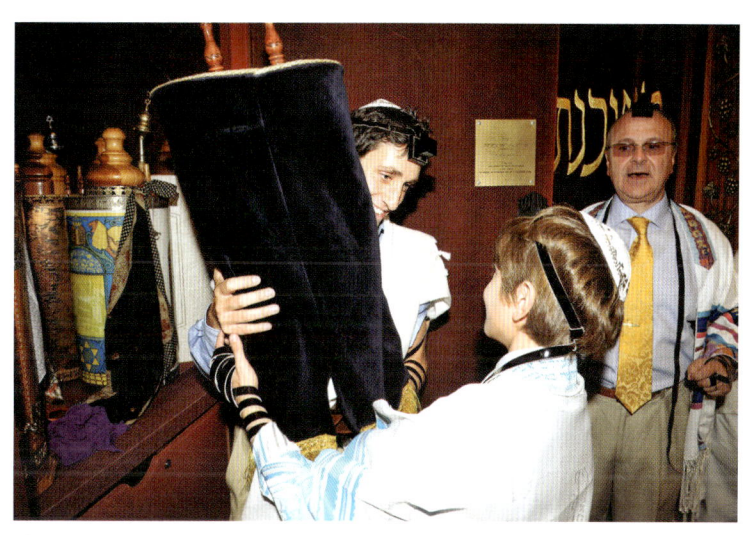

▲ The Torah is dressed with a cover before it is paraded around the synagogue

The Torah is held in front of the congregation while verses from scripture are chanted, after which it is paraded around the synagogue. This represents the march through the wilderness, when the Jews carried the holy Ark (containing the Ten Commandments) from Mount Sinai to Jerusalem. It also gives the congregation an opportunity to be close to the Torah and give thanks for having God's word. As it passes, many touch it with their tzitzit or siddur and then touch their lips. This is done to show that God's words should be on their lips and that his words are sweet like honey (Ezekiel 3:3).

The reading for the day (the sidra) is read from the bimah. Once this is finished the Torah scrolls are dressed again, then paraded around the synagogue once more before being placed back in the Ark.

The rabbi or visiting speaker then gives a sermon, which may be based on the sidra or something important in the news. On leaving the synagogue, Jews wish each other 'Shabbat Shalom' ('have a peaceful Shabbat').

Activities

1. What is Shabbat?
2. Give three reasons why Shabbat is very special to Jews.
3. Describe what Jews do to get ready for the Shabbat celebrations.
4. What services take place in the synagogue during Shabbat?
5. Explain what happens to the Torah during the Shabbat synagogue service.

Discussion activity

In small groups or in pairs discuss the following statement: 'Shabbat is a luxury that is not necessary in the modern world.'

Research activity

Use the Internet or a library to find out some of the particular things that Orthodox Jews are not allowed to do during Shabbat.

★ Study tip

Remember that Shabbat is both a day of rest and a day devoted to God.

Summary

You should now understand some of the reasons why Shabbat is special to Jews, and know how it is celebrated in the synagogue.

243

10.6 Shabbat in the home

■ Shabbat preparations

In Jewish homes, all the work is done and the home is prepared before Shabbat begins on Friday evening. The house is cleaned, the food is prepared, and the family washes and changes into clean, smart clothes.

> **Objective**
> - Understand how Shabbat is celebrated in the home.

Shabbat is often seen as being like welcoming a special bride or queen into the home. The table is set with the best cutlery and crockery, and at least two candles: these represent the two commandments to remember and observe Shabbat. Many homes also have an additional candle for each member of the family.

Wine or grape juice and two loaves of challah bread are also placed on the table; the loaves are covered with a special cover whenever possible. (Challah bread is a type of bread made with eggs that is usually braided before baking; it is eaten on Shabbat and other special occasions.) Shabbat wine is sweet and is usually drunk from a special goblet known as the Kiddush cup. Drinking this wine on Shabbat symbolises joy and celebration. The loaves represent the two portions of manna (a type of food) that God provided for the Israelites on Shabbat while they were in the wilderness.

▲ *Welcoming in the Shabbat*

■ Lighting the candles

A female member of the family (usually the wife and mother) has the honour of lighting the candles. She lights them about eighteen minutes before sunset and once they are lit she welcomes in the Shabbat. She does this by waving or beckoning with her arms around the candles, and then covers her eyes to recite a blessing: 'Blessed are You, Lord, our God, King of the Universe, who sanctifies us with his commandments, and commands us to light the candles of Shabbat'. She also says a prayer asking God to bless the family. (If no women are present, a man lights the candles instead.)

■ The Friday meal

After the evening service in the synagogue, once a family has returned home, the parents bless their children and the head of the household recites the Kiddush blessings while holding up the Kiddush cup. The family say 'Amen' at the end of each blessing. Each family member then washes their hands as an act of purification before taking their place ready for the meal.

> **Activities**
> 1. Describe four things that are done to prepare the home for Shabbat and explain why these actions are taken.
> 2. Describe how Shabbat is welcomed into the home.
> 3. Explain what happens at the Friday meal.
> 4. Why do you think that the Friday meal takes a long time?
> 5. Explain what happens in the ceremony that ends Shabbat.

Chapter 10   Judaism: practices

Once everyone is seated, the head of the household removes the cover from the challah loaves and lifts them up while saying a blessing. The bread is cut into slices or broken into pieces, dipped or sprinkled in salt and passed around to each person so that everyone has a piece. Then the meal begins, which might last for a few hours. After each course, stories from the scriptures might be told to the children or songs might be sung. There is no rush as it is a time to relax and enjoy the company of the family and any friends whom they have invited. The meal ends with a prayer of thanksgiving for the food.

▲ *A Jewish family performing the havdalah service*

■ Saturday

After the morning service in the synagogue, the family enjoys another special meal in their home. During the afternoon parents may spend time with their children and study the Torah. Then there is another smaller meal before sunset.

The end of Shabbat is marked by the havdalah service. This is performed in the home after nightfall, once three stars can be seen in the sky.

Celebrating Shabbat

Ruth Cohen, an Orthodox Jew, describes how Shabbat ends:

'As the Shabbat finishes there is a bittersweet atmosphere – excitement for the coming week mixed with sadness that Shabbat has just finished. We mark the end of Shabbat with a ceremony called Havdalah. Havdalah consists of blessings performed over a cup of wine, sweet smelling spices, and a candle with several wicks. The besamim is meant to soothe the soul now that the Shabbat queen has left, and the candle is to provide a light now that the light of Shabbat has left the home.

▲ *The Havdalah candle, Kiddush cup and spices*

After the ceremony normal weekday activities may be resumed, although some Jews remain dressed in their Shabbat finest and have a meal.'

Discussion activity

In pairs or small groups discuss the following statement: 'Getting prepared, as if to welcome royalty into the home, is a good way to get everything ready for Shabbat.'

⭐ Study tip

Make sure you know, in the right order, what happens when Jews celebrate Shabbat in the home. A simple diagram or flowchart might help you to remember the different steps.

Summary

You should now be able to describe how Jews observe Shabbat in the home, and explain the significance of their actions.

245

10.7 Worship in the home; the written and oral law

Worship in the home and private prayer

Jews believe that every day brings the opportunity to worship God. Prayers are said three times each day either in the home or in the synagogue. Jews traditionally stand to pray, and if they are alone they pray silently. Each house has reminders to obey God's commandments, such as a kitchen that is designed to meet the requirements of the Jewish food laws, and mezuzot. The mezuah is a small box that contains a handwritten scroll of verses from the Torah, which is fixed to a doorpost. Jews touch the mezuzah as a sign of respect and a reminder of God's laws.

> ### Worshipping in the home
>
> Janet Berenson describes what happens in her home:
>
> 'I am a member of Finchley Reform Synagogue and a Jewish Renewal community, the Ruach Chavurah, so prayer and mindfulness are important to me. I start each day with the Modeh Ani prayer, giving thanks that my soul has been returned to me, followed by the blessing thanking God that my body works as it should. I say the Shema every morning and at night. It doesn't matter where I am when I pray, as I believe that it is the practice that matters, and God hears my prayers wherever I may be.
>
> I have a mezuzah on my front doorpost and on my bedroom door, and every time I leave and come home, I touch it to remind myself of the words of the Shema and to live my day in a way that demonstrates loving God with all my heart, soul and strength. Daily prayer helps me to stay conscious of the way I treat people, animals and the planet, and reminds me to live responsibly and ethically as a steward of God's world.'

Study of the sacred writings

Tenakh: the written law

The Jewish sacred scriptures are known as the **Tenakh**. The Tenakh consists of 24 books (which can all be found in what Christians call the Old Testament), grouped into three main parts. The word TeNaKh is formed from taking the first letter of the Hebrew names for each of these three parts. They are:

1. the **Torah**: the five books of Moses, which form the basis of Jewish law
2. the **Nevi'im** (the Prophets): eight books that continue to trace Jewish history and expand on the laws in the Torah
3. the **Ketuvim** (the Writings): eleven books that contain a collection of poetry, stories, advice, historical accounts and more.

Objectives

- Understand how Jews worship and pray in the home.
- Understand what the Tenakh and Talmud contain, and why they are important to Jews.

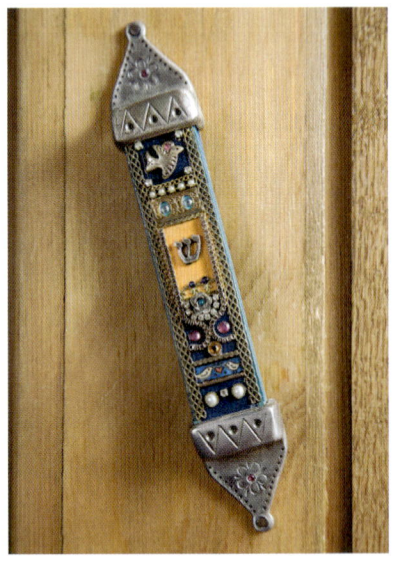

▲ A mezuzah on the doorpost of a house

Activities

1. What is a mezuzah and what is its purpose?
2. Why do you think some Jews pray at home rather than in the synagogue?
3. Name the three parts of the Tenakh and explain what each part contains.
4. Explain why and how the Mishnah and Gemara were formed.
5. Explain the importance of the Talmud to Orthodox Jews.

Chapter 10 Judaism: practices

Talmud: the oral law

Understanding the Torah (the law) is an important part of Jewish life. For the early Jews, teachings on how to interpret the Torah and apply its rules to life were passed from generation to generation by word of mouth, and became known as oral law. There was a danger that these teachings would get altered or misinterpreted and so it was important that they were written down. Rabbi Judah Hanassi did this in 200 CE by bringing together all the oral law into one document known as the **Mishnah**. It was formed of six sections, each one of which is known as a 'seder', dealing with subjects such as dietary laws, marriage and divorce, and laws of Shabbat.

The Mishnah caused much debate. These discussions were written down, organised and brought together in 500 CE and became known as the **Gemara**. The Mishnah and Gemara were then combined to form the **Talmud**.

The Torah and the Talmud are studied extensively by Orthodox Jews, as they are regarded as the source for all Jewish laws, legal teachings and decisions that affect their daily life. Regular lessons and lectures are held to help with this, including in colleges of advanced Jewish studies called Yeshivot. Reform Jews regard the authority of the Torah and the Talmud in a different way and may not study them as much.

> ### Key terms
> - **Tenakh:** the 24 books of Jewish scriptures
> - **Torah:** (1) the five books revealed by God to Moses (2) the first section of the Tenakh (the Jewish Bible), and the Jewish written law
> - **Nevi'im:** the second section of the Tenakh; the prophets
> - **Ketuvim:** the third section of the Tenakh; the writings
> - **Mishnah:** the first written version of Jewish oral law; part of the Talmud
> - **Gemara:** a commentary on the Mishnah; part of the Talmud
> - **Talmud:** a commentary by the rabbis on the Torah – it consists of the Mishnah and Gemara together in one collection

▲ *Studying the sacred writings is important for many Jews*

⭐ Study tip

To help you remember how Jews worship in the home, make a bullet-point list of everything this involves (including at Shabbat).

> **Summary**
> You should now know how Jews worship in the home. You should also know what the Tenakh and Talmud contain, and understand their importance for Jews.

💬 Discussion activity

In pairs or in a small group discuss the following statements:

'Both the written law (Tenakh) and the oral law (Talmud) were written so long ago that they cannot be very relevant for daily life today.'

'The Talmud teaches Jews all they need to know to follow the Jewish way of life.'

10.8 Ceremonies associated with birth

■ The importance of rituals in Jewish family life

For Jews, family life is very important. The family is where the Jewish faith is preserved and passed on to the next generation. Four important events in the life of the family are celebrated with religious **rituals**. These stages in life are sometimes called 'rites of passage' because they involve moving from one phase of life to another. These are birth, coming of age, marriage and death. The wider Jewish community helps families to celebrate and observe these rites of passage.

■ Ceremonies associated with birth

For Jews the birth of a child is a happy event, especially because it fulfils the commandment in Genesis 1:28 to have children:

> God blessed them and God said to them, 'Be fertile and increase, fill the earth and master it.'
>
> Genesis 1:28

There are three Jewish rituals associated with birth: naming, circumcision, and the redemption of the firstborn son.

Naming ceremony

Boys are named at their circumcision, usually eight days after their birth. For a girl, it was traditional for her father to announce her name in the synagogue about a month after her birth. This would formally introduce her to the community and to God.

Nowadays it is common for both boys and girls born into Orthodox families to be blessed in the synagogue on the first Shabbat after their birth. The father goes forward to recite the Torah blessing, and to ask God for the good health of his wife and baby. A baby girl's name will be announced at this point, but a boy will be named later at his circumcision. In Reform synagogues both parents will take part in the ceremony, which may not necessarily happen on the first Shabbat after the child's birth.

▲ Strictly Orthodox Jews preparing for a Brit Milah ceremony

Brit Milah

Circumcision recalls the covenant that God made with Abraham. It is a lifelong reminder of membership of God's chosen people.

Objectives

- Consider the importance of rituals in Jewish family life.
- Know about ceremonies associated with birth, including Brit Milah, and understand their importance to Jews.

Key terms

- **rituals:** religious ceremonies that are performed according to a set pattern
- **Brit Milah:** ceremony of male circumcision; the removal of the foreskin for religious reasons

Links

To read more about the covenant with Abraham see page 223.

Chapter 10   Judaism: practices

> You shall circumcise the flesh of your foreskin, and that shall be the **sign of the covenant** between Me and you. And throughout the generations, every male among you shall be circumcised at the age of eight days … **any male who is uncircumcised** … shall be cut off from his kin; he **has broken My covenant.**
>
> *Genesis* 17:11–14

Baby boys have the **Brit Milah** ceremony when they are eight days old. Traditionally, a close friend or relative is given the honour of placing the baby on an empty chair that symbolises the presence of the prophet Elijah. A trained circumciser (the mohel) picks up the baby and places him on the knee of a person chosen to be the 'companion of the child' (sandek). This is an honoured role often given to the baby's grandfather or a respected member of the synagogue congregation. The boy's father blesses his son with the words: 'Blessed are you Lord our God, King of the Universe, who sanctified us with his mitzvot and commanded us to enter my son into the covenant of Abraham.'

The others respond, 'Just as he has entered into the covenant, so may he enter into Torah, into marriage, and into good deeds.'

A blessing is said over wine and the baby is formally named. The foreskin of the baby's penis is removed in a simple operation that quickly heals. The family and guests then enjoy a festive meal to celebrate.

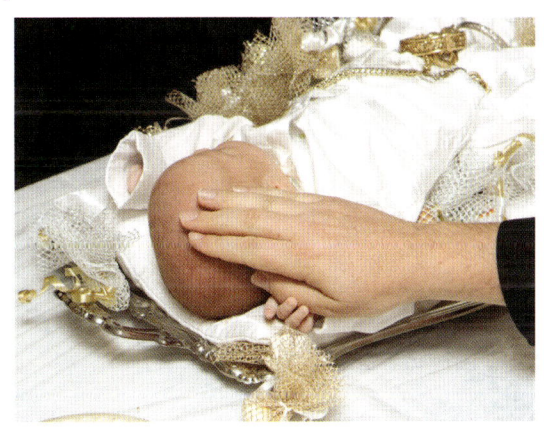

▲ *A Jewish boy is often presented for redemption on a silver tray*

Redemption of the firstborn son

Some Orthodox Jews give a small amount of money 31 days after the birth of their firstborn son, to 'redeem' him from Temple service. The Temple in Jerusalem no longer exists, but some Orthodox parents keep up the tradition in a ceremony known as Pidyon Ha-Ben. Five silver coins are given to a kohen: a descendent of the priests who used to work in the Temple. Prayers are also said asking that the child may 'enter into Torah, into marriage, and into good deeds.'

This tradition comes from a command in Numbers 18:15–16:

> The first issue of the womb of every being, man or beast, that is offered to the LORD, shall be yours; **but you shall have the first-born of man redeemed** … **Take as their redemption price,** from the age of one month up, **the money equivalent of five shekels.**
>
> *Numbers* 18:15–16

Activities

1. Explain why rituals are important in Jewish family life.
2. Explain how the birth of a baby girl is announced in the synagogue.
3. In your own words, describe what happens at the Brit Milah ceremony, and explain why it is important to Jewish families.

Research activity

Find out how Reform Jews celebrate the birth of a child, including whether there are differences between celebrations for boys and girls.

Discussion activity

Discuss whether circumcision should be permitted in Britain today.

⭐ Study tip

It is helpful to note the similarities and differences in the way rituals are carried out in different Jewish communities, and the importance of these rituals for each community.

Summary

You should now be able to explain the importance of rituals in Jewish family life, and the purpose and meaning of ceremonies associated with birth, including Brit Milah.

10.9 Bar and Bat Mitzvah

■ Coming of age for Jews

When Jewish boys reach 13 and girls reach 12, they are considered old enough to take full responsibility for practising their faith. Boys have their **Bar Mitzvah** ceremony at 13 and become a 'son of the commandment'. Girls aged 12 may also have a **Bat Mitzvah** ceremony and become a 'daughter of the commandment'. Although there is no mention of ceremonies to mark coming of age in the Torah or Talmud, they are implied elsewhere, for example in Mishnah Berurah 225:6.

Objectives
- Know how Jews celebrate the Bar and Bat Mitzvah ceremonies.
- Understand the meaning and importance of these ceremonies.

Key terms
- **Bar Mitzvah:** celebration of a boy coming of age at 13; literally 'son of the commandment'
- **Bat Mitzvah:** celebration of a girl coming of age at 12, in Reform synagogues; literally 'daughter of the commandment'

▲ *A Jewish boy is helped to put on tefillin before his Bar Mitzvah*

Celebrating a Bar Mitzvah

At the first opportunity after his thirteenth birthday (usually the first Shabbat), the boy is called to read from the Torah at the normal service in the synagogue. Many synagogues hold classes to prepare boys for this occasion. He will wear a tallit for the first time, may lead part of the service or prayers, and make a short speech. His father thanks God for bringing his son to maturity and declares that he is now responsible for his own actions. Many Jewish families then hold a celebratory meal or party in honour of the Bar Mitzvah boy and he receives gifts.

Celebrating a Bat Mitzvah

Reform Jews often have a Bat Mitzvah ceremony and celebrations for girls that are very similar to a Bar Mitzvah. The girl will read from the Torah, give a short speech, and may lead part of the prayer service. This will often be followed by a celebratory meal or party.

Since Orthodox Jewish women do not take an active role in leading synagogue worship, Orthodox Jews sometimes mark a girl's Bat Mitzvah with a family meal and small religious gifts. The girl may make a speech or give a brief Torah lesson at the end of a synagogue service. The girl's future role in keeping a Jewish home is part of Bat Mitzvah preparation for girls.

Giving a Bar Mitzvah speech

Sam Podolsky, a young American Jew, made a speech at his Bar Mitzvah explaining what it meant to him. Here is part of what he said:

'Thank you all for coming and sharing this special day with me – the day I become a Bar Mitzvah. My Torah portion … includes some of the most fundamental principles of the Jewish faith. It talks about the unity of Israel, future redemption, freedom of choice and the practicality of the Torah. It is this last principle that stands out to me … the Torah is not some far-off ideal that is beyond our reach. Rather, it is something down here on earth – that we all can relate to in our day-to-day lives … Becoming a Bar Mitzvah doesn't only mean I am becoming an adult in the Jewish religion. It also means that I am taking on the responsibilities of the Torah. Preparing for my Bar Mitzvah, such as studying, putting on tefillin and writing this speech has been meaningful to me, and I have learned so much from it. Also, becoming a Bar Mitzvah has helped me strengthen my relationship with Hashem [God] and the Torah. It has also brought me closer to my family, who were involved in my studies and have helped bring me to this day. I also found that my heritage is very important to me. I hope one day to pass along my knowledge of Judaism to my future children.'

▲ *A Jewish girl practises reading from the Torah in preparation for her Bat Mitzvah*

Activities

1. Explain the different ways in which Orthodox and Reform Jews mark boys' and girls' coming of age.
2. Read the case study. In your own words explain what Sam's Bar Mitzvah meant to him.
3. 'Bar Mitzvah and Bat Mitzvah celebrations are no longer relevant in modern Britain.' Evaluate this statement. Be sure to include different points of view and refer to Jewish teachings in your answer.

Research activities

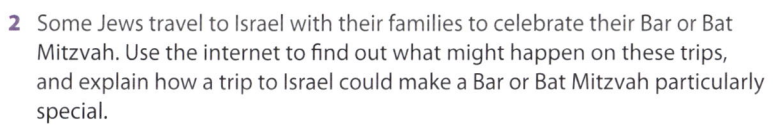

1. Find out more about how Jewish girls prepare for their Bat Mitzvah in Reform Judaism.
2. Some Jews travel to Israel with their families to celebrate their Bar or Bat Mitzvah. Use the internet to find out what might happen on these trips, and explain how a trip to Israel could make a Bar or Bat Mitzvah particularly special.

Discussion activity

With a partner or in a small group, discuss the different ages when people are allowed to do certain things in Britain, such as drive, vote, watch certain films or drink. When do you think a young person 'comes of age'?

★ Study tip

It is important to be able to explain the impact of a Bar or Bat Mitzvah on an individual and for the Jewish community as a whole.

Summary

You should now be able to explain how Jews celebrate their coming of age, and why the Bar and Bat Mitzvah ceremonies are important to them.

10.10 Marriage

■ The importance of marriage for Jews

According to Jewish law, **marriage** is a two-step process. The first stage is betrothal: a period of time, traditionally the 12 months before the wedding ceremony, when the couple are engaged or promised to each other. The second stage is the wedding itself.

It was traditional for Jewish parents to choose a partner for their children, often with the help of a matchmaker. Some Orthodox Jews still do this because they believe the matchmaker is working on God's behalf to find a soulmate for each person. For Jews, marriage is more than just two people choosing to spend their lives together: it is a spiritual bond, where two souls are fused to become one. Marriage is the way of experiencing holiness in everyday life.

> ❝ Hence a man leaves his father and mother and clings to his wife, so that they become one flesh. ❞
>
> *Genesis* 2:24

Objectives

- Know what happens during a Jewish marriage ceremony.
- Consider the meaning and importance of the ceremony.

Key term

- **marriage:** a legal union between a man and a woman (or in some countries, including the UK, two people of the same sex) as partners in a relationship

Discussion activity

Discuss what takes place when a couple get engaged in Britain today. Are there special celebrations or certain rituals involved?

■ Betrothal

The Hebrew word for betrothal is 'kiddushin'. It comes from a word meaning 'made holy' or 'set aside'. The couple are set aside for each other and no other. Betrothal has legal status in Jewish law and cannot be broken except by death or divorce.

Traditionally a special kiddushin ceremony was held a year before the wedding, but now this ceremony is held at the wedding itself. During the year of betrothal the couple will not live together, but they do prepare for their future lives together.

During the betrothal part of the ceremony, a wedding contract (ketubah) is drawn up. For Orthodox Jews this covers aspects

▲ Jewish weddings take place under a canopy (chuppah) that symbolises the couple's home

such as the husband's duties to his wife, the conditions of inheritance upon his death, how the couple's children will be supported, and how he will provide for his wife if they get divorced. For Reform Jews the ketubah usually focuses on spiritual aspirations rather than legal rights. It often describes mutual hopes for the marriage, which are the same for both husband and wife. It might also include a promise not to oppose divorce if the couple should separate.

At the last Shabbat service in the synagogue before the wedding day, the husband-to-be takes part in the Torah blessing and announces his intention to marry. The congregation joins in a small celebration after the service with food, drink and wine. The couple and their families may then have a celebratory lunch together. This may be the last time the couple see each other before the wedding day.

■ The wedding

Weddings take place in the synagogue, or elsewhere such as in a hotel, on any day except Shabbat or a festival. The ceremony is led by a rabbi and held under a canopy called a chuppah, which symbolises the couple's home.

The couple may fast on their wedding day to cleanse themselves of sin and come to the ceremony with the right attitude. The betrothal ceremony takes place first. While the groom stands under the chuppah facing Jerusalem, the bride is brought to join him by her mother. The bride circles the groom, they recite two blessings over wine, and the groom places a plain ring on the bride's finger, saying 'Behold, you are consecrated to me by means of this ring, according to the rituals of Moses and Israel.' Reform couples usually both exchange rings.

After the betrothal ceremony, the marriage contract is signed in the presence of witnesses, then read out and given to the bride. An important wedding guest, family member or the rabbi recites seven wedding blessings, then the rabbi makes a short speech and blesses the couple in front of the congregation.

The groom breaks a glass (wrapped in paper or cloth for safety) under his heel to show regret for the destruction of the Temple in Jerusalem. This symbolises that in life there is hardship as well as joy. The congregation shout 'Mazel Tov', which means 'good luck'. Finally the couple spend a short time together in a private room to symbolise their new status as a married couple. A joyous wedding reception follows that includes music and dancing.

> **Summary**
>
> You should now know what happens during a Jewish betrothal and wedding, and be able to explain its significance.

Activities

1. Explain why marriage is so important for Jews.
2. How is the Jewish community involved in a couple's marriage rituals?
3. Write down three conditions you would want in a marriage contract. Explain why.
4. Explain two symbols used in a Jewish wedding ceremony.

Research activity

Look up more detailed information about Jewish wedding ceremonies on the BBC Religion website. Make a note of any other customs mentioned.

▲ The groom breaks a glass with his heel

★ Study tip

Remember that marriage customs can vary depending on local traditions, and whether the couple are Orthodox or Reform Jews.

10.11 Mourning for the dead

Customs surrounding death

When a Jew is nearing death, their family tries to visit them and makes sure someone stays with them so they do not die alone. Just before they die, the person makes a final confession and recites the Shema if they are able to do so.

When Jews first hear of the death of a close family member, they follow the example of Jacob by making a small tear in their clothes. For a parent, they make a tear over their hearts; for any other close relative they make a tear on the right side of the chest. When Jews hear of a death, they say a blessing that refers to God as the true judge ('Blessed are You, Lord, our God, King of the Universe, the True Judge'). This shows that they accept God's taking of the person's life.

> Jacob rent his clothes, put sackcloth on his loins, and observed mourning for his son many days.
>
> *Genesis 37:34*

Mourning

For Jews there are clear set periods for **mourning** that decrease in intensity. This allows a family to grieve fully but also helps them to get back to normal life.

Jews believe that the soul does not fully leave the person until the burial takes place. It is important for the soul to feel the comfort and support of family members before this happens. During this first period of mourning, close family are left to grieve without having to follow certain religious rules.

Once the burial takes place, a meal of condolence consisting of bread and eggs (symbols of new life) is prepared by a close friend or relative. This marks the end of the immediate mourning period.

Shiva (seven days of intense mourning) begins on the day of burial. The mourners stay at home and sit on low stools or on the floor rather than on chairs. They do not wear leather shoes, shave or cut their hair, wear make-up or do work. Mirrors are covered so they cannot focus on their appearance, and they wear the clothes they tore. Prayer services are held three times a day in the home. Relatives, friends and neighbours make up the minyan (ten people required for certain prayers). The mourners recite the **kaddish** to praise God and pray for the coming age of eternal peace.

Objective
- Know about Jewish practices associated with death and mourning, and understand their importance.

Key terms
- **mourning:** a period of time spent remembering a person who has died
- **shiva:** an intense period of mourning that lasts for seven days
- **kaddish:** a prayer said by Jewish mourners that praises God and asks for peace

Links
To read more about Jewish beliefs in the afterlife see pages 218–219.

▲ During shiva, Jews sit on low stools or the floor and pray regularly

Chapter 10 Judaism: practices

After shiva has finished, the lesser period of mourning begins and lasts until 30 days after the person's death. During this time, normal life resumes but mourners do not listen to music, go to parties or shave or cut their hair. Male mourners say the kaddish daily in the synagogue.

The final period of mourning lasts for 11 months. Mourners do not attend parties and children continue to say the kaddish for a parent that has died. Formal mourning stops when this final period is over, but sons continue to mark the anniversary of a parent's death by reciting the kaddish and, if possible, making a Torah blessing. As a memorial, both sons and daughters light a candle that burns for 24 hours.

The funeral

While some Reform Jews accept cremation, most Jews are buried as soon after death as possible, usually within 24 hours. Before the burial, someone stays with the body and candles are lit beside it. The body is prepared for burial by being carefully washed. It is wrapped in a plain linen cloth, as well as a tallit for men. A corner fringe of the tallit is removed to show it will no longer be used in this life. The body is placed in a simple coffin to show that everyone is equal in death.

Funerals do not usually take place in the synagogue, which is considered a place of the living. The body is transported directly to the cemetery for burial. The service lasts about 20 minutes. Psalms are recited, prayers are said, scriptures are read and a rabbi says a few words about the person. Once the coffin is lowered, mourners shovel earth on top of it. After offering condolences, everyone washes their hands before leaving the cemetery to show that they are leaving death behind.

In Jewish law, a tombstone must be placed on the grave so that the person is remembered. Some families wait until the end of the 12-month mourning period, and may have a small ceremony to mark the unveiling of the headstone. Jews do not use flowers to remember the dead but visitors often place a small stone to show they have visited the grave.

▲ Jews often mark their visit to a grave by placing a small stone there

Discussion activity

With a partner or in a small group, discuss whether you think having fixed periods of mourning is helpful. Give reasons for your opinions.

Research activity

Use the internet to read the mourners' kaddish prayer. What is the prayer asking for?

Activities

1. What does a Jewish family do before and just after the death of a loved one?
2. Explain what happens in a Jewish home during shiva.
3. Describe what takes place at a Jewish funeral.

★ Study tip

Remember that customs may vary between Orthodox and Reform Jews.

Summary

You should now know how Jews mourn a death and understand the importance of Jewish mourning practices.

10.12 Dietary laws

Jewish dietary laws

Jews have strict rules (**dietary laws**) about what they can and cannot eat. Food that is permitted is called **kosher**. Food that is unacceptable is called **trefah**, which means 'torn'. Trefah originally described animals whose flesh had been torn by a predator and so couldn't be eaten.

The kosher laws are found in the Torah, particularly in Leviticus 11 and Deuteronomy 14. The Talmud explains in more detail how Jews should put these laws into practice.

Although the Torah itself gives no logical reason for the dietary laws, some people think that the rules seem to have originally been for hygiene or health reasons, or because an animal was more valuable for uses other than food. For example, the prohibition against pork was sensible in a hot climate where pigs could carry many diseases. Camels were more valued for transporting goods across deserts than as a source of food. Not eating animals that had been killed by predators or that were already unconscious reduced the chances of getting a disease.

Orthodox Jews follow the dietary laws strictly. They believe the laws have come from God to test their obedience and mark out the Jewish people as different from others. The laws are also a call to holiness that helps people to develop self-control and reminds them daily of their faith. However, many Reform Jews think the laws are outdated in modern British society and it should be up to the individual whether or not they follow them.

Kosher butchers

Meat that is permitted must be killed in the prescribed way. The animal must be healthy and slaughtered with a very sharp knife by a trained Jew. The animal's throat is cut so that the animal does not suffer. However, the animal is not stunned first as then it would be unconscious. Blood is drained from the animal as it is forbidden to Jews. Certain parts of the animal, like the intestines and kidneys, must also be removed.

> **Objective**
> - Know about Jewish dietary laws and understand their significance.

> **Key terms**
> - **dietary laws:** rules that deal with foods permitted to be eaten, food preparation, food combinations, and the utensils and dishes coming into contact with food
> - **kosher:** food that meets the requirements of Jewish laws
> - **trefah:** food that Jews are forbidden to eat; means 'torn'

▲ Jews have to be careful about how they prepare food in kitchens to make sure it is kosher

> **Discussion activity**
>
> 'The Jewish food laws are no longer relevant in modern British society.' Discuss this statement. Be sure to include more than one point of view and refer to Jewish beliefs and teachings in your answer.

Chapter 10 Judaism: practices

Examples of kosher food	Examples of trefah food
Cows, sheep, goats, deer	Pork, camel, rodents, reptiles
Fish that has scales and fins, such as salmon, tuna, carp, herring and cod	Seafood without fins and scales, such as crabs, prawns, lobsters, oysters and clams
Cheese that has been officially certified as kosher	Cheese that has not been declared kosher
Any fruit and vegetables, so long as they are free of insects	Any insects or amphibians such as frogs

> **❝** But make sure that you do not partake of the blood; for the blood is the life, and you must not consume the life with the flesh. **❞**
>
> *Deuteronomy* 12:23

■ A Jewish kitchen

Certain combinations of foods, particularly dairy products and meat, are not allowed to be eaten at the same time. After eating meat, several hours must pass before anything containing milk is eaten. Jews debate the reasons for this, but most believe it stems from the instruction in Exodus 23:19: 'You shall not boil a kid in its mother's milk.'

Many Orthodox homes have kitchens with two sinks and two food preparation areas. This is so they can keep milk and meat separate. They may also colour-code their utensils, cutlery and crockery so that the ones used for meat dishes stay separate from the ones used for dairy products.

Most synagogues have kosher kitchens in which food can be prepared according to the dietary laws for functions held there. It can be difficult for Jews who live in non-Jewish communities to ensure that when they eat out, not only is the food kosher but it is also prepared with kosher crockery and utensils. To make it easier when buying food at a supermarket, a number of Jewish authorities will certify foods as kosher and put a label on the packaging.

Activities

1. Explain the terms kosher and trefah.
2. Explain how kosher meat is prepared. Why might some animal welfare groups oppose this method?
3. Make up a menu that would be permitted for a Jewish family dinner.
4. How is a Jewish kitchen organised to follow the dietary laws?

Research activities

1. Find out what the RSPCA has said about kosher methods of butchering meat in an information sheet called 'Slaughter without pre-stunning (for religious purposes)'. Consider how the Jewish community might respond to this report. The Shechita website (www.shechitauk.org) might help you.
2. Many Reform Jews believe that the eco-Kashrut movement, demanding the ethical treatment of animals and workers in the food industry, is a modern way of approaching the dietary laws. Use the internet to find out more about the eco-Kashrut movement and make a note of some of the issues it raises about food production.
3. Divide the class in half: one group to look in Leviticus chapter 11 and the other in Deuteronomy chapter 14 for rules about clean and unclean food. Compare your findings. Do you think these rules were helpful to the Jewish people at the time they were written?

Summary

You should now understand Jewish dietary laws and be able to explain how they affect Jewish life today.

⭐ Study tip

It is helpful to know several examples of kosher and trefah foods.

10.13 Rosh Hashanah and Yom Kippur

Rosh Hashanah is a festival that is celebrated over two days to mark the start of the Jewish new year. The ten days beginning with **Rosh Hashanah** and ending with **Yom Kippur**, the Day of Atonement, are sometimes called 'Days of Awe'. It is a time when Jews think seriously about their lives, consider their actions over the past year, and ask for forgiveness for their sins.

■ Origins of Rosh Hashanah

Rosh Hashanah recalls the creation story from the book of Genesis; it is considered to be the anniversary of the day on which God created humans. It is also a day of judgement. Some Jews believe that God keeps a record of people's good and bad deeds, and on Rosh Hashanah God weighs them up, judges them and makes a decision about what people's fortune will be in the coming year. The judgement can be influenced by the actions taken during the festival, so Jews pray, do works of charity and try to atone for (make up for) any harm or upset they have caused another person. Other Jews see God's record-keeping as representing the idea that all actions have consequences, so people should reflect on and take responsibility for their own actions.

▲ Giving to charity is an important way that Jews can show repentance before Yom Kippur

■ Celebrating Rosh Hashanah in Britain today

The month before Rosh Hashanah, a ram's horn (shofar) is blown daily in the synagogue (except on Shabbat) to announce the coming day of judgement. Special prayers for forgiveness are said all month. On the day before, preparations are made similar to those made for Shabbat, including buying fruit that the family has not eaten for a long time to symbolise renewal. Candles are lit just before sunset. At the usual evening synagogue

Objective
- Consider the origins and importance of Rosh Hashanah and Yom Kippur.

Key terms
- **Rosh Hashanah:** the Jewish new year
- **Yom Kippur:** the Day of Atonement; a day of fasting on the tenth day after Rosh Hashanah

> Despite the fact that **repentance and crying out to G-d** are always timely, **during the ten days between Rosh Hashanah and Yom Kippur** it is exceedingly appropriate, and **is accepted immediately**.
>
> Rabbi Moses Ben Maimon, *Mishneh Torah*

Links
To read more about how Shabbat is celebrated see pages 242–245.

service, prayers are focused on asking God to continue to be the king of the world for the coming year. The service ends with a Kiddush blessing over wine.

At home a festive meal begins with the Kiddush blessing, and apples dipped in honey are eaten: a symbol of hope for a sweet new year. A fish head is sometimes eaten to show the desire for good deeds to grow in number like fish. Other symbolic foods, such as pomegranates, may also be eaten.

Next morning at the synagogue the shofar is blown 100 times. The service is longer than usual with special prayers for the occasion and it attracts a large congregation. Many Jews who do not regularly go to the synagogue will attend on this special day.

▲ The shofar calls Jews to repentance

■ Origins of Yom Kippur

Yom Kippur is the holiest and most important day in the Jewish calendar. Its origins come from Leviticus 16, which describes how it must be observed. One original custom involved symbolically putting the people's sins on a goat and driving it into the desert.

> ❝ You shall practice self-denial; **and you shall do no manner of work … For on this day atonement shall be made for you to cleanse you of all your sins**; you shall be clean before the Lord. **It shall be a sabbath of complete rest for you, and you shall practice self-denial; it is a law for all time.** ❞
>
> *Leviticus* 16:29–31

This Day of Atonement is when God seals the Book of Judgement, so it is the last chance to repent for any sins. It is expected that Jews will have already mended relationships with other people in the days before Yom Kippur. Atonement that takes place on this day concerns the Jews and God; it is an occasion when Jews repent of their sins and God forgives them, enabling the relationship between them and God to be restored.

■ Observing Yom Kippur in Britain today

- No work is done.
- Jews fast (have no food or drink) for 25 hours.
- Bathing, wearing leather shoes, and sexual intercourse are forbidden.
- Jews wear white as a symbol of purity. (Isaiah 1:18 speaks of sins becoming 'like snow'.)

Many Jews spend much of Yom Kippur in the synagogue, where services will be held throughout the day. One of the most important parts is a general confession of sins as a community. The word 'we' is used rather than 'I' in expressing sorrow for sins. During the final service the doors of the Ark are open, requiring all to stand. This is the last chance for people to make confession before the door of the Ark is closed to show that God's judgement is now sealed. The service ends with the blowing of the shofar to signal the end of the fast.

Activities

1. Write down three actions Jews take to influence God's judgement upon their lives.
2. Explain how Rosh Hashanah is celebrated in the home and in the synagogue in Britain today.
3. Why is Yom Kippur such an important holy day for Jews?
4. Explain the impact of these festivals on individual Jews and on the Jewish community.

Discussion activity

With a partner or in a small group, discuss whether you have ever gone without food and drink for 25 hours. How difficult do you think it would be? Why do you think fasting is part of the observance of Yom Kippur?

⭐ Study tip

When studying festivals in Judaism it is important to consider their influence both on individual Jews and on the Jewish community as a whole.

Summary: You should now understand the origins and meaning of Rosh Hashanah and Yom Kippur, and know how they are celebrated in Britain today.

10.14 Pesach

■ Origins of Pesach

Pesach is also called 'Passover' because it recalls the night when God 'passed over' the houses of the Jewish slaves but killed the firstborn children and animals of the Egyptians. The story is found in Exodus 12:1–30.

God told Moses to ask the Pharaoh (ruler of Egypt) to let the Israelites go into the desert for three days to make offerings to God (Exodus 3). The Pharaoh refused, so God sent a series of plagues on Egypt. The final plague, the death of the firstborn, including Pharaoh's own son, finally succeeded in persuading him to allow the Israelites to leave. They miraculously crossed the Sea of Reeds to escape and eventually, after 40 years wandering in the desert, entered the land of Canaan that God had promised them.

■ Preparations for Pesach

God commanded the Jews to celebrate their escape from Egypt by eating unleavened bread (bread without yeast) for seven days each year (Exodus 12:15). The most important preparation for Pesach is to remove leaven (chametz) from the home. This includes wheat, barley, oats, or any grain that has been allowed to ferment or rise. Some Jews also avoid rice, corn, peanuts and beans. Removing leaven recalls how the escaping Israelites did not have time to let their bread rise.

Jews clean their homes thoroughly so that not a trace of leaven can be found. Usually the house is so clean that either parents or children deliberately hide some bread crumbs to find and burn to show that all leaven has been removed. Some firstborn males fast on this day in thanksgiving for their escape from death.

■ The Passover Seder

Pesach lasts for seven or eight days. On the first evening of Pesach, families hold a Seder service and celebrate with a special meal.

The mother lights candles to welcome the festival into the home. Often some family members visit the synagogue to offer thanks to God. When they return, the meal begins with the Kiddush blessing over the wine. On the table there is red wine, three pieces of matzo (unleavened bread), the Seder plate, and a copy of a special book (the Haggadah) which should be read during the Seder service. The middle matzo is broken and the largest piece is hidden for children to hunt for later. The finder receives a small prize.

On the Seder plate there is usually:
- a green vegetable, often parsley, to dip in salt water
- bitter herbs made from horseradish

> **Objective**
> - Understand the origins of Pesach and know how it is celebrated.
> - Understand the importance of Pesach for Jews in Britain today.

> **Key term**
> - **Pesach (Passover):** festival in remembrance of the Jewish exodus from Egypt that is celebrated in spring

▲ The story of the exodus is told when the youngest child asks four questions about the meaning of Pesach rituals

- a second bitter herb, such as romaine lettuce
- charoset (a paste of chopped apples, walnuts and wine)
- a roasted egg
- a lamb bone.

The different elements of the meal symbolise different things:

- Red wine reminds Jews of the lambs' blood the Israelites smeared on their doorposts to save their children from the final plague.
- The unleavened bread fulfils God's command, and recalls that the Israelites did not have time to let the bread rise before their escape.
- The salt water represents the bitter tears shed in slavery.
- The green vegetable may symbolise new life in the Promised Land.
- Bitter herbs, representing the bitterness of slavery, are dipped in the sweet charoset that symbolises the mortar used by the Jewish slaves. It reminds Jews that life is now sweet by comparison.
- The roasted egg and lamb bone are two reminders of sacrifices made in the Temple of Jerusalem.

▲ A Seder plate holds symbolic foods

Usually the youngest family member asks four questions and in reply the story of the escape from Egypt is retold from the Haggadah. During the meal, four small glasses of wine are blessed and shared to represent the four freedoms God promised in Exodus 6:6–7.

A fifth cup of wine is poured out and the door left open for the prophet Elijah, who is expected to reappear at Pesach to announce the coming of the Messiah. The Passover Seder ends with a wish that those present may celebrate next year in Jerusalem.

■ The importance of Pesach

Pesach has great significance for the Jewish community in the UK and elsewhere. It is a joyful festival as it celebrates the birth of the Jewish nation, freedom from slavery, entering the Promised Land and being given the law that made the Jews God's chosen people. The celebration of Pesach with their families gives Jews a chance to show gratitude to God for their redemption. The retelling of the Passover story to the next generation ensures Jewish faith and traditions are passed on. Jews are encouraged to relive the exodus through the Seder rituals and feel empathy with those who still live under political or religious oppression.

> **I am the Lord. I will free you from the labors of the Egyptians** and deliver you from their bondage. I will redeem you with an outstretched arm and through extraordinary chastisements. **And I will take you to be My people, and I will be your God.**
>
> Exodus 6:6–7

Research activity

Read the story of Moses and the exodus in Exodus 3:1–12:42. What do you think the Jews learned about God through these events?

⭐ Study tip

You can use either the term 'Pesach' or 'Passover' when referring to this festival.

Summary

You should now understand the origins and importance of Pesach, and be able to describe how Jews celebrate Pesach.

Activities

1. Explain how Jewish families prepare for Pesach.
2. Give two ways that Jews involve their children in Passover celebrations.
3. Draw a table with three columns. List all the foods and actions from the Seder meal in the first column, explain what they represent in the second column, and draw a picture or symbol to help you remember these in the third column.

10 Assessment guidance

The synagogue and worship – summary

You should now be able to:

✔ explain the meaning and importance of the synagogue for Jews

✔ explain the design and religious features of synagogues, including the reading platform (bimah), Ark (Aron Hakodesh), and ever-burning light (ner tamid)

✔ explain religious practices associated with these features

✔ explain differences between Orthodox and Reform synagogues, including differences in how worship is carried out

✔ explain the significance of prayer in public acts of worship, including the Amidah, the standing prayer

✔ describe the celebration of Shabbat in the home and in the synagogue, and explain its significance

✔ describe and explain worship in the home and private prayer

✔ explain what is meant by the written law (Tenakh) and the oral law (Talmud), and why they are important to Jews

Family life and festivals – summary

You should now be able to:

✔ describe and explain the meaning of ceremonies associated with birth, including Brit Milah

✔ describe and explain the meaning of Bar Mitzvah and Bat Mitzvah

✔ describe and explain the marriage ceremony and its importance

✔ describe and explain Jewish rituals associated with death and mourning and their importance

✔ explain Jewish dietary laws and their significance, including different Jewish views about their importance

✔ explain the origins and importance of Rosh Hashanah and Yom Kippur, and describe how they are celebrated in Britain today

✔ explain the origins and importance of Pesach, and describe how it is celebrated in Britain today

---

Sample student answer – the 12 mark question

1. Write an answer to the following question:

   'The most important religious festival for Jews is Yom Kippur.'
   Evaluate this statement. In your answer you should:
   - give reasoned arguments in support of this statement
   - give reasoned arguments to support a different point of view
   - refer to the teaching of Judaism
   - reach a justified conclusion.   [12 marks]

2. Read the following sample student answer:

   "Yom Kippur is the holiest day of the Jewish year therefore it is the most important religious festival. It is the Day of Atonement for sin. In olden times the Hebrews used to put the people's sins on a goat and drive it into the desert. This showed that the people were cleansed of their sins and could begin a new year with a clean slate. Nowadays Yom Kippur comes at the end of a time of repentance when people try to mend relationships with other people whom they may have hurt in the previous year. On Yom Kippur God will seal the book of judgement and so it is the last chance for Jews to tell God they are sorry for their sins. This is very important because it is the way Jews restore their relationship with God and avoid his bad judgement in the future.

However some Jewish families might think that Pesach is more important because it is celebrated with their families. It is also a reminder of the most important part of Jewish history: their escape from slavery in Egypt. Pesach lasts eight days and involves eating special foods. The Seder meal is a happy occasion, although tinged with sadness because of the oppression of the Jewish people, which has continued into the present day. There are also fun activities for children like searching for a piece of matzo. The youngest child gets to ask questions about the importance of the festival."

3. With a partner, discuss the sample answer. Consider the following questions:
   - Does the answer refer to Jewish teachings and if so what are they?
   - Is there an argument to support the statement and how well developed is it?
   - Is a different point of view offered and how developed is that argument?
   - Has the student written a clear conclusion after weighing up both sides of the argument?
   - Are there logical steps in the argument?
   - What is good about this answer?
   - How do you think it could be improved?

4. What mark (out of 12) would you give this answer? Look at the mark scheme in the Introduction (AO2). What are the reasons for the mark you have given?

5. Now swap your answer with your partner's and mark each other's responses. What mark (out of 12) would you give the response? Refer to the mark scheme and give reasons for the mark you award.

Practice questions

1 Which one of the following is the written law in Judaism?

   A) Torah   B) Tefillin   C) Tzitzit   D) Talmud   **[1 mark]**

2 Give two features of an Orthodox synagogue. **[2 marks]**

3 Explain two contrasting ways in which Jews mourn for the dead. **[4 marks]**

> ⭐ **Study tip**
>
> Remember to develop the points you are making. This may be done by giving detailed information, such as referring to examples. Be sure to include contrasting ways in your answer. The contrasts could be between ways in which Orthodox and Reform Jews carry out mourning rituals.

4 Explain two ways in which Shabbat is celebrated in the home. Refer to Jewish teachings in your answer. **[5 marks]**

5 'The most important duty of Jews is to attend the synagogue.'

Evaluate this statement. In your answer you should:
   - give reasoned arguments in support of this statement
   - give reasoned arguments to support a different point of view
   - refer to the teaching of Judaism
   - reach a justified conclusion. **[12 marks]**

Part 3: Themes

11 Theme A: religion, relationships and families

11.1 Human beings as sexual, male and female

■ Foundational biblical understanding

The creation stories in Genesis 1 and 2 both stress the importance of human beings within creation, and also the male and female aspects of humanity.

> So God created humankind in his image, in the image of God he created them; male and female he created them. God blessed them, and God said to them, 'Be fruitful and multiply.'
>
> *Genesis* 1:27–28 (NRSV)

These verses show that both men and women are made in the image of God and blessed by him, making them equal. This idea of equality is emphasised in Genesis 2, where God takes 'Adam' (humanity) and splits it into two complementary parts. (Complementary means that each person gives to the other what the other lacks, and that they produce a harmony together which is not possible in isolation.)

In Genesis 1, the command to multiply shows the importance of sexual love as part of God's plan. Jesus also stressed its importance when he said:

> From the beginning of creation, 'God made them male and female.' 'For this reason a man shall leave his father and mother and be joined to his wife, and the two shall become one flesh.' … Therefore what God has joined together, let no one separate.'
>
> *Mark* 10:6–9 (NRSV)

■ Catholic teaching about the nature and purpose of sexual love

The Catholic Church has a great respect for the role of sex within relationships. The Church's emphasis on the role of sex as **marital**, **unitive** and **procreative** sees the sexual relationship as being on a divine basis.

Objectives

- Know what the Bible says about human beings as male and female.
- Understand how the Catholic Church views sex as marital, unitive and procreative.

Key terms

- **marital:** to do with marriage
- **unitive:** something that joins or unites people together
- **procreative:** open to creating new life; life-giving
- **consummated:** completed or fulfilled, especially when talking about a marriage
- **adultery:** voluntary sexual intercourse between a married person and a person who is not their spouse (husband or wife)

▲ Men and women complement each other

264

Marital

When two people are in love, they usually want to commit themselves fully and exclusively to each other. In the Catholic Church, this commitment is expressed through the sacrament of marriage. The couple make promises that they will be together for life and will accept children lovingly from God. The promises form the verbal commitment between the couple; this commitment is then **consummated** in the physical union of sex, in which the couple totally give themselves to each other.

The Catholic Church teaches that the commitment expressed in sex is such a holy union that it should not take place before the couple have committed themselves to each other verbally and in public. There should be no sex either before or outside marriage; however, for a marriage to be valid there has to be sexual intercourse.

Unitive

Sexual love expresses and deepens the couple's love for each other. It is through the physical union of sex that the couple come closest to each other: 'and the two shall become one flesh' (Mark 10.24). They find fulfilment in each other and they enter a new phase of life as a couple.

One of the main reasons why **adultery** is forbidden both in the Ten Commandments and by Church teaching is that it destroys the unity that is expressed in sex. Sex is a creative act as it strengthens the couple's commitment to each other. It is a point at which the couple hold nothing back from each other and learn to value the intensity of the other person and the meaningfulness of their relationship.

Procreative

All life comes from God, but God acts through sex to create new life. The Church believes a couple that allow sex to be open to new life find there is much more intensity in their self-giving. One of the commitments accepted in the Catholic marriage ceremony is that the couple will accept children lovingly from God.

> Each and every marriage act must remain open to the transmission of life ... This particular doctrine ... is based on the inseparable connection ... between the unitive significance and the procreative significance which are both inherent to the marriage act.
>
> *Humanae Vitae* 11–12

▲ Catholics agree to accept children lovingly from God as part of their marriage

> According to God's will, husband and wife should encounter each other in bodily union so as to be united even more deeply with one another in love and to allow children to proceed from their love.
>
> *Youcat* 417

Activities

1. Explain what the Bible teaches about sex and the relationship between men and women.
2. 'The Catholic Church has a negative attitude to sex.' Evaluate this statement. Be sure to include more than one point of view, and refer to Catholic beliefs and teachings in your answer.

Extension activity

Choose one of the following terms: 'marital', 'unitive' or 'procreative'. Examine the importance of what recent Church teachings have said about the term you have chosen.

★ Study tip

Try to follow the logic in the Catholic Church's teachings, even if you disagree with them.

Summary

You should now know what the Bible says about humans as being sexual, male and female. You should also understand what the Catholic Church teaches about sex as being marital, unitive and procreative.

11.2 Pope John Paul II's 'Theology of the Body'

In a series of talks during the first ten years of his reign as Pope, Pope John Paul II presented a view of the human body and the relationship between the sexes that some people believe gives new insights into traditional Catholic thinking about sexual relationships.

Some key ideas that Pope John Paul II presented in 'Theology of the Body' include:

- God loves each and every human being for his or her own sake.
- People discover and express their dignity through the body; this includes their ability to think and to choose.
- God created human beings as male and female. Both sexes have inherent dignity and value.
- The full meaning of the body and the person can only be appreciated when there is a deep relationship with a member of the opposite sex. Pope John Paul called this 'the **nuptial** meaning of the body'.
- God established marriage to bring two people together as a form of **communion** of persons.
- In sex, which is an essential aspect of marriage, the man and the woman give themselves to each other completely. In this self-giving, they discover who they are both as individuals and as a united couple.
- Through sex, the couple show that they live for each other in mutual love and respect.
- The body and marital sex are good. However, **extramarital** sex and the use of contraception damage the significance and role of sex.
- Sin distorts God's original plan for human beings. It makes people selfish and self-centred. Extramarital sex can stop sex from being a sign of total commitment and love, and instead it can become a form of exploitation for personal pleasure. In the case of adultery, it is also the breaking of a promise, so it becomes an issue of justice rather than just of sexual morality.
- The way men and women are made shows that sexual intercourse leads to both greater intimacy and the possibility of creating new life. This means that there is an inseparable connection between these two functions.

Objectives

- Know the key features of Pope John Paul II's 'Theology of the Body'.
- Compare the teachings of Pope John Paul II with contrasting positions.

Key terms

- **nuptial:** to do with a marriage
- **communion:** sharing together
- **extramarital:** occurring outside marriage, either before marriage or with someone other than your husband or wife

▲ *In marriage, two become one*

> **❝ In Christianity, the body, pleasure and erotic joy enjoy a high status ... [but] pleasure, of course, is not an end in itself.** When the pleasure of a couple becomes self-enclosed and is not open to the new life that could result from it, it no longer corresponds to the nature of love. **❞**
>
> *Youcat* 417

- Sex in marriage is a fulfilment of the love of the husband and wife. Rather than seeing each person as an object for personal pleasure, it enriches each partner as it is a sincere gift of love.
- True mutual love includes responsible parenthood, and not having more children than the couple can lovingly provide for. The female body naturally has periods of fertility and of infertility. It is perfectly acceptable to make use of nature's cycles to reduce the chances of pregnancy. At times it is more loving to express fondness through non-sexual acts.
- The warning of Jesus – 'everyone who looks at a woman with lust has already committed adultery with her in his heart' (Matthew 5:28) – reminds all people that unfaithfulness starts in the mind. If people remain in control of their thoughts, they will not reduce other people to sex objects but will always value them as individuals who have great personal dignity and value.

▲ *Pope John Paul II in 1979*

> It is typical of rationalism to make a radical contrast in man between spirit and body, between body and spirit. **But man is a person in the unity of his body and his spirit. The body can never be reduced to mere matter.**
>
> John Paul II, *Letter to Families*

Contrasting views

There are a wide variety of views about sexual relationships in British society today. Some people treat sex with a similar respect and consideration as Catholics; others are willing to have casual sex with many different partners. Most people fall somewhere in-between these two opposites.

The topics of sex before marriage and contraception are where many people's views differ to those of the Catholic Church. Sex before marriage is discussed on the next page. Many people in British society do not place as much importance on the need for sex to be open to the creation of new life; instead they view the use of contraception as a responsible way of preventing sexually transmitted diseases and unplanned pregnancies.

Summary

You should now know what Pope John Paul II taught in his 'Theology of the Body', and understand contrasting viewpoints.

Activities

1. In your own words, explain five of the points made by Pope John Paul II in his 'Theology of the Body'.
2. 'Pope John Paul II's teachings about the body give no greater value to sexual relationships than any other approach.' Evaluate this statement. Be sure to include more than one point of view, and refer to Catholic beliefs and teachings in your answer.

Discussion activity

Discuss whether sex should occur only within a marriage.

⭐ Study tip

To understand the Catholic viewpoint, think of the physical union that occurs in sex as a sign that something with deeper meaning is happening.

267

11.3 Human sexuality and its expression

■ Sex before marriage

The teaching of the Catholic Church

The Catholic Church teaches that as sex is the total commitment of a man to a woman, it should be an exclusive act, shared only with the person you have pledged to spend your life with. Sex is the final step in joining the husband and wife in a lasting bond.

The Church believes that having sex before marriage trivialises it. But when a husband and wife both know that they have reserved the gift of their virginity so that they can offer it to each other in marriage, they both feel special, privileged and loved. There is also another benefit of preserving virginity until marriage: if neither person has had sex with anyone else, there is no chance of them passing on sexually transmitted diseases.

Contrasting views

Other Christian denominations generally share the Catholic Church's view that sex should be saved until marriage. However, many people in British society (including many Christians) do have sex before marriage.

Many people wait to find someone they love before having sex. Others think casual sex is fine, providing it doesn't cause any emotional harm. The use of contraception has allowed sex before marriage and casual sex to become more common; its use and how it affects people's approaches to sex is one of the main differences between Catholics and non-Catholics regarding this topic.

■ Adultery

The teaching of the Catholic Church

Adultery occurs when a person who is married has sex with someone who is not their husband or wife. For Catholics, adultery breaks the commitment that is made in the marriage promises: 'To have and to hold from this day forward, for better, for worse'. It is an act of betrayal, and can make the innocent partner feel rejected and a failure. It can destroy trust between the married couple and bring tensions and distress into their family, affecting any children they have.

> **Adultery is an injustice. He who commits adultery fails in his commitment.** He does injury to the sign of the covenant which the marriage bond is, transgresses the rights of the other spouse, and undermines the institution of marriage by breaking the contract on which it is based. He compromises the good of human generation and the welfare of children who need their parents' stable union.
>
> *Catechism of the Catholic Church* 2381

Objectives

- Know what the Catholic Church teaches about sex before marriage, adultery and homosexuality.
- Understand contrasting views on these topics.

> Because **love is so great, so sacred, and so unique,** the Church teaches young people to wait until they are married before they start to have sexual relations.
>
> *Youcat* 407

> Morality that is not God-based need not be anti-social, subjective, or promiscuous, nor need it lead to the breakdown of moral standards … Nor do we believe that any one church should impose its views of moral virtue and sin, sexual conduct, marriage, divorce, birth control, or abortion, or legislate them for the rest of society.
>
> *A Secular Humanist Declaration* 5

▲ Arguments can affect the whole family

Chapter 11 Theme A: religion, relationships and families

Contrasting views

Many non-Catholics share the view that adultery is wrong for very similar reasons to Catholics: they believe that if two people make a commitment to each other, then the commitment should be honoured, and that adultery has the potential to cause great harm to those involved.

Some people would argue that adultery could be forgiven under certain circumstances: for example, in a very unhappy marriage where it seems to be the only way to change or improve the situation. Some might argue that personal happiness is important, even if seeking it inadvertently causes harm to someone else.

▲ *Two men celebrating their marriage*

■ Homosexuality

The teaching of the Catholic Church

The Catholic Church's starting point on anything to do with sexual relationships is the link between sex and reproduction. The Church believes that sex should be open to the possibility of new life. This means that physical homosexual relations are not acceptable to the Church. While the Church accepts that some people are homosexual, it believes these people should live celibate lives.

The Church also believes that Christians owe all people respect and love, regardless of their sexual orientation, because all people are loved and respected by God.

Contrasting views

Same-sex marriage was legalised in England and Wales in 2014. This allows homosexual couples to get married, although not in a church. The Church of England does however support the idea of same-sex civil partnerships (although again does not allow them to be carried out in a church). Civil partnerships give homosexual couples similar legal rights to those of married couples.

The legalisation of same-sex marriage reflects the views of many in British society, which is that homosexuals should have same rights as anyone else, including the entitlement to marry and the right have sexual relationships. There has been considerable debate in the UK about whether Christian Churches should carry out same-sex marriages or not.

Activities

1. Explain the position that the Catholic Church takes on sex before marriage.
2. 'The Catholic Church is unfair to homosexuals.' Evaluate this statement. Be sure to include more than one point of view, and refer to Catholic beliefs and teachings in your answer.

Research activity

Research British laws that deal with either adultery or homosexuality: for example, the Equality Act of 2010 or the Marriage (Same Sex Couples) Act of 2013. Do you think these laws are good for society?

★ Study tip

Remember that the Catholic Church values sex as the ultimate commitment between two people, and all its teachings about adultery, homosexual relations and so on are linked to this central point.

Summary: You should now know what the Catholic Church teaches about sex before marriage, adultery and homosexuality. You should also be able to compare the Church's teaching with contrasting views.

11.4 A valid marriage in the Catholic Church

The conditions for a valid marriage

For any **marriage** to be acknowledged as valid by the Catholic Church (meaning it is officially accepted by the Church), certain conditions have to be met. These are covered by the questions and promises that each of the two people has to publicly answer or make before they give their **consent**:

- The two people have to be free to marry. This means they must not already be married to someone who is still alive. They also must not be bound by final or permanent vows to the priesthood or to a religious community. If they are under temporary vows, they cannot marry before the vows have expired.
- The two people must be getting married of their own free will. If any pressure is being put on the couple to marry, for whatever reason, there might be grounds for the marriage to be declared **null and void**.
- The two people must not be closely related to each other. This means, for example, that first cousins cannot marry.
- The moment of marriage is the consent. If the consent is lacking, there is no valid marriage.

> ❝ The consent consists in a 'human act by which the partners mutually give themselves to each other': 'I take you to be my wife' – 'I take you to be my husband.' **This consent that binds the spouses to each other finds its fulfilment in the two 'becoming one flesh.'** ❞
>
> *Catechism of the Catholic Church* 1627

Objectives

- Know what the Catholic Church requires for a marriage to be valid.
- Understand the religious and non-religious arguments surrounding same-sex marriages.

Key terms

- **marriage:** the sacrament by which the couple commit themselves to each other for life
- **consent:** give permission for something to happen; in Catholicism, the moment of marriage when the couple commit themselves to each other for life
- **null and void:** the marriage did not take place because something was not correct when the commitment happened

- The couple give the sacrament to each other, but the promises must be made in the presence of a Catholic priest or deacon, who leads the prayers and acts as a witness for God and the Church.
- The couple must declare that they are willing to accept children lovingly from God. This promise commits the couple to allowing God to decide if and when they have children. If a couple use contraceptives when having sex, they are showing that they do not take this promise seriously.
- There is no valid marriage until the couple have given themselves to each other physically through sex.
- The couple promise to each other that they will be together 'for richer for poorer, in sickness and in health, to love and to cherish, till death do us part.'

▲ In a Catholic marriage, the couple must make the marriage promises in the presence of a Catholic priest or deacon

> ❝ **Love seeks to be definitive;** it cannot be an arrangement 'until further notice.' The 'intimate union of marriage … demand[s] total fidelity from the spouses and require an unbreakable union between them.' ❞
>
> *Catechism of the Catholic Church* 1646

270

Chapter 11 Theme A: religion, relationships and families

■ The extension of marriage laws to same-sex couples

Because being open to having children naturally is an important part of marriage for Catholics, the Catholic Church has always insisted that marriage is a sacrament between a man and a woman. Two people of the same sex cannot meet the requirements for a valid marriage as they cannot promise to accept children lovingly from God. This means that there is no room for change in Catholic teaching about the nature of same-sex relationships.

Many people in contemporary British society believe that homosexuals should be entitled to exactly the same rights as heterosexuals, including the right of marriage. Unlike Catholics, they do not see having children as an essential part of marriage. In 2014, the British government legalised marriage between two people of the same sex, recognising the position supported by many people in the UK (including some Christians). Same-sex marriage was legalised in Ireland in 2015 after a referendum (a public vote asking Irish citizens to choose whether they wanted same-sex marriage to be legalised or not). The Catholic Church has not been able to accept these unions as marriages.

▲ The Catholic Church does not view same-sex marriages as valid

Pope Francis on homosexuality

In 2013, Pope Francis gave an interview in which he was asked questions about homosexuality. His response made headlines in the media: 'If a person is gay and seeks God and has good will, who am I to judge?' He said that homosexuals should be integrated into society, rather than being marginalised.

His response reaffirmed the teaching of the Catholic Church that while homosexual acts are sinful, homosexuality in itself is not. Did the media take such an interest in his reply because his wording suggested a more open approach and a new attempt by the Church to reach out to and accept homosexuals? Or did Pope Francis make headlines simply because many people had previously misunderstood the Church's position on this matter, so that what was in fact nothing new was taken as newsworthy material?

Activities

1. Explain the importance of the questions and promises in a Catholic marriage service for the validity of the marriage.
2. 'The Catholic Church is right to forbid same-sex marriages.' Evaluate this statement. Be sure to include more than one point of view, and refer to Catholic beliefs and teachings in your answer.

Research activity

Research some countries that allow same-sex marriages – for example the UK, France, and Canada – and some countries that forbid them – for example Hungary, Kenya and Poland. Examine the arguments given by both sets of countries for their decisions on this issue.

★ Study tip

Try to learn the conditions needed for a valid marriage according to the Catholic Church's teaching.

Summary

You should now know what makes a marriage valid for the Catholic Church. You should also understand different views on same-sex marriage.

11.5 The nature of marriage, marriage promises, and cohabitation

◼ The nature of marriage

The Catholic Church values marriage as:

- an exclusive union of two people
- a sacrament and a sign of God's love and blessing on and through the couple
- a sign of the love of Christ for the Church.

The Church believes that marriage is never a private affair. Everybody needs to be aware that the two people are committed to each other, otherwise they might unwittingly do things that could put pressure on the relationship, leading to tension and arguments.

For Catholics, marriage is not just something that happens on the day that the couple make their promises, but is an everyday lived-out commitment. A marriage should get stronger and change as the husband and wife discover more about themselves and each other. A good marriage is an example to the rest of society, showing that people can be happy together in a committed relationship. It can help other couples who are having difficulties to persevere. A happy, loving relationship can also create a warm atmosphere in which children can develop and flourish as individuals.

◼ The marriage promises

> I call upon these persons here present to witness that I, (full name), take you (full name) to be my lawful wedded husband/wife, to have and to hold from this day forward, for better for worse, for richer for poorer, in sickness and in health, to love and to cherish, till death do us part.

The marriage promises, which are made after the consent is given in a marriage ceremony, spell out the commitment that both the husband and wife are making. The promises are the same for both people, showing that marriage is an equal commitment. The promises stress the following points:

- The marriage takes place in public. This means that both the husband and wife are ready to declare their love in front of other people so that both of them can be assured that the declaration of love is genuine. The public announcement is also asking for the community's acceptance and support of the marriage.
- The full names and 'here present' are used to ensure that there can be no question about exactly who is making the commitment and to whom.

Objectives

- Know what the Catholic Church teaches about the nature of marriage.
- Understand what the marriage promises mean.
- Understand different views on cohabitation.

Key term

- **Cohabitation:** a couple living together and having a sexual relationship without being married to one another

> The well-being of the individual person and of both human and Christian society is closely bound up with the healthy state of conjugal and family life.
>
> *Gaudium et Spes* 47

▲ *For Catholics it is important that the marriage takes place in public*

- The promises accept that marriage is a leap into the unknown. Nobody knows what the physical and mental health of anybody, including themselves, will be in the future. The financial position of the couple may change drastically over the years. The husband and wife say that they will accept any changes in life, and work through those changes together.
- The commitment is 'till death do us part'. Once this commitment is made in full freedom of choice, it is not possible to marry another person. For Catholics, only death can end a marriage.

The total self-giving commitment that is first verbally expressed in the promises is then physically expressed in the sexual union of the husband and wife.

▲ *In Britain many couples cohabit before getting married*

The Catholic Church would argue that marriage itself can give strength and hope to the couple. They are not alone in facing the future as Christ is with them and is working through their relationship.

■ Cohabitation

Cohabitation is when two people in a relationship live together, but have not made any formal commitment to each other. Some people claim that this is a good way to help the couple decide if they want to commit themselves to each other for life. The Catholic Church disagrees with cohabitation as it believes:

- it breaks the sanctity of marriage and the sexual union
- it is removing any sense of commitment from the sexual union
- since there is no expressed commitment, the two people might not feel as though they need to make the effort to ensure the relationship lasts, destroying the sense of faithfulness
- the relationship might end at any point when either partner decides to move on
- it can destroy the sense of family, with potentially disastrous results for any children.

Many young couples in Britain choose to cohabit, although many get married when they want to start a family. Some live together for financial reasons, or because they want to see if the relationship will work. Others never marry but live in committed relationships throughout their lives. Same-sex couples may cohabit until they decide to seek a civil partnership or to get married.

> ❝ Because God himself forms the bond of sacramental marriage, it is binding until the death of one of the partners. ❞
>
> *Youcat* 261

Activities

1. Explain the differences between cohabitation and marriage.
2. 'The marriage promises strengthen a marriage.' Evaluate this statement. Be sure to include more than one point of view, and refer to Catholic beliefs and teachings in your answer.

Summary

You should now know what the Catholic Church teaches about the nature of marriage. You should understand the importance of the marriage promises, and know why people hold different views about cohabitation.

⭐ Study tip

Talking to a married person about how they view the marriage promises may help you to understand their significance and meaning.

11.6 Annulment, divorce and remarriage

■ Annulment

Annulment is a statement by the Catholic Church that there was no valid marriage in the first place. This is because something was wrong with the 'commitment' the couple made. Examples of possible reasons for annulment are:

- One of the couple continued having affairs with other people after the marriage had taken place, showing that this person was not taking the exclusive nature of marriage seriously.
- The couple either did not have sex at all or always insisted on using contraception, showing that neither of them were prepared to live by the promise that they would accept children lovingly from God.
- The couple were forced to get married, possibly under pressure from other members of the family. This would mean that the couple did not get married freely and willingly.

Since there was no proper marriage in the first place, anybody who is granted an annulment is free to marry again in the Catholic Church.

■ Divorce

According to UK law, when a couple **divorce** they are no longer married and so each is free to marry someone else. The Catholic Church does not accept the possibility of remarriage in a valid sacramental marriage after a divorce. The Church's position is based on three main points:

- The couple made promises which included the words 'till death do us part'. Since these promises were made before God and in front of witnesses, they cannot be broken.
- God made man and woman to be united as one and no human has the ability to break this bond.
- Jesus taught that anyone who divorced and then married another person was committing adultery.

Objectives

- Know what the Catholic Church teaches about annulment, divorce and remarriage.
- Understand contrasting views.

Key terms

- **annulment:** a statement by the Catholic Church that there was no valid marriage in the first place
- **divorce:** legal ending of a marriage
- **remarriage:** when a person who has been married before goes on to marry another person

▲ Does divorce make it too easy to end a marriage, instead of trying hard to make it work?

> [Jesus] said … 'Whoever divorces his wife and marries another commits adultery against her; and if she divorces her husband and marries another, she commits adultery.'
>
> Mark 10:11–12 (NRSV)

The Church accepts that there are times when people who marry realise that they have made a serious mistake and that they cannot continue to live together. The Church accepts the need for the couple to live apart and that this might involve a legal divorce, so that financial and other matters can be resolved. However, the Church does not accept that either one of the couple can marry again in church, until the other spouse has died.

Many people in Britain today would claim that if a couple have fallen out of love, there is little point in them remaining married, particularly if the atmosphere in the house is hurting the children. In England and Wales, around 43 per cent of all marriages end in divorce. Some people would argue that this proves the need for divorce laws. Others would argue that when it is easy to get a divorce, fewer people try hard enough to make their marriages work.

Ethical arguments

Some people, especially Catholics, would argue that once a couple has made the marriage promises they should stick by them, regardless of how their relationship develops. The promises are sacred and were made in full awareness of what the couple were committing themselves to. Others would argue that it is impossible for anyone to know how the future will work out, and that if the couple end up in a situation where they are causing each other (as well as any children they have) great emotional pain, divorce may be the best and most compassionate solution.

▲ *Are there situations where divorce would benefit the children in a family?*

■ Remarriage

Remarriage happens when a person who has been married before goes on to marry another person. The only time that this can happen according to Catholic teaching is when the original husband or wife has died. This means that the first marriage ended naturally and so the remaining partner is free to remarry. (When a person has their first 'marriage' annulled, they are free to marry as if for the first time, and therefore it is not classed as a remarriage.)

The Church wants to support people whose marriages have ended in divorce and who choose to remarry. However, if the first marriage is valid in the view of the Catholic Church and if the original partner is still alive, a person who divorces and remarries cannot receive Communion. This reflects the Church's belief in the sanctity of (valid) marriage. Other Christian Churches, for example Methodists and Anglicans, do sometimes marry people who have been divorced and will not stop them from receiving Communion.

> ❝ Today there are numerous Catholics … who have recourse to civil divorce and contract new civil unions. In fidelity to the words of Jesus Christ … **the Church maintains that a new union cannot be recognized as valid, if the first marriage was.** If the divorced are remarried civilly, they find themselves in a situation that objectively contravenes God's law. Consequently, they cannot receive Eucharistic communion as long as this situation persists. ❞
>
> *Catechism of the Catholic Church* 1650

Activities

1. Explain the Catholic Church's views on annulment and divorce.
2. 'Catholics should be allowed to get divorced.' Evaluate this statement. Be sure to include more than one point of view, and refer to Catholic beliefs and teachings in your answer.

⭐ Study tip

Check that you know the difference between a divorce and an annulment.

Summary

You should now understand what the Catholic Church teaches about annulment, divorce and remarriage, and you should be aware of contrasting views on this matter.

11.7 Family planning and contraception

Catholic teaching on family planning and contraception

The Catholic Church places great importance on the role of sex within marriage, which is seen as the final expression of the total commitment that the couple make to each other. During the wedding, the couple promise that they will accept children lovingly from God. This means they promise that they will allow God to work through their relationship to create new life. The Catholic Church believes that every act of sex must be both unitive and procreative, and that these two purposes cannot be separated. **Artificial contraception** makes sexual intercourse non-procreative, and therefore brings about the separation of these two purposes.

> ❝ The teaching of the Church 'is founded upon the inseparable connection ... between the two meanings of the conjugal act: the unitive meaning and the procreative meaning.' When couples, by means of recourse to contraception, separate these two meanings that God the Creator has inscribed in the being of man and woman and in the dynamism of their sexual communion, they act as 'arbiters' of the divine plan and they 'manipulate' and degrade human sexuality – and with it themselves and their married partner – by altering its value of 'total' self-giving. ❞
>
> *Familiaris Consortio* 32

Some people think the Catholic Church has a very negative attitude to **family planning** because it opposes artificial contraception. However, recent popes have stressed the need for responsible parenthood. This means that the husband and wife must be aware of their family situation and take appropriate actions to ensure that they can provide for and take care of any children they have.

Pope Francis has followed the example of all his predecessors in supporting the use of natural family planning. This means taking advantage of the woman's natural monthly cycle in which there are times of high fertility and others of low fertility. By monitoring this cycle, the couple can choose when they are more likely to conceive or not conceive, without introducing artificial, outside factors that guarantee there will be no chance of a child being conceived. The Catholic Church believes that natural family planning does not prevent the work of God, but it makes use of

Objectives
- Know what the Catholic Church teaches about family planning.
- Understand different views on the use of artificial contraception.

Key terms
- **artificial contraception:** artificial (unnatural) methods used to prevent a pregnancy from taking place
- **family planning:** the practice of controlling how many children couples have and when they have them

> ❝ A Christian married couple may and should be responsible in using the gift and privilege of transmitting life. ❞
>
> *Youcat* 420

▲ The Catholic Church supports the need for responsible parenthood

God's gift of the woman's monthly cycle to reduce or increase the chance of conception, always leaving the final decision up to God.

■ Contrasting views

Some people argue that contraceptives are essential to stop the spread of sexually transmitted diseases (STDs). The Catholic Church does not accept this as a valid argument. If sex is preserved for marriage and if there is no sex with another person either before or during marriage, there is little chance of either the husband or wife contracting an STD. Therefore, there is no need to use contraceptives to prevent STDs within a marriage.

▲ Many different types of contraception are available to people in Britain today

However, in Britain today many people do have sex before marriage, sometimes with a number of different partners, and there is widespread acceptance of the use of contraception. Many people think it is responsible to use contraception to prevent unwanted pregnancies, particularly if the child would be born into an environment where it could not be properly cared for. Some people also acknowledge concerns about global overpopulation; they believe families should not have too many children because there is a limit to how many people the world can support.

While all Christian Churches agree that having children is a great gift from God, not all Churches agree on the methods families should use to limit the number of children they have. For example, the Church of England accepts the use of contraception and, unlike the Catholic Church, does not believe that using it goes against the will of God.

Some people think that certain forms of contraception should not be used because the egg may already be fertilised and therefore conception has already taken place. For example, the morning-after pill prevents the egg from developing, which some people see as causing an abortion. Those who believe in the protection of human life from the moment of conception are opposed to these methods.

> ❝ The Catholic Church recommends the refined methods of self-observation and natural family planning (NFP) as methods of deliberately regulating conception. These are in keeping with the dignity of man and woman; they respect the innate laws of the female body; **they demand mutual affection and consideration and therefore are a school of love.** ❞
>
> *Youcat* 421

Activities

1. Explain the Catholic Church's view on the use of contraception.
2. 'The Church's teaching on the use of contraception ignores the needs of the modern world.' Evaluate this statement. Be sure to include more than one point of view, and refer to Catholic beliefs and teachings in your answer.

Summary

You should now understand Catholic teaching about family planning and contraception, and be able to give examples of contrasting views.

Discussion activity

Discuss whether ignoring the Catholic Church's views on contraception will lead to a greater misuse of sex.

★ Study tip

Try to keep an open mind on this topic. If you are very critical of the Church's position, you may miss the logic of the Church's teaching.

11.8 The nature and purpose of the family

The Catholic Church values the family as a Church in miniature.

> ❝ The Christian family … is the first community called to announce the Gospel to the human person during growth and to bring him or her, through a progressive education and catechesis [sharing of the faith], to full human and Christian maturity. ❞
>
> *Familiaris Consortio* 1

The Catholic Church teaches that the family has four tasks:

- to form a community
- to support the life and personal development of each individual
- to share in the development of the wider society
- to share in the life and mission of the Church.

The family is composed of a number of related individuals. Sometimes 'the family' might just refer to the parents and their children, and at other times 'the family' could also include additional relatives such as grandparents or aunts and uncles.

In either case the task of the family remains the same: to be mutually supportive. Each person within the family has different gifts to offer and different roles to play. These roles will change over the years as people develop, weaken with age or sickness, make new relationships with people who are then brought into the family through marriage, and so on. The Church teaches that the care, love and support given within the family and by each member is vital (life-giving) for the whole community.

■ Procreation

The Catholic Church teaches that the family is the best environment in which to bring up children, who are visible signs of the love the parents have for each other. It is through having children that the couple make their own family, adding another level to the families in which they themselves were raised and nourished.

■ Security

Children need a stable, safe environment in which to develop. Development comes through experiencing life and responding to challenges. In a loving family environment, these challenges can be presented in a way that ensures the child will be not be harmed. The parents and older siblings play their part in helping a younger member of the family learn how take part in the life of the community.

The parents' role is always to be supportive, though at times this may translate into 'tough love', creating conditions where the risk of failure or hardship ultimately helps the child to develop.

Objectives

- Know what the Catholic Church teaches about the nature and purpose of the family.
- Understand how **procreation**, security and education play a role within the family.

Key term

- **procreation:** producing children

▲ *The Catholic Church teaches that the family is a Church in miniature*

> ❝ The welfare and future of a State depend on the ability of the smallest unit, the family, to live and develop. ❞
>
> *Youcat* 370

> ❝ The fundamental task of the family is to serve life, to actualize in history the original blessing of the Creator – that of transmitting by procreation the divine image from person to person. ❞
>
> *Familiaris Consortio* 28

Education

The Catholic Church believes that parents are the first and most important teachers of their children. Children should be able to grow and flourish, supported by the actions, teachings and examples of their parents. Parents should help their children to appreciate different aspects of life, particularly the differences between right and wrong, and how to live according to Christian principles.

▲ One of the main duties of parents is to educate their children

Parents need to be conscious of their authority over their children as well as their love for their children. The end product of a child's education is an independent, balanced human being, who has great self-respect as well as immense respect for their parents and the rest of society. The family atmosphere should be one in which each individual is valued, offering an environment where peace and forgiveness are experienced on a regular basis. When children experience these qualities in a deeply meaningful way as they grow up, they will continue to practise them throughout their lives.

Contrasting views

The traditional idea of a 'nuclear family' – a married man and woman with their children – is becoming less common in Britain, although it is still the norm. Less traditional types of families include single parents and same-sex couples with or without children.

Some people argue that the standards, morals and values that are learned in a traditional family ('family values') are harder to absorb in a less traditional family. Others argue that such values can still exist regardless of who makes up the family. In addition, a more fluid understanding of 'family' can allow people to feel as though they belong to a family even if it is not a traditional one.

Many people in Britain still value the family for the support it can give to each individual. However, some people place less emphasis on the importance of the family, arguing that emotional attachments to people are often more important than blood connections. Some might argue that the 'family' who provides your support should consist of only the people you want it to.

> **Summary**
> You should now know what the Catholic Church teaches about the nature and purpose of the family, including the roles of procreation, security and education.

> ❝ In the family … special attention must be devoted to the children by developing a profound esteem for their personal dignity, and a great respect and generous concern for their rights. ❞
> *Familiaris Consortio* 26

> ❝ **Family communion [sharing] can only be preserved and perfected through a great spirit of sacrifice.** It requires, in fact, a ready and generous openness of each and all to understanding, to forbearance, to pardon, to reconciliation. ❞
> *Familiaris Consortio* 21

Activities

1. Explain the nature and purpose of family life for Catholics.
2. 'Education of children is the most important task for parents.' Evaluate this statement. Be sure to include more than one point of view, and refer to Catholic beliefs and teachings in your answer.

Extension activity

Examine what other religious and non-religious groups say about the nature and purpose of the family. Compare their views with those of the Catholic Church.

⭐ Study tip

Remember that every family is different, with its own strengths and weaknesses. This can be helpful to bear in mind when answering evaluation questions.

11.9 Roles and responsibilities within the family

■ Roles within the family

The Catholic Church has always acknowledged that people play different roles within the family, and believes that these roles should be respected and supported. The different roles do not presume that one person is better than another; instead they mutually work together to produce a harmonious whole. One of the earliest expressions of these roles comes from Paul's letter to the Ephesians:

> **Be subject to one another out of reverence for Christ.** Wives, be subject to your husbands as you are to the Lord. For the husband is the head of the wife just as Christ is the head of the church … Husbands, love your wives, just as Christ loved the church and gave himself up for her …
>
> Children, obey your parents in the Lord, for this is right. 'Honour your father and mother' — this is the first commandment with a promise: 'so that it may be well with you and you may live long on the earth.' And, fathers, do not provoke your children to anger, but bring them up in the discipline and instruction of the Lord.
>
> *Ephesians* 5:21–6:4 (NRSV)

Some people think that Paul was being sexist in these comments but, for the time he was writing, his views were fairly progressive. The main points that Christians can take from Paul's teachings are:

- Family life is lived in the love of Christ. What people do for each other, they also do for Christ.
- Husbands should love their wives unconditionally, even to the point of dying for them.
- Wives show their love for their husbands in doing what the husband asks, but the husband's love should mean that they only ask reasonable things of their wives.
- Children should obey their parents, as this is God's command. This obedience is a way for children to honour to their parents.
- Fathers should show love and kindness to their children and not use any form of extreme discipline.

■ The dignity of work in the home

The Catholic Church has always stressed the importance of the mother's role in looking after the home and children. This does not mean that women have no other function in life, but it does mean that women should be given every possible help to fulfil their duties within the family. The Catholic Church believes the importance of this work is often overlooked by society, making it harder for women to fulfil this role, but

---

Objectives

- Know what the Catholic Church teaches about the roles and responsibilities of men and women in the family.
- Understand contrasting views on the roles in the family.

▲ The Catholic Church teaches that women should be supported in their role as mothers

> **Jesus was a child who received love and affection from his parents and was brought up by them** … The fact that God in Jesus willed to be born into a human family and to grow up in it has made the family a place where God is present and a prototype of a helping community.
>
> *Youcat* 86

this should not have to be the case.

For the Catholic Church, the roles of both men and women in the family are important as each contributes different qualities to the upbringing of children, and to the security and stability of the home. The role of the man in the family should be to provide for the needs of the family, protect the family, and teach by word and example.

In Britain today, the majority of mothers work part- or full-time, often because it is necessary in order to help provide for the family financially. Many people accept that roles within a family can vary depending on what is best for their individual situation. For example, a family might be in a position where it makes more sense for the mother to work while the father stays at home to look after young children. Increasing gender equality has meant that roles traditionally reserved for women and men are now being shared or switched.

Families with single or same-sex parents

The Catholic Church teaches that marriage is limited to the union of one man and one woman. Therefore, any family that is not founded on this relationship, at least initially (accepting that death and separation change the situation), is not encouraged by the Catholic Church.

Outside of the Church, there is a growing acceptance in Britain today of same-sex parents, who are able to acquire the same legal rights as other parents. Many would argue that the love between the children and the parents is what matters most. However, some argue that children need both a mother and a father. Others worry that a child with same-sex parents will be harmed through having to encounter prejudice and intolerance as they grow up.

▲ *Can same-sex parents show the same quality of love as a mixed-sex couple?*

While the Catholic Church would not encourage single people to have children, around a quarter of all children in Britain today have single parents. This is usually because the parents' relationship has ended, but sometimes it is because a single person wanted to adopt or have a child. A single parent may find it harder to support a child, and there are a number of charities and organisations in the UK that aim to help provide the support that might be lacking as a result of not having two parents.

> **❝** While it must be recognized that women have the same right as men to perform various public functions, society must be structured in such a way that **wives and mothers are not in practice compelled to work outside the home,** and that their families can live and prosper in a dignified way even when they themselves devote their full time to their own family. **❞**
>
> *Familiaris Consortio* 23

Activities

1. Explain Catholic teachings about different roles within the family.
2. 'The Catholic Church should support families that have same-sex parents.' Evaluate this statement. Be sure to include more than one point of view, and refer to Catholic beliefs and teachings in your answer.

Research activity

Research how two different cultures or religions – for instance Islam and Christianity – understand the nature and role of the family.

Summary

You should now know what the Catholic Church teaches about different roles and responsibilities within the family. You should also understand contrasting views about same-sex and single parents.

⭐ Study tip

Remember that the Catholic Church teaches about the 'ideal' family but understands that every family will have different strengths and weaknesses.

11.10 Gender equality in the Bible

■ The creation of men and women as equal

Often people think that in the Bible the only important people are men, while women are reduced to a position that is little better than a slave. The Bible often reflects the cultural standards of the time it was written. However, women do have an important role to play in the Bible and in Christianity. The roles of men and women are different but neither is subservient to the other.

In both creation stories from Genesis, it is clear that God made man and woman equal:

> God created humankind in his image, in the image of God he created them; male and female he created them.
>
> *Genesis* 1:27 (NRSV)

> The man said, 'This at last is bone of my bones and flesh of my flesh; this one shall be called Woman, for out of Man this one was taken.' Therefore a man leaves his father and his mother and clings to his wife, and they become one flesh.
>
> *Genesis* 2:23–24 (NRSV)

Though the story in Genesis 2 might suggest that woman was made second, from man, the true meaning comes out in verse 24 where it stresses that a man and woman combined are the full form of a human being. The story means that God took one human being and divided it into two equal parts that complement and complete each other.

■ The importance of women in the Bible

Throughout the Old Testament, women play special roles on the same level as men. For example, Deborah acted as a judge (Judges 4:4–10) and played a similar role to Gideon. Esther was the person who brought about the freedom of the Jews from the Persians (Esther 4–5). Ruth showed the Jews how to be faithful (Ruth 1–4).

In the New Testament, the importance and dignity of women is symbolised in Mary, the mother of Jesus. She is the perfect disciple as she shows how all people should be open to the will of God when she says, 'Here am I, the servant of the Lord' (Luke 1:38).

Jesus showed great respect for women. In his teachings about divorce and adultery, he showed that the same standards apply to men and women, which was an unusual position to take in those days.

An important event that shows how Jesus regarded women as being equal to men is the fact that he first appeared to a woman after the resurrection, and that Mary of Magdala was given the task of announcing the resurrection to Jesus' male followers (see John 20:17).

Objectives

- Understand that both men and women are important in the Bible.
- Understand how the role of women in Christianity reflects the Christian understanding of equality.

> In the Lord, woman is not independent of man or man independent of woman. For just as woman came from man, so man comes through woman; but all things come from God.
>
> *1 Corinthians* 11:11–12 (NRSV)

▲ Jesus' first appearance after his resurrection was to a woman

> He [Jesus] said to them [his disciples], 'Whoever divorces his wife and marries another commits adultery against her; and if she divorces her husband and marries another, she commits adultery.'
>
> *Mark* 10:11–12 (NRSV)

In the early Christian community, the role of women was recognised. They were prominent among the leaders and preachers.

> I commend to you our sister Phoebe, a deacon of the church at Cenchreae, so that you may welcome her in the Lord as is fitting for the saints, and help her in whatever she may require from you, for she has been a benefactor of many and of myself as well.
>
> *Romans* 16:1–2 (NRSV)

These verses bear witness to Paul's teaching that:

> There is no longer Jew or Greek, there is no longer slave or free, there is no longer male and female; for all of you are one in Christ Jesus.
>
> *Galatians* 3:28 (NRSV)

From the earliest days of Christianity, women have been valued as witnesses for the faith, as is seen in Paul's comment to his disciple, Timothy:

> I am reminded of your sincere faith, a faith that lived first in your grandmother Lois and your mother Eunice and now, I am sure, lives in you.
>
> *2 Timothy* 1:5 (NRSV)

▲ Jesus' 12 apostles were all men

The importance of men in the Bible

The importance of men in the Bible is illustrated by the fact that most events recorded are about men. Even in the New Testament, men appear to dominate. Jesus' 12 apostles, who Catholics believe were made the first priests at the Last Supper, were all men. It was largely male followers who travelled round the Roman Empire spreading the teachings of Jesus.

The main reason for the focus on men was connected to the structure of society at the time. Most people would not have accepted women who went from town to town preaching. Christians had to be careful how far they challenged the structure of society in the Roman Empire if they wanted people to listen. However, the importance of women, particularly as the first witnesses of the resurrection, was an essential fact in Christianity.

Discussion activity

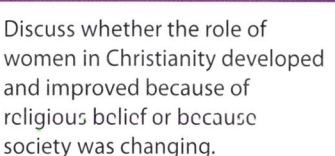

Discuss whether the role of women in Christianity developed and improved because of religious belief or because society was changing.

★ Study tip

Remember that the relative importance of men and women in the Bible is not necessarily connected with the number of times men and women are mentioned.

Activities

1. Explain two ways in which the Bible shows that men and women are considered to be of equal importance.
2. 'Christianity has always undervalued women.' Evaluate this statement. Be sure to include more than one point of view, and refer to Catholic beliefs and teachings in your answer.

Summary

You should now know that men and women are portrayed in the Bible as equal and complementary.

283

11.11 Catholic teaching on the equality of women and men

Catholic teaching on equality

The foundation for Catholic teachings about the equality of women and men comes from the Bible. God made both man and woman in his image and likeness (Genesis 1:27):

> The human race, which takes its origin from the calling into existence of man and woman, crowns the whole work of creation; **both man and woman are human beings to an equal degree,** both are created *in God's image*. This image and likeness of God, which is essential for the human being, is passed on by the man and woman, as spouses and parents, to their descendants.
>
> *Mulieris Dignitatem* 6

Objectives
- Know what the Catholic Church teaches about the equality of women and men.
- Understand why the Catholic Church distinguishes between treating men and women equally and treating them the same.

The belief in the equality of women and men is stated constantly in Church teachings. However, the Church also stresses that equality is not the same as uniformity.

> **In the 'unity of the two', man and woman are called from the beginning not only to exist 'side by side' or 'together',** but they are also called *to exist mutually 'one for the other'*.
>
> *Mulieris Dignitatem* 7

▲ *The Catholic Church teaches that women and men are equal but have different, complementary roles to play*

The Church believes that women and men cannot be the same and yet be mutually supportive. There are differences between men and women that are obvious in their physical traits but which also occur in many aspects of their psychology, responses and actions. The fact that men and women are not identical is a very positive factor as it enables each of them to reinforce the other, and to value the gifts and qualities that are more prominent in the other.

The Church teaches that women and men have different roles in life, which each individual plays out in their own way. When a man and a woman unite, they create a natural bond that strengthens and completes them as individuals and as a couple. This is highlighted in the physical union of sex but it also applies throughout their whole relationship.

> The personal resources of femininity are certainly no less than the resources of masculinity: they are merely different.
>
> *Mulieris Dignitatem* 10

Chapter 11 Theme A: religion, relationships and families

> ❝ Man and woman were made 'for each other' – not that God left them half-made and incomplete: he created them to be a communion of persons, in which each can be "helpmate" to the other, for they are equal as persons … and complementary as masculine and feminine. ❞
>
> *Catechism of the Catholic Church* 372

The Catholic Church believes that the differences between men and women must be respected, as these differences are essential to a healthy appreciation of all that life has to offer. The Church does not place men higher than women or women higher than men; it stresses that women and men have different yet complementary roles to perform. Men and women are to be valued for what they are and for what they contribute to the family and to the world. Both are irreplaceable.

▲ The Catholic Church believes that some roles, like the priesthood, are better suited to a particular gender

> ❝ **God endowed men and women with identical dignity as persons.** Both men and women are human beings created in God's image and children of God, redeemed by Jesus Christ. It is just as unchristian as it is inhumane to discriminate unjustly against someone because he is male or female. **Equal dignity and equal rights, nevertheless, do not mean uniformity.** The sort of egalitarianism that ignores the specific character of a man or a woman contradicts God's plan of creation. ❞
>
> *Youcat* 401

■ Contrasting views

While few people would argue against the Catholic Church's teaching that men and women are equally important, many would argue that this does not mean men and women should have different, predefined roles. For example, the Catholic Church does not allow women to be priests, and believes the mother should be allowed to fulfil her role in the family of looking after the home and children.

Many people in Britain today would view this as sexist, as they believe that treating women as equals means allowing them equal opportunities. Some would argue that men and women are equally capable of fulfilling the same roles; others might argue that even though women and men overall may be suited to particular roles, this does not mean that individuals should be expected to fulfil particular roles or denied the opportunity to fulfil others.

Activities

1. Explain what the Catholic Church teaches about the equality of men and women.
2. 'The Catholic Church is trying to cover up its sexist attitude with meaningless explanations.' Evaluate this statement. Be sure to include more than one point of view, and refer to Christian beliefs and teachings in your answer.

Research activity

Research one situation where women have demanded equal rights to men, such as the right to equal pay or the right to vote. How do you think Catholic teaching would apply in this situation?

Summary

You should now know what the Catholic Church teaches about the equality of women and men. You should also understand contrasting views on whether treating men and women as equal means treating them the same.

⭐ Study tip

Think about how men and women are treated. Does this suggest they are equal or identical?

11.12 Gender prejudice and discrimination

What are gender prejudice and discrimination?

Gender prejudice is the attitude that women are not as good as men, or men are not as good as women. Prejudice is built on stereotypes: a set idea that a person or group of people should behave in a particular way. Gender prejudice assumes that men or women should behave in a certain way, or have certain strengths or weaknesses because of their gender.

Gender discrimination turns this attitude into action and affects how people treat others. For example, the manager of a building site might be prejudiced against women because he does not think they are as strong as men; if he decides not to employ any women as a result, this is an example of gender discrimination.

Catholic teachings on gender discrimination

The Catholic Church believes that discrimination can do great damage as it can prevent people from developing their God-given talents. It can hurt those who are being discriminated against, making them feel like they have less worth and value. Widespread discrimination can affect society as a whole. For example, in Britain in the first half of the twentieth century, women were usually paid much less than men, even for similar jobs.

In 2015, Pope Francis spoke about women who were being paid less than men for a piece of work. He said: 'Why is it expected that women must earn less than men? No! They have the same rights. The disparity is a pure scandal.' This example sums up the Church's attitude to gender discrimination. The Church believes is not acceptable to treat men and women differently in the same situation.

The Catholic Church has championed the rights of women in the home and family, in the workplace, and within society. The Church believes that women should be entitled to fulfil their primary role in society as mothers who bring up their children in safety. This role must not be taken from them for political or financial reasons. The Church believes that all societies should support the role of women in this regard, while also allowing those women who choose to go to work the full opportunity to do so.

> ❝ The recognition and defence of women's rights in the context of work generally depend on the organization of work, which must take into account the dignity and vocation of women, whose 'true advancement ... requires that **labour should be structured in such a way that women do not have to pay for their advancement by abandoning what is specific to them**'. This issue is the measure of the quality of society and its effective defence of women's right to work. ❞
>
> *Compendium of the Social Doctrine of the Church* 295

Objectives
- Understand what is meant by gender prejudice and discrimination.
- Understand Catholic teachings on gender prejudice and discrimination.

Key terms
- **gender prejudice:** expecting someone to behave in a particular way because of their gender
- **gender discrimination:** taking actions that treat one person differently to another because of their gender

> ❝ An urgent need to recognize effectively the rights of women in the workplace is seen especially under the aspects of pay, insurance and social security. ❞
>
> *Compendium of the Social Doctrine of the Church* 295

▲ Does gender prejudice and discrimination make it harder for women to succeed in more senior positions?

286

The Church acknowledges that the rights of men also need to be protected. It teaches that there should be 'objective equality', which means that no distinction should be made between the sexes in any particular situation.

However, the Catholic Church does not agree that men and women should be treated identically, unless the situation being dealt with requires this. Men and women have their own roles that must be respected. Certain roles, notably the priesthood, belong to one gender rather than the other.

▲ Why is it much more usual for the mother to stay at home and look after the children than the father?

> **'Male' and 'female' differentiate two individuals of equal dignity, which does not however reflect a static equality,** because the specificity of the female is different from the specificity of the male, and this difference in equality is enriching and indispensable for the harmony of life in society.
>
> *Compendium of the Social Doctrine of the Church* 146

As well as negative discrimination there can also be positive discrimination. This happens when – in an attempt to counteract negative discrimination – people who have previously been discriminated against are given preferential treatment. An example might be for a company to have a certain number of people from ethnic minorities that they need to employ, to help overcome prejudice that might be present in the workplace. Some people approve of the good intentions behind the policy, but claim that positive discrimination is actually as bad as negative discrimination in practice.

Gender discrimination in Britain today

While most people in Britain are against gender discrimination, which has been illegal in the UK since the Sex Discrimination Act of 1975, it still occurs in a number of different situations. For example, on average women are still paid less than men, and while women make up roughly half the workforce, men hold a higher proportion of senior positions.

As discussed on the page 285, many people in Britain today would disagree with the Catholic Church's teaching that men and women should fulfil particular roles. They would argue that not allowing women to become priests, for example, is a form of gender discrimination.

Activities

1. Explain what is meant by gender prejudice and gender discrimination.
2. Give two examples of gender discrimination.
3. 'People will always be gender prejudiced.' Evaluate this statement. Be sure to include more than one point of view, and refer to Catholic beliefs and teachings in your answer.

Extension activity

Find three examples of positive discrimination. How positive do you consider these particular examples to be for society?

⭐ Study tip

Make sure you know the difference between prejudice and discrimination. It would help to be able to give examples of each.

Summary

You should now know the meaning of the terms gender prejudice and gender discrimination, and be able to explain the Catholic Church's views on the topic.

287

11 Assessment guidance

Theme A: religion, relationships and families – summary

You should now be able to:

- ✔ explain how the Bible shows that people are sexual, male and female
- ✔ explain Catholic teaching about sexual love as being marital, unitive and procreative
- ✔ explain the main ideas of John Paul II's 'Theology of the Body'
- ✔ explain different view held in Britain, both Christian and non-religious, about sex before marriage, adultery and homosexuality
- ✔ explain the conditions for a valid marriage according to the Catholic Church
- ✔ explain what marriage and the marriage promises mean for Catholics
- ✔ explain what the Catholic Church teaches about annulment, divorce and remarrying
- ✔ explain different views held in Britain, both Christian and non-religious, on cohabitation and same-sex marriage
- ✔ explain what the Catholic Church teaches about family planning
- ✔ explain what the Catholic Church teaches about the family, including procreation, security and education of children, and the roles of men and women
- ✔ explain what the Catholic Church teaches about work within the home
- ✔ explain different views held in Britain, both Christian and non-religious, on the use of artificial contraception, and the rights of same-sex parents and single people to have children
- ✔ explain what the Bible and the Catholic Church teach about the equality of women and men
- ✔ explain ways in which the Catholic Church opposes gender prejudice and discrimination
- ✔ explain different views held in Britain, both Christian and non-religious, on the view that treating men and women equally means treating them the same.

Sample student answer – the 4 mark question

1. Write an answer to the following question:

   Explain two contrasting beliefs in contemporary British society about the issue of sex before marriage.
   - You must refer to Christian belief.
   - You must refer to contrasting religious and/or non-religious belief.

   [4 marks]

2. Read the following sample student answer:

   "The Catholic Church says that as sex is the final part of the marriage sacrament, it is a holy thing. Therefore, a person should not have sex before they commit themselves in words at the wedding ceremony. It is seen as a misuse of human sexuality, especially if contraceptives are used, as it is not using sex to show true love and devotion and being open to children. Many other Christian churches respect sex as a bond between the husband and wife, but also accept that people often do not want to wait to express their love for someone else until they are married, as long as the love is sincere, and they are not just using each other."

3. With a partner, discuss the sample answer. What are its good points and are there any weaknesses? How do you think the answer could be improved?

4. What mark (out of 4) would you give this answer? Look at the mark scheme in the Introduction (AO1). What are the reasons for the mark you have given?

5. Now swap your answer with your partner's and mark each other's responses. What mark (out of 4) would you give the response? Refer to the mark scheme and give reasons for the mark you award.

Sample student answer – the 5 mark question

1. Write an answer to the following question:

   Explain two Christian beliefs about the roles and responsibilities in a family. Refer to scripture or sacred writings in your answer. **[5 marks]**

2. Read the following sample student answer:

   "The father and mother are there to produce and look after the children. They should give the children what they want as this is one way that the parents can show their love for their children. Children should respect their parents until they leave home. The father should make money and the mother should go out to work once the children are old enough to go to school so that the family has a good income. Before that time the children should play their part in the family by helping to take care of younger children and cleaning the house."

3. With a partner, discuss the sample answer. Is the focus of the answer correct? Is anything missing from the answer? How do you think it could be improved?

4. What mark (out of 5) would you give this answer? Look at the mark scheme in the Introduction (AO1). What are the reasons for the mark you have given?

5. Now swap your answer with your partner's and mark each other's responses. What mark (out of 5) would you give the response? Refer to the mark scheme and give reasons for the mark you award.

Practice questions

1. Which of the following is NOT regarded by the Catholic Church as being the nature of sexual love?

   A) unitive   B) procreative   C) selfish   D) marital **[1 mark]**

2. Give two teachings about the human body from Pope John Paul II's 'Theology of the Body'. **[2 marks]**

3. Explain two contrasting beliefs in contemporary British society about the issue of annulment.
   - You must refer to Christian belief.
   - You must refer to contrasting religious and/or non-religious belief. **[4 marks]**

4. Explain two Christian beliefs about the nature of marriage. Refer to scripture or sacred writings in your answer. **[5 marks]**

5. 'A family is still a family, no matter what gender the parents are.'

   Evaluate this statement.

   In your answer you:
   - should give reasoned arguments in support of this statement
   - should give reasoned arguments to support a different point of view
   - should refer to Christian arguments
   - may refer to non-religious arguments
   - should reach a justified conclusion. **[12 marks]**

> ⭐ **Study tip**
>
> Remember to include Christian arguments, for example teachings from the Catholic Church or references to what the Bible says.

12 Theme B: religion, peace and conflict

12.1 Biblical perspectives on violence and bullying

■ Ideas about violence in the Bible

Christians believe that God made the world 'very good' (Genesis 1:31): a state of paradise and harmony in the Garden of Eden (Genesis 2). However, shortly after humans turned against God – by insisting on making their own decisions rather than following God's rules (Genesis 3) – humans turned against each other. While many Christians believe the early chapters of Genesis are myths, so should not be taken literally, they still make important points about human nature. They tell us that anger is an integral part of human nature, and if it is not controlled then it will lead to **violence**. For Christians, violence is a rejection of the ideals that God wants for the world.

> **Objective**
> - Understand what the Bible says about violence, including bullying.

> **Key terms**
> - **violence:** using actions that can threaten or harm others
> - **bullying:** the deliberate intimidation of a person through words or physical actions

> " Cain was very angry, and his countenance fell. The Lord said to Cain, 'Why are you angry, and why has your countenance fallen? If you do well, will you not be accepted? And if you do not do well, sin is lurking at the door; its desire is for you, but you must master it.' Cain said to his brother Abel, 'Let us go out to the field.' And when they were in the field, Cain rose up against his brother Abel and killed him. Then the Lord said to Cain, 'Where is your brother Abel?' He said, 'I do not know; am I my brother's keeper?' And the Lord said, 'What have you done? Listen; **your brother's blood is crying out to me from the ground!** And now you are cursed from the ground, which has opened its mouth to receive your brother's blood from your hand.' "
>
> *Genesis* 4:5–11 (NRSV)

However, while anger and violence are a part of human nature, which has been corrupted by sin, Jesus taught that they should nearly always be avoided. Jesus said to his disciples: 'Peace I leave with you; my peace I give to you' (John 14:27). Peace does not just mean a lack of violence. It means a deep feeling of wellbeing and inner calm that enables people to accept the changes and challenges in life with a feeling of security and trust. It is when this quality is lacking that trouble and violence break out.

▲ *Genesis 4 describes how Cain killed his brother Abel*

In the Sermon on the Mount, Jesus taught that if the seeds of bitterness, anger and jealousy are not controlled from the start, they will increase and end up destroying relationships between people, particularly through the use of violence (Matthew 5:21–22).

■ Bullying

One very destructive form of violence is **bullying**. This is when one person or a group of people uses intimidation against another person or group. Bullying might not appear frightening from an onlooker's perspective as there is often no physical violence involved. However, being the recipient of negative behaviour and comments can destroy a person's self-esteem, and may reduce them to living in a state of fear and with a sense of powerlessness. There are many current examples of people whose lives have been ruined by negative comments on social media; the internet has made it much easier for bullying to be played out in front of a public and potentially global audience, causing even more distress for those involved.

▲ *Bullying can make the victim feel isolated and worthless*

In the Bible, James talked about the power of the tongue and words. He reminds Christians that, although the tongue is only a small part of the body, the power of speech – which the tongue represents – can do great damage to other people. As a result, people should be very careful about what they say.

> ❝ But **no one can tame the tongue** – a restless evil, full of deadly poison. With it we bless the Lord and Father, and with it we curse those who are made in the likeness of God. From the same mouth come blessing and cursing. My brothers and sisters, this ought not to be so. ❞
>
> *James* 3:8–10 (NRSV)

There are also many passages in the Bible which show that God is on the side of the defenceless, for example:

> ❝ Father of orphans and protector of widows is God in his holy habitation. ❞
>
> *Psalms* 68(67):5 (NRSV)

> ❝ You have heard that it was said to those of ancient times, 'You shall not murder'; and 'whoever murders shall be liable to judgement.' But I say to you that if you are angry with a brother or sister, you will be liable to judgement; and if you insult a brother or sister, you will be liable to the council; and if you say, 'You fool', you will be liable to the hell of fire. ❞
>
> *Matthew* 5:21–22 (NRSV)

Activities

1. Explain what the Bible teaches about violence.
2. 'Bullying is the worst form of violence.' Evaluate this statement. Be sure to include more than one point of view, and refer to Catholic beliefs and teachings in your answer.

Research activity

Research cases of bullying that have led to serious outcomes for those involved. Suggest how religious teachings might have prevented the situation.

⭐ Study tip

Try to understand the underlying reasons for violence and bullying as this will help you to make sense of why it happens.

Summary

You should now know what the Bible teaches about violence and bullying.

291

12.2 Forgiveness and reconciliation

Forgiveness

Forgiveness is a central message in Jesus' teachings. Jesus practised it himself, for example:

- When he was being nailed to the cross, he prayed: 'Father, forgive them; for they do not know what they are doing' (Luke 23:34).
- After the resurrection, he forgave Peter for his denial of him (see John 21:15–17).

When Peter asked Jesus about forgiveness, Jesus suggested that forgiveness should be without limits: 'Then Peter came and said to him, "Lord, if another member of the church sins against me, how often should I forgive? As many as seven times?" Jesus said to him, "Not seven times, but, I tell you, seventy-seven times"' (Matthew 18:21–22 (NRSV)).

▲ *From the cross, Jesus asked for forgiveness for the people who had crucified him*

Jesus taught that forgiveness towards a fellow human being is essential if a person wants to be forgiven by God. This is stated in the Lord's Prayer: 'And forgive us our debts, as we also have forgiven our debtors' (Matthew 6:12).

This approach to forgiveness is also expressed in the Parable of the Unforgiving Debtor (Matthew 18:23–35). In this parable, the king forgave a servant a debt of billions of pounds. Then this servant met another servant who owed him £100. The first servant insisted on having the money repaid, and when the second servant could not do this, the first servant put him into the debtors' prison along with his family. When the king heard about this, he demanded that the first servant repay all his debt to him, and put the servant into prison until all the billions of pounds were repaid. In this parable Jesus taught that God will only forgive someone who is willing to share this forgiveness.

Gee Verona Walker on forgiveness

In 2005, 18-year-old Anthony Walker was killed in a racially motivated attack. Jesus' teaching about forgiving 77 times was quoted both by his mother and his sister. They found the courage to forgive the teenagers who had killed Anthony. Five months after the murder, Anthony's mother Gee said: 'Do I forgive them? At the point of death Jesus said "I forgive them because they don't know what they did". I've got to forgive them. I still forgive them. My family and I still stand by what we believe: forgiveness.'

Objectives

- Understand the concepts of forgiveness and reconciliation.
- Know what Jesus taught about forgiveness and reconciliation.

Key terms

- **forgiveness:** showing grace and mercy; pardoning someone for what they have done wrong
- **reconciliation:** (1) the restoring of harmony after relationships have broken down (2) a sacrament in the Catholic Church

Activities

1. Explain how forgiveness and reconciliation are linked.
2. Explain why forgiveness is important within religions and societies.
3. 'Reconciliation can never be truly effective.' Evaluate this statement. Be sure to include more than one point of view, and refer to Catholic beliefs and teachings in your answer.

Research activity

Research a Biblical passage about reconciliation, such as Matthew 18:23–35 or Colossians 3:12–15. What does this passage teach about reconciliation?

■ Reconciliation

Reconciliation refers to bringing back together two parties that have been torn apart by some kind of difference. Jesus taught that people have to be reconciled to each other before they can offer suitable praise to God:

> So when you are offering your gift at the altar, if you remember that your brother or sister has something against you, leave your gift there before the altar and go; **first be reconciled to your brother or sister, and then come and offer your gift.**
>
> Matthew 5:23–24 (NRSV)

What are the best ways to reconcile young offenders, to help them to form a better relationship with the rest of society?

Once forgiveness and reconciliation have taken place, a relationship is much stronger because the two parties have learned to appreciate and accept each other for what they are. Forgiveness and reconciliation do not mean denying the difficulties of the past, but learning from the past to build a better, more peaceful future. Reconciliation leads to the peace that Jesus prayed for at the Last Supper: 'Peace I leave with you; my peace I give to you. I do not give to you as the world gives. Do not let your hearts be troubled, and do not let them be afraid' (John 14:27 (NRSV)).

In all his travels to countries that have been torn apart by conflict, Pope Francis has called for reconciliation. Without reconciliation, there can be no peace, and without peace people will live unsecure lives in fear. There has been an increased awareness of the need for reconciliation between different religions in recent times. The Catholic Church stated its awareness of the respect due to other religions in *Lumen Gentium*:

> Those who have not yet received the Gospel are related in various ways to the people of God … the plan of salvation also includes those who acknowledge the Creator. **In the first place amongst these there are the Muslims, who, professing to hold the faith of Abraham, along with us adore the one and merciful God, who on the last day will judge mankind.**
>
> *Lumen Gentium* 16

For both forgiveness and reconciliation, understanding and empathy are important. As one example, when a teenager vandalises the property of an older person, one of the aims of the local police and justice system might be to get the teenager to meet the victim and do something to help them. The hope is that the teenager will begin to appreciate what harm they have done. If the victim can also learn to know the teenager as someone who has problems in their life which have caused their anger, understanding and sympathy can arise. This is the foundation for reconciliation, and a springboard for deeper trust and respect within the community.

Discussion activity

Discuss whether reconciliation between different groups within a society (such as Catholics and Protestants in Northern Ireland) is necessary.

⭐ Study tip

Forgiveness is a common theme in plays and soap operas. Relating Christian teachings to a dramatised situation might help you to understand more fully the teaching of Jesus.

Summary

You should now know what Jesus taught about forgiveness and reconciliation. You should also understand how forgiveness and reconciliation lead to peace.

12.3 Justice

The importance of justice

The Bible teaches that establishing **justice** is one of the ways in which Christians help God's Kingdom to spread on earth. Therefore, creating justice is an important concern for the Catholic Church. The Church teaches that justice means ensuring fairness for all people, establishing what is right, and ensuring things are as God wants them to be.

In the Old Testament, creating justice is more important than ensuring that worship is done correctly, as Amos taught (Amos 5:23–24).

▲ Occupy London was a peaceful protest against the abuse of capitalist monetary policies held in 2011, during which protesters camped outside St Paul's Cathedral for a number of months

When people are treated unjustly, they can lose their sense of self-worth and self-respect. There are many examples in history where groups of people have been denied their human dignity because they have been unfairly treated by those in power. One well-known example is the apartheid era in South Africa, when the government introduced laws to segregate and discriminate against black people.

The Catholic Church has made many statements about the importance of justice. Among the more recent was Pope Benedict XV's encyclical *Deus Caritas Est*:

> **Building a just social and civil order, wherein each person receives what is his or her due, is an essential task which every generation must take up anew.** As a political task, this cannot be the Church's immediate responsibility. Yet, since it is also a most important human responsibility, the Church is duty-bound to offer … her own specific contribution towards understanding the requirements of justice and achieving them politically.
>
> *Deus Caritas Est* 28

Objectives

- Understand the concept of justice and why it is important to Catholics.
- Understand contrasting views on the best ways to respond to injustice.

Key terms

- **justice:** bringing about what is right and fair, according to the law, or making up for a wrong that has been committed
- **righteous anger:** anger against an injustice; some Christians use the term to describe anger that they believe is acceptable

> Take away from me the noise of your songs; I will not listen to the melody of your harps. But let justice roll down like waters, and righteousness like an ever-flowing stream.
>
> *Amos* 5:23–24 (NRSV)

> Mighty King, lover of justice, you have established equity; you have executed justice and righteousness in Jacob.
>
> *Psalms* 99(98):4 (NRSV)

Chapter 12   Theme B: religion, peace and conflict

■ Righteous anger as a response to injustice

We saw on pages 290–291 that Jesus taught anger should be avoided wherever possible. However, some Christians believe that in certain situations **righteous anger** can be effectively used to help create justice. It refers to anger that Christians feel is acceptable because it is directed against something that God would not agree with. Jesus himself showed righteous anger when he drove the sellers from the Temple (John 2:13–17).

For Christians, an important element of righteous anger is that it is controlled and used positively to change a situation. It can be easy to make mistakes when responding emotionally or impulsively in anger; righteous anger should be channelled into positive action that will improve a situation.

> **❝** So then, putting away falsehood, let all of us speak the truth to our neighbours, for we are members of one another. Be angry but do not sin. **❞**
>
> *Ephesians* 4:25–26 (NRSV)

■ Violent protest as a response to injustice

Many people would argue that injustice must be visibly opposed in order to stop it. Some believe that one of the best ways to do this is to take part in protests. The law in the UK allows individuals and groups to peacefully protest in public to demonstrate their point of view. If the protest involves a procession or a march, the police must be told at least six days before it takes place. The police can request alterations to the route or even apply to a court for an order to ban the march. They may do this if they feel that the march might intimidate other people or if they predict that violence will be involved.

Violent protest is illegal in the UK, and many people do not support it because they believe it is an ineffective and damaging way to create change, particularly if people lose their lives in the violence. Others believe that violent protest is sometimes necessary to make a government take notice, particularly if a government is abusing their position of power and refusing to pay attention to people's needs (such as the suffragette movement in the early twentieth century in Britain). In 2015, the Catholic Church supported the protests in the Democratic Republic of Congo against a government that was unjustly delaying elections, even though the protests turned violent.

▲ *At what point does protest become too violent to be acceptable?*

Activities

1. Explain why some Catholics would agree with the idea of righteous anger.
2. 'The only way to defend human dignity is to ensure there is justice in the world.' Evaluate this statement. Be sure to include more than one point of view, and refer to Catholic beliefs and teachings in your answer.

Summary

You should now know why justice is important and how it is linked to human dignity. You should also understand different approaches to combatting injustice.

Extension activity

Research a situation in which religious believers used violent protest, such as the Christian protest in Pakistan in March 2015. How effective do you think their approach was? Explain your answer.

⭐ Study tip

There are many examples in the world where justice is denied and this causes tension. Investigating some of these examples, and finding out how people have tried to improve the situation, will help you to better understand this topic.

12.4 The just war theory

Background to the just war theory

The New Testament contains teachings that suggest there are situations where the limited use of violence is acceptable. For example, towards the end of his ministry, Jesus said to his disciples: 'The one who has no sword must sell his cloak and buy one' (Luke 22:36). This statement suggests that Jesus realised his followers would need to be able to protect themselves.

In the early days of Christianity, Christians refused to fight in wars or disputes as they did not accept they had the right to take the life of another person. However, once the Roman Empire made Christianity the official religion after 370 CE, this situation had to change. The Empire was attacked by invaders. Christians faced the choice of either fighting or allowing their country to be overrun.

Christian thinkers – in particular St Augustine and St Thomas Aquinas – devised a list of conditions that made fighting a war justifiable. Over the centuries, these conditions were refined and became known as the **just war theory**.

Conditions for a just war

The official position of the Catholic Church on going to war is stated in the *Catechism of the Catholic Church*:

> The strict conditions for *legitimate defense by military force* require rigorous consideration. The gravity of such a decision makes it subject to rigorous conditions of moral legitimacy. At one and the same time:
> - **the damage inflicted by the aggressor** on the nation or community of nations **must be lasting, grave, and certain;**
> - all other means of putting an end to it must have been shown to be impractical or ineffective;
> - there must be serious prospects of success;
> - **the use of arms must not produce evils and disorders graver than the evil to be eliminated.** The power of modern means of destruction weighs very heavily in evaluating this condition.
>
> These are the traditional elements enumerated in what is called the 'just war' doctrine.
>
> The evaluation of these conditions for moral legitimacy belongs to the prudential judgment of those who have responsibility for the common good.
>
> *Catechism of the Catholic Church* 2309

Objectives
- Understand the just war theory.
- Understand contrasting attitudes towards fighting.

Key term
- **just war theory:** a set of criteria that a war needs to meet before it can be justified

▲ In 2015, many Syrians were forced to flee a civil war and live in refugee camps such as this one. Is it possible to fight a war without harming any civilians?

> Those who wage war justly aim at peace, and so they are not opposed to peace … Hence Augustine says: **'We do not seek peace in order to be at war, but we go to war that we may have peace**. Be peaceful, therefore, in warring, so that you may vanquish [overcome] those whom you war against, and bring them to the prosperity of peace.'
>
> St Thomas Aquinas, *Summa Theologica*

Chapter 12 Theme B: religion, peace and conflict

These conditions mean that:
- Only a legitimate authority, such as a government, can declare war.
- A country should not go to war without a serious and just reason for doing so. A just reason might include self-defence; a non-just reason might be to gain territory or resources.
- War should only be declared if all other means of settling the dispute have been tried and have failed.
- A country should not go to war if there is not a reasonable chance of success. It is unjust to ask people to fight a war if it is probable that the war will be lost and they will be killed.
- Any use of weapons has to be limited to only what is needed to bring about a lasting peace. Weapons must not be too destructive.
- Innocent people or civilians should not be attacked.

The aim of the just war theory is to limit the use of war to settle disputes. The Catholic Church accepts that there are times when force has to be used. However, it believes that when a country goes to war, it should be because there is no workable alternative.

The invasion of Kuwait

In 1990 Iraq invaded Kuwait. The Iraqi leader defied the continuous demands to leave Kuwait that were made by the United Nations. Eventually, a United Nations force, which was led by the United States of America and included British forces and forces from many Arab nations, invaded and freed Kuwait, driving the Iraqi army back into Iraq. When asked if this was a just war, Cardinal Hume of Westminster said: 'I am not sure if it is a just war, but it is definitely a justified war.'

■ Contrasting views on the just war theory

Many people in Britain think the British army should only go to war in a country when there has clearly been a major abuse of power or there exists a serious, lasting threat to the security of Britain. While few people may talk explicitly about a just war, in practice many will not support or approve of a war that does not meet the just war criteria.

Of course many people believe that it is much better if there is no war, just or not, and that working together to avoid situations where war is a possible outcome is preferable to fighting. The United Nations, founded in 1945, encourages countries to resolve disputes peacefully.

Some people think that the just war theory is dangerous as it could be seen to endorse or defend the concept of war. Others think that the just war theory is no longer relevant to warfare in the twenty-first century.

Activities

1. In your own words, list the main conditions that make a war 'just'.
2. Explain the importance of the just war theory for Christians.
3. 'No war can ever be just.' Evaluate this statement. Be sure to include more than one point of view, and refer to Catholic beliefs and teachings in your answer.

Discussion activity

Discuss whether the world needs a just war theory.

Research activity

Examine one recent war and see how many of the just war criteria applied to it.

★ Study tip

Try to learn and remember the main conditions of the just war theory.

▲ The sculpture outside the United Nations headquarters in New York

Summary

You should now know the criteria for a just war. You should also understand how the just war theory can help people to decide whether a particular conflict is acceptable or not.

12.5 Nuclear war and weapons of mass destruction

■ Catholic attitudes to nuclear war and weapons of mass destruction

The basic Catholic attitude to modern warfare was laid out in 1963 by Pope John XXIII in his encyclical *Pacem in Terris*. Later statements by other popes and bishops have simply developed the central ideas presented by Pope John XXIII.

▲ The first nuclear bomb to be used in warfare was dropped on the Japanese city of Hiroshima in 1945; the bomb itself and the radiation it produced killed around 130,000 people in the first few months after it was dropped

There are five main reasons for the Catholic Church's opposition to **nuclear war**. These reasons also apply to using other **weapons of mass destruction (WMD)**, such as **chemical** and **biological weapons**.

- The effects of these weapons are completely indiscriminate. Innocent civilians and people in any countries that neighbour the area where the fighting is taking place could all be affected, not only by the initial release of the weapon but also through its long-term effects, which could include it having an impact on future generations.
- The effects of these weapons are totally disproportionate to any possible success that might follow on from their use. This applies both to the initial effects of the weapon but also to the escalation that might follow: for instance, if other countries release their WMD in retaliation.
- With WMD the possibility of success is small. The effect of these weapons is so devastating that the survivors might end up living in a world that is in a state of chaos. Pope Benedict XVI said in 2006 that in a nuclear war there would be no 'victors, only victims' (*Message for the World Day of Peace*, paragraph 13).
- The cost of researching, building and maintaining WMD is so great that a considerable amount of a country's military budget has to be spent on them. This means that governments are spending people's money on weapons that destroy rather than on things that improve

Objectives
- Understand Catholic attitudes to nuclear war and weapons of mass destruction.
- Understand contrasting views about the possession of weapons of mass destruction.

Key terms
- **nuclear war:** war that makes use of nuclear weapons: weapons that work by creating a nuclear reaction in order to devastate huge areas and kill large numbers of people
- **weapons of mass destruction (WMD):** weapons that can kill large numbers of people and/or cause great damage
- **chemical weapons:** weapons that use chemicals to harm humans and destroy the natural environment
- **biological weapons:** weapons that use living organisms to cause disease or death

> ❝ As long as there are nuclear weapons in the world there is always the danger they will be used, whether by accident or intention. ❞
>
> Campaign for Nuclear Disarmament

Chapter 12 Theme B: religion, peace and conflict

people's lives. Even countries with low incomes may feel that they have to protect themselves with this type of weapon.
- The possession of WMD by any country increases tension and fear. This fear in itself is a factor in making the world a less safe and stable place.

> " We are deeply distressed to see the enormous stocks of armaments that have been, and continue to be, manufactured in the economically more developed countries. This policy is involving a vast outlay of intellectual and material resources, with the result that **the people of these countries are saddled with a great burden, while other countries lack the help they need for their economic and social development.**
>
> **Consequently people are living in the grip of constant fear.** They are afraid that at any moment the impending storm may break upon them with horrific violence.
>
> **Hence justice, right reason, and the recognition of man's dignity cry out insistently for a cessation to the arms race.** The stock-piles of armaments which have been built up in various countries must be reduced all round and simultaneously by the parties concerned. **Nuclear weapons must be banned.**
>
> Everyone, however, must realize that, unless this process of disarmament be thoroughgoing and complete, and reach men's very souls, it is impossible to stop the arms race, or to reduce armaments, or – and this is the main thing – ultimately to abolish them entirely. Everyone must sincerely co-operate in the effort to banish fear and the anxious expectation of war from men's minds.
>
> The warning of Pope Pius XII still rings in our ears: **'Nothing is lost by peace; everything may be lost by war.'** "
>
> *Pacem in Terris* 109–116

■ Contrasting views

In Britain today there are major differences of opinion about the possession and use of WMD. Britain already has a number of nuclear weapons. Some people (including some Catholics) argue these are necessary to deter aggressive attacks from other countries, and are important for effective self-defence (particularly when other countries have WMD too). Other people maintain that Britain should get rid of all its WMD; they oppose WMD for similar reasons to those given by the Catholic Church. They would argue that somebody has to start the process of disarmament and it is Britain's responsibility to do this.

Activities

1. Explain why many people are opposed to the use of weapons of mass destruction.
2. 'It is acceptable for a country to own nuclear weapons.' Evaluate this statement. Be sure to include more than one point of view, and refer to Catholic beliefs and teachings in your answer.

Extension activity

Examine recent papal teachings on warfare. Assess whether the recent statements have changed the teachings of *Pacem in Terris* (paragraphs 109–116) in any fundamental way.

▲ Modern nuclear weapons are far more powerful than the bomb dropped on Hiroshima in 1945

★ Study tip

There are some interesting films and programmes on nuclear weapons, both about the effects of the nuclear bombs on Hiroshima and Nagasaki and about the possible effects of a future nuclear war (for example, the 2005 film *Hiroshima* or the 1984 drama *Threads*). Watching these will help you to understand the issues more clearly.

Summary

You should now know why the Catholic Church opposes the use of weapons of mass destruction. You should also understand the arguments for and against the possession of these weapons.

299

12.6 The consequences of modern warfare

Due to the development of more powerful weapons, modern warfare has the potential to be far more destructive than any previous form of war. The consequences of any fighting usually last far longer than the fighting itself, and can have devastating, wide-reaching effects on the whole of society. This situation has become worse due to the use of modern weapons, including weapons of mass destruction.

■ Civilian casualties

Civilian casualties refer to the people who do not fight in the war but are still killed or injured by the fighting. The methods of fighting and the weapons used in modern warfare mean that civilian deaths now often greatly outnumber military deaths.

The *Catechism of the Catholic Church* states that 'Non-combatants, wounded soldiers, and prisoners must be respected and treated humanely.' The Church believes that any person who is not directly involved in the fighting should not be attacked or threatened in any way, and aims to help protect as many people as it can. For example, during the Second World War, many Jews were given shelter in the Vatican and other Church buildings to protect them from the Nazis.

The Church supports all efforts to bring about a peaceful solution to fighting, but it works especially to gain agreement that the rights of non-combatants will be protected.

▲ Civilians can be affected in many different ways by warfare, even if they are not directly injured by the fighting

■ Refugees

In a war, civilians are often forced to flee their homes, either because their lives have already been destroyed or because they face a serious risk of death. Often refugees escape a war zone with very few

Objectives
- Understand the consequences of modern warfare.
- Understand contrasting opinions on how to deal with the effects of modern warfare.

> ❝ We cannot insist too much on **the duty of giving foreigners a hospitable reception.** It is a duty imposed by human solidarity and by Christian charity, and it is incumbent upon families and educational institutions in the host nations … This must be done … that they may be shielded from feelings of loneliness, distress and despair that would sap their strength. ❞
>
> *Populorum Progressio 67*

> ❝ **Delicate ecological balances are upset by the uncontrolled destruction of animal and plant life or by a reckless exploitation of natural resources.** It should be pointed out that all of this, even if carried out in the name of progress and well-being, is ultimately to mankind's disadvantage. ❞
>
> *Message for the World Day of Peace*

possessions and struggle to find somewhere new to rebuild their lives. Many end up living in refugee camps with very poor conditions.

The Catholic Church believes that refugees should be welcomed and protected by all countries, and has made a number of statements urging everyone, from individuals to governments, to help refugees.

The Syrian refugee crisis

In 2015, at the height of the Syrian refugee crisis, Pope Francis preached: 'May every parish, every religious community, every monastery, every sanctuary in Europe host a family, starting with my diocese of Rome.' The Vatican provided homes for two refugee families. When some found it too impractical to host a family, they found other ways to help. For example, a small community of three Benedictine nuns in Herefordshire realised that in practice it would be impossible for them to take in a refugee family. Instead, they gave a month's income to a charity that helps refugees.

▲ Many Syrian refugees have risked drowning in order to flee from the fighting in their country

■ Environmental damage

Modern warfare has the potential to do great damage to the environment. For example, an army might destroy huge areas of land in order to wipe out an enemy's cover, using chemical weapons that can affect the vegetation for decades after the war has ended.

Catholics believe that, as stewards of the earth, they have a responsibility to limit the damage done to the environment. Recent popes have condemned the harm that humans have caused to the environment, whether through a careless attitude or the deliberate use of practices that cause environmental damage (such as chemical weapons in war).

■ Contrasting views

Opinions differ on the methods that are acceptable in warfare. Some people argue that if more powerful and destructive weapons can bring a war to an end more quickly, they should be used, even if they cause greater harm, for example by causing more civilian deaths or greater environmental damage.

Many individuals and governments have differing opinions on how refugees should be treated, in particular regarding whether they should be accepted into a country or not. In Britain, some people argue that there are not enough resources to support taking in large numbers of refugees. Others argue that providing asylum to people whose lives are in danger is the humane thing to do, and that refugees can positively contribute to the economy of a country.

Activities

1 In your own words, explain contrasting views about whether a country should accept refugees or not.
2 'The greatest damage done by modern warfare is to the environment.' Evaluate this statement. Be sure to include more than one point of view, and refer to Catholic beliefs and teachings in your answer.

Discussion activity

Discuss whether it is either possible or desirable to prevent civilians becoming casualties of war.

★ Study tip

Find a news story or watch a documentary about the problems people face in a modern war zone, in order to better understand the issues involved in modern warfare.

Summary

You should now know about the effects of modern warfare. You should also understand differing opinions on how these effects can be dealt with.

12.7 Religion as a reason for violence and war

■ Religion and belief as a reason for war and violence

A common statement that is made about wars is that most are caused by religion. Examples of such wars might include the Crusades; the wars of religion in the seventeenth century, including the Thirty Years War; the Troubles in Northern Ireland; and the current unrest in the Middle East. On the surface there appears to be some truth in this claim, but the reality is far more complex: wars are caused by a number of complicated, interrelated reasons. Politics, economics, self-defence, retaliation, and the desire to gain territory or resources might all play a part. While religion may be a difference between the two sides, it is rarely the sole or main reason for the conflict.

For most Christians, the teachings of Jesus make it quite clear that the use of violence is very rarely justified. For example, in Matthew's gospel he said:

> You have heard that it was said to those of ancient times, 'You shall not murder'; and 'whoever murders shall be liable to judgement.' But I say to you that **if you are angry with a brother or sister, you will be liable to judgement.**
>
> *Matthew* 5:21–22 (NRSV)

Objectives

- Understand views on whether religion is or should be a cause for violence and war.
- Understand what the Old Testament says about violence and war.
- Understand the concept of a holy war.

Key term

- **holy war:** fighting for a religious cause or God, probably controlled by a religious leader

■ War and violence in the Old Testament

People often claim that the Old Testament is full of violent war waged on behalf of God. The Old Testament certainly describes a number of battles that the Israelites fought in order to establish themselves in the Promised Land, and the killing of many enemies to defend the country (see Samuel 15:1–33). However, these conflicts should be considered in their historical context: it could be argued that they were necessary for a persecuted group of people to establish themselves at a time when many disputes were settled through violence. There are a number of passages in the Old Testament that show that peace is what God wants for all people. For example:

▲ *How far can the conflict in the Middle East be seen as religious war?*

> He shall judge between the nations, and shall arbitrate for many peoples; they shall beat their swords into plowshares, and their spears into pruning hooks; nation shall not lift up sword against nation, **neither shall they learn war any more.**
>
> *Isaiah* 2:4 (NRSV)

302

A verse that is often quoted from the Old Testament is 'eye for eye, tooth for tooth' (Exodus 21:24), which is sometimes taken to mean that it is acceptable to return violence with violence. When this was first written over 3000 years ago, individual wrongs were punished by taking violent action against the families or tribes of the offenders. The 'eye for an eye' teaching tried to reduce this violence by suggesting only the individuals involved should be punished and not a larger group of people, most of whom were innocent.

Holy war

There are some wars that have been fought on behalf of a religious belief. For Christians, a **holy war** must be approved by a religious leader who has great authority. The purpose of the war should be to defend the Christian faith from attack. Those who take part believe they will gain spiritual rewards.

▲ Crusaders believed they were fighting on the side of God

The Crusades are the best-known examples of a holy war. Between the eleventh and fifteenth centuries, various popes called upon Christians to go to the Holy Land to free the holy places, particularly Jerusalem, from the control of Muslim Turks. Christians were promised that since they were fighting for God, if they died in battle they would go straight to heaven.

Arguments in favour of the Crusades were strongly presented by St Bernard in the twelfth century, who built his case on two points of the just war theory:

- The Crusaders were aiming to fight injustice, particularly the injustice done to Christians by the 'infidel' (those who were not Christians).
- The Crusades were authorised by the Pope, God's representative on earth, so they must have been God's will.

St Bernard argued that the Crusaders were fighting on the side of Christ, against the powers of darkness, to protect and spread the Kingdom of God on earth. However, this initial religious intention quickly disappeared beneath political and power struggles as the war developed.

The concept of holy war does not feature widely in current Christian belief, but that does not mean that Christians are happy to see their faith attacked. Christians will still stand up for their faith but are much more likely to use the power of argument than military strength.

> ❝ O grant us help against the foe, for human help is worthless. With God we shall do valiantly; it is he who will tread down our foes. ❞
>
> *Psalms* 60(59):11–12 (NRSV)

Links

For more on the just war theory see pages 296–297.

Extension activity

Choose either the Thirty Years War or one of the Crusades. Examine to what extent this was a holy war.

★ Study tip

Remember that the reasons for war are very complex, even in the case of religious wars.

Summary

You should now understand views about religion as a cause of violence and war. You should also understand the concept of a holy war.

Activities

1. Explain to what extent religion can be seen as a cause of war.
2. 'People should never use violence to defend religion.' Evaluate this statement. Be sure to include more than one point of view, and refer to Catholic beliefs and teachings in your answer.

12.8 Pacifism

■ Christian views on pacifism

Pacifism is the belief that violence and war can never be justified, and that peaceful means should always be used to resolve disputes.

Some Christians claim that Jesus was a pacifist for the following reasons:

- He taught that force should not be used. For example, he said 'Do not resist an evildoer. But if anyone strikes you on the right cheek, turn the other also,' (Matthew 5:39) and 'Blessed are the peacemakers, for they will be called children of God' (Matthew 5:9).
- He nearly always refused to allow violence to be used. For example, when he was arrested, 'one of those with Jesus put his hand on his sword, drew it, and struck the slave of the high priest, cutting off his ear. Then Jesus said to him, "Put your sword back into its place; for all who take the sword will perish by the sword"' (Matthew 26:51–53 (NRSV)).

The early Christians were pacifists. A typical example was Martin of Tours (336–397 CE) who resigned from the Roman army when he became a Christian, saying: 'It is not right for me to fight'. When he was accused of cowardice, Martin offered to go at the front of the army unarmed to face the enemy. But the enemy asked for peace before this offer could be taken up.

There have been some influential Christians who refused to use violence, the most prominent of these during the twentieth century was Martin Luther King. The Religious Society of Friends (Quakers) strongly promotes pacifism. Despite their refusal to fight, during the First World War many Quakers acted as stretcher-bearers and some went to treat the wounded of both sides in the no man's land between the trenches, even when shells and bullets were flying. In the Second World War, pacifist Christians from different denominations joined the Friends Ambulance Unit to help provide medical support.

After the Second World War, a group of Catholics founded the organisation Pax Christi (The Peace of Christ) to try to reconcile the war-torn countries of Europe. Today it is a global organisation that works to bring about justice, peace and reconciliation. The validity of their efforts has been greatly strengthened by papal encyclicals, including *Pacem in Terris* (1963).

■ Teachings of the Catholic Church

While the popes' and the Church's teachings have always acknowledged that every person and nation has the right to protect itself, over the past

Objectives

- Understand what the Catholic Church teaches about pacifism.
- Understand contrasting views about pacifism.

Key term

- **pacifism:** the belief of people who refuse to take part in war and any other form of violence

★ Study tip

Remember the difference between a pacifist and a peacemaker. A pacifist does not accept the use of violence to solve disputes; a peacemaker works to bring about peace in a conflict. A pacifist may be a peacemaker and vice versa but this is not always the case.

▲ *Pacifists believe that disputes should be solved through non-violent means such as negotiation*

few decades there has been an increasing emphasis on the use of non-violent approaches to resolving conflicts.

> Men nowadays are becoming more and more convinced that any disputes which may arise between nations must be resolved by negotiation and agreement, and not by recourse to arms.
>
> We acknowledge that this conviction owes its origin chiefly to the terrifying destructive force of modern weapons. It arises from fear of the ghastly and catastrophic consequences of their use. Thus, **in this age which boasts of its atomic power, it no longer makes sense to maintain that war is a fit instrument with which to repair the violation of justice.**
>
> We are hopeful that, by establishing contact with one another and by a policy of negotiation, nations will come to a better recognition of the natural ties that bind them together as men.
>
> *Pacem in Terris* 126–129

▲ *Pacifists believe that the death and destruction caused by war cannot be justified*

On 2 September 2013, Pope Francis wrote in a social networking post: 'War never again! Never again war!' Pope Francis has spoken strongly against the use of unnecessary force and has urged people to pray for peace. However, he has not taken a purely pacifist stance. He has acknowledged that there are times that force has to be used in self-defence or to defend the weak, but he is of the opinion that the force must be of a limited nature. This approach is supported in many Church teachings.

> **The Church strives for peace but does not preach radical pacifism.** Indeed, no one can deny the individual citizen or particular governments and alliances the fundamental right of armed self-defence.
>
> *Youcat* 398

Activities

1. Explain the reasons why some Christians are pacifists.
2. 'Christians should set the example for the rest of the world by refusing to support the use of violence.' Evaluate this statement. Be sure to include more than one point of view, and refer to Christian beliefs and teachings in your answer.

■ Contrasting views

Some people in Britain believe that it is always wrong to fight, even in self-defence, while others concede that in practice sometimes a war is a better alternative to the consequences of defeat. There are people who are pacifists for religious reasons: some because they have a moral (though non-religious) belief in the sanctity of life, and others because they think that war is not a practical solution to solving problems. People who agree with pacifism, whether to a greater or lesser extent, argue that war causes such destruction and damage that it is always preferable (and possible) to solve problems through more peaceful, humane means.

In contrast, many people believe that force is necessary to solve certain disputes. They may fear that a pacifist approach will invite attack from others, so they argue that it is the duty of a country to defend its people. Some argue that peace can only be built on solid mutual respect, and that this is unlikely to come about if one of the parties is not prepared to use violence to defend itself and is therefore seen to be weak.

Discussion activity

Discuss whether pacifism could ever bring about a just society.

Summary

You should now know what the Catholic Church teaches about pacifism, and you should understand why some people are pacifists.

12.9 The role of religion in conflicts of the twenty-first century

The Catholic Church believes it is important both to try to prevent war and to help the victims of war. It aims to do this through a number of ways, some of which are outlined below.

■ The efforts of the Pope

Recent popes have worked hard to bring about peaceful resolutions to conflict situations. The following are just a few examples of how the Pope can influence people's attitudes, which is an important starting point for achieving peace.

- Every week the Pope leads the crowd in the Vatican Square in prayer. Often, before the prayer starts, Pope Francis brings people's attention to conflicts and asks them to pray for peace. For example on 25 January 2013, he said 'I follow with deep concern the escalation of fighting in eastern Ukraine, which continues to cause many casualties among the civilian population … I renew a heartfelt appeal so that efforts for dialogue can resume and an end to all hostilities [can occur]'.
- In June 2014, Pope Francis organised a meeting of prayer between the presidents of Israel and Palestine. He said that he was not trying to mediate between two countries that have been in conflict with one another for decades. However, by bringing the leaders together in a quiet, prayerful atmosphere, using Jewish, Muslim and Christian prayers, he hoped to help bring the two leaders into a position that might lead to change. Pope Francis said: 'Peacemaking calls for courage, much more so than warfare. Instill in our hearts the courage to take concrete steps to achieve peace.'

> **Objective**
> - Know how the Catholic Church responds to modern conflicts, including providing help to the victims of war.

> " War is madness. Whereas God carries forward the work of creation, and we men and women are called to participate in his work, war destroys. It also ruins the most beautiful work of his hands: human beings. War ruins everything, even the bonds between brothers. **War is irrational; its only plan is to bring destruction: it seeks to grow by destroying.** "
>
> Pope Francis, 13 September 2014

▲ *Pope Francis with the presidents of Israel and Palestine in 2014*

Chapter 12 Theme B: religion, peace and conflict

- In September 2014, Pope Francis organised an international football match in Rome's Olympic stadium to raise funds for children in need, particularly those affected by war. The match included international football stars and players with Jewish, Christian, Muslim, Hindu and Buddhist backgrounds. The Pope was praised by Jewish leaders for using an unconventional yet effective method to break down the barriers that cause tension and division, thus helping all people to work together for a common good.

■ The work of Catholic agencies

Catholic agencies such as CAFOD, Aid to the Church in Need and Caritas International help to support the victims of war. They do not take sides in the conflict; they just try to help people to survive during the fighting and to rebuild their lives after the war. The following are examples of the type of help that these agencies give.

- After 11 years of bitter civil war in Sierra Leone between 1991 and 2002, there were many children who had been separated from their parents or kidnapped by terrorists and forced to become child soldiers. CAFOD established orphanages to rescue these children. They also started education and rehabilitation programmes, to help these victims regain a sense of normality in their lives.
- The civil war in Syria has caused many people, including persecuted Christians, to flee to neighbouring countries like Lebanon and Jordan. In 2014, Aid to the Church in Need spent almost a million pounds providing shelter, blankets, medicine and food to those still in Syria and to the thousands of refugees who had been compelled to leave the country.
- In 2015, Caritas International went to the aid of the victims of the fighting in Niger. Some of these victims were living under trees out in the open, trying to escape the violence of the extremists in their country. They had no food, water or shelter and they were badly affected by the cold nights. Caritas International provided water, food and tents, even in conditions under which the aid workers themselves could have been attacked by the extremists.

■ Individual contributions

Many Christians and non-Christians in Britain find their own ways to provide support for the victims of war. Some might donate money or goods to charities that provide aid to refugees and war victims; some might volunteer for these charities; some might provide support through prayer.

Activities

1. Give two examples of the work of Catholic agencies in helping the victims of war.
2. 'Christian leaders can do nothing to end wars.' Evaluate this statement. Be sure to include more than one point of view, and refer to Catholic beliefs and teachings in your answer.

▲ Many children became orphans as a result of the civil war in Sierra Leone

Research activity

Research the work of one religious organisation that is trying to help the victims of a war. What has the organisation done to help, and how successful has it been?

★ Study tip

It is easier to see how religion can help in conflict situations through specific examples.

Summary

You should now know how the Catholic Church tries to help prevent war and provide support to the victims of war.

12.10 Terrorism

What is terrorism?

Terrorism is where an individual, or a group of people who share certain beliefs, uses terror as part of a campaign to further their cause. Their violence is usually committed against innocent civilians and takes place in public. Terrorism can create a climate of fear in which people are afraid to go about their daily lives because they believe their safety is at risk. Terrorism is used in particular to try to undermine governments and force authorities into giving way to certain demands.

▲ Terrorism is rejected by most people regardless of their religion

Biblical perspectives

The Bible makes it clear that a state of terror goes against the state of peace that God wishes for all people.

Since terrorist activities are usually against the government, Paul's teaching to obey the civil authorities (as they have been put in power by God) could apply to terror groups (see Romans 13:1–2).

Equally, Paul's command not to take vengeance suggests terrorist groups should reject the use of violence:

> Beloved, never avenge yourselves, but leave room for the wrath of God; for it is written, 'Vengeance is mine, I will repay, says the Lord.'
>
> *Romans* 12:19 (NRSV)

However, it is possible to see the methods of the Jewish Maccabees in the first century BCE as a form of terrorism. The Maccabees rebelled against a

Objectives

- Know what terrorism is and what it aims to achieve.
- Understand religious and non-religious responses to the use of terrorism.

Key term

- **terrorism:** the unlawful use of violence, usually against innocent civilians, to achieve a political goal

> O Lord, you will hear the desire of the meek; you will strengthen their heart, you will incline your ear to do justice for the orphan and the oppressed, so that those from earth may strike terror no more.
>
> *Psalms* 10(9):17–18 (NRSV)

> Let every person be subject to the governing authorities; for there is no authority except from God, and those authorities that exist have been instituted by God. Therefore **whoever resists authority resists what God has appointed,** and those who resist will incur judgement.
>
> *Romans* 13:1–2 (NRSV)

Discussion activity

Discuss whether terrorism can ever bring about change.

Gentile (non-Jewish) power that was trying to force the Jews to abandon their religious beliefs and practices. The Maccabees resorted to violent terrorist attacks to defeat the enemy (see 1 Maccabees 2:44–48). Some would argue that without their work, Judaism would not have survived. If this argument is accepted, terrorism might be seen as justifiable in the cause of truth. The underlying question here would be: who decides what is the cause of truth?

Contemporary Catholic teachings

The Catholic Church opposes any form of the use of terror in any situation.

Pope Francis has recently spoken out against acts of terrorism, particularly those that are claimed to be carried out in the name of God. Typical of his statements is one made on 11 January 2015 after a terrorist attack in Paris: 'Religious fundamentalism, even before it eliminates human beings by perpetrating horrendous killings, eliminates God himself, turning him into a mere ideological pretext.'

> **❝** Kidnapping and hostage taking bring on a reign of terror; by means of threats they subject their victims to intolerable pressures. They are morally wrong. **Terrorism threatens, wounds, and kills indiscriminately; it is gravely against justice and charity. ❞**
>
> *Catechism of the Catholic Church* 2297

Terrorism in Britain

Since the Second World War, there have been a number of occasions when people in the UK have been affected by terrorist activities. For example, the Irish Republican Army (IRA) detonated bombs, killing innocent people at random, in Warrington (1993), London (1993), Manchester (1996) and Omagh (1998). Terrorist attacks have also been carried out by Islamic extremists in central London (2005) and at Glasgow airport (2007).

Some people in Britain blame religion for these terrorist attacks. They believe the terrorists have religious motivations, which have been inflamed by the beliefs of the faith they claim to follow. Many other people accept that terrorists are isolated individuals who have highly distorted and inaccurate views of the world (and what God would want), which have been completely rejected by the religion they claim to represent.

▲ *This memorial in Hyde Park, London, consists of 52 columns to remember the 52 people killed in the 2005 London suicide bombings*

7 July London bombings

On 7 July 2005, there were four suicide bombings in London that killed 52 people and injured over 700. Even though the terrorists involved in the bombings attached themselves to the religion of Islam, most Muslims, including their religious and community leaders, strongly condemned the attacks. They often shared platforms with leaders of other faiths, especially Christianity, to show their solidarity against terrorism.

⭐ Study tip

Try to be non-emotional when dealing with the issue of terrorism, and consider as objectively as possible the underlying motives of terrorists and whether they are justifiable.

Activities

1. Explain what terrorism is and what it aims to achieve.
2. 'Terrorist activities are sinful.' Evaluate this statement. Be sure to include more than one point of view, and refer to Catholic beliefs and teachings in your answer.

Summary

You should now know what is meant by terrorism. You should also understand contrasting responses to the issue of terrorism, including what the Catholic Church teaches.

12.11 Torture, radicalisation and martyrdom

■ Torture

Torture is the use of severe physical or mental pain, usually as a punishment or to force the person being tortured to do or say something. The use of torture is illegal under international law, even in a war.

The Catholic Church has rejected the use of torture as inhuman.

Many people, including Catholics and non-Catholics, believe that torture is always wrong regardless of the situation, as it is a barbaric, inhuman practice that denies the victim their basic human rights. It is also considered to be an ineffective way to obtain information.

However, torture is still used around the world. Some might argue that if torture can be used to obtain information that will prevent a greater wrong (such as a terrorist bombing that could potentially kill a large number of people), there are rare situations where its use could be justified.

■ Radicalisation

Radicalisation is the process by which people adopt increasingly extreme positions on religious, social or political issues. It often leads people to a point where they are unwilling to accept any alternative views, and may use violence to perpetrate their own views. Radicalisation tends to take place among younger people who feel rejected by their society or religion.

▲ People light candles to remember those killed in a terrorist attack in Paris in 2015. Is radicalisation to blame for this?

The Catholic Church tries to focus on mutual respect and understanding. It urges people to reject radicalisation because it encourages tension in the world.

> **Objectives**
> - Know the meanings of torture, radicalisation and martyrdom.
> - Understand different perspectives on these practices.

> **Key terms**
> - **torture:** the use of severe physical or psychological pain to punish someone or force them to do or say something
> - **radicalisation:** adopting extreme views on religious, social or political issues
> - **martyrdom:** the suffering or death of a martyr (a person who suffers or dies because of their beliefs)

> "Torture which uses physical or moral violence to extract confessions, punish the guilty, frighten opponents, or satisfy hatred is contrary to respect for the person and for human dignity."
>
> *Catechism of the Catholic Church* 2297

Chapter 12 Theme B: religion, peace and conflict

> " In the past, cultural differences have often been a source of misunderstanding between peoples and the cause of conflicts and wars. Even now, sad to say, in different parts of the world we are witnessing with growing alarm the aggressive claims of some cultures against others. In the long run, this situation can end in disastrous tensions and conflicts. At the very least it can make more difficult the situation of those ethnic and cultural minorities living in a majority cultural context which is different from their own. "
>
> *Message for the World Day of Peace*

Most people in Britain oppose radicalisation, as they see it as a threat to the unity and stability of society. In recent years, radicalisation has come to be seen as a bigger threat to the security of Britain, as it can potentially lead to terrorism. This concern was reflected by a change to the law in 2015, which states that schools in the UK now have a legal duty 'to prevent people from being drawn into terrorism'. However, while extremist groups have always existed within Britain, they have so far been a minority and have not had much influence on society as a whole.

There are many different opinions about what causes radicalisation and how to tackle it. Some would argue that it is largely the fault of specific groups or individuals, who need to be stopped from radicalising others. Some would argue that people are drawn to an extremist position because they feel rejected by the rest of society, and therefore society itself needs to change. This might mean rethinking the education system, tackling inequality, and trying to ensure that nobody experiences rejection.

■ Martyrdom

Some radicals claim that by killing themselves in suicide bombings they are martyrs for their religion and for God. The Catholic Church would not accept that these people are martyrs.

A martyr is a person who suffers pain or death because of their beliefs. In a religious context, it is usually used to describe someone who is killed because of their faith. The suffering or death of a martyr is known as **martyrdom**.

The Catholic Church has always valued martyrs. Martyrs follow the teachings and example of Jesus, who said: 'If any want to become my followers, let them deny themselves and take up their cross and follow me' (Matthew 16:24). The Church believes that Christians should reject standards that are against the teachings of Jesus. Through their examples, martyrs bear witness to the truth of their faith and encourage others to reject standards that are wrong.

Many people in Britain admire others who stand up for their beliefs. Some would argue however that no belief is worth dying for, and that there are more effective ways to change or challenge other people's beliefs than by dying for a cause.

Activities

1. Explain why the Catholic Church rejects the use of torture.
2. 'Radicalisation always distorts religion.' Evaluate this statement. Be sure to include more than one point of view, and refer to Catholic beliefs and teachings in your answer.

Extension activity

Examine the idea of martyrdom through some examples of martyrs who lived and died during the twentieth century. Explain the positive impact of martyrs on other believers.

> " A Christian martyr is a person who is ready to suffer violence or even to be killed for Christ, who is the truth, or for a conscientious decision made on the basis of faith. "
>
> *Youcat*

★ Study tip

These topics cover experiences beyond those that people normally go through, but there are plenty of examples in the present world of each of them. Use news reports and articles to give you some examples.

Summary

You should now know what is meant by torture, radicalisation and martyrdom. You should also understand different attitudes to these issues.

311

12.12 Conflict resolution and peacemaking

■ Biblical perspectives and Christian teaching

Christians believe that the end of warfare will be one of the signs that God's kingdom has come on earth. A lasting peace that is built on mutual acceptance and obedience to the will of God is promised in both the Old and New Testaments.

Paul reminds Christians that it is their duty to be at peace with one another. Christians also have a duty to help other people to resolve their differences. In one of his letters, Paul speaks to the community about an argument between two of its members, Euodia and Syntache. He asks them for peace and also for the whole community to help them to be reconciled.

> " I urge Euodia and I urge Syntyche to be of the same mind in the Lord. Yes, and I ask you also, my loyal companion, help these women. "
>
> *Philippians* 4:2–3 (NRSV)

This appeal shows all Christians that they should help to bring about reconciliation. The Bible teaches that living in harmony with one another will be a sure sign to all people that God is present in their lives.

> " Put things in order, listen to my appeal, agree with one another, live in peace; and the God of love and peace will be with you. "
>
> *2 Corinthians* 13:11 (NRSV)

The Catholic Church encourages all people to work together to ensure there is lasting peace built on mutual respect and trust.

> " **Peace, however, is not merely a gift to be received: it is also a task to be undertaken.** In order to be true peacemakers, we must educate ourselves in compassion, solidarity, working together … seeking adequate mechanisms for the redistribution of wealth, the promotion of growth, cooperation for development and conflict resolution. "
>
> *Message for the World Day of Peace*

Objectives

- Understand what the Bible and Catholic Church teach about peacemaking and conflict resolution.
- Know how two Christian organisations work to bring about peace.
- Understand why some Christians prefer the use of non-violent resistance.

Key terms

- **peacemaking:** the action of trying to establish peace
- **conflict resolution:** creating peace between two parties that have been at war or in a dispute with each other
- **non-violent resistance:** resisting a government without using violence, for example through peaceful protest or non-cooperation

▲ A Christian march to support peace efforts

■ Catholic organisations working for peace

The Church asks all Catholics to be involved in **peacemaking** and **conflict resolution** at a local level, within the family and the neighbourhood. However, the Church also believes that there needs to be a commitment to working for peace on a global scale. Here are two examples of Catholic organisations that try to bring different groups together.

Pax Christi

Pax Christi was founded after the Second World War with the intention of creating understanding between French and German people in the aftermath of the violence. The organisation works in more than 50 countries to establish peace based on mutual respect, justice and reconciliation.

Pax Christi supports the efforts of groups working at the local level by sharing experience and resources. It rejects the use of violence as a means of solving disputes, and tries to become involved in disputes at an early stage so a peaceful resolution can be found without resorting to violence. It encourages all people to bring justice and fairness to every society.

Justice and Peace Commission

The Justice and Peace Commission was founded in 1978. It is a national organisation that works within each diocese of the Catholic Church in England and Wales. Its aim is to help reduce violence and tension by focusing on respect for the individual and for the whole of creation. It campaigns to remove nuclear weapons from the world and to reduce the arms trade. It raises awareness of situations where people are deprived of their rights and needs. The Commission aims to remove war by removing the causes of war.

■ Non-violent resistance

People who use **non-violent resistance** want to make a stand against injustice without resorting to violence. The first notable use of non-violent protest was made by Ghandi in his efforts to gain independence for India in 1945–1948. Martin Luther King, who was a Christian, also made use of non-violent resistance in his efforts to get equal rights for black people in the United States.

▲ In 2016, students in New York remembered Martin Luther King's achievements and calls for change through peaceful protest

Many Christians would claim that Jesus supported non-violent protest when he said: 'Love your enemies, do good to those who hate you, bless those who curse you, pray for those who abuse you' (Luke 6:27–28). The Catholic Church commends the efforts of people who use non-violent resistance to pursue justice.

Activities

1. Explain what the Bible teaches about peace and peacemaking.
2. 'Christians must do all they can to prevent individuals and nations getting caught up in disputes.' Evaluate this statement. Be sure to include more than one point of view, and refer to Catholic beliefs and teachings in your answer.

Discussion activity

Discuss the strengths and weaknesses both of non-violent and violent protests.

Research activity

Investigate the work of two organisations involved in peacemaking, for example Pax Christi and the Justice and Peace Commission. What actions do they take to create peace, and how effective have these actions been?

★ Study tip

Consider tensions within your own family or among your friends, and think about how these could be or have been resolved. Once you have thought about the idea of reconciliation in your own life, you might find it easier to apply this to the world as a whole.

Summary

You should now know what the Bible and the Catholic Church teach about peacemaking. You should be able to give examples of the work of two Christian organisations involved in peacemaking, as well as examples of Christian non-violent resistance.

12 Assessment guidance

Theme B: religion, peace and conflict – summary

You should now be able to:

- ✓ explain what the Bible teaches about violence and human nature, including bullying
- ✓ explain what Jesus taught about forgiveness and reconciliation
- ✓ explain what is meant by justice, and what the Catholic Church teaches about justice and human dignity
- ✓ explain different views held in Britain, both Christian and non-religious, on righteous anger and violent protest as responses to injustice
- ✓ explain the importance of the just war theory
- ✓ explain what the Catholic Church teaches about nuclear war and weapons of mass destruction
- ✓ explain Catholic views about civilian casualties, refugees and environmental damage in modern warfare
- ✓ explain different views held in Britain, both Christian and non-religious, on the use of weapons of mass destruction
- ✓ explain different views on how religion and war are linked, and explain the concept of holy war
- ✓ explain what the Old Testament teaches about war
- ✓ explain different views held in Britain, both Christian and non-religious, on pacifism
- ✓ explain how religions try to help the victims of war in conflicts of the twenty-first-century
- ✓ explain different religious teachings and viewpoints about the use of terrorism
- ✓ explain Catholic views on torture, radicalisation and martyrdom
- ✓ explain how and why the Catholic Church tries to bring about conflict resolution
- ✓ explain the work of two Christian organisations that are active in conflict resolution and peacemaking.

Sample student answer – the 12 mark question

1. Write an answer to the following question:

   'All citizens should be prepared to fight when their government declares a war.'

   Evaluate this statement.

   In your answer you:
   - should give reasoned arguments in support of this statement
   - should give reasoned arguments to support a different point of view
   - should refer to Christian arguments
   - may refer to non-religious arguments
   - should reach a justified conclusion. **[12 marks]**

2. Read the following sample student answer:

   "One of the conditions of a just war is that it is waged by a legitimate authority. The officially recognised government is a legitimate authority so people should respect its call to go and fight. St Paul tells Christians that they must do what the government tells them as it is in power because God has put it there. Also, as a member of the country, a person has a duty to play their part. They take all the benefits from the country, like education and hospitals, so they should defend the country as a form of pay back.

   However, a person also has a duty to follow their conscience as that is the voice of God. Just because a government declares war, it does not mean that it is the correct action. Sometimes, governments declare war as a means of uniting the country behind an unpopular government. Sometimes, the government goes against God's will and abuses its power, like Hitler or Mugabe. If a person fights for a corrupt government, they are supporting corruption. Many atheists and humanists would argue that the rights and dignity of human beings take precedence over the rights of a government to claim obedience from its citizens.

People have a duty to defend their own country against an unjust attack from an enemy force. This is one of the just war conditions. However, people who are pacifists and who do not believe that violence solves anything, whether they are Christians, Buddhists, humanists or whatever, should have their views respected. They should not be forced to fight, nor should they be imprisoned or treated badly, just because they disagree with the government's policy."

3. With a partner, discuss the sample answer. Consider the following questions:
   - Does the response answer the question?
   - Does the answer refer to Catholic teachings and if so what are they?
   - Is there an argument to support the statement and how well developed is it?
   - Is a different point of view offered and how developed is that argument?
   - Has the student written a clear conclusion after weighing up both sides of the argument?
   - What is good about this answer?
   - How do you think it could be improved?

4. What mark (out of 12) would you give this answer? Look at the mark scheme in the Introduction (AO2). What are the reasons for the mark you have given?

Practice questions

1. What does 'reconciliation' mean?
   A) Bringing together people who have been enemies
   B) Refusing to use violence
   C) Insisting that everybody agrees with your opinion
   D) Ensuring that the enemy is completely defeated [1 mark]

2. Give two Old Testament ideas or teachings about war. [2 marks]

3. Explain two contrasting beliefs in contemporary British society about the use of nuclear weapons.
   - You must refer to Christian belief.
   - You must refer to contrasting religious and/or non-religious belief. [4 marks]

4. Explain two Christian beliefs about the use of torture. Refer to scripture or sacred writings in your answer. [5 marks]

> ⭐ **Study tip**
>
> The question only asks for Christian beliefs, so do not provide any views that are not clearly Christian. You must include some material from the Bible or Church documents in your answer.

5. 'It is impossible for Catholics to support the use of terrorism.'

   Evaluate this statement. In your answer you:
   - should give reasoned arguments in support of this statement
   - should give reasoned arguments to support a different point of view
   - should refer to Christian teaching
   - may refer to non-religious arguments
   - should reach a justified conclusion. [12 marks]

13 Theme C: religion, human rights and social justice

13.1 Human dignity and religious freedom

Biblical teaching about human dignity

The starting point for any Christian understanding about the dignity of the individual is found in the opening chapter of the Bible:

> God created humankind in his image, in the image of God he created them; male and female he created them.
>
> *Genesis* 1:27 (NRSV)

Christians believe that God created each human being in his own image. This does not mean that human beings look like God, but that they share in the qualities of God. These qualities make human beings superior to all other creatures, and they give humans a sense of **dignity**.

▲ *Church walking days, such as the Warrington walking day, allow Christians to gather together as a witness to their faith*

For Christians, this basic belief underlines all their teachings about human beings. However, there is a further belief that increases the dignity of every person. Christians believe that God became man in Jesus and died to save all human beings. All people are united and given dignity by the love that God has for everyone. In Colossians 3:11, Paul reminds his readers that this means there should be no division of any type between people.

Following on from this belief is Jesus' teaching that the second commandment – 'You shall love your neighbour as yourself' (Mark 12:31) – is an essential foundation for Christian beliefs and actions.

Objectives

- Understand Biblical teachings about human dignity and loving your neighbour.
- Understand Catholic teachings about freedom of religion.

Key term

- **dignity:** being worthy of honour and respect

Activities

1. Explain what the Bible teaches about human dignity.
2. 'The right to freedom of religion is an essential part of what it means to be human.' Evaluate this statement. Be sure to include more than one point of view, and refer to Catholic beliefs and teachings in your answer.

⭐ Study tip

If you find it hard to relate to the idea of being denied the freedom to follow a religion, think of a parallel case. For example, how would you feel if you were not allowed to support your favourite football team or band?

> There is no longer Greek and Jew, circumcised and uncircumcised, barbarian, Scythian, slave and free; but Christ is all and in all!
>
> *Colossians* 3:11 (NRSV)

It teaches Christians that they should put the needs of other people on the same level as their own needs, and that they should not be selfish but strive for justice and equality. It puts into practice the teaching of Micah in the Old Testament (see Micah 6:8).

Freedom of religion or belief

One way in which people can show that they accept their fellow human beings is to recognise their right to have a different set of beliefs. What a person believes is an integral part of who they are, and no person should be forced to accept a belief system or even specific beliefs. For most people this is an important part of human freedom.

Since the Second Vatican Council (1962–65), the Catholic Church has taught that religious freedom is a basic right of every human being:

> This Vatican Council declares that the human person has a right to religious freedom. This freedom means that all men are to be immune from coercion on the part of individuals or of social groups and of any human power, in such wise that **no one is to be forced to act in a manner contrary to his own beliefs,** whether privately or publicly, whether alone or in association with others.
>
> *Dignitatis Humanae* 2

In 2013, Pope Francis said that 'In today's world, religious freedom is more often affirmed than put into practice.' He called for a world where 'believers and non-believers can work together to promote a society where injustice can be overcome, and each person can contribute to the common good according to his or her dignity, and make the most of his or her abilities.' The Church believes this society will only come about when people recognise and respect the rights and differences of every individual.

The respect for individual beliefs must also acknowledge the right of religious believers to put their faith into practice in their own lives. However, the Catholic Church teaches that religious believers must also accept that there are limitations to their expression of freedom. Freedom of religion must never be used in such a way that other people feel threatened.

The right to freedom of belief applies equally to religious and non-religious beliefs. It is part of the International Covenant on Civil and Political Rights, which most countries in the world have agreed to legally uphold:

> **Everyone shall have the right to freedom of thought, conscience and religion.** This right shall include freedom to have or to adopt a religion or belief of his choice, and freedom, either individually or in community with others and in public or private, to manifest his religion or belief in worship, observance, practice and teaching … No one shall be subject to coercion which would impair his freedom to have or to adopt a religion or belief of his choice.
>
> *International Covenant on Civil and Political Rights* 18

> What does the Lord require of you but to do justice, and to love kindness, and to walk humbly with your God?
>
> Micah 6:8 (NRSV)

Extension activity

Examine one example of how a denial of freedom of religion has led to problems within a country. How was religious freedom denied, and what were the results? Examples include religious persecution in England in the seventeenth and eighteenth centuries, or the treatment of Jews during the Second World War.

> Society has the right to defend itself against possible abuses committed on the pretext of freedom of religion.
>
> *Dignitatis Humanae* 7

▲ Some Christians in Britain can feel uncomfortable displaying their faith publicly. Is this a sign that religious freedom is not widely respected?

Summary

You should now know what the Bible teaches about human dignity and loving your neighbour. You should also understand Catholic attitudes towards freedom of religion.

13.2 Human rights

Catholic teachings on human rights

The Catholic Church has championed the rights of the individual since the time of Pope Leo XIII's encyclical *Rerum Novarum* (1891).

In *Pacem in Terris*, Pope John XXIII started his teachings on peace by recognising that ensuring the rights and dignity of each person is fundamental to creating a peaceful society:

> ❝ Any well-regulated and productive association of men in society demands the acceptance of one fundamental principle: that **each individual man is truly a person. His is a nature, that is, endowed with intelligence and free will.** As such he has rights and duties, which together flow as a direct consequence from his nature. These rights and duties are universal and inviolable, and therefore altogether inalienable … Men have been ransomed by the blood of Jesus Christ. Grace has made them sons and friends of God, and heirs to eternal glory. ❞
>
> *Pacem in Terris* 9

Objectives

- Understand what the Catholic Church teaches about human rights.
- Understand how human rights are important for human dignity.

Key term

- **human rights:** the basic rights and freedoms to which all human beings should be entitled

The Catholic Church's teaching on **human rights** is clearly spelled out in *Gaudium et Spes* 26:

> ❝ Every day human interdependence grows more tightly drawn and spreads by degrees over the whole world. As a result the common good … today takes on an increasingly universal complexion and consequently **involves rights and duties with respect to the whole human race. Every social group must take account of the needs and legitimate aspirations of other groups, and even of the general welfare of the entire human family.**
> At the same time, however, there is a growing awareness of the **exalted dignity proper to the human person**, since he stands above all things, **and his rights and duties are universal and inviolable. Therefore, there must be made available to all men everything necessary for leading a life truly human, such as food, clothing, and shelter;** the right to choose a state of life freely and to found a family, the right to education, to employment, to a good reputation, to respect, to appropriate information, to activity in accord with the upright norm of one's own conscience, to protection of privacy and rightful freedom even in matters religious.

▲ *Basic human rights that many take for granted – such as the rights to food, shelter and education – are still not adequately available to all*

318

Chapter 13 Theme C: religion, human rights and social justice

> … This social order requires constant improvement. It must be founded on truth, built on justice and animated by love; in freedom it should grow every day toward a more humane balance. An improvement in attitudes and abundant changes in society will have to take place if these objectives are to be gained.
>
> God's Spirit, Who with a marvellous providence directs the unfolding of time and renews the face of the earth, is not absent from this development. The ferment of the Gospel too has aroused and continues to arouse in man's heart the irresistible requirements of his dignity.
>
> *Gaudium et Spes* 26

▲ *Protection of privacy is a basic human right. Does the rise of social media make privacy harder to protect?*

The Catholic Church believes that a person who is deprived of any of these human rights is being treated as less than human, and therefore loses their human dignity. The Church teaches that human rights belong to every individual, regardless of status, race or religion. Pope Paul VI stressed this point when in 1972 he wrote to the Secretary-General of the UN: 'The Church feels wounded in her own person whenever a man's rights are disregarded or violated, whoever he is and whatever it is about.'

It is important to note that while some of the rights stated in *Gaudium et Spes* 26 are more theoretical (such as the right to respect), most of them are very practical. They are similar to the basic human needs expressed in the Parable of the Sheep and the Goats (Matthew 25:31–46), showing that Jesus' teachings about people's rights and needs are still relevant today.

■ Ensuring human rights

All countries are legally required to uphold the UN Declaration of Human Rights. This covers similar rights to those expressed in *Gaudium et Spes* 26. While few would argue with the importance of these rights, making sure everyone has equal access to them is another matter: many people throughout the world are still being denied certain basic rights (such as the right to education), and opinions differ greatly about how to tackle this very complex global problem. The Church asks Catholics to help by working to create a greater equality than currently exists. In 1984, Pope John Paul II permitted the following statement to be made on behalf of the Church: 'The fight for the rights of man … constitutes the authentic fight for justice.'

⭐ Study tip

An easy starting point for this topic is to think about how you expect to be treated and why. Consider what you think you should be allowed to do, or what you should have access to, as part of your everyday life.

Links

To read more about the Parable of the Sheep and the Goats see page 51.

Research activity

Compare the UN Declaration of Human Rights with *Gaudium et Spes* 26. In what ways are the two documents similar and in what ways are they different?

Activities

1 Examine the human rights presented in *Gaudium et Spes* 26. Choose five of them and explain why each of these rights is important for an individual.
2 'Human rights have no meaning if they do not have a basis in religion.' Evaluate this statement. Be sure to include more than one point of view, and refer to Catholic beliefs and teachings in your answer.

Summary

You should now know what the Catholic Church teaches about human rights, and understand how these rights are related to human dignity.

13.3 Rights and responsibilities

The relationship between rights and responsibilities

It is impossible to insist on basic human rights for everyone without acknowledging the responsibilities and duties that people have to help make those rights available. This includes the responsibility to respect other people's rights, and the responsibility to help create access to those rights.

> **"** The natural rights of which We have so far been speaking are inextricably bound up with as many duties, all applying to one and the same person. These rights and duties derive their origin, their sustenance, and their indestructibility from the natural law, which in conferring the one imposes the other. Thus, for example, the right to live involves the duty to preserve one's life; the right to a decent standard of living, the duty to live in a becoming fashion; the right to be free to seek out the truth, the duty to devote oneself to an ever deeper and wider search for it.
>
> Once this is admitted, it follows that in human society **one man's natural right gives rise to a corresponding duty in other men; the duty, that is, of recognizing and respecting that right.** Every basic human right draws its authoritative force from the natural law, which confers it and attaches to it its respective duty. Hence, to claim one's rights and ignore one's duties, or only half fulfil them, is like building a house with one hand and tearing it down with the other. **"**
>
> *Pacem in Terris* 28–30

Nobody can insist on their own rights without also acknowledging that other people should be able to have the same rights. This means there are sometimes limits to what any one person is allowed to do. For example, if someone encourages violence through their right to free speech, this might take away someone else's right to live without fear. The person encouraging violence is not acknowledging their responsibility to respect other people's rights.

People also have a responsibility to help make sure everyone has access to human rights. For example, it is not possible to give everyone a right to education without many people being willing to help provide that education. The right to education also includes a responsibility to be willing to learn.

It is usually the most vulnerable members of society who are deprived of their human rights, yet are not able to defend or claim those rights for themselves. The Catholic Church teaches that other people, especially Christians, must show their solidarity with the weak by demanding that they are given their just rights.

Objectives

- Understand the links between rights and responsibilities.
- Understand how Catholics work to support human rights.

> **"** It is the destiny and duty of each human being to become more fully human. **A society which observes human rights will be a society in which this true human growth is encouraged.** Every member of the community has a duty to the common good in order that the rights of others can be satisfied and their freedoms respected. Those whose rights and freedoms are being denied should be helped to claim them. **"**
>
> *The Common Good* 37

▲ *What responsibilities do people have to acknowledge in order to give everyone a right to education?*

Chapter 13 Theme C: religion, human rights and social justice

■ The pursuit of human rights in action

Individual Catholics might not feel they are in a position to demand human rights for themselves or for other people, either in Britain or in other parts of the world. However, the Church teaches that Catholics, as members of the Body of Christ on earth, should work together with others to try to bring about change, especially in unjust situations.

▲ Catholic volunteers helping with charity activities

There are Catholic agencies that work to bring human rights to those who do not have them. For example:

- The Justice and Peace Commission works on behalf of the Church. It tries to ensure all people that it comes into contact with have their human rights respected. This is partly done through raising awareness of situations that abuse human rights, but the Commission also takes practical action, such as through providing food and shelter for the homeless.
- Caritas International raises awareness of situations such as human trafficking and takes action to limit the negative impact of this type of abuse. It also puts pressure on international organisations such as the United Nations to bring about measures that can help to improve access to human rights around the world.

Catholics can also work with agencies from other religions, such as Islamic Aid, to help people in non-Christian countries to get justice and aid. Sometimes local governments prevent Christian agencies from working in their land but they are happy to allow agencies of the national religion to work there. The Church believes that Catholics should work with whatever agency can be most effective in any particular area to help defend people's rights.

> **Summary**
> You should now understand how people have to take responsibility for providing human rights. You should also know how Catholics work to support the rights of individuals.

Activities

1. Explain the Catholic view of the link between human rights and individual responsibilities.
2. 'There is no point in an individual Catholic taking any action against a government's abuse of human rights.' Evaluate this statement. Be sure to include more than one point of view, and refer to Catholic beliefs and teachings in your answer.

Discussion activity

Discuss whether Catholics should work with agencies that take a non-Catholic stance on issues like abortion and euthanasia in order to defend human rights.

> ❝ For the word of the Lord is upright, and all his work is done in faithfulness. He loves righteousness and justice; the earth is full of the steadfast love of the Lord. ❞
>
> *Psalms* 33(34): 4–5 (NRSV)

⭐ Study tip

Think about what your school would be like if everybody demanded their own rights but refused to do anything to support the rights of other people.

13.4 Responsibilities of wealth

■ Teachings in the Bible

Some Christians believe that the Bible urges them to be poor. To support this argument they might quote passages such as Jesus' instruction to his disciples: 'He ordered them to take nothing for their journey except a staff; no bread, no bag, no money in their belts; but to wear sandals and not to put on two tunics' (Mark 6:8–9 (NRSV)). Some people think this means Jesus wants his followers to reject money. However, many Christians believe that the New Testament as a whole shows that it is not wealth itself which is the problem, but people's use of wealth and their attachment to it.

Some Christians see wealth as a gift from God but one that has to be used wisely. The Parable of the Talents (Matthew 25:14–30) is often used to warn people that they will be judged by God according to how they have used their wealth. The first letter of John confirms that wealth should be used to help others:

> How does God's love abide in anyone who has the world's goods and sees a brother or sister in need and yet refuses help?
>
> *1 John* 3:17 (NRSV)

The Bible shows how wealth can distort people's values and perspectives. In the Parable of the Rich Man and Lazarus, for example, the rich man was condemned because he did not even notice the poor man at his gate.

Objectives

- Understand Catholic teachings about wealth.
- Understand the concept of stewardship of wealth.

> For the love of money is a root of all kinds of evil … As for those who in the present age are rich, command them not to be haughty, or to set their hopes on the uncertainty of riches, but rather on God who richly provides us with everything for our enjoyment. **They are to do good, to be rich in good works, generous, and ready to share.**
>
> *1 Timothy* 6:10, 17–18 (NRSV)

Links

The Parable of the Rich Man and Lazarus is discussed in more detail on pages 154–155.

■ Teachings of the Catholic Church

The Catholic Church has strongly spoken out against the imbalance of wealth in the world, and the way in which poor people are deprived of their dignity by those who are trying to make even greater profits for themselves.

> **While an immense mass of people still lack the absolute necessities of life, some, even in less advanced countries, live sumptuously or squander wealth.** Luxury and misery rub shoulders. While the few enjoy very great freedom of choice, the many are deprived of almost all possibility of acting on their own initiative and responsibility, and often subsist in living and working conditions unworthy of human beings.
>
> *Gaudium et Spes* 63

Catholic teachings about wealth can be summarised by Paul's words to the Corinthians:

▲ The imbalance of wealth can be seen in cities around the world, where rich areas are contrasted with much poorer areas

Chapter 13 Theme C: religion, human rights and social justice

> **For if the eagerness [the desire to be of help] is there, the gift is acceptable according to what one has** — not according to what one does not have. I do not mean that there should be relief for others and pressure on you, but it is a question of a fair balance between your present abundance and their need.
>
> *2 Corinthians* 8:12–14 (NRSV)

Paul is saying here that Christians are not expected to make themselves poor in order to help other people, but they should share with others the money that they do have.

■ Stewardship of wealth

The idea that the wealthy have a responsibility to share their wealth with the poor, as a way to help correct the imbalance of wealth in the world, is called **stewardship of wealth**.

In the same way that many Christians believe they are stewards of God's creation – tasked with looking after the world on behalf of God – a large number of Christians also believe they are stewards of God's wealth. They believe that wealth is a gift from God, so should be used wisely and responsibly as God would want. This involves sharing God's wealth with those who are poorer. There is enough food in the world for everybody to have a decent amount of food every day, but the food needs to be shared out fairly. Equally, if everyone was willing to share their wealth, everybody would be able to have a reasonable standard of living.

In 2013, Pope Francis clearly called for the better stewardship of wealth when he referred to 'solidarity':

> The word 'solidarity' is a little worn and at times poorly understood, but it refers to something more than a few sporadic acts of generosity. It presumes the creation of a new mindset which thinks in terms of community and the priority of the life of all over the appropriation of goods by a few. Solidarity is a spontaneous reaction by those who recognize that the social function of property and the universal destination of goods are realities which come before private property. **The private ownership of goods is justified by the need to protect and increase them, so that they can better serve the common good;** for this reason, solidarity must be lived as the decision to restore to the poor what belongs to them.
>
> *Evangelii Gaudium* 188–189

Activities

1. Explain, using examples, what the Bible says about wealth.
2. 'People should enjoy the wealth that God has given them.' Evaluate this statement. Be sure to include more than one point of view, and refer to Catholic beliefs and teachings in your answer.

Key term

- **stewardship of wealth:** using wealth, which has been given by God, in such a way that all people may benefit from it

Discussion activity

Discuss whether all people in Britain, including the poor, should make efforts to live more simply to help people in other parts of the world.

▲ Some people in Britain depend on charitable food banks to provide food for themselves and their families

Links

To read more about stewardship of creation see page 18.

★ Study tip

Many people in Britain think of themselves as poor, but have a much higher standard of living than those who officially live in poverty. Learning about families in the UK who do struggle with poverty can help you to appreciate the amount of wealth you have.

Summary

You should now know what the Bible and the Catholic Church teach about wealth. You should also understand the concept of stewardship of wealth.

13.5 Wealth creation and exploitation

■ Catholic teachings about wealth creation

In a world that runs on money, wealth creation (making money) is essential for people's survival and prosperity. The Catholic Church teaches that Catholics have a duty to do what they can to ensure that people can live in a stable, supportive environment. Part of this means helping to create wealth and using that wealth to help others.

In 2 Thessalonians 3:10–12, Paul gave the early Christians the basic guideline that urges all Christians to be productive. In Genesis 41, Joseph stored the surplus from the more productive years to help the whole nation survive the years of shortage that followed. The Church teaches that Catholics should take a similar approach to wealth: they should use it positively to provide for times of less prosperity and to help people who are in need.

■ Exploitation of the poor

The Catholic Church teaches that wealth creation must not be done at the expense of depriving other people of their rights. In the Old Testament, the prophets voiced God's strong criticism of the **exploitation** of the poor (see for example Amos 8:4–7).

▲ Sweatshops – factories in the clothing industry where workers are paid very little to work long hours – are a form of exploitation of the poor

Exploitation of the poor takes place both at an individual and national level. Rich nations and international companies often take advantage of the needs and weaknesses of poorer people, who cannot easily stand up for themselves. The Catholic Church insists that the rights of all people should be respected and supported, so they are not abused or exploited in any way.

Objectives
- Understand what the Catholic Church teaches about wealth creation and exploitation of the poor.
- Know how the Catholic Church is helping to combat human trafficking.
- Understand views about the wealth of the Catholic Church.

Key terms
- **exploitation:** misuse of power or money to get others to do things for little or unfair reward
- **human trafficking:** the illegal movement of people, typically for the purposes of forced labour or commercial sexual exploitation

> ❝ For even when we were with you, we gave you this command: **Anyone unwilling to work should not eat.** For we hear that some of you are living in idleness, mere busybodies, not doing any work. Now such persons we command and exhort in the Lord Jesus Christ to do their work quietly and to earn their own living. ❞
>
> *2 Thessalonians* 3:10–12 (NRSV)

The *Catechism of the Catholic Church* explains that wealth should not be created out of the greed for more wealth, but in order to help provide for a family and, where possible, the wider community:

> **Work is for man, not man for work.** Everyone should be able to draw from work the means of providing for his life and that of his family, and of serving the human community.
>
> *Catechism of the Catholic Church* 2428

■ Human trafficking

Human trafficking is a form of modern-day slavery. It can happen to people who want to leave their homes in search of a better quality of life, often as a result of war or persecution. These people are often vulnerable and they are sometimes exploited by groups that promise help but who in the end simply sell them into prostitution or slavery.

In the nineteenth century an African girl named Bakhita was caught by slavers. She eventually managed to escape that life to become a nun and a saint. An institute has been set up by the Catholic Church in England and Wales called the Bakhita Foundation. This aims to help people who have been caught up in human trafficking with both practical and emotional support. It is also working with international agencies to enforce the laws regarding those responsible for human trafficking.

■ The wealth of the Church

In *Evangelii Gaudium* Pope Francis said:

> Any Church community, if it thinks it can comfortably go its own way without creative concern and effective cooperation in helping the poor to live with dignity and reaching out to everyone, will also risk breaking down, however much it may talk about social issues or criticize governments.
>
> *Evangelii Gaudium* 207

Many people criticise the Catholic Church for its wealth. However, this criticism often doesn't take into account the nature of the wealth. For example, the value of the land owned by the Church is significant, but the only way to sell the land would be to sell the buildings that stand on it, including hospitals, schools and churches that provide important services for people.

Popes since John XXIII have been gradually selling works of art owned by the Church, but this has to be done carefully, otherwise the true value of the art will not be obtained. Profits from these sales have been used to help in situations of great need. The Church has to keep a balance between being able to operate successfully and meaningfully in the world – which necessarily requires a certain amount of wealth – versus not being able to share its wealth to help others.

Activities

1. Explain the Catholic Church's teachings on wealth creation and exploitation.
2. 'The Catholic Church should sell off all its works of art.' Evaluate this statement. Be sure to include more than one point of view, and refer to Catholic beliefs and teachings in your answer.

Research activity

Research the life of St Bakhita, then look at how the Bakhita Institute is working against human trafficking.

▲ Some of the Catholic Church's most valuable works of art cannot easily be sold because they are part of the buildings themselves

⭐ Study tip

The linking question for these topics is: which is more important, the dignity and wellbeing of everyone or the wealth of a few people?

Summary

You should now understand Catholic teachings on wealth creation and exploitation. You should also be able to explain different views on the wealth of the Church

13.6 Greed, materialism and the sacrifice of wealth

■ Greed

Jesus told his disciples: 'Take care! Be on your guard against all kinds of greed; for one's life does not consist in the abundance of possessions' (Luke 12:15). Greed is the desire to have more, regardless of the need. Greedy people tend to put their own desires before the needs of other people. For Christians, this goes against Jesus' teachings and the commandment to love your neighbour.

Greed is one of the seven deadly sins. The Church teaches that the deadly sins destroy a person's relationship with God as they put the delights of the body central to a person's life, ignoring the more important spiritual side of the individual.

Some people would argue that greed is necessary to fuel the economy and society as a whole, particularly in a world that is largely capitalist. Some believe that if people work hard for their wealth they should be able to spend it however they wish, even if that means putting their own needs before other people's needs.

■ Materialism

Materialism is an approach to life that places greater value on the possession of material, physical objects rather than spiritual or intellectual things. The Catholic Church believes that materialism can give a false sense of purpose to life, and can make people seem important simply because they have possessions. In 2013, Pope Francis said:

> ❝ **Whenever material things, money, worldliness, become the centre of our lives, they take hold of us, they possess us; we lose our very identity as human beings** … [with a materialist approach, humans] end up becoming self-absorbed and finding security in material things which ultimately rob us of our face, our human face. ❞
>
> Pope Francis, 29 September 2013

The Catholic Church teaches that when people are only valued for their possessions, they become little more than objects to be used and abused until they no longer have a role or any value. This leads to a shallowness of life that destroys any appreciation of the beauty of creation; things and people that have no obvious immediate value might be discarded as worthless. If people are judged on what they earn, people who earn a lot of money (like footballers and film stars) are unfairly given far greater status than people who are paid much less but who put the needs of others first (like nurses). People should be valued for who they are, not for what money they can extract from other people.

In Britain today, the possession of goods is important to many people to a greater or lesser extent. This is partly because a capitalist society encourages

Objectives

- Understand contrasting views on greed and materialism, including the teachings of the Catholic Church.
- Understand why some Catholics take the vow of poverty.

Key term

- **materialism:** the belief that physical objects matter far more than other things

▲ How would the world and economy change if people were not so greedy?

Activities

1. Explain why Christians reject greed and materialism.
2. 'There is no value in the vow of poverty.' Evaluate this statement. Be sure to include more than one point of view, and refer to Catholic beliefs and teachings in your answer.

Extension activity

Examine how people who have committed to live in poverty have challenged the attitudes of the times in which they live or lived. Examples might include Francis of Assisi or Clare of Assisi.

people to value material things. For some atheists and humanists who do not believe that people have a spiritual side, materialism can become an important focus. However, many people would agree that a total focus on possessions can distort a person's sense of value, and that it is important to embrace less material things to make life more meaningful and enriched.

■ The vow of poverty

Many religious people take the vow of poverty. Monks, nuns, priests, and religious brothers and sisters commit their lives to the service of God and their neighbours. They willingly go without wealth and possessions as a sign that they have committed themselves to something that has far greater value, which cannot be reduced to money or status. They recognise that possessions can be distracting and have a tendency to take over a person's life. Instead they follow the advice of Jesus to the rich young man:

> ❝ If you wish to be perfect, go, sell your possessions, and give the money to the poor, and you will have treasure in heaven; then come, follow me. ❞
>
> Matthew 19:21 (NRSV)

By taking a vow of poverty, these Catholics are showing the value of the Kingdom of God by trying to live by the Beatitudes. They are proof of the fact that humans do not need many possessions. The Catholic Church believes that simplicity in life often leads to deep happiness, as it removes the mentality of being jealous of others and having to match the possessions of other people. Members of religious communities are committed to sharing their talents, time and spare money with people in need.

Most Catholics do not take a vow of poverty because they believe that God has given them a particular role in life, which cannot be fulfilled without using money. The call to live a life of poverty can only really apply to people who have limited family responsibilities. As discussed above, many people in Britain value their wealth and possessions, which they believe they should be allowed to keep if they have worked hard to earn them. However, some people agree with the idea of living very simply – including Christians, atheists and humanists – because they believe it is important for individuals to do what they can to help solve the imbalance of wealth in the world.

▲ How many possessions do you own that it would be easy to live without?

Links

To read more about the Kingdom of God and Beatitudes see pages 50–51.

Summary

You should now know what the Catholic Church teaches about greed, materialism and the vow of poverty, and you should be able to give contrasting views on these.

⭐ Study tip

Think of how much money you spend on yourself and ask yourself what life would be like, and how you would feel, if you chose to do without this money.

13.7 Catholic teachings about poverty

Poverty is the condition of not having enough money to be able to meet basic daily needs. It exists in all countries, but particularly in the developing world. The Catholic Church teaches that all human life is sacred as it comes from God, and that humans are created in God's image and likeness (Genesis 1:27). Anything that prevents people from living in a way that respects this dignity is unjust.

The Church also teaches that humans are not just individuals; they are part of a much larger social group. It is therefore the responsibility of the whole group to remove any factors that threaten the dignity of any one person in that group, including poverty.

■ The preferential option for the poor

One of the main teachings of the Catholic Church that is related to poverty is the idea of 'the preferential option for the poor'. This means that the needs of poor people should be put first: they should be given preferential treatment to make up for the fact that they have been deprived of basic requirements.

The Church believes that Catholics should follow the example of Christ. As Paul says: 'Let each of you look not to your own interests, but to the interests of others. Let the same mind be in you that was in Christ Jesus' (Philippians 2:4). Paul then praises the way that Jesus humbled himself for the sake of all people.

> " For the Church, the option for the poor is primarily a theological category rather than a cultural, sociological, political or philosophical one. God shows the poor 'his first mercy'. This divine preference has consequences for the faith life of all Christians, since we are called to have 'this mind … which was in Jesus Christ' (*Phil* 2:5). Inspired by this, the Church has made an option for the poor which is understood as a 'special form of primacy in the exercise of Christian charity, to which the whole tradition of the Church bears witness'. This option – as Benedict XVI has taught – 'is implicit in our Christian faith in a God who became poor for us, so as to enrich us with his poverty'.
>
> **This is why I want a Church which is poor and for the poor.** They have much to teach us. Not only do they share in the *sensus fidei* [the sense or feeling of the faith], but in their difficulties they know the suffering Christ. We need to let ourselves be evangelized [have the Gospel preached] by them. The new evangelization is an invitation to acknowledge the saving power at work in their lives and to put them at the centre of the Church's pilgrim way. **We are called to find Christ in them, to lend our voice to their causes, but also to be their friends, to listen to them, to speak for them** and to embrace the mysterious wisdom which God wishes to share with us through them. "
>
> *Evangelii Gaudium* 198

Objectives

- Know what the Catholic Church teaches about the Christian duty to take action against poverty.
- Understand the significance of the teaching that the needs of the poor should be put first (the preferential option for the poor).

Key term

- **poverty:** being without money, food, or other basic needs of life (being poor)

▲ Poverty affects people all around the world, including in the UK

▲ The Catholic Church teaches that it is important for Catholics to help those living in poverty

Chapter 13 Theme C: religion, human rights and social justice

In this passage, Pope Francis teaches that:

- Caring for the poor is a demand on Christians because of their faith, not just because it fits in with political or economic ideals.
- Christians should put the needs of other people first, especially those in most need, just as Jesus offered his life for all people.
- The Catholic Church must focus on the needs of the poor, as they are in most need of help.
- There is much that poor people can teach richer people because they are closer to the spirit of Jesus, in terms of sharing his rejection and suffering.
- Richer Christians must be willing to listen to and go to the aid of the poor if they really want to appreciate and put into practice the message of Jesus.

▲ *What are the best ways to help the many people who struggle to meet basic daily needs, including access to food and water?*

The Church teaches that Catholics have a duty to protest and work against the forces in society that create poverty. Poverty degrades everybody: not just the poor, but also those who exploit the poor and those who do nothing to stop the exploitation.

> **Poverty in the world is a scandal.** In a world where there is so much wealth, so many resources to feed everyone, it is unfathomable that there are so many hungry children, that there are so many children without an education, so many poor persons. Poverty today is a cry.
>
> Pope Francis, 7 June 2013

> **A way has to be found to enable everyone to benefit from the fruits of the earth,** and not simply to close the gap between the affluent and those who must be satisfied with the crumbs falling from the table, but above all to satisfy the demands of justice, fairness and respect for every human being.
>
> Pope Francis, 20 June 2013

Activities

1. Explain why the 'preferential option for the poor' is important for Catholics.
2. 'There is no point in trying to get rid of poverty as it will always exist.' Evaluate this statement. Be sure to include more than one point of view, and refer to Catholic beliefs and teachings in your answer.

Discussion activity

Discuss whether there is any real difference in the aims and attitudes of different religious and non-religious groups regarding poverty.

★ Study tip

Think about how hard life is for someone who has almost nothing and struggles to meet basic daily needs. Then think about how much attention should be given to helping them meet those needs.

Summary

You should now know what the Catholic Church teaches about the Christian duty to take action against poverty. You should also understand the concept of the preferential option for the poor.

13.8 Contrasting views on fighting poverty

■ The duty to take action on poverty

The Catholic Church teaches that Christians should always be aware that they are part of the Body of Christ on earth, and that they have a duty to help care for the whole Body. When one part is hurt, the other parts should take action to support it. Similarly, Christians who have more money are expected to support those who are not as well off.

For Christians, there is no point in claiming to love your neighbour at the same time as ignoring people in need. James 2:15–17 and 1 John 4:20 are two passages in the New Testament that stress this point.

> If a brother or sister is naked and lacks daily food, and one of you says to them, 'Go in peace; keep warm and eat your fill', and yet you do not supply their bodily needs, what is the good of that? **So faith by itself, if it has no works, is dead.**
>
> *James* 2:15–17 (NRSV)

The Church teaches that love is not shown in words but in deeds. It is therefore important for individual Christians to take actions to help reduce poverty. This might either involve directly helping those in poverty, or trying to tackle the root causes of poverty.

■ Directly helping the poor

One way to help overcome poverty is by giving money and aid to the poor, either directly (for example to homeless people on the streets) or through charities that support the poor (such as the Salvation Army).

Some Christians refer to the Parable of the Good Samaritan (Luke 10:29–37), in which Jesus praised the man who came to the help of the person who had been beaten up on the road. They believe that by giving money and support to those living in poverty, they are following Jesus' example and are likewise being Good Samaritans.

Some argue that it is important to show compassion and kindness towards the poor through providing direct help, and that trying to give them access to their basic human rights is a responsibility that should be shared by everyone. Some acknowledge that poverty is often a result of unfortunate circumstances and bad luck, and know that if they ended up in a similar situation they would also want and need other people's help.

Most people who live in poverty desperately wish to become self-sufficient but lack the initial means to do so. Charities such as the St Vincent de Paul Society (SVP) and the Salvation Army help by providing money, support and aid to the poor to help them escape poverty.

Objectives
- Understand why Christians believe it is important to take action against poverty.
- Understand different opinions about how best to solve poverty.

★ Study tip
A good parallel here might be to think about how the other players in a football team have to work harder in a match to compensate for a friend who is playing while injured.

> Those who say, 'I love God', and hate their brothers or sisters, are liars; for those who do not love a brother or sister whom they have seen, cannot love God whom they have not seen.
>
> *1 John* 4:20 (NRSV)

▲ Buying Fairtrade products ensures that the farmers who do the work gain a fair share of the profits

Tackling the root causes of poverty

Some argue that providing the poor with limited basic needs – such as spare change to homeless people on the street, or sacks of grain to farmers in Africa – only helps to keep them in the poverty trap, and makes them reliant upon whoever is giving out the aid. It does not solve the problems causing their poverty, or do enough to help them to get out of poverty.

Poverty is a complex global problem that has many causes, from how society is structured to environmental issues such as drought. Some people think it is more important to direct their energies towards solving these underlying causes of poverty, as this is the only way to completely put an end to it. While some might argue that poverty is a problem that can only really be solved by governments and organisations with power, there are ways that individuals can help. For example:

▲ Is it better to give someone in poverty enough food to feed their family, or the means to grow their own food?

- There are many multinational companies who abuse their power by paying poor wages so they can make a profit. If people boycott these companies and make their reasons known to others, this could force the companies to change their policies and pay fair wages. Once people have a fair wage, there is less likelihood of them being stuck in poverty.
- Organisations such as Fairtrade ensure that workers receive a fair amount of the profits from the sale of their goods. If a greater number of people paid a little bit extra for Fairtrade products, this would help more people in the developing world to become self-sufficient.

> ❝ **The rich countries have a moral obligation to help the underdeveloped nations** out of poverty through developmental aid and the establishment of just economic and commercial conditions. ❞
>
> *Youcat* 448

The responsibility to help those in poverty

Who is responsible for poverty: those who live in poverty themselves, or the social systems that have caused their poverty? Some would argue that most people are in poverty through unfortunate circumstances that are a result of how society works, therefore it is society's responsibility to help them. Others think that more responsibility should be placed on the individuals in poverty, either not to get into poverty in the first place or to make more of an effort to improve their situation.

To take just one example: a homeless person on the streets has an alcohol addiction. Is this purely the fault of the homeless person, who should take the responsibility to stop drinking in order to spend his money on more important requirements? Or is the addiction the result of his desperate situation, making it unfair to expect him to solve his addiction before society has helped him out of his poverty?

Extension activity

Compare the work of one charity that helps homeless people in Britain (such as the Salvation Army or Shelter) with the work of a charity that helps the poor in South America (such as Christian Aid or LAMP, the Liverpool Archdiocesan Missionary Project). In what ways are they similar in theory and practice, and in what ways are they different?

Summary

You should now understand why taking action against poverty is important for Christians. You should also know about the different approaches to dealing with poverty, including their potential benefits and effects.

Activities

1. Explain why Christians think it is important to take action against poverty.
2. 'The poor have a responsibility to get themselves out of poverty.' Evaluate this statement. Be sure to include more than one point of view, and refer to Catholic beliefs and teachings in your answer.

13.9 The work of CAFOD and Christian Aid

■ Taking action against poverty as an expression of Christian values

The Catholic Church is very aware of the needs of the poor and teaches that it is important for the whole of society, rich and poor alike, to help combat poverty with genuine, sustained action.

There are a number of Christian agencies that provide aid for the poor as a way of showing Christian love, and also as a way of showing that all people are equal and should be treated fairly. Christians accept the need to be Good Samaritans (Luke 10:29–37), not just to individuals in need but also to whole sections of society. In a real way, Christian agencies realise that they have to accept they should be 'my brother's keeper' (Genesis 4:9). Ignoring the plight of the poor and the causes of poverty is not an option.

■ The work of CAFOD

CAFOD tries to relieve the burden of poverty through direct action that supports the efforts of poor people. Here are some of the ways that they help:

- By supporting Fairtrade, CAFOD tries to ensure that people get a fair price for their goods and a fair share of the profit. This means that farmers and labourers can invest in better equipment and techniques to help improve their crops or products, allowing them to bring in more profit. Using this profit to pay for their children to receive an education is one way that their families can escape the poverty trap.
- While CAFOD provides aid to deal with immediate difficulties, poor people want to be able to provide for themselves rather than depend on handouts. The financial systems and companies that encourage low wages and exploitation have to be challenged. CAFOD puts pressure on major multinational companies to change the policies that have negative effects on poor people. CAFOD has also helped in the campaign to make the British government accept by law that 0.7 per cent of its income will be spent on international aid. This means that, no matter which government is in power, international aid will not be a target when the government needs to cut its spending.
- A lack of clean water and poor sewerage systems means that many people living in poverty in the developing world fall victim to crippling and deadly diseases like diarrhoea and typhoid. By helping to provide access to clean water supplies, CAFOD helps poor people to increase the quality of their health and lifestyles.

■ The work of Christian Aid

Like CAFOD, Christian Aid tries to help all people to overcome the problems that keep them in poverty, regardless of their faith. Christian Aid is founded on the teachings of Jesus and unites Christians of all

Objectives

- Understand how Christian agencies express Christian values through their work.
- Understand how CAFOD and Christian Aid help those living in poverty.

> **"** In all places and circumstances, Christians, with the help of their pastors, are called to hear the cry of the poor. **"**
>
> *Evangelii Gaudium* 191

> **" Love for the poor must be in every age the distinguishing mark of Christians.** The poor deserve not just a few alms; they have a claim to justice. For Christians there is a special obligation to share their goods. Our example in love for the poor is Christ. **"**
>
> *Youcat* 449

▲ *Poor water supplies are a major problem for many people living in poverty in the developing world*

denominations through its work. Christian Aid and CAFOD join with many other charities in Britain to form the Disasters Emergency Committee (DEC). This organisation responds immediately to provide aid when natural disasters or similar crises occur.

Examples of Christian Aid's work include:

- Christian Aid workers go to areas devastated by floods and monsoons. They provide immediate relief with food and shelters. Once the flood waters have subsided, Christian Aid helps people to re-establish their farmland, providing seed for the next year's planting so that the crisis does not last beyond the immediate growing season.
- In areas of drought, Christian Aid workers go to help people who have been forced to leave their homes to find food elsewhere. Christian Aid helps to provide food, water and shelter. Where the situation is made worse by local wars, Christian Aid tries to make the refugees feel more secure and hopeful about restarting their lives.
- Christian Aid works with local organisations around the world. These groups are often better able to understand the problems facing the local people and how best to solve them. Christian Aid provides funds and physical assistance for these groups so that people may get the help they want, rather than what outsiders think might be best. This is part of an approach that values individual cultures and belief systems, and recognises that all people have a right to decide their own future.

▲ Providing enough humanitarian aid after a natural disaster is a huge operation that requires the cooperation of many different charities and governments

In Britain today many people support the work of charities such as Oxfam, Save the Children and Live Aid. These groups do not have an explicit religious outlook or foundation to their work. They see people in need and respond on a humanitarian basis.

Some people do not donate to these types of charities because they believe they are not the most effective way to solve the underlying causes of poverty. They would prefer to direct their energies into trying to change the governmental policies and financial systems that help to perpetuate poverty, particularly in the developing world.

Research activity

Research one of CAFOD's or Christian Aid's recent projects, examining the problems the agency addressed and the actions it took.

★ Study tip

You only need to study either CAFOD or Christian Aid, although the work of both agencies is very similar.

Activities

1. Explain how either CAFOD or Christian Aid tries to fight poverty.
2. 'All Christians should donate 10 per cent of their income to the work of aid agencies.' Evaluate this statement. Be sure to include more than one point of view, and refer to Christian beliefs and teachings in your answer.

Summary

You should now know how the work of Christian agencies reflects Christian values. You should also know how CAFOD and Christian Aid help to fight poverty.

13.10 Racial prejudice and discrimination

■ Christian teachings about prejudice and discrimination

The fundamental Christian teaching is that all human beings are created in the image and likeness of God (Genesis 1:27), and that all people are saved by the death and resurrection of Jesus. God is present in each individual, regardless of gender, nationality, colour, faith, disability, sexual orientation or any other quality that might be used as grounds for negative **discrimination**.

> ❝ Created in the image of the one God and equally endowed with rational souls, all men have the same nature and the same origin. Redeemed by the sacrifice of Christ, all are called to participate in the same divine beatitude: all therefore enjoy an equal dignity.
> **The equality of men rests essentially on their dignity as persons and the rights that flow from it:** 'Every form of social or cultural discrimination in fundamental personal rights on the grounds of sex, race, colour, social conditions, language, or religion must be curbed and eradicated as incompatible with God's design.' ❞
>
> *Catechism of the Catholic Church* 1934–1935

Racial prejudice

Racial **prejudice** is having a negative attitude towards another person based on the race or ethnic group to which they belong. This is often linked to the colour of a person's skin, which is one of the more obvious indicators that a person belongs to a different race.

Most Christians acknowledge that skin colour, eye colour, gender and so on are all simply genetic factors that differentiate one person from another. While they make people different to each other, they do not make any one person better than another. Therefore there is no justification for any person to be treated as having less value than another, based on these genetic traits.

The Catholic Church teaches that every individual should be judged as a child of God. Since God loves each person into existence, each person has infinite value in God's eyes. God values the individuality of everyone, so each person's dignity as an individual should be respected by all people.

Objectives

- Understand Christian teachings about racial prejudice and discrimination.
- Understand different views about racism in Britain today.

Key terms

- **discrimination:** actions or behaviour that result from prejudice
- **prejudice:** unfairly judging someone before the facts are known; holding biased opinions about an individual or group

> ❝ The differences among persons belong to God's plan, who wills that we should need one another. These differences should encourage charity. ❞
>
> *Catechism of the Catholic Church* 1946

▲ *Is peer pressure the best way to challenge racism?*

Racial discrimination

Where negative attitudes lead to negative actions, prejudice turns into discrimination. Racial discrimination occurs around the world, and can affect individuals or whole groups of society.

334

Chapter 13 Theme C: religion, human rights and social justice

Racial discrimination leads to people being treated as less than full human beings. This is not acceptable for the Catholic Church, which believes that each person should be treated fairly, given full value for the work they perform, and given every opportunity to develop their full potential, regardless of their race.

> **The equal dignity of human persons requires the effort to reduce excessive social and economic inequalities. It gives urgency to the elimination of sinful inequalities.**
>
> *Catechism of the Catholic Church* 1947

Racial prejudice and discrimination can cause great harm to those being discriminated against, and may also create tensions within society that can have much wider negative effects.

> **Whatever insults human dignity … poison[s] human society, but [the insults] do more harm to those who practise them than those who suffer from the injury.**
>
> *Evangelium Vitae* 34

Activities

1. Explain what the Catholic Church teaches about racial prejudice and discrimination.
2. 'Every person should be treated in the same way.' Evaluate this statement. Be sure to include more than one point of view, and refer to Catholic beliefs and teachings in your answer.

Discussion activity

Discuss the value of having a wide range of racial groups living and working closely together.

In Britain today

Throughout the history of the British Isles, there have been groups from a number of different races working together, marrying regardless of their race. Different races and cultures have contributed to both the genetic make-up of the British people and to their culture. Today, there is a wide range of racial groups in Britain, most of whom accept and celebrate the diversity produced by this mixture, as well as helping people of other cultures to feel at home. However, some people have a more insular attitude, wrongly believing that there is only one racial group that historically belongs to the British Isles. This misunderstanding can lead to tensions between different groups in society.

Racism is illegal in the UK but it still occurs on a daily basis. For example, figures published in 2015 show that black people in Britain are much more likely to be stopped and searched by the police than white people. Racist abuse is often a problem at football matches, affecting both the players and those attending the matches. A study published by NatCen in 2013 suggested that around 30 per cent of people in Britain admit to having some level of racial prejudice.

Racial prejudice is often based on a lack of knowledge and understanding about people who are in some way different – not just because of their race, but because of their customs, beliefs, values and so on. It can occur when people feel threatened. For example, some fear Britain's security and prosperity is threatened by the increase in immigration to the UK; as many immigrants are not white, this can lead to racial prejudice against British ethnic minorities. However, most people in Britain believe that racism is unacceptable and that it is important to oppose it.

▲ *Is the acceptance of ethnic and cultural differences one of the strengths of British society?*

⭐ Study tip

The main ideas that underline Catholic teachings on racial prejudice and discrimination also apply to all other forms of prejudice and discrimination.

Summary

You should now understand Christian teachings about racial prejudice and discrimination. You should also understand different views about racism and its place in British society today.

13.11 Equality

Equality in the Bible

Genesis 1:27 teaches that God created humankind in his image and likeness. Genesis 2 stresses that men and women are complementary to each other as they complete each other. Neither is subservient or inferior to the other, though each has a different role to play.

The idea of the equality of human beings is stressed throughout the Bible, and it is not limited to sexual equality. For example, when Peter had a vision that showed he had to preach to non-Jews as well as Jews, he said 'I truly understand that God shows no partiality' (Acts 10:34).

Paul echoed the same idea that God treats everyone equally in Colossians 3:11.

The Catholic Church teaches that as all people are united in Christ and all people are children of God, there is no excuse for any Christian to treat another person unequally, no matter what their differences. Everyone is equal in Christ.

Equality and gender

The Catholic Church has always supported the idea that men and women are of equal dignity with equal rights, but 'equal dignity and equal rights do not mean uniformity' (Youcat 401). The role of the woman within the family is irreplaceable, and the Catholic Church has always opposed efforts to force women into work.

This does not mean that the Church expects women to stay at home. The Church supports the involvement of women in all types of professional work. It believes that women have special talents that enable the whole of society to benefit, and society must allow women to play a full part while always respecting the demands of their home life.

Tradition is an important element in the Catholic faith. The Catholic Church teaches that Jesus ordained his male followers, the apostles, as priests during the Last Supper. For this reason the Catholic and Orthodox Churches have always limited ordination to men, following Jesus' example. The Catholic Church believes this is not seen as diminishing the role and status of women; it is just another example of how men and women are equal but different.

In contrast, the Church of England has allowed women to become priests since 1993, and bishops since 2014. The Archbishop of Canterbury believes that this now allows the Church to select people for ordination 'on the basis simply of our sense that they are called by God to be in that position without qualification as to their gender'. This reflects a widely held opinion in Britain that access to equal opportunities is an important part of equality.

Objectives

- Understand Catholic teachings about equality.
- Understand contrasting views about how equality applies to gender and sexuality.

> In that renewal there is no longer Greek and Jew, circumcised and uncircumcised, barbarian, Scythian, slave and free; but Christ is all and in all!
>
> *Colossians* 3:11 (NRSV)

> **All men are equal in God's sight insofar as all have the same Creator,** all were created in the same image of God with a rational soul, and all have the same Redeemer.
>
> *Youcat* 330

Links

The Catholic Church's teachings on gender and equality are discussed in more detail on pages 284–285.

Activities

1. Explain Catholic teachings about the role and status of women.
2. 'There is no sign of equality in the Catholic Church's position on homosexuals.' Evaluate this statement. Be sure to include more than one point of view, and refer to Catholic beliefs and teachings in your answer.

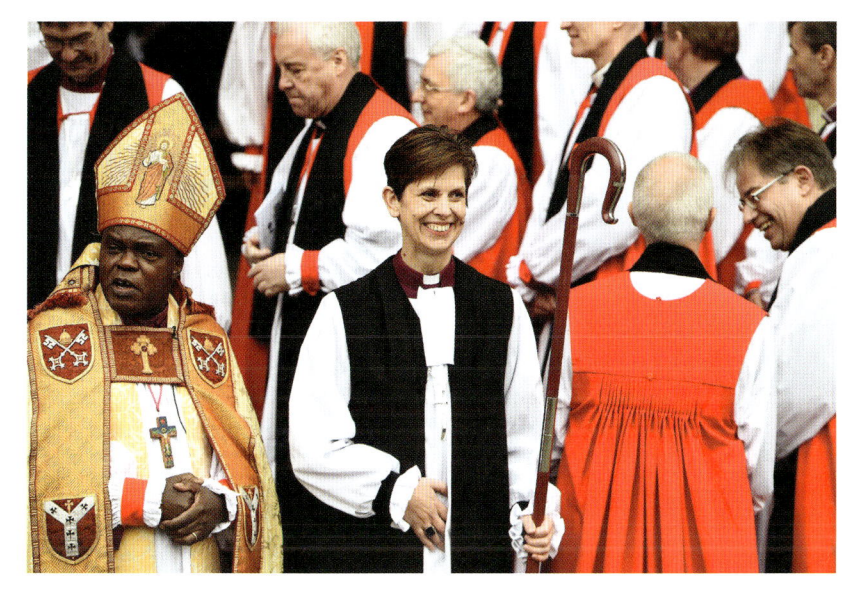

Chapter 13 Theme C: religion, human rights and social justice

▲ Libby Lane became the Church of England's first female bishop in January 2015

Extension activity

Examine the role women have played in the Catholic Church over time. You could include references to Mary the Mother of Jesus, Mother Julian of Norwich, St Catherine of Siena, and St Theresa of Avila, among many other women.

▲ The rainbow flag is a symbol of lesbian, gay, bisexual and transgender (LGBT) pride, with the different colours representing the diversity (and equality) within the LGBT community

■ Equality and sexuality

The Catholic Church's teaching on homosexuality is based around its teaching on the meaning and purpose of sex. Through a sexual union, God can bless the couple by creating new life. This cannot happen when the two people are of the same sex. Therefore the Church has stated that any sexual union that is not open to new life is sinful as it distorts the purpose of sex.

> Homosexual acts … are contrary to the natural law. They close the sexual act to the gift of life. They do not proceed from a genuine affective and sexual complementarity. Under no circumstances can they be approved.
>
> Catechism of the Catholic Church 2357

The Catholic Church does not deny that homosexuals should have their rights and dignity as human beings, but it does call on them to live chaste lives as they cannot be open to the possibility of conceiving children, which is an integral part of sex.

> [Homosexuals] **must be accepted with respect, compassion, and sensitivity.** Every sign of unjust discrimination in their regard should be avoided. These persons are called to fulfil God's will in their lives and, if they are Christians, to unite to the sacrifice of the Lord's Cross the difficulties they may encounter from their condition.
>
> Catechism of the Catholic Church 2358

As explained on page 269, it is not currently possible for homosexual couples to marry in most churches in Britain, although the Church of England supports the idea of same-sex civil partnerships and does not teach that homosexuals should be celibate.

Links

Equality and sexuality are discussed in more detail on page 271.

★ Study tip

Be prepared to balance an argument on one side of the debate with an opposing argument on the other side. Do not limit yourself to one viewpoint only, even if you have very strong feelings about one side of the debate.

Summary

You should now know what the Catholic Church teaches about equality. You should also understand contrasting views on the equality of different genders and sexual orientations.

13.12 Justice, racial equality and racial prejudice

■ Justice

For Christians, justice can be encouraged at an individual level by treating others fairly and following the commandment to 'love your neighbour'. Christians can also contribute to campaigns that try to improve justice at a wider level in society. Promoting equality is an essential part of creating justice. The Catholic Church teaches that seeking justice is important for all Catholics.

> **Social justice comes about where the inalienable dignity of every person is respected** and the resulting rights are safeguarded and championed … Among these is also the right to active participation in the political, economic, and cultural life of the society.
>
> **A society is not perfected by laws, however, but rather by the love of neighbour** which makes it possible for everyone to look upon his neighbour (without any exception) as 'another self'
>
> *Youcat* 329

Objectives

- Understand how the Catholic Church values and promotes justice and tolerance.
- Understand how support can be given to victims of racial prejudice.

■ The promotion of tolerance and racial equality

Christians have a duty to work towards creating a society where everyone is treated justly and fairly. To allow this to happen, the laws of any country must respect the rights of every member of society, whether they are native or immigrant. Christians should strongly oppose any measures that could be used to undervalue any group or individual.

> If a state should establish laws and procedures that are racist, sexist or destructive of human life, **a Christian is obliged in conscience to refuse to obey, to refrain from participation, and to offer resistance.**
>
> *Youcat* 377

> A peaceful society is one built upon justice. The guiding principle of justice is: 'To each his due'.
>
> *Youcat* 302

Links

The importance of justice is discussed in more detail on pages 294–295.

There are various ways that the Catholic Church helps to promote tolerance and racial equality. For example:

- Children of all ethnicities and religions are welcomed into Catholic schools in the UK. Both Catholics and non-Catholics value the atmosphere of tolerance that they experience in Catholic schools; in some Catholic schools in Britain, for example, there are significant numbers of Muslim students. The sharing of education in an atmosphere of mutual trust and respect helps to create understanding and acceptance among different groups. The Catholic Church believes this

▲ *How does education help equality?*

Chapter 13 Theme C: religion, human rights and social justice

is an important step in helping to create a society that is just and fair.

- There has been a long tradition within the Catholic Church of clergy, particularly priests and bishops, going to work in other countries. The fact that recent popes have been Italian, Polish, German and Argentinian, and that each one has been accepted worldwide by believers, shows that there are no racial distinctions made in Catholicism. The College of Cardinals is made up of over 120 senior bishops from every continent. The diversity among the Church leaders sets an example for how all Catholics should treat people from different ethnic groups. This is a clear example of how 'all nations form but one community' (*Catechism of the Catholic Church* 842).

▲ *Racial equality is important to the Catholic Church*

Support for victims of racial prejudice

The *Catechism of the Catholic Church* lays out the duty of all Catholics to support efforts to bring injustice to an end. This includes providing support for people who have been targeted by racial prejudice or abuse.

> **"** Respect for the human person entails respect for the rights that flow from his dignity as a creature … It is the Church's role to remind men of good will of these rights. **"**
>
> *Catechism of the Catholic Church* 1930

The Catholic Church has a long tradition of offering individual support through the sacrament of reconciliation and through private conversations with a priest. Churches of all denominations can also offer group discussions so victims can see that they are not alone, and can be strengthened by the support and prayers of the community.

One way in which victims of racial prejudice are helped is by the Church bringing different groups together so that they can learn to appreciate and accept each other. Racial prejudice will only end if the attitudes of the racists themselves are changed. Many churches in the UK support youth clubs and other societies that enable people of different races to meet on an informal basis. Once people have learned to value what different cultures can offer, tensions often diminish. Victims of racial prejudice can also be publicly supported by other people, so the racist can realise that they do not express the views of the majority of the population.

Research activity

1. Use the internet to research a specific case of racism that happened recently in the UK. What happened, and how did the victim, authorities or public respond?
2. Research the help offered to victims of racial abuse by an organisation in Britain that assists in fighting racism (such as Show Racism the Red Card or Race Equality First). What type of help is available and how have people benefitted from it?

⭐ Study tip

It is often easier to understand the effects of racial prejudice and how best to combat it by studying specific cases rather than general theory.

Activities

1. Explain how justice is linked with racial tolerance.
2. 'The only thing that Catholics can do about racial prejudice is to support the victims of racial prejudice on an individual basis.' Evaluate this statement. Be sure to include more than one point of view, and refer to Catholic beliefs and teachings in your answer.

Summary

You should now know how the Catholic Church helps to promote tolerance and racial equality. You should also understand how Catholics and others can help the victims of racial prejudice.

339

13 Assessment guidance

Theme C: religion, human rights and social justice – summary

You should now be able to:

- ✔ explain what the Bible teaches about human dignity and the importance of 'loving your neighbour'
- ✔ explain what the Catholic Church teaches about human rights and their importance for human dignity
- ✔ explain Catholic attitudes to freedom of religion or belief
- ✔ explain different views held in Britain, both Christian and non-religious, on how rights and responsibilities are linked, and how human rights should be achieved
- ✔ explain what the Catholic Church teaches about the responsibilities of wealth
- ✔ explain what the Catholic Church teaches about wealth creation, exploitation of the poor and human trafficking
- ✔ explain the importance of Catholic attitudes to wealth, including the wealth of the Church
- ✔ explain different views held in Britain, both Christian and non-religious, on greed and materialism, and the religious vow of poverty
- ✔ explain what the Catholic Church teaches about the Christian duty to fight poverty, and explain the idea of the preferential option for the poor
- ✔ explain different views about the best ways to fight poverty, including giving money to the poor
- ✔ explain the work done by CAFOD or Christian Aid to combat poverty
- ✔ explain different views held in Britain, both Christian and non-religious, on who should be responsible for helping the poor, and the responsibilities of the poor
- ✔ explain what the Catholic Church teaches about racial prejudice and discrimination
- ✔ explain what the Catholic Church teaches about equality and justice
- ✔ explain different views on whether there is prejudice and discrimination within religion, in relation to equality of gender and sexuality
- ✔ explain different views held in Britain, both Christian and non-religious, on how religion actively promotes tolerance and racial equality, and supports victims of racial prejudice.

Sample student answer – the 12 mark question

1. Write an answer to the following question:

    'It is impossible for every person to have all their human rights.'

    Evaluate this statement.

    In your answer you:
    - should give reasoned arguments in support of this statement
    - should give reasoned arguments to support a different point of view
    - should refer to Christian arguments
    - may refer to non-religious arguments
    - should reach a justified conclusion.

    [12 marks]

2. Read the following sample student answer:

    "The Catholic Church believes that every human being is made in the image and likeness of God. As such, any attempt to deprive a person of his human rights is denying them their dignity both as a human being and as a child of God. Pope John XXIII taught that humans are intelligent persons whose rights and duties flow from their human nature. Every Christian has a duty to ensure that each person is fed, clothed, welcomed and cared for in their times of need. This is to put into practice Jesus' teachings in the Parable of the Sheep and Goats.

The rights enshrined in the United Nations Declaration of Human Rights are accepted by most people of all religions and none as central to what it means to be a human being. It is wrong for any person or country to refuse an individual any of these rights. However, these rights in themselves have their limits. If a person has freedom of speech, he should be able to say anything that he likes. However, if a person is to have the right to live without fear, he cannot be threatened by what another person says. This means that either people have to live in fear or they have to have their right of freedom of speech limited. This does not mean the rights are bad, just that people have to apply the Christian ideal of love and recognise where other people's rights have to take precedence."

3. With a partner, discuss the sample answer. Consider the following questions:
    - Does the response answer the question?
    - Does the answer refer to Catholic teachings and if so what are they?
    - Is there an argument to support the statement and how well developed is it?
    - Is a different point of view offered and how developed is that argument?
    - Has the student written a clear conclusion after weighing up both sides of the argument?
    - What is good about this answer?
    - How do you think it could be improved?

4. What mark (out of 12) would you give this answer? Look at the mark scheme in the Introduction (AO2). What are the reasons for the mark you have given?

Practice questions

1 What does 'the exploitation of the poor' mean?
   A) Rich people can ignore those who don't have anything
   B) Christians should make sure governments spend taxes on health services
   C) Rich people do not pay a fair wage since the poor cannot defend themselves
   D) Everybody should have a proper meal each day   **[1 mark]**

2 Give two Catholic teachings about equality.   **[2 marks]**

3 Explain two contrasting beliefs in contemporary British society on freedom of religion.
   - You must refer to Christian belief.
   - You must refer to contrasting religious and/or non-religious belief.   **[4 marks]**

4 Explain two Christian beliefs about the preferential option for the poor.   **[5 marks]**
   Refer to scripture or sacred writings in your answer.

> ⭐ **Study tip**
>
> Remember that you need to explain two distinct teachings. You can refer to passages from the Bible or teachings of the Catholic Church. You do not have to quote the passages exactly, but the meaning of the passages you refer to must be clear.

5 'Applying Christian teachings on stewardship is the only way to remove world poverty.'

Evaluate this statement. In your answer you:
   - should give reasoned arguments in support of this statement
   - should give reasoned arguments to support a different point of view
   - should refer to Christian teaching
   - may refer to non-religious arguments
   - should reach a justified conclusion.   **[12 marks]**

Glossary

A

abortion: the removal of a foetus from the womb to end a pregnancy, usually before the foetus is 24-weeks-old

acclamation: praising with great enthusiasm

Adalat: the concept of justice in Shi'a Islam

Adam: the Hebrew word for humanity, which many people see as the name of the first man

adultery: voluntary sexual intercourse between a married person and a person who is not their spouse (husband or wife)

Akhirah: everlasting life after death

Allah: the Arabic name for God

Alleluia: meaning 'Praise God', it is the Easter proclamation (the announcement of the resurrection) and is used before the reading of the Gospel at Mass

Alpha and Omega: a symbol made from the first and last letters of the Greek alphabet, which are used to show that God and Jesus are eternal – the beginning and end of all things

Amidah: also known as the 'standing prayer', it is the central prayer of Jewish worship

angel: a spiritual being believed to act as a messenger of God

annulment: a statement by the Catholic Church that there was no valid marriage in the first place

annunciation: when the angel Gabriel asked Mary to accept the role of the mother of the Son of God

apostles: one who is 'sent out'; the name given to those disciples who became leaders of the early Church

apostolic: based on what the apostles taught

apostolic authority: the authority of the apostles, as leaders of the early Church, that is passed on to the bishops

apostolic exhortation: a letter or document from the Pope encouraging Catholics in their religion

apostolic succession: the power of the apostles passed on to the next generations of bishops

Aramaic: the language that Jesus spoke

Aron Hakodesh: the Ark – the holiest part of the synagogue, which contains the Torah scrolls

artificial contraception: artificial (unnatural) methods used to prevent a pregnancy from taking place

ascension: the event, 40 days after the resurrection, when Jesus returned to God the Father in heaven

atone: make amends for something that has gone wrong

atonement: restoring the relationship between people and God through the life, death and resurrection of Jesus

B

baptism: the sacrament in which a person becomes a child of God and a Christian

Bar Mitzvah: celebration of a boy coming of age at 13; literally 'son of the commandment'

Bat Mitzvah: celebration of a girl coming of age at 12, in Reform synagogues; literally 'daughter of the commandment'

Benediction: meaning 'blessing'; a service at which the Blessed Sacrament is exposed and Catholics worship Christ in the sacrament

beneficent: benevolent, all-loving, all-good; a quality of God

Bible: the sacred book of Christianity, containing the Old and New Testaments

bimah: a platform in a synagogue from where the Torah is read

biological weapons: weapons that use living organisms to cause disease or death

bishops: high-ranking clergymen who have the power to confirm and ordain

Blessed Sacrament: a term that refers to the consecrated Bread and Wine

bowing: bending from the waist as a sign of respect

Brit Milah: ceremony of male circumcision; the removal of the foreskin for religious reasons

bullying: the deliberate intimidation of a person through words or physical actions

C

Caliph: a person considered to be a political and religious successor to the prophet Muhammad, and the leader of the Sunni Muslim community

cantor (chazzan): a person who leads or chants prayers in the synagogue

Catholic: (1) a term used to describe something that is worldwide and all-inclusive (2) referring to the Roman Catholic Church

charity: (1) providing help and love to those in need (2) an organisation that does not make a profit, whose main purpose is to help those in need (3) another term for 'love'

chemical weapons: weapons that use chemicals to harm humans and destroy the natural environment

Chi-Rho: a symbol to represent Jesus, made up of the first two letters of his name in Greek

Church: (1) the holy people of God, also called the Body of Christ, among whom Christ is present and active (2) a building in which Christians worship

circumcision: the removal of the foreskin from the penis

cohabitation: a couple living together and having a sexual relationship without being married to one another

commendation of the dying: the prayers that are said when a person is at the point of death

Communion: (1) sharing together (2) sharing in a meal that unites people with each other and with Christ

conception: when the male sperm fertilises the female ovum, seen by Catholics as the start of life

conciliar: when the authority of the Magisterium is expressed through the Pope in a council

conflict resolution: creating peace between two parties that have been at war or in a dispute with each other

conscience: for Christians, the voice of God in the heart and soul of a person

consecration: the point in the Mass when the bread and wine are blessed (consecrated) and become the Body and Blood of Christ

consent: give permission for something to happen; in Catholicism, the moment of marriage when the couple commit themselves to each other for life

consubstantial: literally 'of one being', showing that the Father, Son and Spirit are not separate entities but one God

consummated: completed or fulfilled, especially when talking about a marriage

contemporary worship songs: religious songs that have been written recently for the praise of God, often using modern instruments

cosmic reconciliation: the time when all things in creation will be brought together in harmony

Council: a gathering of bishops to make decisions about important issues for the Church

covenant: an agreement; in Judaism it refers to an agreement between individuals, often on behalf of the Jews, and God

creation: the act by which God brought the universe into being

creator: the one who makes things and bring things about

creed: a statement of faith

cremation: the burning of the bodily remains of a person

crucified: executed by being fixed to a cross

crucifix: a representation of Jesus on the cross on which he died

D

Day of Ashura: a festival that is important for Shi'a Muslims in particular, who remember the battle of Karbala and death of Husayn on this day

Day of Judgement: a time when the world will end and every soul will be judged by God, and either rewarded or punished

Denominations: distinct groups within the Christian faith, with their own organisation and traditions

dietary laws: rules that deal with foods permitted to be eaten, food preparation, food combinations, and the utensils and dishes coming into contact with food

dignity: being worthy of honour and respect

disciple: a follower of Jesus; one who learns

discrimination: actions or behaviour that result from prejudice

Divine Office: a collection of psalms and readings that every priest, monk and nun has to say at least four times a day

divorce: legal ending of a marriage

doctrine: official Church teaching

dramatised prayer: a form of prayer that includes actions, like moving from one place to another or acting out the intention of the prayer

dynamic: full of energy and creativeness

E

Easter Vigil: the service that takes place in the hours of darkness between Holy Saturday and Easter Sunday, during which the resurrection of Jesus is proclaimed and celebrated, and the first Mass of Easter is held

Eastertide: the 50-day period between Easter Sunday and Pentecost

Emmanuel: a Jewish name meaning 'God is with us'

epistles: the letters written by the apostles to the early churches

eschatology: the study of what will take place at the end of time

eternal: without beginning or end

eternal life: life after death, that exists forever

Eucharist: meaning 'thanksgiving', it is especially used about the Mass as a thanksgiving sacrifice to God

Eucharistic Prayer: the prayer of thanksgiving that is the central part of the Mass, during which Jesus' words from the Last Supper are said over the bread and wine

euthanasia: killing someone painlessly and with compassion, to end their suffering

evangelism: preaching the good news about Jesus to other people

evangelists: the writers of the Gospels (Matthew, Mark, Luke and John)

exploitation: misuse of power or money to get others to do things for little or unfair reward

extramarital: occurring outside marriage, either before marriage or with someone other than your husband or wife

F

fairness: the idea that God treats people fairly and impartially without favour or discrimination

family planning: the practice of controlling how many children couples have and when they have them

fasting: not eating or drinking for a certain length of time, usually for a religious reason

final judgement: sometimes called the Last Judgement; when Christ comes at the end of time and the whole of creation is judged

forgiveness: showing grace and mercy; pardoning someone for what they have done wrong

free will: belief that God gives people the opportunity to make decisions for themselves

fundamentalist: someone who believes the Bible is a factual record that describes events exactly as they happened; fundamentalists believe that the Bible is divinely inspired and without error

funeral: a ceremony to mourn the dead person

G

Gemara: a commentary on the Mishnah; part of the Talmud

gender discrimination: taking actions that treat one person differently to another because of their gender

gender prejudice: expecting someone to behave in a particular way because of their gender

Genesis: the first book of the Bible, in which the stories of creation are found

genuflecting: going down on one knee as a sign of respect

Gloria: a hymn of praise of God's glory and goodness, which is sung early in the Mass

God's Kingdom: the reign of God, when everyone will accept God and live forever in peace and harmony

God's will: the things that God wants people to do

Gospel: (1) in Christianity, a reading from one of the four Gospels (Matthew, Mark, Luke and John), which tells of the life and teachings of Jesus (2) in Christianity, the good news of the teaching of Jesus and the message that God loves all people (3) in Islam, a holy book revealed by God to Jesus

grace: God's free gift of his unconditional love to the believer

greater jihad: the personal inward struggle of all Muslims to live in line with the teachings of their faith

H

Hajj: the annual pilgrimage to Makkah that every Muslim should try to make at least once in their life

Hajji: someone who has completed Hajj

healing the world: being involved in God's work to sustain the world; it can involve work to increase social justice or to preserve the environment

heaven: the state of eternal happiness in the presence of God

heavenly banquet: a symbol of the unity and joy of the Kingdom of God, pictured as everyone joining together in one great meal

hell: the state of total separation from God

heresy: a belief that goes against the accepted teaching of the Church

hierarchy: a ranking system that gives structure to the Church

Holy Spirit: the Third Person of the Trinity whom Christians believe is the inspiring presence of God in the world

holy war: fighting for a religious cause or God, probably controlled by a religious leader

holy water: blessed water that is used in baptism

hosts: the small Communion breads that are given out at Communion

human rights: the basic rights and freedoms to which all human beings should be entitled

human trafficking: the illegal movement of people, typically for the purposes of forced labour or commercial sexual exploitation

343

I

Iblis (Satan): a spiritual being, created from fire, who was thrown out of paradise for refusing to bow to Adam

Ichthus (fish): a symbol of a fish, based on a Greek acronym that translates as 'Jesus Christ, Son of God, Saviour'

iconostasis: the screen that divides the holy part of an Orthodox church, including the altar, from the congregation; it represents the meeting place and division between heaven and earth

Id-ul-Adha: a Muslim festival that celebrates the prophet Ibrahim's willingness to sacrifice his son for God

Id-ul-Fitr: a Muslim festival that celebrates the end of Ramadan

imago dei: 'the image of God', the Latin term used to show that God made humans in his image and likeness

Imam: (1) a person who leads communal prayer (2) in Shi'a Islam, the title given to Ali and his successors

Imamate: the divine appointment of the Imams

Immaculate Conception: a title given to Mary that refers to the belief that Mary was conceived without original sin

immanent: the idea that God is present in and involved with life on earth and in the universe; a quality of God

immanent theology: the study of the internal life of God

incarnation: God taking on the human condition in Jesus

inspiration: the guidance that God gives to people

Islam: the name of the religion followed by Muslims; to surrender to the will of God; peace

J

Jibril: the Arabic name for Gabriel, the archangel who brought God's message to the prophets, particularly to Muhammad

jihad: a struggle against evil; this may be an inward, personal struggle or an outward, collective struggle

judgement: the belief that God judges a person based on their actions, and either rewards or punishes them as a result

Jummah prayer: a weekly communal prayer performed after midday on Friday, which includes a sermon

just war theory: a set of criteria that a war needs to meet before it can be justified

justice: bringing about what is right and fair, according to the law, or making up for a wrong that has been committed

K

Ka'aba: the black, cube-shaped building in the centre of the Grand Mosque in Makkah; the holiest place in Islam

kaddish: a prayer said by Jewish mourners that praises God and asks for peace

Ketuvim: the third section of the Tenakh; the writings

Khums: a 20 per cent tax paid by Shi'a Muslims on their excess income

kindness to others: positive, caring actions that should be shown to all living things

Kingdom of God: also called the Reign of God, where all people live as God intends

Kingdom values: the standards of living that God wants his people to follow

kneeling: being on both knees as a sign of humility

kosher: food that meets the requirements of Jewish laws

L

Last Supper: the final meal that Jesus ate with his disciples before he died; it is the basis of Holy Communion

law: the commandments and rules laid down in the Old Testament

laying on of hands: a symbolic gesture that passes on the power of the Holy Spirit

lectern: the reading stand from which the Bible readings are given and the word of God is proclaimed

Lent: the 40 days before Easter, during which Christians reflect on the sufferings of Jesus

lesser jihad: the outward struggle to defend one's faith, family and country from threat

liturgy: the practices and rituals that make up the communal worship of God

M

magisterial teachings: the decisions of the Magisterium that should be accepted by Catholics

Magisterium: the teaching authority of the Catholic Church, exercised by the Pope and the bishops

Magnificat: the name of the prayer that Mary said when Elizabeth greeted her during her visit

marital: to do with marriage

marriage: the sacrament by which the couple commit themselves to each other for life

martyrdom: the suffering or death of a martyr (a person who suffers or dies because of their beliefs)

Mass: a ceremony, also called Eucharist, in which the sacrificial death and resurrection of Jesus is celebrated using bread and wine

materialism: the belief that physical objects matter far more than other things

menorah: a many-branched candlestick that holds either seven or nine candles

merciful: the quality of God that shows compassion or forgiveness to humans, even though he has the power to punish them

Messiah: 'the anointed one'; a leader of the Jews who is expected to live on earth at some time in the future

Messianic age: a future time of global peace when everyone will want to become closer to God, possibly through the intervention of the Messiah

mihrab: a niche in a wall that indicates the direction of Makkah

Mika'il: the Arabic name for Michael, the archangel of mercy who rewards good deeds and provides nourishment to people

minyan: a group of at least 10 adults; the minimum number of Jews required for a Jewish religious service

Mishnah: the first written version of Jewish oral law; part of the Talmud

mission: 'sending out' people with a job or function to perform

mitzvot: Jewish rules or commandments

monotheism: belief in one God

monotheistic: a religion that believes there is only one God

monument: something that is built to remember an important person or event

morality: a system of ethics about what is right and wrong

mortal sins: offences against God, yourself or other people that totally destroy the relationship with God

mourning: a period of time spent remembering a person who has died

Muslim: one who has submitted to the will of God and has accepted Islam

Mystery of Faith: the acclamation after the consecration, when people acknowledge what Christ has done for them

myth: a story that intends to convey a deep truth or message, but not in a literal way

N

natural law: moral principles and values that are considered to be inherent to all humans

ner tamid: eternal light; a light that is kept burning in the synagogue above the Ark

Nevi'im: the second section of the Tenakh; the prophets

Nonconformist: Christians who do not follow the rules laid down by a central authority but are organised at a local level; the Bible forms a central part of their worship

non-violent resistance: resisting a government without using violence, for example through peaceful protest or non-cooperation

nuclear war: war that makes use of nuclear weapons: weapons that work by creating a nuclear reaction in order to devastate huge areas and kill large numbers of people

null and void: the marriage did not take place because something was not correct when the commitment happened

nuptial: to do with a marriage

O

omnipotent: almighty, having unlimited power; a quality of God

omnipresent: being everywhere at all times; a quality of God

omniscient: knowing everything; a quality of God

ordained: made a priest

Orthodox: A branch of Christianity mainly, but not entirely, practised in Eastern Europe

Orthodox Jews: Jews who emphasise the importance of following the laws and guidance in the Torah; they believe the Torah was given directly by God to Moses so should be followed as closely as possible

P

pacifism: the belief of people who refuse to take part in war and any other form of violence

parable: a story with a religious message; particularly used for the stories told by Jesus

particular judgement: the time when a person is judged by God after they die, and has to accept the responsibility for their actions when alive

Paschal: relating to Easter, so the Paschal candle is the Easter candle

Paschal sacrifice: a term that refers to the Last Supper, suffering, death and resurrection of Jesus

peacemaking: the action of trying to establish peace

Pesach (Passover): festival in remembrance of the Jewish exodus from Egypt that is celebrated in spring

pikuach nefesh: the obligation to save a life, even if doing so breaks Jewish law

pilgrim: a person on a religious journey, which reflects the journey through life to heaven

pilgrimage: a journey by a believer to a holy site for religious reasons; an act of worship and devotion

plainchant: an ancient form of song, usually unaccompanied, which uses a limited range of notes

pontifical: when the teachings of the Church are presented by a pope

Pope: the Head of the Catholic Church, the successor to St Peter

poverty: being without money, food, or other basic needs of life (being poor)

praise: an expression of respect, honour and thanks to God

prayer: the raising of the heart and mind to God

preach: publicly announcing a religious message

predestination: the idea that God knows or determines everything that will happen in the universe

prejudice: unfairly judging someone before the facts are known; holding biased opinions about an individual or group

priest: an ordained minister of the Catholic Church; one who is chosen to celebrate Mass, preach and forgive sins

procreative: open to creating new life; life-giving

Promised Land: the land of Canaan that God promised to the Jews

prophet: a person who proclaims the message of God

prophethood: when God makes someone a prophet to communicate his message to people

prostration: (1) for Catholics, lying flat as a sign of total submission (2) for Muslims, kneeling with the forehead, nose, hands, knees and toes touching the floor, in submission to God

Psalms: (1) in Christianity, a book in the Old Testament containing pieces of poetry that are sometimes set to music (2) in Islam, a holy book revealed by God to David

purgatory: a state of cleansing to remove the effects of sin, to help a person accept the full presence of God

Q

qiblah wall: the wall in a mosque that contains the mihrab

Quakers: a religious group founded in the seventeenth century; instead of celebrating the Eucharist they gather together for prayer and wait to be inspired by the Holy Spirit

Qur'an: the holy book revealed to Muhammad by the angel Jibril; God's final revelation to humankind

R

rabbi: a Jewish religious leader and teacher

radicalisation: adopting extreme views on religious, social or political issues

rak'ah: a sequence of movements in ritual prayer

Ramadan: the ninth month of the Muslim calendar, during which Muslims have to fast from dusk to sunset

Real Presence: Christ is truly present in the consecrated Bread and Wine

reconciliation: (1) the restoring of harmony after relationships have broken down (2) a sacrament in the Catholic Church

redemption: making up for the wrongs done by other people, to bring humans back into a relationship with God

Reform Jews: Jews who believe the laws and guidance in the Torah can be adapted for modern times; they believe the Torah was inspired by God but written by humans, so can be interpreted according to the times

relational: having a personal, direct link with another person or with other people

remarriage: when a person who has been married before goes on to marry another person

restoration: when things are brought back to the way that God intended them to be

resurrection: (1) rising from the dead or returning to life (2) Jesus' rising from the dead after dying on the cross

righteous anger: anger against an injustice; some Christians use the term to describe anger that they believe is acceptable

Risalah: the belief that prophets are an important channel of communication between God and humans

Rosh Hashanah: the Jewish new year

S

sacrament: rites and rituals through which the believer receives a special gift of grace; for Catholics, Anglicans and many Protestants, sacraments are 'outward signs' of 'inward grace'

Sacred Heart: a representation of Jesus that focuses on his burning love for everybody

Sacred Scripture: the holy writings of a religion that are believed to be inspired by God

Sadaqah: good actions or voluntary payments that are undertaken for charitable reasons

salah: prayer with and in worship of God, performed under conditions set by the prophet Muhammad

salvation: freedom from sin, and from the eternal separation from God that is brought about by sin

Salvation Army: a Christian group founded in the nineteenth century who see the main purpose of religion as going out to serve and help those in need

sanctify/sanctification: being made holy

sanctity of life: all life is holy as it is created and loved by God; human life should not be misused or abused

Sanctus: a hymn of praise to the three-fold Holy God, which is used before the Eucharistic Prayer in Mass

Sanhedrin: the Jewish Council that looked after all aspects of Jewish life and religion at the time of Jesus

Second Vatican Council: a series of important gatherings of all the Catholic bishops between 1962 and 1965, which updated many Catholic teachings

self-revelation: the idea that humans can only know God through what God has chosen to show about himself

Sermon on the Mount: Jesus' teachings found in Matthew 5–7, which give Christians a set of rules and values to apply in their lives

Shabbat: the Jewish holy day of the week; a day of spiritual renewal starting shortly before sunset on Friday and continuing to sunset on Saturday

Shahadah: the Muslim declaration of faith

Shekhinah: the divine presence of God

Shema: a Jewish prayer affirming belief in the one God, found in the Torah

Shi'a (Shi'i): Muslim who believe in the Imamate, the successorship of Ali

shiva: an intense period of mourning that lasts for seven days

sign of initiation: an action to show that a person has become a formal member of the Church

sinful: when humans turn away from God and do what they want, rather than what God wants

Son of Man: a title that could refer to either just a human being, or a human who is given power by God

Star of David (Magen David): a symbol of Judaism said to represent the shield of King David, who ruled Israel in the tenth century BCE

Stations of the Cross: a series of 14 images that remind Catholics of Jesus' final journey to the cross

stewardship: the idea that believers have a duty to look after the environment on behalf of God

stewardship of wealth: using wealth, which has been given by God, in such a way that all people may benefit from it

Sunnah: the teachings and deeds of Muhammad

Sunni: Muslims who believe in the successorship to Muhammad of Abu Bakr, Umar, Uthman and Ali

supremacy: supreme power or authority; a quality of God

sustainability: only using natural resources at a rate at which they can be replaced

synagogue: a building for Jewish public prayer, study and gathering

T

tabernacle: the place in the church where the consecrated hosts are kept

tallit: a prayer shawl

Talmud: a commentary by the rabbis on the Torah – it consists of the Mishnah and Gemara together in one collection

Tawhid: the Oneness and unity of God

tefillin: small leather boxes containing extracts from the Torah, strapped to the wearer's arm and forehead for morning prayers

Temple: the centre of Jewish worship at the time of Jesus; the meeting place between God and the priest

Ten Commandments: ten laws given by God to Moses over 3000 years ago

Tenakh: the 24 books of Jewish scriptures

terrorism: the unlawful use of violence, usually against innocent civilians, to achieve a political goal

the anointing of the sick: one of the seven sacraments that gives healing, strength and forgiveness

the Body of Christ: (1) the consecrated host (Bread) in the Eucharist (2) a community of believers, the Church

the divine life: the shared love of the Father and the Son in the Holy Spirit

the Five Pillars: the five most important duties for all Muslims: to believe, to pray, to give to charity, to fast and to go on pilgrimage

the last day: the end of time, when the earth will be destroyed and all people will face judgement

the Last Judgement: the time when all people will have to account for their actions and will be rewarded or condemned by God

The Lord's Prayer: the prayer taught to the disciples by Jesus; also known as the 'Our Father'

the Night of Power: (1) the night when the first revelation of the Qur'an was made to Muhammad (2) the festival that marks the start of God's revelation to Muhammad

the Ten Obligatory Acts: ten important duties for Shi'a Muslims, which include the Five Pillars

theologian: a person who studies things related to God and religion

tombstone: a large carved stone that is placed (either lying or standing) over a burial site

Torah: (1) in Judaism and Islam, the five books revealed by God to Moses (2) in Judaism, the first section of the Tenakh (the Jewish Bible), and the Jewish written law

torture: the use of severe physical or psychological pain to punish someone or force them to do or say something

totally immersed: being under the water at a baptism so the whole body and head are covered

traditional hymns: religious songs that have been used by believers over generations

transcendent: the idea that God is beyond and outside life on earth and the universe; a quality of God

trefah: food that Jews are forbidden to eat; means 'torn'

Trinity: the belief that there are three Persons in one God; the Father, the Son and the Holy Spirit are separate, but are also one being

Triune God: within the one God there is a three-ness

U

Ultra-Orthodox Jews: Jews who are even more committed than Orthodox Jews to strictly following the laws and guidance in the Torah

V

Viaticum: meaning 'with you on the way'; the last Communion before death to show that Christ is with the person in death

virgin birth: the belief that Jesus was fully human but did not have a human father

vocation: a call from God to fulfil a particular role in life

W

weapons of mass destruction (WMD): weapons that can kill large numbers of people and/or cause great damage

witness: when someone shows their faith in their words and actions

Word of God: the Second Person of the Trinity, God the Son, who became flesh in Jesus

wudu: ritual washing before prayer

Y

Yom Kippur: the Day of Atonement; a day of fasting on the tenth day after Rosh Hashanah

Z

Zakah: purification of wealth by giving 2.5 per cent of savings each year to the poor

Acknowledgements

The publisher would like to thank the following for permission to use their photographs:

cover: Hands of God and Adam, detail from The Creation of Adam, from the Sistine Ceiling, 1511 (fresco) (pre restoration), Buonarroti, Michelangelo (1475-1564)/Vatican Museums and Galleries, Vatican City/Bridgeman Images; **p9:** 123RF/Cosmin-Constantin Sava; **p10:** jorisvo/Shutterstock.com; **p11t:** Universal Images Group/Getty Images; **p11b:** DEA / A. DAGLI ORTI/Getty Images; **p12:** 123RF/olan; **p14:** jorisvo/Shutterstock.com; **p16:** Shutterstock; **p17:** 123RF/Jean-Marie Guyon; **p18-21:** iStockphoto; **p22:** Shutterstock; **p23:** Zheltyshev/Shutterstock.com; **p24 & p25:** Shutterstock; **p26:** 123RF/mihtiander; **p27:** 123RF/Marin Veraja; **p28 & p29:** iStockphoto; **p30:** cafod.org.uk; **p31:** viacampesina.org; **p34:** Nancy Bauer/Shutterstock.com; **p35:** 123RF/Jozef Sedmak; **p36:** Shutterstock; **p37:** iStockphoto; **p38:** Renata Sedmakova/Shutterstock.com; **p39 & p40:** iStockphoto; **p41:** Mary Evans Picture Library/Alamy Stock Photo; **p42:** iStockphoto; **p43 & p44:** Shutterstock; **p45:** Gary S Chapman/Getty Images; **p46t:** 123RF/rafcha; **p46b:** Shutterstock; **p47:** imageBROKER/Alamy Stock Photo; **p48:** Zvonimir Atletic/Shutterstock.com; **p50:** World History Archive/Alamy Stock Photo; **p51:** Freedom Studio/Shutterstock.com; **p52:** 123RF/Zvonimir Atletic; **p53:** Renata Sedmakova/Shutterstock.com; **p54:** iStockphoto; **p55:** Shutterstock; **p58:** Peter Muhly/Stringer/Getty Images; **p59:** Shutterstock; **p62:** Mondadori Portfolio/Getty Images; **p63:** iStockphoto; **p64:** 123RF/Simone Buehring; **p65:** Shutterstock; **p66:** iStockphoto; **p67:** Bridgeman Images; **p68:** Shutterstock; **p69 & p70:** Renata Sedmakova/Shutterstock.com; **p71:** iStockphoto; **p72:** AFP/Stringer/Getty Images; **p73:** Alf Ribeiro/Shutterstock.com; **p74:** Zvonimir Atletic/Shutterstock.com; **p75 & p76:** Shutterstock; **p77:** Holmes Garden Photos/Alamy Stock Photo; **p78:** LiamMcArdle.com/Alamy Stock Photo; **p79 & p80:** Shutterstock; **p81:** ChameleonsEye/Shutterstock.com; **p82 & p83:** iStockphoto; **p89:** David Levenson/Getty Images **p88:** NaughtyNut/Shutterstock.com; **p90:** Pontino/Alamy Stock Photo; **p91:** 123RF/neftali77; **p92:** iStockphoto; **p93t:** Shutterstock; **p93b:** 123RF/Richard Faenza; **p94:** Renata Sedmakova/Shutterstock.com; **p95 & p96:** Shutterstock; **p97:** 123RF/Jozef Sedmak; **p99:** iStockphoto; **p100:** Shutterstock **p102:** iStockphoto; **p105:** Shutterstock; **p104:** bibiphoto/Shutterstock.com; **p106:** iStockphoto; **p107:** 123RF/Magdalena Kucova; **p108:** iStockphoto; **p109:** John Morrison/Alamy Stock Photo; **p110:** iStockphoto; **p115:** Zvonimir Atletic/Shutterstock.com; **p116:** 123RF/Richard Faenza; **p117:** CountrySideCollection - Homer Sykes/Alamy Stock Photo; **p119:** ScreenProd/Photononstop/Alamy Stock Photo; **p120:** SuperStock/Getty Images; **p123:** John Davidson Photos/Alamy Stock Photo; **p124:** RealyEasyStar/Fotografia Felici/Alamy Stock Photo; **p125:** iStockphoto; **p127:** 123RF/portokalis; **p128:** Art Kowalsky/Alamy Stock Photo; **p129:** 123RF/Jozef Sedmak; **p130:** David Lees/Corbis; **p131:** giulio napolitano/Shutterstock.com; **p132:** Wayne Hutchinson/Alamy Stock Photo; **p135:** Tim Graham/Alamy Stock Photo; **p136:** giulio napolitanoShutterstock.com; **p137:** WENN UK/Alamy Stock Photo; **p140:** 123RF/thamkc; **p141:** Shutterstock, **p142 & 143:** World History Archive/Alamy Stock Photo; **p145t:** 123RF/Antonio Ribeiro; **p145b:** iStockphoto; **p146:** DEA/A. DAGLI ORTI/Getty Images; **p149:** valeriiarnaud/Shutterstock.com; **p148:** iStockphoto; **p150:** 123RF/Daria Belozerova; **p151-154t:** Shutterstock; **p154b:** Mary Evans Picture Library/Alamy Stock Photo; **p156:** 123RF/ Marin Veraja; **p158:** Agencja Fotograficzna Caro/Alamy Stock Photo; **p159:** Zvonimir Atletic/Shutterstock.com; **p160:** George Sweeney/Alamy Stock Photo; **p161:** Agencja Fotograficzna Caro/Alamy Stock Photo; **p162:** Shutterstock; **p166:** iStockphoto; **p167 & p168:** Shutterstock; **p169:** Hasan Mroue/Getty Images; **p170:** Shutterstock; **p171:** iStockphoto; **p173t & p173b:** Shutterstock; **p174:** 123RF/Jennifer Keddie De Cojon; **p175:** Sorin Vidis/Shutterstock.com; **p176 & p177:** iStockphoto; **p178:** Fedor Selivanov/Alamy Stock Photo; **p179:** Shutterstock; **p181:** 123RF/Ramzi Hachicho; **p180:** ZUMA Press, Inc/Alamy Stock Photo; **p182:** artpixelgraphy Studio/Shutterstock.com; **p183:** enciktat/Shutterstock.com; **p184:** Ahmad Faizal Yahya/Shutterstock.com; **p185 & p188:** Shutterstock; **p189:** iStockphoto; **p190:** RosaBetancourt 0 people images/Alamy Stock Photo; **p191t:** Shanti Hesse/Shutterstock.com; **p191b:** iStockphoto; **p192:** hikrcn/Shutterstock.com; **p193:** 123RF/Eray Haciosmanoglu; **p194 -196:** Shutterstock; **p197:** Agencja Fotograficzna Caro/Alamy Stock Photo; **p198:** Shutterstock; **p199:** shahreen/Shutterstock.com; **p200:** Kami Kami/Getty Images; **p201:** Mawardi Bahar/Shutterstock.com; **p202:** Jim West/Alamy Stock Photo; **p203:** thomas koch/Shutterstock.com; **p204 & p205:** Shutterstock; **p206:** iStockphoto; **p207:** Gapper/Alamy Stock Photo; **p210:** TravelCollection/Alamy Stock Photo; **p211:** Ira Berger/Alamy Stock Photo; **p212:** Shutterstock; **p213:** iStockphoto; **p215:** Mary Evans/Grenville Collins Postcard Collection; **p216:** 123RF/Josef Muellek; **p217:** epa european pressphoto agency b.v/Alamy Stock Photo; **p218:** Mary Evans Picture Library; **p219:** Richard Levine/Alamy Stock Photo; **p220:** Mary Evans/Sueddeutsche Zeitung Photo; **p222:** iStockphoto; **p223:** Shutterstock; **p224:** Jim West/Alamy Stock Photo; **p225:** Jason Moore/Alamy Stock Photo; **p226:** Nir Alon/Alamy Stock Photo; **p227:** iStockphoto; **p228:** Israel images/Alamy Stock Photo; **p229:** Ruby/Alamy Stock Photo; **p232l:** Shutterstock; **p232r:** robertharding/Alamy Stock Photo; **p233:** Chameleons/EyeShutterstock.com; **p234:** Shutterstock; **p235:** Martin Metsemakers/Shutterstock.com; **p237:** PS-I/Alamy Stock Photo; **p238:** Shutterstock; **p239:** Robert Hoetink/Shutterstock.com; **p240:** iStockphoto; **p241:** ChameleonsEye/Shutterstock.com; **p242:** ASAP/Alamy Stock Photo; **p243t:** OUP; **p243b & p244:** iStockphoto; **p245:** ChameleonsEye/Shutterstock.com; **p246:** Ira Berger/Alamy Stock Photo; **p247:** Shutterstock; **p249:** Anders Ryman/Alamy Stock Photo; **p248:** 123RF/Rafael Ben-Ari; **p250:** David Grossman/Alamy Stock Photo; **p251:** Robert Mulder/Alamy Stock Photo; **p252:** Ira Berger/Alamy Stock Photo; **p253:** ChameleonsEye/Shutterstock.com; **p254:** Ruby/Alamy Stock Photo; **p255:** Alpha and Omega Collection/Alamy Stock Photo; **p256:** Shutterstock; **p257:** iStockphoto; **p258:** ASAP/Alamy Stock Photo; **p259 & p262:** Shutterstock; **p263:** 123RF/Natalii Sdobnikova; **p264:** Shutterstock; **p265:** Henryk T. Kaiser/Getty Images; **p266 & p267:** iStockphoto; **p268:** 123RF/maximkabb; **p269:** Jim West/Alamy Stock Photo; **p270:** Alamy; **p271 - 279:** iStockphoto; **p280:** Renata Sedmakova/Shutterstock.com; **p281:** The Art Archive/Alamy Stock Photo; **p282:** iStockphoto; **p283:** robertharding/Alamy Stock Photo; **p284 & p285:** iStockphoto; **p288:** 123RF/ruskpp; **p289:** 123RF/Mandy Godbehear; **p290:** 123RF/mikekiev; **p291:** Shutterstock; **p292:** Padmayogini/Shutterstock.com; **p293:** 1000 Words/Shutterstock.com; **p294:** iStockphoto; **p295:** Songquan Deng/Shutterstock.com; **p296:** Everett Historical/Shutterstock.com; **p297:** Goran Bogicevic/Shutterstock.com; **p298:** Volodymyr Borodin/Shutterstock.com; **p299:** Anjo Kan/Shutterstock.com; **p300:** Shutterstock; **p301:** 123RF/Luis Louro; **p302:** Drop of Light/Shutterstock.com; **p303:** Shutterstock; **p304:** Vatican Pool/Getty Images; **p305:** Flirt/Alamy Stock Photo; **p306:** Bettina Strenske/Alamy Stock Photo; **p307:** robertharding/Alamy Stock Photo; **p308:** Frederic Legrand - COMEO/Shutterstock.com; **p310:** iStockphoto; **p311:** Frances Roberts/Alamy Stock Photo; **p314:** CountryCollection - Homer Sykes/Alamy Stock Photo; **p315:** Shutterstock; **p316 - 321:** iStockphoto; **p322:** Purepix/Alamy Stock Photo; **p323:** 123RF/isogood; **p324:** iStockphoto; **p325:** Shutterstock; **p326t & p326b:** iStockphoto; **p327:** Sadik Gulec/Shutterstock.com; **p328:** Realimage/Alamy Stock Photo; **p329:** iStockphoto; **p330:** Martchan/Shutterstock.com; **p331:** US Air Force Photo/Alamy Stock Photo; **p332:** AGIF/Shutterstock.com; **p333:** roger askew/Alamy Stock Photo; **p335l:** Jeff J Mitchell/Getty Images; **p335r:** Bikeworldtravel/Shutterstock.com; **p336:** Friedrich Stark/Alamy Stock Photo; **p337:** Vincenzo Pinto/Getty Images

We are grateful to the authors and publishers for use of extracts from their titles and in particular for the following:

The Scripture quotations contained herein are from the **New Revised Standard Version Bible**, copyright © 1989, Division of Christian Education of the National Council of Churches of Christ in the U.S.A. Used by permission. All rights reserved. The New Revised Standard Version Catholic Edition of the Bible, Harper Catholic Bibles – a division of Harper Collins.; Excerpts from **Catechism of the Catholic Church**, http://www.vatican.va/archive/ccc_css/archive/catechism/ccc_toc.htm (Strathfield, NSW: St Pauls, 2000). Reproduced with permission from The Vatican. © Libreria Editrice Vaticana; Excerpts from the English translation of the Non-Biblical Reading from **The Liturgy of the Hours** © 1973, 1974, 1975, International Commission on English in the Liturgy Corporation. All rights reserved. Reproduced with permission from the International Committee on English in the Liturgy and from the Catholic Bishops' Conference of England and Wales.; Excerpts from the English translation of **The Order of Celebrating Matrimony** © 2013, International Commission on English in the Liturgy Corporation. All rights reserved. Reproduced with permission from the International Commission on English in the Liturgy and from the Catholic Bishops' Conference of England and Wales.; Excerpts from the English translation of **Pastoral Care of the Sick: Rites of Anointing and Viaticum** © 1982, International Commission on English in the Liturgy Corporation. All rights reserved. Reproduced with permission from the International Committee on English in the Liturgy and from the Catholic Bishops' Conference of England and Wales.; Excerpts from the English translation of **Rite of Baptism for Children** © 1969, International Commission on English in the Liturgy Corporation. All rights reserved. Reproduced with permission from the International Committee on English in the Liturgy and from the Catholic Bishops' Conference of England and Wales.; Excerpts from the English translation of **The Roman Missal** © 2010, International Commission on English in the Liturgy Corporation. All rights reserved. Reproduced with permission from the International Committee on English in the Liturgy and from the Catholic Bishops' Conference of England and Wales.; Excerpts from **The Qur'an OWC** translated by M. A. S. Abdel Haleem (Oxford University Press, 2008). Reproduced with permission from Oxford University Press. Excerpts from the **Mass**. English Language Liturgical Consultation http://englishtexts.org/ The English translation of (text) prepared by the English Language Liturgical Consultation (ELLC), 1998.; **P. Binet:** *The Divine Favours Granted to St Joseph*, (TAN Books & Publishers, 1983). TAN Books, Charlotte, NC (www.tanbooks.com). Reproduced with permission from TAN Books.; **Rabbi Benjamin Blech:** *Life after Death: What matters most is maximizing our life before death*, (Aish, 2009). Reproduced with permission from Benjamin Blech.; **N.Bunyan:** I forgive you, mother tells racist thugs who killed son, The Telegraph, December 1st 2005 (The Telegraph, 2005). Reproduced with permission from Telegraph Syndication.; **CAFOD:** *Sustainable Development*, http://cafod.org.uk/index.php/News/Campaigning-news/Sustainable-development (CAFOD, 2015). Reproduced with permission from CAFOD.; **CND:** *Global Abolition*, http://www.cnduk.org/campaigns/global-abolition (CND, 2015). Reproduced with permission from CND.; **Catholic Bishops' Conference of England and Wales:** *The Common Good and the Catholic Church's Social Teaching*, Statement (Catholic Bishops' Conference of England and Wales, 1996). Reproduced with permission from the Catholic Bishops' Conference of England and Wales.; **Catholic Bishops' Conference of England and Wales:** *The Complete Order of Celebrating Matrimony*, (Catholic Truth Society, 2016). Reproduced with permission from the Catholic Bishops' Conference of England and Wales.; **Catholic Truth Society:** *A Catechism of Christian Doctrine*, (Catholic Truth Society, 1978). Reproduced with permission from the Catholic Truth Society.; **Julian of Norwich:** *Love's Trinity: a companion to Julian of Norwich*, translated by John-Julian. (Liturgical Press, 2009). Copyright 2009 by Order of Saint Benedict. Reproduced with permission from Liturgical Press.; **P. Kurtz:** *A Secular Humanist Declaration*, (Prometheus Books, 1980). Reproduced with permission from Prometheus Books.; **Mother Theresa:** Speech December 11th 1979. (Nobel Foundation, 1979). Reproduced with permission from the Nobel Foundation.; **S. Podolsky:** *Bar Mitzvah Speech*, September 24th 2011 (Chabad of Port Washington, 2011). Reproduced with permission from Chabad of Port Washington.; **Pontifical Council for Justice and Peace:** *Compendium of the Social Doctrine of the Church*, May 26th 2006 (The Vatican, 2006). Reproduced with permission from The Vatican. © Libreria Editrice Vaticana; **Pope Benedict XVI:** *Deus Caritas Est*, December 25th 2005 (The Vatican, 2005). Reproduced with permission from The Catholic Truth Society, London.; **Pope Benedict XVI:** *Verbum Domini, On the Word of God in the Life and Mission of the Church*, September 30th 2010 (The Vatican, 2010). Reproduced with permission from The Vatican. © Libreria Editrice Vatican; **Pope Benedict XVI:** *Message for the World Day of Peace*, January 1st 2012 (The Vatican, 2012). Reproduced with permission from The Vatican. © Libreria Editrice Vaticana; **Pope Francis:** Speech, January 25th 2013, (The Vatican, 2013). Reproduced with permission from The Vatican. © Libreria Editrice Vaticana; **Pope Francis:** Speech, June 7th 2013, (The Vatican, 2013). Reproduced with permission from The Vatican. © Libreria Editrice Vaticana; **Pope Francis:** Speech to the 38th Conference of the FAO, June 20th 2013, (The Vatican, 2013). Reproduced with permission from The Vatican. © Libreria Editrice Vaticana; **Pope Francis:** Speaking at a meeting with Italian President Giorgio Napolitano, June 8th 2013, (The Vatican, 2013). Reproduced with permission from The Vatican. © Libreria Editrice Vaticana; **Pope Francis:** Interview, July 28th 2013, (The Vatican, 2013). Reproduced with permission from The Vatican. © Libreria Editrice Vaticana; **Pope Francis:** Twitter post, September 2nd 2013, https://twitter.com/pontifex/status/374466943312330753 (The Vatican, 2013). Reproduced with permission from The Vatican. © Libreria Editrice Vaticana; **Pope Francis:** Speech, September 29th 2013, (The Vatican, 2013). Reproduced with permission from The Vatican. © Libreria Editrice Vaticana; **Pope Francis:** *Evangelii Gaudium, On the Proclamation of the Gospel in Today's World*, November 24th 2013, (The Vatican, 2013). Reproduced with permission from The Vatican. © Libreria Editrice Vaticana; **Pope Francis:** *Invocation for Peace*, Speech at the Vatican Gardens, June 8th 2014, (The Vatican, 2014). Reproduced with permission from The Vatican. © Libreria Editrice Vaticana; **Pope Francis:** *Homily*, Mass at the Military Memorial of Redipuglia, September 13th 2014, (The Vatican, 2014). Reproduced with permission from The Vatican. © Libreria Editrice Vaticana; **Pope Francis:** Speech at the Pontifical Academy of Sciences, October 27th 2014, (The Vatican, 2014). Reproduced with permission from The Vatican. © Libreria Editrice Vaticana; **Pope Francis:** Speech, January 12th 2015 (The Vatican, 2015). Reproduced with permission from The Vatican. © Libreria Editrice Vaticana; **Pope Francis:** Speech in St Peter's Square, April 29th 2015 (The Vatican, 2015). Reproduced with permission from The Vatican. © Libreria Editrice Vaticana; **Pope Francis:** *Laudato Si*, May 24th 2015, (The Vatican, 2015). Reproduced with permission from The Vatican. © Libreria Editrice Vaticana; **Pope Francis:** Speech, September 6th 2015, (The Vatican, 2015). Reproduced with permission from The Vatican. © Libreria Editrice Vaticana; **Pope Francis:** Speech to US Congress, September 24th 2015, (The Vatican, 2015). Reproduced with permission from The Vatican. © Libreria Editrice Vaticana; **Pope John XXIII:** *Pacem in Terris, On Establishing Universal Peace in Truth*, April 11th 1963 (The Vatican, 1993). Reproduced with permission from The Vatican.

© Libreria Editrice Vaticana; **Pope John Paul II:** *Familaris Consortio, On the Role of the Christian Family In The Modern World*, November 22nd 1981 (The Vatican, 1981). Reproduced with permission from The Vatican. © Libreria Editrice Vaticana; **Pope John Paul II:** *Mulieris Dignitatem, On the Dignity and Vocation of Women on the Occasion of the Marian Year*, August 15th 1988 (The Vatican, 1988). Reproduced with permission from The Vatican. © Libreria Editrice Vaticana; **Pope John Paul II:** *Message for the World Day of Peace*, January 1st 1990 (The Vatican, 1990). Reproduced with permission from The Vatican. © Libreria Editrice Vaticana; **Pope John Paul II:** *Evangelium Vitae*, March 25th 1995 (The Vatican, 1995). Reproduced with permission from The Vatican. © Libreria Editrice Vaticana; **Pope John Paul II:** *Message for the World Day of Peace*, January 1st 2001 (The Vatican, 2001). Reproduced with permission from The Vatican. © Libreria Editrice Vaticana; **Pope Paul VI:** *Inter Mirifica*, Decree on the Media of Social Communications, December 4th 1963 (The Vatican, 1963). Reproduced with permission from The Vatican. © Libreria Editrice Vaticana; **Pope Paul VI:** *Sacrosanctum Concilium*, Constitution on the Sacred Liturgy, December 4th 1963 (The Vatican, 1963). Reproduced with permission from The Vatican. © Libreria Editrice Vaticana; **Pope Paul VI:** *Lumen Gentium*, Dogmatic Constitution on the Church, November 21st 1964 (The Vatican, 1964). Reproduced with permission from The Vatican. © Libreria Editrice Vaticana; **Pope Paul VI:** *Dei Verbum*, Dogmatic Constitution on Divine Revelation, November 18th 1965 (The Vatican, 1965). Reproduced with permission from The Vatican. © Libreria Editrice Vaticana; **Pope Paul VI:** *Gaudium et Spes*, Pastoral Constitution on the Church in the Modern World, December 7th, 1965 (The Vatican, 1965). Reproduced with permission from The Vatican. © Libreria Editrice Vaticana; **Pope Paul VI:** *Dignitatis Humanae*, On the Right of the Person and of Communities to Social and Civil Freedom in Matters Religious, December 7th, 1965 (The Vatican, 1965). Reproduced with permission from The Vatican. © Libreria Editrice Vaticana; **Pope Paul VI:** *Populorum Progressio*, On the Development of Peoples, March 26th 1967 (The Vatican, 1967). Reproduced with permission from The Vatican. © Libreria Editrice Vaticana; **Pope Paul VI:** *Humanae Vitae*, On the Regulation of Birth, July 25th 1968 (The Vatican, 1968). Reproduced with permission from The Vatican. © Libreria Editrice Vaticana; **Pope Paul VI:** Letter to the Secretary-General of the UN, 1972 (The Vatican, 1972). Reproduced with permission from The Vatican. © Libreria Editrice Vaticana; **Sacred Congregation for the Doctrine of the Faith:** *Declaration on Euthanasia*, May 5th 1980 (The Vatican, 1980). Reproduced with permission from The Vatican. © Libreria Editrice Vaticana; **Sacred Congregation for the Doctrine of the Faith:** *Instruction on Certain Aspects of the "Theology Of Liberation"*, August 6th 1984 (The Vatican, 1984). Reproduced with permission from The Vatican. © Libreria Editrice Vaticana; **St Thomas Aquinas:** *Summa Theologica*, translated by Fathers of the English Dominican Province (Benziger Bros, 1947). Reproduced with permission from Ave Maria Press.; **St Vincent de Paul Society:** *Spiritual Values/Ethos*, http://svp.org.uk/spiritualvaluesethos (St Vincent de Paul Society, 2013). Reproduced with permission from the St Vincent de Paul Society (England & Wales); **United Nations:** *Universal Declaration of Human Rights*, (United Nations, 1948). Reproduced with permission from the United Nations.; **P. Wallace:** *Roman Catholicism*, (Oxford University Press, 2009). Reprinted with permission from Oxford University Press.; **Justin Welby, Archbishop of Canterbury:** Speech to reporters, November 17th 2014. (Lambeth Palace, 2014). REprodcued with permission from Justin Welby, Archbishop of Canterbury.; **YOUCAT:** *YOUCAT*, (Ignatius Press, 2011). Reproduced with permission from Ignatius Press.

We have made every effort to trace and contact all copyright holders before publication, but if notified of any errors or omissions, the publisher will be happy to rectify these at the earliest opportunity.

Excerpts from **The Divine Office Volume 2** © 2006, HarperCollins. Copyright holder not established at time of going to print. **Augustine:** *On the Trinity: Bk. 8-15*, edited by Gareth B. Matthews, translated by Stephen McKenna (Cambridge Texts in the History of Philosophy, 2008). Copyright holder not established at time of going to print. **C. LaCugna:** *God For Us: The Trinity and Catholic Life*, (HarperOne, 2000). Copyright holder not established at time of going to print. **Rabbi Moshe Ben Maimon:** *Mishneh Torah*, (Moznaim Pub Corp, 2010). Copyright holder not established at time of going to print.

The publishers and authors would like to thank Dr Deborah Herring, Revd Francis Loftus, Sohail Ahmed Siddiqui (Peace Education Programme), Mohammad S. Bahmanpour, Ann Angel and Philip Robinson, RE Adviser to the Catholic Education Service, for reviewing this book.

Index

A

ablution 192–3
abortion 60, 61
Abraham 222–3
acclamations 68–9
Acts of the Apostles 21
Adalat (justice) 172, 173
Adam 10–12, 16, 25, 156, 180–1
adoration 112–13
adultery 264, 265, 268–9
afterlife 148–53, 178–9, 218–19
akhirah 178
Aleinu prayer 241
Allah 168
Alleluia 68–9
almsgiving 198–9
Alpha symbols 44–5, 143
altar 90, 92, 94
Amidah (standing prayer) 240, 241
Ancillaries of the Faith 190–1
angels 36, 69, 144, 174–5
annulment 274
annunciation 36, 37
anointing of the sick 160–1
Anselm, salvation 105
apostles 20–21, 54–5, 80, 130–1, 283
Arabic calligraphy 180
Arafat 201, 202
Aramaic 76, 77
architecture 90–1
Aron Hakodesh (The Ark) 236–7
art 10–13, 37, 46–7, 56, 71, 148
artefacts 94–5
artificial contraception 276
ascension 96–9, 105
Ashura festival 208–9
Asr (times of prayer) 192
atonement 96, 105
St Augustine 64, 78–9, 296
authority 80

B

baptism 58–9, 76–7, 82–3
Bar & Bat Mitzvah 250–1
Beatitudes 50–1
Benediction 112, 113
beneficence 172, 173
betrothal 252–3
Bible
    Beatitudes 50–1
    bullying 290–1
    conflict resolution/peacemaking 312
    definition 20
    equality 336
    evangelism 75
    gender equality 282–3
    Genesis 10, 14–15, 16–17, 24–5
    human dignity 316–17
    New Testament 21, 70–1
    Old Testament 20–21, 70, 302–3
    origins and structure 20–21
    redemption 102–3, 104–5
    terrorism 308–9
    Trinity 76–7
    Triune God 70–1
    violence 290–1
    warfare 302–3
    wealth 322
    word of God 22–3
bimah platform 236, 237
biological weapons 298–9
birth 38–9, 248–9, 264–5
    see also children
bishops 126, 337
Blessed Sacrament 112, 113
Body of Christ 118, 119, 130, 134–5
Book of Genesis *see* Genesis
Book of Revelation 21
Brit Milah ceremony 248, 249
British terrorism 309
bullying 290–1
burial 98–9, 146

C

CAFOD *see* Catholic Agency for Overseas Development
Caliph 185
calligraphy 180
candles 142–3, 234, 244
care of the dying 164–5
cathedrals 47, 91, 294
Catholic, definition 130
Catholic Agency for Overseas Development (CAFOD) 32–3, 135, 307, 332
cemeteries 147
charitable giving 190–1, 198–9
charity 134–5, 197, 323
chemical weapons 298–9
Chi-Rho symbol 44, 45, 147
children 264–5, 268, 275, 277, 280–1, 307
    see also birth
Christ *see* Jesus
Christian Aid 332–3
Christian denominations 94
Church 20, 90–1
    adultery 268
    architecture 90–1
    Body of Christ 130, 134–5
    conciliar/pontifical nature 132–3
    contraception 276–7
    discrimination/prejudice 334
    divorce 274–5
    end of time 158–9
    four marks 130–1
    freedom 317
    gender equality 284–5, 336–7
    hierarchy 126–7
    homosexuality 269
    human rights 318–19
    Kingdom of God 116–41
    laying on of hands 80
    main parts 92–3
    marriage 270–1
    modern warfare 298–9, 300–1
    pacifism 304–5
    post-1965 architecture 91
    poverty 328–9
    pre-1965 architecture 90
    racial equality 338–9
    roles of family 280–1
    sex before marriage 268
    sexuality 268–9
    terrorism 309
    walking days 316
    wealth 322–3, 325
circling the Ka'aba 200, 201
circumcision 222, 223, 248–9
civilian casualties 296, 300
cohabitation 272, 273
Commandments 216, 224–5, 230–1, 250–1
commemoration, Ashura festival 208–9
commendation of the dying 160, 161
commitals 163
Communion 108, 109, 266
conception 60–1
conciliar nature of Church 132
condemnation 145, 148
confirmation 58–9
conflict 290–315
conscience 50–1, 106–7, 226–7
consecration 68, 69, 92
Constantinople Council 81
consummated relationships 264, 265
contemporary worship songs 66–7
contraception 266, 276–7
cosmic disasters 148
cosmic reconciliation 156–7
Councils 26–7, 80–1, 126–7, 132, 158–9, 317
covenant 222–5
creation 10–35, 214–15, 324–5
creator 10, 214–15
creed 72–3
cremation 146, 147
crematorium 162, 163
cross 94, 95, 116–17
crucifix 48, 49, 92–5, 102, 292
Crusades 303

D

David, Star of 218, 221, 234
Day of Ashura 208
Day of Judgement 174, 177, 178–9
death 96, 98, 146–53, 160–1, 178–9, 218–19, 228, 254–5, 305
Dei Verbum document 127
denominations 94
Deuteronomy 70
devil *see* Satan
Die Verbum 4 54
dietary laws 256–7
dignity 18–19, 316–17
direction of prayer 193
disciples 128
discrimination 286–7, 334–5
divine life 56
Divine Office 64, 65
divine presence 216, 217
divorce 274–5

349

dove and Holy Spirit 78
drama 120–1
dramatised prayer 116
duties of Islam 190–211

E

Easter Vigil 68–9, 142–3
Eastertide 142, 143
Eden, Garden of 16, 25
education 279, 338–9
Egypt 224
Emmanuel 38
end of Mass 109
end of time 158–9
environment 28–9, 32–3, 226–7, 301
Epistles 21, 22, 76, 77
equality 282–5, 336–7, 338–9
eschatology 142–67
ethics 50–1, 106, 107, 226–7
Eucharist 58–9, 68–9, 92, 108–9, 110–1
euthanasia 164–5
evangelism 42, 43, 74, 75, 120–1
Eve 12, 16, 25, 156
evil 214–15
exhortation 54–5
exodus 260
exploitation 324–5
extramarital sex 266

F

fairness 172, 173
faith 68, 69, 145, 148, 177, 317
Fajr (times of prayer) 192
family 136–7, 248, 264–89
fasting 190–1, 196–7
Father, Trinity 22, 56, 71, 72–3, 78, 104
fatherhood *see* parenthood
female sexuality 264–5
festivals 182, 183, 190–211
final judgement 152–3
Five Pillars 182–3, 190–203
five roots of Usul ad-Din 171
food 135, 181, 196, 207, 231, 244–5, 256–7, 261, 323, 329, 331
forgiveness 292–3
Francis, Pope 28, 126, 133, 138–9, 306–7
freedom 16, 96, 159, 176–7, 214–5, 230, 317
fresco 13, 150–1, 155
fundamentalist 24, 25
funerals 162–3, 255

G

Galatians 71, 77
gardens 16, 25, 146, 147, 179
Gaudium et Spes 127
gender 282–5, 286–7, 336–7
Genesis 10, 14–15, 16–17, 24–5, 72–3, 290
glass breaking 253
global charities 134
Gloria 68
God 168–9, 172–3, 212–5, 216–7
    faith 177
    Genesis 16–7
    God's Kingdom 100
    greatness 172

images 180
inspiration and Bible 22–3
Jesus/incarnation 36–7
Joseph 38–9
Kingdom of 116–41
mitzvot 231
mosaic of hand 13
names 172
Son of God 42–3
Triune God 64–89
will of 50
Word of God 40–1
Gospels 21, 22, 68, 74, 75, 187
grace 36, 37, 56–7, 100
Grand Mosque 183, 200, 201
gravesites 163, 218, 305
greater jihad 204–5

H

Hades 154–5
Hajj pilgrimage 182, 183, 190–1, 200–3
Hajji 202, 203
harmony 124–5, 138–9, 156–7, 290–315
havdalah service 245
healing the world 226–7
heaven 150–1, 154, 155, 178, 179, 218
heavenly banquet 100, 101
hell 144–5, 150–1, 154–5, 159, 178, 179, 218
heresy 54, 80, 81
hierarchy of the Church 126–7
history books 21
holy books 186–7
holy days 214, 242–5
Holy Spirit 22, 56, 71, 72–3, 78, 104
Holy Trinity *see* Trinity
holy war 204, 205, 303
home life 195, 244–5, 246–7, 280–1
homelessness *see* poverty
homosexuality 269, 271
hosts 92, 93
human dignity 18–19, 316–7
human incarnation 42–3
human nature 16–7
human rights 316, 318–9, 320–1
human trafficking 324, 325
humanitarian aid 332–3
humility 53
Husayn shrine 208
hymns 66

I

Iblis (Satan) 180–1
Ibrahim 182–3
Ichthus (fish) 44
iconostasis 110
Id-ul-Adha 182, 183, 206–7
Id-ul-Fitr festival 206
idol worship 182
Ihram 201
images of Jesus 49
imago dei 60–1
Imam 184
Imamate 184, 185
Immaculate Conception 118
immanence 172

immanent theology 78, 79
incarnation 36–63
individual judgement 152–3
Injil 187
inspiration, word of God 22–3
interdependence 30
Irenaeus 52–3, 105
Isha (times of prayer) 192
Ishmael 183
Islam
    beliefs/teachings 168–89
    worship, duties, festivals 190–211
Israel 306

J

Jamarat 202
Jerusalem 117
Jesus 36–7
    apostles 283
    apostolic succession 131
    ascension 96–9
    baptism 76–7
    birth 38–9, 69
    Body of Christ 118, 119
    burial 98–9
    cosmic reconciliation 156–7
    crucifix 48, 49, 92–5, 102, 292
    death 96, 98
    different understandings 54–5
    example 103
    Irenaeus' writings and tradition 52–3
    Joseph 38–9
    The Last Judgement 144–5
    lectern 92
    moral teachings 50–1
    mosaic 47
    nailing to cross 117
    restoration/sacrifice 96–7
    restorer 103
    resurrection 96–7, 98, 99, 103, 282
    risen Christ 94, 95
    Son of God/Son of Man 42–3
    statues 46, 48–9
    victor 103
    Word of God 40–1
Jibril (Gabriel) 174–5, 184
Jihad 190–1, 204–5
John Paul II, Pope 266–7
John XXIII, Pope 298–9
Joseph 38–9
Judaism 212–33, 234–63
judgement 150, 152–3, 174, 177, 178–9, 216–7
Julian of Norwich 157
Jummah prayer 194, 195
just war theory 296–7
justice 124, 138, 172, 173, 226, 294–5, 313, 338

K

Ka'aba 182–3, 200–1
kaddish 254
Ketuvim 247
Khums 198, 199
kindness to others 226, 227

Kingdom of God 100, 116–41
Kingdom values 136–9
kosher food 256–7

L

La Pieta statue 46
LaCugna, C. 79
Lane, L. 337
the last day 144, 145
The Last Judgement 144–5, 147
last rites 160–1
Last Supper 53, 94, 131
law 20–1, 26–7, 50, 187, 214, 216, 230, 236–7, 243, 246–7, 251, 256–7, 271
laying on of hands 58, 59, 80
Lazarus 154–5
lectern 92
Lent 116
Les Miserables 120–1
lesbian, gay, bisexual and transgender (LGBT) pride 337
lesser jihad 204, 205
life after death 148–53, 178–9, 218–9
life of a Catholic (Kingdom values) 136–9
liturgy 66–7, 100–1
local charities 134
Lord's Prayer 122–3
Lourdes, pilgrimage 118–9
love 41, 53, 74–5, 78–9, 264–5, 281
Luke 39
Lumen Gentium document 127

M

Magen David 218, 221, 234
Maghrib (times of prayer) 192
magisterial teachings 80
Magisterium 22, 23, 26, 27, 54, 80–1, 130, 131, 133
Magnificat 128–9
Makkah 183, 200, 201
male sexuality 264–5
marriage 58–9, 252–3, 264, 265, 268, 269, 270–1
martyrdom 310, 311
Mary 41, 46, 118–9, 128, 144, 145
Masjid al-Haram mosque 183, 200, 201
Mass 64, 66, 67, 68–9, 108–9, 162–3
materialism 326–7
Matthew 39, 70–1, 154
memorials 146–7, 309
menorah candlestick 234
mercifulness 172, 173
Messiah 220–1
see also Jesus
Messianic age 220, 221
metaphor 105
Michelangelo Buonarotti 10–11, 46, 144–5
Middle East conflict 302
mihrab 192, 193
Mika'il (Michael) 174, 175
Mina 183, 201, 202
minyan 234
Mishnah 247
mission 74, 75, 120–1
mitzvot/mitzvah 216, 230–1, 250–1
modern warfare *see* warfare

monks 136, 137
monotheism 212, 222
monuments 146–7
morality 50–1, 106, 107, 226–7
mortal sins 159
Moses 224–5
mosques 169, 180, 183, 185, 190, 193–4, 200–1, 203
Mother Teresa 137
motherhood *see* parenthood
Mount Hira 184
mourning 146–7, 254–5
Muhammad 184–5, 203
music 64–5, 66–7
Muslims 168, 226, 308
see also Islam
mystery 68, 69, 70–1
myth 24

N

naming ceremonies 248
national charities 134
natural law 26–7
natural resources 28, 29
negotiation 304
ner tamid (ever-burning light) 236, 237
Nevi'im 247
New Testament 21, 70–1
Nicea Council 81
Nicene Creed 72–3
Night of Power 196, 197
non-violent resistance 312, 313
Nonconformist Christians 110
nuclear weapons 298–9
nuns 136, 137

O

Obligatory Acts 190–1
Old Testament 20–1, 70, 302–3
Omega symbols 44–5, 143
omnipotence 14, 172, 173, 214–5
omnipresence 214–5
omniscience 214–5
oral law 246, 247
ordained 126
ordination 58–9
Orthodox Christians 110–1
Orthodox Jews 214
Orthodox synagogues 238–9
Our Father and Communion 109

P

pacifism 304–5
paintings 37, 56, 71, 148
Palestine 306
parables 51, 145, 154–5
paradise *see* heaven
parenthood 176, 276–81, 284, 287
see also children
particular judgement 152
Paschal candle 142–3
paschal sacrifice 92
Paul, St 77, 149, 294
Pax Christi 313
peace 124–5, 138–9, 290–315

peer pressure 334
Persons of the Trinity 22, 56, 71, 72–3, 78, 104
Pesach (Passover) 260–1
pikuach nefesh (saving a life) 228, 229
pilgrimage 116–9, 182–3, 184, 190–1, 200–3
Pillars of Islam *see* Five Pillars
plainchant 66
planning, family 276–7
pollution 28–9
pontifical nature of Church 132–3
popes 28, 126, 133, 138–9, 266–7, 298–9, 306–7, 339
posture 86–7
poverty 226, 322–3, 327–35
praise 64
prayer
　Aleinu 241
　Amidah 240, 241
　dramatised 116
　Du'a 195
　Eucharist 68, 69, 108–9
　Jewish services 240–1
　Kingdom of God 122–3
　Mass and adoration 112–3
　mosques 169, 180, 183, 185, 190, 193–4, 200–1, 203
　posture 86–7
　private worship 246
　salah 190–1, 192–5
　Shema 70, 212, 213, 240
　shiva 254
　spontaneous 84–5
　statues 49
　synagogues 213, 234–9, 242–3
　traditional 84–5
preaching 74, 75, 184–5
predestination 176–7
prejudice 286–7, 334–5, 339, 340
priests 136, 160, 162–3, 270, 285
private prayer 246
procreation 278
procreative relationships 264, 265
Promised Land 222–3
promises 272–3, 275
prophets 21, 22, 180–1, 184–5, 203
prostration 194
protest 129, 294–5
Psalms 64–5, 187
public worship 238–9
purgatory 152–3

Q

qiblah wall 192, 193
Quakers 110, 111
Qur'an 169–70, 174–5, 184, 186–7, 197

R

rabbi 218, 219, 236
racial equality/prejudice 334–5, 338–9
radicalisation 310–1
rak'ah 194–5
Ramadan 196–7
readings 85, 108, 236, 237

reality, sacramental nature of 56–7
reception of the body 162
recitations 194
reconciliation 58–9, 124, 125, 139, 156–7, 292–3
redemption 90–115, 249
Reform synagogues 238–9
refugees 205, 296, 300–1
relationships 264–89
religious life 137
remarriage 274, 275
remembrance gardens 146, 147
repentance (shofar horn) 258–9
requiem 162
responsibilities 320–1, 322–3
restoration 96–7
resurrection 68–9, 96–9, 103, 149, 178–9, 218–9, 282
Revelation, Book of 21
Rich Man and Lazarus parable 154–5
righteous anger 294, 295
rights 316, 318–9, 320–1
Risalah 180
risen Christ 94, 95
rites 160–1, 162–3
rituals 248–9
Rome, pilgrimage 118
rosary 84
Rosh Hashanah 258–9

S

sacraments 56–7, 58–9, 112, 113, 160–1
Sacred Heart 48–9
Sacred Scripture 24
sacred writings 24, 246–7
sacrifice 92, 96–7
Sacrosanctum Concilium 127
Sadaqah 198, 199
St Augustine 64, 78–9, 296
St Paul 77, 149, 294
St Vincent de Paul (SVP) Society 134–5
saints 144–5
salah prayer 190–1, 192–5
salvation 54, 100–1, 105
Salvation Army 111
same-sex relationships 269, 271, 281
sanctify/sanctification 59
sanctity of life 18, 19, 164, 228–9
Sanctus 68, 69
Sanhedrin 42–3
sarcophagus 147
Satan 180–1
Saul & Samuel 220
sawm fasting 190–1, 196–7
science 26–7
sculptures 49, 147
Second Vatican Council 26, 27, 126–7, 132, 158–9, 317
security, family 278
Sedar plates 261
self-revelation 78, 79
Sermon on the Mount 50
sex before marriage 268
sexuality 264–9, 337
Shabbat 214, 242–5

Shahadah 190, 191
Sheep and Goats Parable 51, 145
Shekhinah (divine presence) 216, 217
Shema prayer 70, 212, 213, 240
Shi'a Islam 170–1, 191, 208–9
shiva 254
shofar horn 258–9
sick, anointing 160–1
sick, sacrament of 58–9
sign of initiation 82–3
sin 96
Sinai 224–5
sinful 56, 57
sins 159
Sistine Chapel 64, 144–5
six articles of Faith of Sunni Islam 170–1
social justice 316–41
social teaching 133
Solomon's Temple 217
Son of God/Man 42–3
Son, Trinity 22, 56, 71, 72–3, 78, 104
spontaneous prayer 84, 85
stained-glass windows 12, 14, 16, 36, 76, 161
standing prayer (Amidah) 241
Star of David 218, 221, 234
Stations of the Cross 90, 91, 116–7
statues 46, 48–9, 70
stewardship 18, 30–1, 323
stones 182, 202, 255
succession 130–1
Sunni Islam 170–1
supremacy of God 168–9
sustainability 32–3
SVP *see* St Vincent de Paul Society
symbolism, baptism 82
symbols 44–5, 143, 147, 218, 221, 234, 337
synagogues 213, 234–9, 242–3
Syrian conflict 205, 296, 301

T

tabernacle 92, 93
tables 94
tallit 240
Talmud 228, 246, 247
Tawallah 190–1
Tawhid 168
tefillin 240, 250
temples 102, 217
Ten Commandments 216, 224–5
Ten Obligatory Acts 190–1
Tenakh 246, 247
Teresa, Mother 137
terrorism 308–9, 310–1
The Last Judgement 145, 148
The Mission 121
themes
    human rights and social justice 316–41
    peace and conflict 290–315
    relationships and families 264–89
theologians 78, 79
Theology of the Body 266–7
tolerance *see* equality
tombstones 146
Torah (Tawrat) 20–1, 187, 214, 230, 236–7, 243, 247, 251

torture 310
total immersion 82, 83
tradition 52–3, 66, 84–5
trafficking 324, 325
transcendence 14, 172
transplant surgery 229
trefah food 256–7
Trinity 56, 70, 72–81
Triune God 64–89
twenty-first century conflicts 306–7

U

Ultra-Orthodox Jews 214
unitive relationships 264, 265

V

Vatican 26, 27, 29, 126–7, 132, 158–9, 317
Verbum Domini 12 55
Viaticum 160, 161
violence 290–315
virgin birth 38, 39
vocations and Kingdom values 136–7
volunteer work 205, 226
vows 272–3, 275, 327

W

walking days 316
Walsingham 118, 119
warfare 298–303, 305, 307
washing 192–3
water 162, 196, 329, 332
wealth 322–5
weapons of mass destruction (WMD) 298–9
weddings 154, 252–3
will of God 50
wisdom books 21
witness 59, 74
WMD *see* weapons of mass destruction
word of God 22–3, 40–1
World religions 168–263
worship 66–7, 182, 190–211, 238–9
written law 246, 247
wudu (ablution) 192–3

Y

Yom Kippur 258, 259

Z

Zakah 190–1, 198–9
Zuhr (times of prayer) 192